JOHN BANDLER

CYBERSECURITY FOR THE HOME AND OFFICE

THE LAWYER'S GUIDE TO TAKING CHARGE OF YOUR OWN INFORMATION SECURITY

Cover design by Tahiti Spears/ABA Design

Printed in the United States of America.

21 20 19 18 17   5 4 3 2 1

Library of Congress Cataloging-in-Publication Data
Names: Bandler, John, author.
Title: Cybersecurity for the home and office / By John Bandler.
Description: Chicago : American Bar Association, 2017.
Identifiers: LCCN 2017024695 | ISBN 9781634259071 (print)
Subjects: LCSH: Computer security—Law and legislation—United States. | Computer
    networks—Security measures—United States. | Law offices—United States. | Data
    protection—Law and legislation—United States.
Classification: LCC KF390.5.C6 B34 2017 | DDC 005.8024/34—dc23
LC record available at https://lccn.loc.gov/2017024695

Discounts are available for books ordered in bulk. Special consideration is given to state bars, CLE programs, and other bar-related organizations. Inquire at Book Publishing, ABA Publishing, American Bar Association, 321 N. Clark Street, Chicago, Illinois 60654-7598.

www.ShopABA.org

To my wife, children, and parents.

Contents

CHAPTER 8
Secure Your Devices   **113**

Chapter 9
Secure Your Data   145

Chapter 11
Secure Your Family, Children, and Seniors   223

Chapter 12
Secure Yourself When You Travel   241

Chapter 13
Secure the Work Office 259

CHAPTER 14
The Law, and the Role and
Responsibilities of Lawyers   295

CHAPTER 15
Troubleshooting and Responding
to Your Own Incidents   329

About the Author

John Bandler runs a law firm and a consulting practice that help businesses and individuals with cybersecurity and cybercrime investigations, among other areas. His expertise stems from over twenty years of experience working in law enforcement and the private sector. He served as a state trooper in the New York State Police for eight years, assigned to one of the state's busiest stations that provided full police services to the local community. While serving in the state police he attended law school at the evening program of Pace University School of Law, and then was hired as an Assistant District Attorney by the legendary Robert Morgenthau. At the New York County District Attorney's Office he investigated and prosecuted a wide variety of criminal offenses, ranging from violent crime to identity theft, financial crime, and cybercrime. One investigation into a single incidence of credit card fraud eventually uncovered an international network of cybercriminals and identity thieves who stole data, sold it, and then used it for fraud. This groundbreaking case provided a breathtaking view of the cybercrime economy and its participants. John holds a number of information security and information technology certifications, and writes, lectures, and teaches on cybersecurity and cybercrime.

John can be contacted at:

John Bandler
Bandler Law Firm PLLC
Bandler Group LLC
48 Wall Street, 11th Floor
New York, NY 10005
John@CybersecurityHomeAndOffice.com

You can visit his websites at:

CybersecurityHomeAndOffice.com
BandlerLaw.com
BandlerGroup.com

Acknowledgments

There are many people who made this book possible and contributed to it.

Ben Wilson and Antonia Merzon deserve much of the credit for this book and special thanks for their help and editing. Ben, an information security expert and lawyer, is the former Chair of the Book Publishing Board of the American Bar Association Section of Science and Technology Law. Recognizing the need for such a book for lawyers, he proposed the concept and then shepherded my drafts through to publishing. Antonia, formerly my visionary supervisor at the New York County District Attorney's office, has read more of my writing over the last fifteen years than anyone should have to, and her legal and practical insight and thoughtful editing has been invaluable for this book.

Rob Bandler, my cousin and formerly the Deputy Director of IT Security at Cornell University, read the entire book and gave extensive help in many areas ranging from cybersecurity to grammar and more. Bret Rubin also made it from beginning to end of the book, and offered important suggestions. Now an information security professional, Bret and I worked together at the District Attorney's office, including on the international cybercrime case mentioned.

Many others helped to make this book possible, reading many chapters, providing valuable feedback, and bringing diverse expertise in areas that included cybersecurity, cybercrime, law, business, and editing. They include Nicolette Endara, Stephen Moccia, Richard E. Parke, Christopher Jones, Lawrence C. Montle, Augustine Fou, and Anthony R. Rossabi.

I would also like to thank the Book Publishing Board of the American Bar Association Section of Science and Technology Law, and Sarah Forbes Orwig, Executive Editor, Book Development and Publication for the ABA, and her colleagues, for all they did in moving this book to publication.

Finally, none of this would be possible or worthwhile without the support of my family, and my appreciative thanks go to my wife, children, and parents, including my mother who read it all and provided essential editing assistance and feedback.

Foreword

In December 2015 the Book Board of the ABA Section of Science and Technology Law discussed the concept of a book about cybersecurity in the home. We recognized that many books had been written from the perspective of an information security professional to lawyers and other professionals, but that none of them seemed to address cybersecurity in the home. We solicited suggestions and proposals from members of the ABA's Information Security Committee, and several individuals responded. We received one proposal that stood above the rest. That proposal was a book outline from John Bandler that covered all the bases.

Chapters 1 through 3 of *Cybersecurity for the Home and Office* aim to educate readers about the value of data in their lives and how cybercriminals will try and exploit that value with ransomware and other attacks. Chapter 4 provides an introduction to key principles about data protection, especially the need to protect the confidentiality, integrity, and availability of personal data. Chapters 5 and 6 provide an overview of how computers store and transmit data.

In Chapters 7 through 10, Mr. Bandler provides tips on securing data, whether it is at rest on your home computer or in motion as it is being transmitted over the Internet. Key concepts in these chapters are the "security dial" (personal risk tolerance) and the tools needed to conduct a personal risk assessment of your computing practices. With the growth of cloud storage for personal data, securing access with two-step authentication (strong passwords and one-time codes) is also highlighted. Protecting your family, especially your children and seniors, from attack or other types of abuse is the subject of Chapter 11.

Chapters 12 and 13 tell readers how to secure their data when outside the home, while traveling or at the office. Chapter 13 provides added security considerations for the small office, and Chapter 14 covers ethical obligations specific to lawyers. Finally, Chapter 15 provides a methodology for solving problems you might have with your computer, and the appendices provide helpful forms and templates to organize and protect your data.

There are two types of people—those who have been hacked and those who don't know they've been hacked. Most of us have already been hacked, and we just don't know it. *Cybersecurity for the Home and Office* is a call to action. Readers of this book will grow to appreciate that personal data protection needs to become a priority in our lives, and effective information security for our personal information requires that we make good choices to secure our devices. Our behavior needs to change. We need to develop better habits concerning our data, and *Cybersecurity for the Home and Office* is a playbook to help readers incorporate "cyber hygiene" into our daily routine.

Ben Wilson, JD CISA CISSP
ABA Section of Science and Technology Law

CHAPTER 1

The Need for Cybersecurity

This book was written to help you take control of your cybersecurity. Every day in the news, we read about cybercrime—a multi-billion-dollar-a-year criminal industry whose actors have little fear of law enforcement. Incidents of cybercrime and cybercrime-related identity theft continue to grow exponentially. As a result, governments, regulators, and professional bodies increasingly require that lawyers and other professionals take reasonable cybersecurity measures. Beyond protecting our workplaces from cybertheft or intrusion, we also need to protect ourselves and our families from these threats.

Why is there so much concern about cybercrime and cybersecurity? Here is the basic problem: When we use the Internet, we drastically increase the odds that private and confidential information in our possession will be stolen. Not long ago, it was nearly impossible for criminals to steal all of your confidential documents, correspondence, photos, and other personal or professional information. They would have had to pick your pocket, burglarize both your home and office, and manage to carry it all away without being caught. Today, vast quantities of documents, data, photos, and personal and professional information are on our phones, laptops, and in the cloud. A cybercriminal can steal it all through the Internet, without you even knowing that anything has happened. The information that was once contained in hundreds of boxes of paper documents—and required a moving van to take—now exists in bits and bytes, and can be stolen with the press of a button, remotely, from thousands of miles away.

This type of data is valuable to criminals. They can use personal information to steal in any number of ways, to include tricking banks and credit card companies into giving them money or credit in the victim's name. Personal data has become a commodity, sold on the black market for its intrinsic value. Criminals even use encryption to "lock up" data, and then extort the data's owner for ransom in exchange for access—so-called ransomware. Imagine if all of your personal and client files were suddenly unavailable to you. And while greed is the main reason cyberthieves want your data, there are other reasons, too, such as harassment, stalking, and corporate espionage.

The Internet makes cybercrime possible. It is the information "super-highway," and our devices are continuously connected and ready to send and receive information from friends, family, employers, colleagues, clients, financial institutions, retailers, advertisers, and many others. Data is being exchanged constantly. This perpetual connection means our electronic door to the Internet is visible to the world, thereby exposing us to criminals. These criminals, like house burglars, are always trying doorknobs, hoping for an unlocked door. If that fails, they will knock on doors to try to talk their way in, see if they can pick the locks, or even kick doors in.

WHY THIS BOOK?

Most of us have neither considered, nor know how "cybersecure" we are. If you are not an information technology (IT) professional, the idea of delving into the technical details of secure computing can create apprehension and confusion. Some people think that if their e-mail system works, and if their documents are accessible, then why bother making any security improvements to their system, which might create complications or cost time and money. Some would prefer not to know the cybercrime risks they are facing, or just haven't thought about it. Cybersecurity is more, though; it is also about protecting data from risks other than cybercrime, such as unanticipated IT issues, hard drive crashes, house fires, and other incidents. Beyond security, this book will also help you use your computers and data more efficiently.

No matter your level of comfort or experience with computers, this book will help you recognize when your electronic "doors" are open to cybercriminals, and help you fully appreciate why you need to take certain security steps. Since cybercriminals are always attacking, trying to steal your data or make your data unusable, this book will help you understand these risks so you can decide where to set your "cybersecurity dial" in your home and office. How much risk feels comfortable? How sensitive or confidential is your data? Are you safeguarding someone else's data and confidential information? What do you risk, professionally and personally, were your data ever stolen or compromised? If you set the dial too low, you may be overly exposed to threats, but if you set the dial too high, you may become frustrated with the inconveniences of the security measures themselves. Appendices 1 through 4 offer some assessments and materials to start your thought process about your cybersecurity posture and awareness. Appendices 1 and 2 have short quizzes you can take to assess your current security, awareness, and threats, and see how your home and work cybersecurity are related. Appendix 3 discusses the concept of the cybersecurity dial, where it is set now, and where you want it to be. Appendix 4 covers some common cybersecurity myths.

Cybersecurity is not one-size-fits-all, but needs to be what works for you. It's how you decide to evaluate and manage your risks. With this book, you can gradually increase your security posture as you learn, by making incremental changes and learning to live with them. For the price of this book, you will learn how to improve your cybersecurity by yourself, without paying anyone else to do it for you, as this book does not recommend any costly services or products. The time you invest now can save you from an expensive disaster later and could make your computing experience much more efficient. By first fixing the cybersecurity of your home and personal devices, you will then be in a position to translate that knowledge and experience to your workplace.

I wrote this book for other lawyers because we all have personal and work-related information on numerous devices and in various locations, and we all should be aware of the risks of loss or theft of that information. I have had the opportunity to learn about cybercrime, cybersecurity, law, and the basic mistakes most people make that puts their information at risk.

You should not wait for the law and other standards to evolve, as they will always lag behind the pace of technology advancements. The basic principles and methods to secure yourself are available now, and you can learn and apply them yourself. Technology will continue to change rapidly, but if you understand the basic principles, you will be able to make sound, ongoing choices to protect yourself.

You need not become a technology expert; however, you should learn about the serious threats you face, the potential consequences, and the steps you can take to mitigate these risks. Technology-related threats and appropriate countermeasures are similar to things you already do in your "brick and mortar" physical life. This book will teach you to secure your computer just as you learned to lock your house's doors and windows, put on your seatbelt while driving, check your car's oil level and tire pressure, and stop at a red light. Yes, computers can be complex, frustrating, and confusing, but everyone can learn how to do this.

WHAT YOU SHOULD DO RIGHT NOW

I hope you will read all of this book—doing so will improve your security to the degree that you choose, even if that is just a little bit. If you read this book in its entirety, you will understand the concepts and risks, improve your own protection, and be able to thoughtfully discuss cybersecurity issues with your clients, friends, and family members. Cybersecurity will no longer be a daunting issue for you.

I know that many things compete for your time, and it might take a while to get through this book in its entirety. There are some important concepts you should remember, and steps you should implement as soon as possible. If you remember nothing else, *remember* these key concepts:

1. Your data has value to cybercriminals—they will try to steal it, sell it, and use it.
2. Your data has value to you. Losing access to your data would be devastating. Cybercriminals may lock you out of your data in order to extort payment for its return, or to use the data themselves.
3. You can make small changes that will greatly increase your security, without interfering with your regular computer usage.

If you do nothing else, *implement* these simple steps to improve your security:

1. Put a password or passphrase on all of your computing devices (smartphones, tablets, laptops, and desktops). Make it easy for you to remember but difficult for a stranger to guess.
2. For your e-mail and cloud accounts, have a more complex password or passphrase, but recognize that a password alone is not always enough. Add a second measure to gain access, such as a one-time code that the provider sends to your cell phone. This is called "two-factor authentication" or "two-step login."
3. Run anti-malware software on your laptop and desktop. You can find free software from reputable companies that works well for this purpose.
4. Disconnect from the Internet (or turn off your devices) when they are not needed.

HOW THIS BOOK IS ORGANIZED

The first half of this book provides a basic understanding of the threats you face from criminals, examines the interests of advertisers in acquiring your personal data, and offers a foundational understanding of information security principles and how computers and networks work. When a threat is discussed, there is a quick tip on how to protect yourself from it; but, mostly, this part provides a basic understanding so that when you read the second part of the book, you will be able to make informed decisions.

The second half of this book starts with Chapter 7, and helps you protect yourself in a systematic, incremental manner, as you gradually learn about and improve your security posture and knowledge of the systems you use. This will help you decide where to set your "security dial," and guide you as you safeguard your computing devices. Then you will effectively protect the data that you maintain on your devices, in the cloud, and in your online accounts, as well as the information that you provide to others. The following chapter will secure your home network, and hone the way you use the Internet and the "Internet of Things." Then it's time to apply what you've learned to protect your family.

Next, you'll learn how to travel securely with technology; then we will look at how all of these principles translate to your work setting. In Chapter 14, you'll learn about the professional responsibilities you have as a lawyer with respect to your own cybersecurity, and you'll get a quick primer on the law as it applies to you and your clients. The last chapter is about troubleshooting for cybersecurity and other IT issues. The appendices have more detailed materials to help with your cybersecurity and IT awareness and implementation, additional resources, and helpful fill-in-the-blank forms. These forms can also be downloaded at CybersecurityHomeAndOffice.com, a website that also contains materials that parallel the book, such as photos of computer components that could not be included here.

YOU *CAN* IMPROVE YOUR OWN CYBERSECURITY

Whoever you are, and whatever your background, you can improve your home and office security by taking simple steps to safeguard your computers and data. You don't have to become a computer expert to protect yourself, and, with the help of this book, can start building some good cybersecurity habits that will translate directly to the workplace. Once they become habits, the steps will be nearly effortless and keep you safer. This book is not meant to scare or shame you, and it will not advise you to take every single precaution to guard against every single threat. Rather, it will empower you to learn and to understand, so you can make your own choices to protect yourself better.

CHAPTER 2

The Black Market for Your Data: The Cybercrime Economy

A. INTRODUCTION

Cybercrime is a fascinating topic because it provides a window into the dark side of the cybereconomy, the motivations of online criminals, and the lengths to which they will go to steal and use your data. This chapter discusses the many ingenious methods cybercriminals use to steal data through the Internet to ultimately steal money. Understanding what the bad guys are trying to do helps you make informed assessments of the threats you face and how to mitigate them. In other words, learning about the context that makes your data valuable to thieves will help you make the right choices for how to protect it. Too many individuals focus on nation-state threats, saying "X government won't want my data, so why should I worry about being hacked," or inverting that, "If X government or Y elite hacker wants my data, there's nothing I can do about that anyway." But this overlooks the fact that cybercrime-for-profit is a serious threat everyone faces, and we can and should reduce our vulnerability.

Think in terms of how you might protect your home or car. If you live in a dangerous neighborhood and are cautious enough to keep your doors triple-locked, but open the door without first looking in the peephole when there's a knock, you make your security measures less effective. Similarly, if you parked your convertible and locked the doors, but left the top down, you wouldn't be protecting your belongings. You understand those principles of physical security, and in order for your cybersecurity to be effective, you need to understand the cyberthreats. It's a great first step to lock the doors to your data, because a lot of people don't even realize these doors are wide open. But locking the door to your data isn't enough. Cybercriminals may knock on your virtual door, pretend to be someone else, and trick you into letting them into your house. A lot of cybercrime relies on social engineering—tricking the user into allowing the bad guy in—and, if you understand the scams, you will better recognize the tricks.

B. IT IS A BIG BUSINESS

The cybercrime-for-profit economy is international, highly profitable, and highly adaptable. It's all about data and its value. For every type of data—e-mail addresses, credit card numbers, bank account numbers, birthdates, Social Security numbers, and more—there are many ways to monetize it. Cybercriminals and identity thieves are extremely creative in trying many ways to steal until something works. Unfortunately, the Internet allows cybercriminals to work anonymously and from afar, and laws and law enforcement haven't kept up. Thus, a young person with a penchant for computers and stealing can hone his or her skills, never have a brush with the law, and evolve into a sophisticated cybercriminal. Subsequently, he or she will continue to innovate, adapt to new technologies and new security measures, and experiment until he or she is successful in earning illicit profits. Again, the chances of any interaction with law enforcement are slim.

Cybercriminals are like salesmen or telemarketers in the sense that they need not be successful every time, but merely enough to earn money. If they e-mail spam, a link to a dangerous website, or even a message from a "Nigerian Prince" (offering a fanciful tale promising vast rewards in exchange for either a small up-front payment or the provision of your financial information), they don't need *everyone* to click on the link or respond, they only need a small percentage of the recipients to do so. If they are trying to guess people's passwords, they don't need to break into every account, they just need to break into some accounts. So, like telemarketers, a success rate that is a small percentage of all efforts made may suffice to remain profitable. Interestingly, some cybercriminals are even using the telemarketer techniques of phone calls to contact potential victims to trick them into giving up control of their computers.

Cybercrime-for-profit is an important economy to consider. It is, by far, the greatest threat to the average person. The criminals want to steal data, monetize it, and launder and then spend the money. Generally, this means that cybercriminals are often not specifically targeting you for who you are—they have no special malice towards you. You are simply a "sales lead," that is, you are within a data set of potential victims. It's important to recognize that the security protection principles are similar, whether you are targeted by profit-motivated actors or other cybercrime threats, such as nation-state sponsored attacks or cybercrime for political ("hacktivism") or personal reasons.

There are, however, some unlucky people who are the repeated target of persistent cybercrime-for-profit actors. If you or your clients work with a financial institution or retailer, hold a sensitive position, or have high net worth, criminals might be willing to spend extra effort to target you specifically (including through "spear-phishing" or "whaling"), hoping to obtain access to your data systems at work and at home. There is even a smaller group of people who might be the potential target of a nation-state or hacktivist group because of their work or who they represent.

If you or your clients face these significant threats, there may be highly organized attackers willing to spend significant time to target, research, and attack you. You need to set your "security dial" much higher, trading easier access to your data in exchange for greater security. These attackers will probe your home computers and devices checking for valuable information, direct access to your work systems, or clues about how to break in. If you have work-related data at home, access work systems from home, or use work devices at home, then the attacker may have the information he or she needs or the ability to directly access your work systems. That's why this book starts in the home. Don't underestimate the value of your own data or the ease of your access.

Some people might be potential targets for more traditional "brick and mortar" criminal actors who commit crime the "old-fashioned" way. These criminals could take a particular interest in you or your client—for example, if your client is suspected of being an informant against organized crime or a violent gang, or if you or your client is being harassed or stalked by another individual. Understanding the cybercrime economy will help you understand that this economy can serve any bad actor; everything is available for sale, including malware and hacker-for-hire services.

Never lose focus of the threat posed by the general cybercrime-for-profit economy and the fact that no one is immune from being targeted by it. It is important to realize that cybercrime and identity theft are part of the same economy, a capitalist endeavor that relies upon stealing and using your personal information. Your personal information is valuable to criminals in order to commit frauds and identity theft, which makes them a profit. That's why your data is prized, and that's why criminals work so hard to get it. With that concept in mind, we will look at the most common cyber frauds being perpetrated today.

C. IT IS INTERNATIONAL

Cybercrime can be committed from anywhere, and the United States is a major target for cybercriminals because of its enormous wealth and robust financial and business systems. While there certainly are cybercriminals born and raised in the United States, some countries overseas have become incubators for cybercrime activities. Some of these countries turn a blind eye to cybercriminals so long as they target people in other countries, such as the United States.

Cybercriminals generally don't meet face to face, and they don't let anyone, including other cybercriminals, know their true identities. Instead, they use made-up nicknames and usernames to conduct business. They need to keep their true identities hidden from associates and law enforcement alike. If they anger another cybercriminal, or if another cybercriminal gets arrested and becomes an informant, it's important that no true identities have been exposed in order to prevent retaliation or investigation. In the cybercrime world, criminals don't keep one another in line with physical intimidation or force. The threat is having one's real identity exposed.

When individuals develop and conduct long-term, anonymous business relationships through the Internet, buying and selling stolen data and sharing profits with criminal partners becomes challenging. How do you pay someone when you have no idea who or where he or she is?

Cybercriminals have adapted to this challenge, coming up with many solutions, such as hiring people to send and receive money (these people are referred to as "money mules") or using shell accounts in countries that don't verify the identities of bank customers. But the ideal system for cybercriminals is one where the payment is instant, irreversible, over the Internet, and anonymous. The invention of digital currency turned out to be the perfect answer.

D. DIGITAL CURRENCY

Digital currency is simply an electronic payment method. Many also call it "virtual currency," to reflect that it's not a currency issued and backed by a government. Instead, it's issued and administered by a private entity or even a group of people. The digital currency everyone has heard of today is Bitcoin, but there are and have been many others through the years, including E-gold, WebMoney, and Liberty Reserve. There are many fascinating issues surrounding digital currencies, but for a criminal, the digital currency is neither an investment nor a movement, but simply a way to pay and accept payments anonymously.

While digital currencies have been used by cybercriminals, that does not mean that such currencies are inherently bad. Cash has been used by criminals for millennia, and that does not make cash inherently bad, and traditional banks and bank wires have been used by criminals as well. Money laundering through digital currency, however, has become a concern that the world has not fully learned how to address. Unfortunately, some early digital currencies have been administered and used by people who turned a blind eye to criminality and who actually profited from the illegal activity.

There is a place for digital currency in the legitimate economy, but law enforcement, regulators, and financial institutions need to understand the threats digital currency poses.

E. PAYMENT CARD FRAUD: AN EXAMPLE OF THE CYBERCRIME ECONOMY

There's plenty of news coverage about the huge data breaches of large retailers, where millions of customers' credit card accounts are stolen, and it's quite likely that you have been a victim of such a breach. While immensely disruptive themselves—not only requiring the companies to change their computer systems, the banks to reissue millions of cards, and the customers to monitor their accounts for fraud, but also leading to lawsuits and regulatory actions—these breaches are actually just the first step of a major form of cybercrime called "payment card fraud."

Mitigate the Risks of Payment Card Fraud for Yourself

We discussed payment card fraud and the cybercrime economy behind it. You or people you know have probably been a victim of this type of identity theft, and it will probably happen again to you. So let's take a moment to look at how you can protect yourself when it comes to credit and debit cards. Simply put, use credit cards, not debit cards, whenever possible. Whichever you use may eventually be compromised, but it is better if your credit card is compromised, rather than your debit card.

Here's why a theft of your debit card account is much worse than a compromise of your credit card. Suppose a thief uses your account information to buy a flat-screen TV at Best Buy. If the thief does this with your debit card account, the fraud has an immediate effect on your finances. The stolen funds are immediately debited from your bank account and put into Best Buy's account, and you must then fight to recover your own funds. Because the money has been stolen from your checking account, you may not have funds available to cover the checks you may have already written or any recurring payments that may have been scheduled. Consequently, checks may bounce and you may incur fees and embarrassment. Further, you may not have funds available to pay your own expenses until the issue is resolved, and that could take days, weeks, or longer. When you fight to recover funds stolen due to fraud on your debit card, you often do not have the same legal rights as with your credit card.

By contrast, if the thief uses your credit card to buy the TV, the funds are immediately paid for by the credit card's issuing bank (such as Chase or Citi), who pays Best Buy. If the issuing bank's internal fraud monitoring system does not detect the fraudulent purchase, it will send you a bill for the charge; however, you are not obligated to pay this. You would simply dispute the charge, refuse to pay, perhaps provide an affidavit, and the matter will be closed. With debit card fraud, you are fighting to get stolen money back, but with credit card fraud, you simply decline to pay a charge that you didn't make. Further, you have consumer rights with a credit card that you don't with a debit card, and usually it is a simple matter to dispute a credit card charge. Resolving payment and fraud loss then takes place without you—the decision as to who bears the fraud loss is a matter between the issuing bank, the card processor (such as Visa, MasterCard, American Express, or Discover), and the merchant.

Payment card fraud is perpetrated by a well-organized capitalist industry. Data relating to credit and debit cards are stolen and then used to
commit fraud on people, retailers, and financial institutions. Those who
specialize in this type of fraud are called "carders." Payment card fraud is a
large part of the global cybercrime economy, and is an excellent illustration
of how the economy works. My education about the cybercrime industry
started while investigating these carders.

You—and millions like you—use credit or debit cards to make online or
in-store purchases at retailers like Target or Home Depot, to name but two of
many corporate data breach victims in the news (and thousands who never
made the news). In 2005, when I began my investigation into an international
cybercrime and identity theft ring, corporations were generally not required
to notify customers or the public about breaches. The public didn't hear about
them, but they were happening nonetheless. Every reader probably knows
about payment card information being stolen and used for fraud through
personal, and unsettling, experience. Today, nearly every state requires corporations suffering a data breach to notify law enforcement, the customers
whose data was stolen, and sometimes even the press. Thus, each week we
hear about the latest and increasingly egregious data breach and theft of data.

It takes many participants to make a data breach happen and be profitable, as Figure 2.1 and following narrative illustrate. The Malware Writer
writes malware—malicious software—or perhaps customizes existing malware and sells it to a Hacker. Malware can be secretly introduced into a computer system for nefarious reasons, like stealing data. This malware might
assist in hacking a retailer, or it might be introduced to the retailer's computers to "sniff" data during processing and then send that data through the
Internet to a specified collection location. The Hacker secretly deploys this
malware to gather payment card data from the targeted United States retailer,
stealing thousands or millions of credit card numbers. The Hacker's data theft
business is "wholesale," after stealing this credit card information he sells it
in bulk quantities to "retail" Card Data Vendors. A Card Data Vendor makes
bulk purchases of credit card account information and then organizes it into
categories, such as the issuing bank, credit limit, and type of information stolen (account holder name and address, account number, PIN number, expi-
ration date, security code, etc.). He then offers his stock for resale, the price
based on its value for fraud.

These three cybercriminals may never set foot within the United States,
safely conducting their business from overseas. Each of them may have partners and associates, or sometimes roles are combined. Generally, however,
the three tasks above require very different skill sets.

The Card Data Vendor will sell the stolen credit card data to anyone
who will buy it. Years ago, a Card Data Vendor might advertise the data on

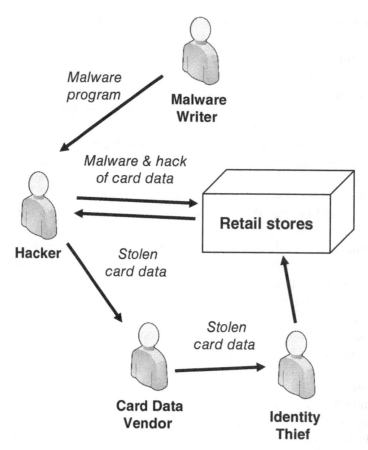

FIGURE 2.1 Participants of the payment card hacking economy.

a criminal website and indicate a method of contact (such as an instant messenger e-mail address). Today, a Card Data Vendor sets up an e-commerce website that works much like a typical Internet shopping site would except for the payment method. Not surprisingly, the criminal will not accept credit card payments. Instead, his customers must pay him in advance, sometimes by digital currency (such as Bitcoin), to establish a balance on his site. Customers can then browse his e-commerce site and buy the credit card data they want. They can choose among thousands of stolen cards, selecting the credit card's issuing bank, credit limit, and even the geographical area where the victim account holder resides.

If the data was stolen from the United States, the customer of the Card Data Vendor is likely to be an Identity Thief who resides in the United States.

That's because the best place to use stolen payment card data is in the country of origination. And, in fact, the best place to use a stolen account is close to where the victim account holder lives, because credit card companies use geographic location as one aspect of fraud detection. Thus, a Card Data Vendor sells the data to the Identity Thief (and hundreds like him) back in the United States. The Identity Thief uses the data for a variety of frauds, including in-store or online fraud to purchase valuable merchandise with the stolen credit card data.

Some hackers steal payment card data hacked from a retailer's database of online purchases, while others steal data collected by retailers from in-store purchases. The type of data stolen will determine how it will be resold and then used for identity theft. Online purchases require the account number, as well as the three- or four-digit CVV code and the account holder's billing address. In contrast, when a purchase is physically made in a store with a "swipe" (where the data is read from the magnetic strip of a credit card), this additional data is not captured. So to successfully commit fraud online, the identity thief needs more detailed account information, should disguise his IP (Internet Protocol) address so his fraudulent online purchase can't be traced, and specify a location to ship the merchandise. To make fraudulent purchases in a store, the identity thief needs to manufacture a forged credit card that is encoded with stolen account information. Because of the risk of being caught buying items with a fake credit card, many thieves employ others to do the shopping and bear the risk of arrest. As a result, the individuals typically caught by law enforcement engaging in payment card fraud are not the masterminds; they are simply people willing to risk arrest in exchange for quick cash.

Anonymity is a critical component of the dealings among cybercriminals and identity thieves. Thus, the three cybercriminals (Malware Writer, Hacker, and Card Data Vendor) and the Identity Thief probably have never met, don't know each other's real names or identities, and make all transactions via the Internet with anonymity. Because they frequently live on other sides of an ocean, they often pay each other anonymously through the Internet using digital currency. Digital currency is not the enemy, but merely one tool used by this innovative group, which also uses conventional payment methods and the conventional banking system.

Thus, this is an innovative, highly functioning, and specialized economy that steals many billions of dollars per year from the United States through fraud and exfiltrates much of that money out of the United States. Business relationships are established and huge profits are made in an environment in which the participants interact anonymously, using only nicknames and other Internet identifiers.

Chip and Signature Payment Cards

You may have read or heard about "chip and pin" or "chip and signature" credit cards, you probably have one or more of them in your wallet, and you may have experienced the confusion of how to make a purchase with this new type of card. You frequently wonder whether you should "swipe" or "insert and hold" when you conduct a transaction. Chip-and-pin technology was created to put an end to counterfeit credit and debit cards.

When we "swipe" our credit card, the account number is read from the magnetic stripe on the credit card, the authorization process begins, and then the charge is approved. But this process is easily compromised by criminals, who obtain that hacked account information, then manufacture forged credit cards using readily available equipment. The account data encoded on the magnetic strip can be stolen without difficulty, either through hacking or by crooked employees at retailers and restaurants. For a few dollars per account, an identity thief has the data he needs; then with a little practice and a small investment for the necessary equipment, he can make a counterfeit card and encode the stolen account data on the magnetic strip. Now the fake card is ready for shopping.

The new "chip" technology within credit and debit cards is supposed to reduce and perhaps even eliminate this type of in-store fraud with forged credit cards. Currently, chip cards are effectively impossible to forge, but chip technology is slow to be adopted, as evidenced by the many credit card transactions we still perform by swiping, rather than inserting. Even a full adoption of chip technology will not mark the end of payment card fraud—cybercriminals and identity thieves are ingenious.

F. OTHER CYBERCRIME AND IDENTITY THEFT SCHEMES

Payment card fraud is merely one example of the global reach of the cybercrime and identity theft economy, and card data is only one type of data that is stolen and trafficked. Cybercriminals and identity thieves covet these types of data, and try to steal it and make money from it. They want your data, including your online usernames and passwords, for e-mail accounts, financial accounts, social media accounts, and more. They want information about you and your contacts, and they want to monitor and control your computer. All of this can be done through the Internet, with automated tools, from next door or half a world away.

1. Financial Account Takeover

In account takeover fraud, the identity thief has your account and personal information and uses this to assume control of one or more of your financial accounts. A criminal can potentially take over your financial account with your online username and password. There are a lot of ways cybercriminals can learn your online usernames and passwords, including through "phishing," guessing, or by infecting your computer with malware and then capturing the information when you log in to your accounts. We'll cover that in greater detail shortly. When committing the simple payment card fraud we discussed in the previous section, the identity thief is trying to make some rapid fraudulent charges before detection, and detection will be swift since you remain in control of your account. When the thief takes over your account, he or she can delay detection of fraud and conduct significantly more theft until it is noticed.

When a criminal gets access to your account, he or she might silently monitor it, waiting for an opportunity, or perhaps lock you out of it, changing the password and the e-mail address and other contact information on file. All of these steps are designed to lengthen the amount of time that elapses before you notice the fraud, allowing time to steal more, escape, and cover his trail before law enforcement has been notified.

2. New Financial Account Opening

The more of your personal information that a cybercriminal can acquire, the more successful and profitable fraud options are available. When he manages to get the golden combination of name, birthdate, Social Security number, address, mother's maiden name, usernames, passwords, and financial account information, the criminal can trick many financial institutions and retailers into believing that he is you. Consider that when accounts are opened online or by phone, it's just a matter of providing the correct personal information when prompted. When accounts are opened in stores, criminals can do this with your personal information plus forged identification such as a fake driver's license. Thus, it's possible for criminals to conduct a wide variety of activities as if they were you, including opening new credit accounts (e.g., obtaining a store credit card), getting a bank loan, or even receiving medical services, all as if they were you.

Many retailers and banks require a customer to present some form of identification to prove identity when opening a new account. With only some minor training and an investment in the proper equipment, criminals can create a forged identification in a victim's identity. Millions of victims' personal information is for sale on the black market, having been hacked through data breaches over the years. Banks, retailers, insurance companies, restaurants, governments, and home computers have been breached and infiltrated. Their data was then stolen, compiled, and put up for sale on the black market for a small fee, and is available for identity thieves.

3. Infected Computers

A large percentage of computers in the world—thirty percent according to some reports[1]—are infected with some form of malicious software, and this can allow the computers to be monitored remotely or controlled by others. This type of malware causes infected computers to be grouped into a network of robots, or "botnet," that is controlled by "botmasters." Later in the book, we will discuss keeping your computing devices free of this malware, and how to avoid using computers with unknown security when you travel outside the home. An infected computer can record everything you are doing, including the websites you visit and the usernames and passwords you enter. Thus, an infected computer can harvest your passwords for resale on the black market, and criminals can then use your password to log in to websites and online accounts as if they were you—unless you have enabled two-factor authentication.

How does a computer get infected in the first place? The criminals break in, sneak in, or trick the user into letting them in, then secretly insert the hidden malware. This can occur when a criminal tricks you into opening a document that will infect your computer or into clicking on a link that takes you to a malicious website that infects your device. There are even ads on compromised websites that require no user action to infect the browser and computer—just visiting the website with a vulnerable web browser can infect the computer. This kind of human mistake is often called the weakest link in computer security. That said, our computers and software were not

---

1. *See, e.g.,* Ted Samson, *Malware Infects 30 Percent of Computers in U.S.,* INFOWORLD (Aug. 8, 2012), http://www.infoworld.com/article/2618043/cyber-crime/malware-infects-30-percent-of-computers-in-u-s-.html. *See also* John P. Mello Jr., *Report: Malware Poisons One-Third of World's Computers,* TECHNEWS-WORLD (July 9, 2014), http://www.technewsworld.com/story/80707.html.

originally built for security, and that is why doing simple things that you are accustomed to doing, such as clicking on a link or opening a document, can compromise a computer if you do it with a dangerous e-mail or attachment.

It seems strange that your computer could be taken over by a software program or by someone across the globe. But every device, operating system, and software application has imperfections that criminals try take advantage of to compromise your system. These imperfections, like holes in your castle wall, are termed "vulnerabilities," and criminals develop "exploits" to take advantage of them. The makers of devices, operating systems, and software constantly try to patch these holes, and encourage users to apply the patches; however, the criminals continue to find more holes to exploit. Every day, criminals find weaknesses in devices, operating systems, and software, and use those weaknesses to exploit and infect your system. Among cybercrime's diverse participants are technical experts who can write tools to capitalize on these vulnerabilities. These tools are then sold or made available to other criminals possessing only average technical skill.

Infected computers are used by criminals for more than just data theft. They also can be used as "proxies" for a criminal's own computer so that a criminal can hide his tracks by routing his Internet use through an infected "proxy" computer before committing Internet crime, whether it's hacking or placing a fraudulent Internet order. Some cybercriminals have a business of selling access to infected computers for use as proxies. Prolific cyber fraudsters may purchase a dashboard of thousands of infected computers through which to route their criminal Internet activity. Imagine that your computer is both infected and part of a criminal's set of proxies, and the criminal uses your computer and your Internet service to hack the government or a company, send a fraudulent e-mail, or make a fraudulent order. When the victim begins investigating, it may seem that the bad act came from you and your computer.

Infected computers that are grouped into a botnet can be used to launch massive Internet attacks against websites and companies, called distributed denial of service (DDoS) attacks, that can flood a website with enough traffic to bring it down, costing the company lost revenue and lost customers. The website may be designed for a few hundred or a few thousand customers who are conducting normal shopping activities, but when a malicious botmaster directs a million computers simultaneously to visit the website and interact with it in a highly resource-consuming way, the surge of traffic can effectively shut the website down. Cybercriminals often threaten and conduct these DDoS attacks to extort ransom from a company. Hacktivists or nation-states might conduct these activities for political reasons.

Botnets can also be used to earn advertising money. Internet advertising is a fascinating area that is discussed in the next chapter and revolves around monetizing information about the user and what the user views, clicks on, or purchases. Often, advertisers get paid per view or per click under the theory that the more humans who view an ad or click on a link, the greater the chance of a sale taking place. Where there is money, there are criminals, so cybercriminals have become involved in advertising fraud, and use the botnets to click on ads. The botnet thereby impersonates humans, tricking advertisers into paying for views or clicks that no human actually performed. Advertisers end up paying for these fake views and clicks, and the botmaster ends up earning a portion of these payments.

Infected computers are also used to send out mass e-mails, or spam, which has its own use in the cybercrime economy, as discussed in the next section. Sometimes, the mail server on a corporate network is compromised, and criminals use this to send mass amounts of e-mail throughout the Internet.

This is where you, as a home user, can do something that not only protects you but also makes the Internet a bit safer for everyone else. By securing your computer and devices, you can make sure that the bad guys don't use your computer to commit fraud against other people. Just as you shouldn't leave your keys in your car for a thief to steal it, you shouldn't let a criminal gain access to your computer. As we will cover in Chapter 8, you need to keep your computer updated, run anti-malware programs, and turn it off or disconnect from the Internet when you are not using it. This keeps you safer and also makes the Internet safer.

4. Phishing, Spam, and Internet Account Takeover

Cybercrime relies on fraudulent spam e-mails, which are e-mails sent to thousands of recipients in the hopes that a few will respond or simply click on the link. Spam is like a massive online telemarketing network to facilitate cybercrime, a method for cybercriminals to reach a large audience and try various cons and scams to steal data and money. Using spam, cybercriminals can embed malicious web links and files that can infect the recipient's computer.

Through spam, cybercriminals can induce the recipient to provide crucial information. One such way is a false warning that the recipient's online account will be suspended unless the recipient clicks the link, visits the imposter site, and enters login credentials (username and password) or perhaps other personal information (like birthdate and social security number). This is a fraud known as "phishing." The e-mail appears to be from a legitimate company, induces you to click on a link to what appears to be the company's website and urges you to log in to your account. In fact, the spam has impersonated the company, and you are being taken to an imposter website that will capture your username and password. In an instant, your credentials are stolen.

The criminal has done a lot of work to make that happen. The cybercriminal has paid to rent a web address, register a domain name that looks like a legitimate company (e.g., YourBankSupport.com), and to host a website. The criminal has purchased a "spam list" of millions of e-mail addresses, and then has obtained access to a compromised e-mail server or compromised e-mail accounts to send the messages. He or she sends out millions of e-mails that appear to be from a legitimate company or bank, trying to trick the recipients into thinking it is a legitimate e-mail, clicking on the link, and then entering information. If the spam is sent to a million recipients, and one percent are tricked by it, that's a success for the cybercriminal.

Phishing is an important method used by criminals to learn your online account credentials, in order to obtain access to your account, monitor it, and then monetize it.

5. Other Ways to Obtain Passwords

Passwords are an important way to keep criminals out of our accounts. Beyond phishing, cybercriminals have other ways to guess or steal usernames and passwords, which they then use to gain access to online accounts, such as financial, e-mail, cloud, or social media accounts.

If a computer device is infected with malware, the infected computer can log all user activity, including websites visited, and usernames and passwords entered. Imagine the amount of information an infected computer could gather, whether it is your own computer, or a hotel computer that thousands of guests have used to check their e-mail or other cloud accounts.

In later chapters we discuss passwords in greater depth, including ways criminals can learn passwords, automated password cracking tools, passwords as a means of identifying the user (authentication), and best practices for your devices and cloud accounts.

Undercover Purchase of Passwords: Many People Don't Ever Change Their Passwords

There is a lucrative cybercrime business in the trafficking of stolen usernames and passwords for online accounts— what are called "logins." Cybercriminals have a number of ways of obtaining victim usernames and passwords, including through phishing schemes and computers infected with malware.

While I was in government investigating cybercrime, we made an undercover purchase of such "logins" for a particular e-commerce site, and the information was frighteningly inexpensive. When we received our contraband, we saw that it was not just logins for that particular e-commerce site, but logs of the Internet activity of each victim, including other websites visited and usernames and passwords entered for each site. This demonstrated that victims were using computers infected with malware that tracked all of their Internet activity and then transmitted it to cybercriminals.

Upon inspecting the logs, it was apparent they were several years old, so I feared the cybercriminal had "ripped us off" by selling us obsolete data. Surely, after all these years, many of these passwords would have been changed and many accounts would have become inactive.

We sent the information to the cybersecurity department of the e-commerce site in question, so that they could confirm whether the user accounts were genuine and if the passwords were still active. The security department advised that about fifty percent of the passwords remained valid, even after the passage of several years. This meant these accounts were not only still active, but the users had not changed their password for years.

Without a doubt, cybercriminals can purchase many online account credentials. You can protect yourself with strong passwords, by periodically changing the passwords (but not so frequently that you can't remember any of them), and with two-step login.

Cybercriminals can also crack passwords through other methods. One way is by "brute force" attacks where they use a software tool to try every possible combination of letters, numbers, and symbols in an attempt to hit upon the correct combination. Most websites will lock them out after a certain number of incorrect guesses, and will also employ some type of "CAPTCHA" challenge to ensure it is a human and not an automated tool trying to log in. But sometimes the criminals try to guess your password without even going to the website. Suppose the criminal has hacked a website and obtained a list of user accounts and encrypted passwords—something that has happened in the past at LinkedIn and Yahoo and will surely happen again. The website should be storing your password in a "hashed" format, which is a one-way encryption mechanism we'll discuss more in Chapter 4. This hashing of passwords, however, is often not as strong as it should be. A criminal with a database of usernames and hashed passwords and who knows the hashing technique can try different password combinations to achieve the same hash result. He can do this offline and with automated tools, and if he eventually guesses the correct password, he can then go to the website and enter the correct username and password to gain access.

Cybercriminals also use a technique called "spraying" that allows them to guess passwords and play the odds without getting locked out because of too many incorrect guesses. With spraying, criminals try one password guess among thousands of user accounts, thus avoiding account lockout for a particular user account. Under this technique, the criminal is not targeting a specific online account, but is playing the odds that a small percentage of the accounts will have a particular password, such as "password" or "123456." Since about ten percent of Internet users choose the top twenty most popular passwords, a sprayer will keep trying these twenty passwords on thousands of accounts, and chances are pretty good that he will unlock some of them.

6. E-mail Account Compromise (Hack)

Cybercriminals are scarily creative in using stolen information and account passwords to earn money. When criminals obtain your e-mail account information and password, they may try to use your contact list to send out spam of various types. One type of spam e-mail often sent to stolen contact lists is a crude type of social engineering scam, where the criminal pretends to be you stranded in a foreign country, in need of an emergency payment via Western Union (for example). It seems like this ruse could not succeed, but a small percentage of people actually do send money, which is why criminals keep doing it. Remember, criminals don't have to be successful every time—they can try the scam on a thousand people each day, and if a tiny fraction of those people are tricked, it is enough to make a living. Unfortunately, there is almost no law enforcement action for these thousands of daily fraud attempts.

Hacked E-mail Account Used for Fraud

Here's an example of one of these less sophisticated scams. It might seem amusing and harmless, but remember that malefactors make a living with this scam, and each compromised e-mail account constitutes commission of a serious hacking offense.

Subject: Painful News !!! ....[victim name]

From: [e-mail hacking victim's e-mail account]

To: [every contact in the victim's address book]

I Hope you get this on time, I made a trip to (Philippines) and had my bag stolen from me with my passport and personal effects therein. The embassy has just issued me a temporary passport but I have to pay for a ticket and settle my hotel bills with the Manager.

I have made contact with my bank but it would take me 5-7 working days to access funds in my account, the bad news is my flight will be leaving in less than 12-hrs from now but I am having problems settling the hotel bills and the hotel manager won't let me leave until I settle the bills of $2,850 USD, I need your help/LOAN financially and I promise to make the refund once I get back home, you are my last resort and hope, Please let me know if I can count on you and I need you to keep checking your e-mail because it's the only way I can reach you.

> Any help is very appreciated,
> Thanks so much.
>
> [Victim name]
>
> If that were your e-mail account that got hacked and sent out this request to all of your contacts, you would be embarrassed. Not only had all of your e-mails and contact information been exposed to the criminals, but all of your contacts know this. Further, you might be required to make data breach related notifications.

The e-mail hacking and impersonation schemes have become very sophisticated, and earn billions of dollars a year. For example, many lawyers and business people transmit and receive bank wiring instructions routinely, as payment for merchandise, settlement payments, or payments for real estate. When a criminal hacks a person's e-mail account, not only can he or she monitor the communications to and from that e-mail account, but also use that e-mail account to impersonate the true account holder. At the appropriate time, the criminal can initiate a wire transfer to a bank account controlled by a criminal associate. This scam illustrates the great creativity of cybercriminals and the use of social engineering to trick people. Law enforcement has termed this kind of fraud as "business e-mail compromise," "CEO fraud," or "CFO fraud," and the fraud losses have been extensive. Chapter 13 will discuss ways to protect your firm from this fraud.

7. Ransomware

Cybercriminals have realized that your data may be worth more to you than it is to them, and they are able to "kidnap" and ransom it. "Ransomware" is malware that infects your computer and encrypts your data, rendering it unreadable without a decryption key. The kidnapping criminals demand a ransom for the password key. If they are "reliable" criminals with a "good business model," you will in fact get the key to unlock your data when you pay the ransom, though you may never know if they have retained a copy of all your data or will analyze and exploit it in the future. And you will never know if you are marked as someone who will pay the ransom, and thus a good future target. Paying the ransom only fuels this type of crime and the overall cybercrime economy, so you should do everything possible to avoid this problem, protect your devices (Chapter 8), and be a knowledgeable computer user so you don't become a victim of ransomware. Back up your data (Chapter 9) so that, if you are so victimized, you can restore your backup rather than pay the ransom and feed the cybercrime economy.

Ransomware and Cryptolocker

In one ransomware case the cybercriminals infected the victim's computer with malware that encrypted every single one of the user's documents, photos, and spreadsheets, so that it was impossible to open them. In each folder were files providing information to the user about what had happened, that the files were protected by unbreakable encryption, and that the user should visit a website where there were instructions for paying the ransom in order to get the key. The ransom was to be paid by the digital currency Bitcoin. It's an impressive criminal business, because it automates cybercrime and takes advantage of the victim's willingness to pay money to regain access to data.

This information provided to the victim is excerpted below:

What happened to your files?

All of your files were protected by a strong encryption with RSA-2048 using CryptoWall 3.0. More information about the encryption keys using RSA-2048 can be found here: http://en.wikipedia.org/wiki/RSA_(cryptosystem).

What does this mean?

This means that the structure and data within your files have been irrevocably changed, you will not be able to work with them, read them or

see them, it is the same thing as losing them forever, but with our help, you can restore them.

How did this happen?

Especially for you, on our server was generated
the secret key pair RSA-2048—public and private.
All your files were encrypted with the public key,
which has been transferred to your computer via
the Internet. Decrypting of your files is only possible with the help of the private key and decrypt
program, which is on our secret server.

What do I do?

Alas, if you do not take the necessary measures
for the specified time then the conditions for
obtaining the private key will be changed. If you
really value your data, then we suggest you do
not waste valuable time searching for other solutions because they do not exist. For more specific
instructions, please visit your personal home
page, there are a few different addresses point-
ing to your home page below.

The way to protect oneself is to try avoid infection
through proper computing practices, regular backups,
and avoiding malware infections. Later chapters cover
this in greater detail (see Chapters 8, 9, and 15).

8. Scareware and Technical Support Scams

Telemarketing scams have been around for a long time, and now those scammers have diversified into computer crime and take advantage of victims'
fears of technology and cybercrime. A typical scenario is for a scammer to
call a victim to "advise" that there is something wrong with the victim's computer, and then induce the victim to allow the scammer into the computer

or pay the scammer money to "fix" the supposed problem. Once the victim allows the scammer access into the computer, the entire computer has been compromised. Then the scammer can convince the victim that a valuable service has been provided for which the scammer should be paid.

There is also "scareware" and "extortionware," malicious software that masquerades as security software and induces a target to pay money to resolve supposed problems with the computer, or to give control of the computer to this malicious software or to crooks waiting to "help" when the target calls the 800 number on the screen.

G. GOVERNMENT AND LAW ENFORCEMENT RESPONSE

Cybercrime schemes are limitless. The point here is to understand the vast underground economy that is devoted to infecting computers, learning passwords, stealing data, and using personal information to earn criminal profits. Cybercriminals are constantly looking for ways to break in, sneak in, or be let in.

While law enforcement has had some successes, they have been quite limited in the context of the enormous rate of cybercrime—thousands of international cybercriminals steal billions of dollars each year. Despite meaningful efforts, law enforcement has not been close to keeping up with the malefactors, as evidenced by the incessant pace of cybercrime. Even local identity thieves, who fuel the cybercrime economy, receive limited law enforcement attention, as the crimes are difficult to investigate and prosecute and the penalties are relatively low. Law enforcement must invest years to develop employees, intelligence, and cases, and that investment of resources can be difficult to sustain. But the problem extends far beyond just law enforcement's reach—the highest levels of government need to address this as a serious national and international problem.

There are law enforcement successes. By way of example, one law enforcement cybercrime victory was a case that I worked on for over eight years. The investigation began when I had barely three years of experience as a prosecutor at the Manhattan District Attorney's Office and started with a single report of identity theft on a single credit card. The case mushroomed into a global investigation of cybercriminals and identity thieves. We partnered with the United States Secret Service and eventually apprehended three international cybercriminals, a dozen or so domestic identity thieves, and a significant money launderer that funneled tens of millions of dollars of illicit funds through it. Most defendants pleaded guilty, but the cases against three of the defendants proceeded to a two-and-a-half-month trial that ended with verdicts of guilty on over 300 felony counts. The case enabled me to sit next to legendary Manhattan District Attorney Robert Morgenthau as we briefed the press at various stages of the prosecution. I had the opportunity to work with some phenomenal and dedicated professionals with a myriad of skills, including analysts, District Attorney's Investigators, Secret Service Special Agents, a visionary supervisor who shepherded the case through investigation, indictment, and beyond, and a superb trial team. As successful as that case was, for all the criminals brought to justice, I was sharply aware of how many others got away and how vast the underground economy was. There were thousands of cybercriminals I learned about, but we lacked the time and resources to pursue them. We brought a handful of cybercriminals, identity thieves, and cybercrime money launderers to justice, but it only made a dent in the overall cybercrime economy. The cybercrime business is still booming, and we need good cybersecurity more than ever.

CHAPTER 3

Advertising: Another Market for Your Data

A. INTRODUCTION

While the prior chapter examined the cybercrime economy and its reliance upon relentless attacks on business networks and home computers to steal data, this chapter examines how legitimate companies obtain, store, and profit from data about us. Companies collect such data every time we use the Internet and look at a website, a fact that has significant privacy implications. A cybersecurity book would be incomplete without addressing how everyday Internet usage may allow businesses to capture important facts about you and your life. Your cybersecurity and privacy are intertwined, so you need to understand both. Further, your practice may include corporate clients who need to develop and administer their own privacy policies properly.

You may not realize it, but daily you are making choices about the information you provide to companies online. There are a lot of great services and products out there, and many don't cost any money at all. We think of these services as a product that we are using. In fact, we are the product that is being used by the companies providing those services. We are tracked constantly, from the information we look up or research to the things we pay to buy or use. Even the providers of expensive services, such as our cellular or cable service, make additional money by learning about our data usage.

These companies and services track our Internet usage carefully because what we do has advertising and marketing value. By analyzing our interests and purchases, retailers and services can target their advertising and marketing efforts toward people who might want their products. They can tailor online ads to include products or information that might entice you, while offering different options to another user with different preferences.

The popular search engine Google is a good example of how our past Internet use turns into tailored suggestions for the future. When you start to type into the Google search bar, it automatically starts suggesting words for you, anticipating what you want. Google does this by tracking each key you type and using predictive analysis and artificial intelligence to suggest what you mean to type. When you hover over buttons on a webpage, it often provides a pop-up text box that describes what the button does, because it is tracking each mouse movement and is trying to help you by explaining what would happen if you decided to click on that button. On the one hand, this type of monitoring can be quite helpful, but on the other hand it can be particularly invasive, as it allows the company to obtain a lot of information about you, your interests, and your habits. Depending on your various privacy settings, it is possible that every Internet search and every web page you have ever visited is being stored somewhere, providing insight into what you were thinking about each day of your life, going back weeks, months, or even years. With all the concern about government surveillance, it is ironic that some seem less concerned about information that private corporations collect from and about us.

Most of us voluntarily give information via social media, or to websites and companies, without understanding the terms under which we have done so. This chapter explains how companies go about obtaining, storing, and using your data.

B. CORPORATE COLLECTION AND USE OF YOUR INFORMATION AND DATA

Retailers, consumer services, and other corporations have always used advertising to try to win new customers and expand business relationships with existing customers. Simply put, advertisements are the primary method businesses use to communicate with prospective buyers or users, letting people know about new products, existing products, sales, and other offerings that might induce them to buy more.

Even in the pre-Internet days, when advertising relied upon paper catalogs and radio announcements, companies collected information about who was buying their products. Using this information, they could make educated decisions about how to entice those customers again and solicit similar new customers. Somewhere along the way, companies realized the information about their own customers might also be valuable to other organizations looking to focus their own advertising efforts. For a long time, retailers, utilities, and many other kinds of companies have made money by selling their customer lists to other businesses. The companies that buy the information use it, with the help of advertising agencies, to develop and implement campaigns to reach the correct demographic market. In the past, the ability to collect and store information about individuals was limited, as were the mechanisms to reach them. Traditionally, names, mailing addresses, and phone numbers were the important pieces of personal information for reaching potential customers with a successful, targeted ad campaign.

Today, it's not just our names and addresses being collected. The amount of data that is obtained and stored about us is unprecedented. Corporations want to analyze our personal information, our connections to family and friends, our purchasing history, and our Internet preferences. By finding out as much as possible about us, companies try to capitalize on the reach of the Internet, using this information to advertise products and services in novel and high-tech ways. Internet advertising is now a $50-billion-a-year industry that uses an entirely different approach from traditional paper or media ads. With traditional advertising, a company would put an ad in the newspaper or on TV and monitor whether sales went up. Advertising agencies were compensated based upon the success of their campaigns in raising sales figures. With Internet advertising, however, they are attempting to quantify the success of ads by collecting more data about individual users' viewing and responding to these ads. Advertising methods have emerged that track and reward each time a user sees or responds to a particular advertisement.

Internet advertising is all around you. It's an ad that displays on your screen, and maybe you look at it, maybe you don't. Maybe it's an annoying pop-up ad that stops you from doing anything until you close it. Maybe you click on the ad, whether deliberately or by accident, and are directed to the website of the company placing the ad. Occasionally, you might click on that ad and go to the company website to visit or even make a purchase.

Internet advertising is monetized in three main ways. First, the advertiser might pay for each "impression," that is, for every website visitor who had the ad displayed onscreen. The second way an advertiser might pay for advertising is via the pay-per-click model. In this scenario, the advertiser pays a certain amount for each user who clicks on the ad and is redirected to the advertising company's website. Here, the advertiser is getting a clearer result; not just someone who might have seen their ad, but someone who actually was directed to their virtual store because of the ad. The third way an advertiser might pay for advertising is with the pay-per-conversion model. The advertiser is paid if a user clicks on the ad, goes to the advertiser's website, and makes a purchase. In this instance, the advertiser is getting a concrete result, since an actual sale was made. There may be many layers of advertising agencies who sell and resell advertising space and referrals, and advertisers are constantly innovating and seeking to present the right advertisement to the right person at the right time.

Given the money to be made in Internet advertising, it should be no surprise that cybercrime exists in this realm, too. Cybercriminals have found another use for their botnets—their army of malware-infected computers that do their bidding. Instead of using the botnets as proxies to commit various frauds or attacks on consumers, retailers, or financial institutions, the malefactors use these botnets to simulate real people viewing digital advertisements, generating advertising income. One form is called "click fraud," where the botnet simulates a real person clicking on an ad to generate pay-per-click advertising income. Criminals have found many other ways to defraud advertising clients in each method of advertising monetization. One study estimated there was eight billion dollars' worth of Internet advertising fraud per year.[1] This criminal involvement undermines the entire online advertising industry.

C. WHAT (OR WHO) IS THE PRODUCT?

Many websites and services on the Internet are free. Most news websites, LinkedIn, Facebook, Pinterest, Twitter, and Google's Gmail, Contacts, Calendar, and Drive, as well as Apple's similar services, are free. But these sites don't exist solely as a public service—the companies behind them still make money somehow. To an extent, these free services could be described as "loss leaders," meaning they get the user to try it, like it, rely upon it, and eventually upgrade to a paid service. To a larger extent, the services are provided for free because the company is able to profit by showing you ads while you use their product or surf their website, as well as by tracking what you do and selling that data to others. Thus, the product is not Facebook or LinkedIn, *the product is you,* your preferences, interests, buying patterns, and the like.

Facebook, LinkedIn, and Twitter are amazing creations for advertisers, because each user voluntarily provides not only basic demographic information that advertisers historically craved (name, age, gender, location, occupation, etc.), but also intimate details about all they do and everyone they know.

D. PRIVACY POLICIES AND THE CONSUMER

There are laws relating to privacy in the United States, but compared to the European Union, our laws are fragmented. Companies are allowed to track us online, store the data they accumulate, and sell it to others because we largely agree to this. Our Internet providers and software suppliers are supposed to provide us with accurate and transparent privacy policies and terms of use that govern our relationships with them. These policies are required to describe how we can use the company's product and how they can use information about us. They are also supposed to advise us about how customer information is collected, stored, and used, and we are supposed to read and agree to the privacy policy before interacting with the company. The privacy policy is generally paired with the company's terms of use, or terms of service, which is, in essence, a contract between the company and customer.

---

1. *See* Ernst & Young LLP, *What Is an Untrustworthy Supply Chain Costing the U.S. Digital Advertising Industry?* (Nov. 2015), http://www.iab.com/wp-content/uploads/2015/11/IAB_EY_Report.pdf (study commissioned by Interactive Advertising Bureau).

These policies create issues. The first problem with these privacy policies is that almost no one reads them. One study from 2008 estimated that it would take about 250 hours per year for the average person to read every privacy policy for every website he or she visited.[2] That's about thirty full work days, or about six full work weeks, and doesn't even include the separate terms of service that we also are supposed to read and "agree" to. Further, that's a 2008 estimate—since then, our use of websites and software with privacy policies has increased, and lawyers have surely lengthened the average policy. The second problem is that even if a seasoned attorney were to read every single privacy policy and terms of service, it might not be understandable. Each policy can be several pages long, and the language can be a confusing jumble of legalese. Frequently, we blindly agree to unread and incomprehensible terms of service and privacy policies. How many privacy policies, terms of service, or end user license agreements have you read? Unless this is part of your legal practice, and you are being paid to read or write them, you probably gloss over them or don't read them at all.

Further, if these policies are unintelligible to us, they are probably equally incomprehensible to the people within the company charged with crafting and following the policies. Assuming the policy was accurate at one point, businesses try to move rapidly to adjust as technology and competition changes, so spending money and time to review and update privacy policies and practices might be a low priority. Nevertheless, the field of privacy is evolving, and companies now have a greater legal responsibility to describe accurately how they will collect, store, and use customer information.

As discussed in the prior chapter, cybercriminals recognize that corporations hold large quantities of data and they know that a breach of a retailer, financial institution, or other company can yield huge troves of personal information for resale or other criminal exploitation. Thus, the more information corporations store about you, the more information is available to be hacked and stolen. When companies retain customers' personal information indefinitely, hoping that it will be of advertising or marketing value, those companies are an even more lucrative target for hackers. In this evolving area of the law, corporations must take some responsibility to keep less data, safeguard stored data, and notify victims if customer data is breached. We cover the legal aspects of privacy policies, cybersecurity, and breach notification in Chapter 14.

---

2. *See* Aleecia M. McDonald and Lorrie Faith Cranor, *The Cost of Reading Privacy Policies*, 4 ISJLP 543, 563 (2008), http://moritzlaw.osu.edu/students/groups/is/files/2012/02/Cranor_Formatted_Final.pdf. *See also* Lorrie Faith Cranor, *Necessary But Not Sufficient: Standardized Mechanisms for Privacy Notice and Choice*, 10 J. Telecomm. & High Tech. L. 273, 274 (2012), http://jthtl.org/content/articles/V10I2/JTHTLv10i2_Cranor.PDF.

E. CORPORATE DATA STORAGE

No matter the laws or regulations, it's troubling to think that companies store information about us indefinitely, but this practice is widely employed in many customer-driven industries. I went to a branch of a major bank to open an account a while back, and though I once had an account with that bank, it had been over ten years since I had any dealings with them. Nevertheless, they had retained all of my personal information, including birthdate, Social Security number, residence address, e-mail address, phone number, employer, and more. The bank employee was easily able to access my file and update it, and I was able to open the account. The bank chose to store personal information about past customers because of its value to the bank. But the mere storing of it also made my data more susceptible to theft. And, unfortunately, my personal information had probably been stolen, because this particular bank has been the subject of several data breaches where hackers had accessed customer information.

Clearly, the storage of personal data by corporations—whether for advertising or internal use—creates a number of areas for concern, even for well-managed and well-meaning companies. Since there are few laws generally preventing most data collection and storage, we are entrusting these companies to use it properly. But even when companies follow the law, they are not immune from data breaches, so whatever data they are storing may be subject to theft. Even well-intentioned corporations may not realize either the masses of data they are storing or where it is, especially with multiple backup mechanisms and corporate mergers and sales. But not every corporation complies with laws, regulations, and principles of good corporate ethics—some corporations have deceitful privacy practices and should not be entrusted with information about us.

The reality is that companies have every incentive to collect and store more and more data about their customers. For example, since you pay hundreds of dollars for your cellular service or cable Internet service, you might think that they are making enough money from you that they wouldn't try to earn even more by monetizing information they have about you. However, the dollar value of this information is too high to pass up, and these service providers make more money by collecting and sharing information about your data usage habits. Some cellular providers insert information into your phone's data stream information that identifies you and your device; thus, when you use your smartphone to surf the web, the website is able to track you better. This type of digital tag that they insert is sometimes called a "super cookie." One cellular provider was fined over a million dollars for conducting this practice in a deceptive manner, failing to give its customers adequate information about what data was being tracked and how. The financial motivation for service providers and other companies to collect and store data remains in place, and super cookie tracking still takes place. It might require a careful reading of the company's privacy policy to see if you can opt out and whether that would affect your service.

The issue of whether to opt out or go along with a company's data collection practices often arises in loyalty programs. Many companies, including supermarkets, airlines, and retailers, offer loyalty programs. When you join a loyalty program, you agree to have your purchases tracked, so that you can earn discounts and points towards a reward. These programs incentivize you to stick with a single retailer or service and to provide information to that company by presenting your loyalty card or identifier number at each purchase, ensuring that all of your purchases can be tracked. While you earned a benefit from this transaction that was exclusive to your loyalty membership, the retailer or service also benefits by continuing to learn about you and your habits.

Consider a supermarket loyalty program, which might give you special discounts on certain products—or even a free turkey for Thanksgiving. In many ways, the Internet as a whole is a supermarket loyalty program on steroids, with companies vying to learn not only what you purchase, but everything you search, read, look at, and click on. Consider Amazon.com as a prime example (no pun intended) of the endless reach of online data. A supermarket has tens of thousands of products for sale, but that's a pittance compared to what Amazon offers. Amazon provides a seamless shopping experience from the convenience of the home to encourage users to purchase almost any consumer item through its site. Amazon tracks and collects data, not only about what their users are buying, but also about items they search for, so that the site can suggest items for purchase and connect the user to vendors of those items. This data is much more detailed than what a supermarket loyalty program can capture, allowing innovation by Amazon in the products it has available, and how it markets and sells them to its huge customer base.

Companies in the business of Internet advertising and marketing are quick to state that they "anonymize" data about customers. Personal information, such as your name, is stripped before the data is shared, analyzed, or monetized. In some cases, this data might actually be anonymized, aggregated, and then used without any connection to the actual individual about whom the data was obtained. In other cases, the advertiser might call the data "anonymized" when it really isn't. Just because the data doesn't have one's name or e-mail address, doesn't mean that it is truly anonymized. If the data still contains hundreds or thousands of personal details about an individual, it's hard to say that removing the name is enough to call it "anonymized." Plus, common sense suggests that if the data were truly anonymized, there would not be as much value to other advertisers and marketers.

F. CONCLUSION

It is important to try and grasp how much information is being collected about us, stored potentially indefinitely, and then used by corporations. Almost every website and application collects and stores data relating to the connected user, and there are a myriad of ways companies do so. As corporations and providers are motivated by profit, their data practices can be contrary to our own interests. Cybersecurity and privacy are interconnected issues, so it makes sense to address them together, and taking control of your personal privacy is important. Further, you may have individual or corporate clients who can use guidance on how such personal information is gathered and used. In sum, any information that is stored can be stolen.

CHAPTER 4

Basic Information Security Principles

A. INTRODUCTION

This chapter will help you understand some basic information security principles. With this foundation, you will be able to make sound cybersecurity decisions in your home, as well as hold an intelligent conversation with a client, information security professional, or vendor. Most importantly, these principles will inform your continuing risk assessments and actions over the coming years, enabling you to develop a cybersecurity posture that is adaptable to changes in technology and your individual needs.

First and foremost is physical security. Preventing your electronic devices from being stolen, carried away, or even falling into the bathtub, will save you a lot of headaches. As we all know, replacing or resurrecting stolen or damaged devices can be a costly, time-consuming undertaking, and there's no guarantee that all the data can be replaced or restored. Physical security is an everyday "brick and mortar" concept, but few things make our electronic data more vulnerable than lost, stolen, or broken devices.

Next come three basic information security principles: confidentiality, integrity, and availability (if you were studying for an information security exam, you would remember the initialism "CIA"). For the home user, confidentiality and availability are paramount, meaning that you want to keep your private information private, and you want to be able to access your data on demand. For the business user, integrity is also essential, because if the data can be tampered with or altered, then the business and others cannot rely upon it.

The goal when creating a successful information security strategy is to find a balance among these three concerns, and often there is no single answer. Confidentiality and availability are frequently at odds, and concessions are needed. Just as putting more locks on your door makes you safer while simultaneously impeding your entry and exit, the higher you turn the "security dial" to protect the confidentiality of your data, the greater the chances that you are decreasing the ease with which you can access it. The object is to find a happy medium, where you can protect yourself appropriately from most of the threats you face while still using your systems with relative ease.

The tradeoff between confidentiality and availability is even more apparent when we look at the trend toward increasing mobility with all of our devices and data, including moving much of our data to the "cloud." In the 1980s, all of our data was on a desktop computer without Internet connectivity, making it safe from theft, but that data was only available to us when we were sitting at that computer. Now, our data is available to us no matter where we go in the world, via smartphone, tablet, laptop, or a borrowed computer. Availability has increased exponentially, but it puts confidentiality at risk, because anyone, anywhere in the world, can reach our data through the Internet and try to hack in. Many of our information technology services—e-mail, documents, social media networks, and workplace remote-computing platforms—grapple with this tradeoff between offering confidentiality and providing availability.

You are embarking upon a holistic endeavor that involves protecting yourself, but first a quick word about the terms "information security" and "cybersecurity," which have differing and evolving definitions. Generally, information security means protecting information, whatever its form, while cybersecurity focuses more on the protection of digital data from digital threats, especially those involving the Internet. We don't need to focus on the terminology, but rather the basic concepts, which we will cover in a prioritized order.

B. PHYSICAL SECURITY

Physical security is the first priority for keeping your data safe. This means making an honest assessment of how you secure your home and office, who has access to your devices in each place, and how you protect these devices when you leave the home. An essential step in assessing the risks involved with having your devices lost or stolen is to ask both what a criminal could do with them and the effect on you of such loss or theft. As we will cover in Chapter 8 (on securing your devices) and Chapter 12 (on travel), one of the most important things you can do to protect yourself is to develop good habits to secure your mobile devices properly. In Chapter 13, this analysis extends to your workplace.

1. Theft and Damage

Electronic devices have value to petty thieves. If they steal a smartphone or laptop, they can resell it for a few dollars. There are more petty thieves than sophisticated cybercriminals, and these thieves generally do not care about data, they just want to make a quick buck selling your stolen property to shady electronics shops or to individuals in their neighborhoods. But the consequences for you are disastrous—you have lost access to your data and will likely never get it back. So always consider the primary risk that a thief can grab your device and run off with it.

As technology and data security regulations advance, the theft of your device may create even deeper concerns. For example, if you have enabled two-step sign-in (also called two-factor authentication) with a cloud service provider that requires use of your smartphone, and that smartphone is stolen, you will have difficulty accessing your cloud data. If there is confidential data on the device that was stolen, you may be obligated to make notifications to clients, customers, and law enforcement, as will be discussed in Chapter 14.

Within your home, you should also consider threats from environmental hazards. Some places are safer than others to place your important computing devices. A hot radiator could fry your device, and a smartphone or laptop could fall off the kitchen counter. Of course, use common sense around any location where the device might drop into water or have liquid spilled on it. No one wants to have valuable data destroyed by a preventable accident.

These physical concerns are multiplied when you leave home with your devices. The risk of losing them, breaking them, or having them stolen increases significantly, so you should evaluate your devices' physical security everywhere you go and act accordingly.

2. Controlling Access to Your Devices at Home

If someone has physical access to your computer or mobile device, then that person has the ability to compromise it. Anyone who uses your devices could intentionally compromise your security, such as stealing or sabotaging your data, or by installing a program that continually monitors the device. We trust that most people allowed into our homes will not try to do something malicious, but compromises can occur accidentally. The user might not be sophisticated with computers, and might accidentally damage your data or install software that exposes you to threats.

Accidental or careless misuse of your devices by others can have serious effects on your data security and professional reputation. The situation might seem as benign as a young child who uses your phone or tablet to send texts or e-mails to your professional contacts. Some recipients might view this scenario as unprofessional or as a sign that your systems are not secure. Taking it a step further, a teenager or careless adult might use your device to engage in risky behavior, such as visiting a questionable or infected site that could end up infecting the device and compromising your data. If your device is provided by your employer, it might also be a violation of company policy to allow others in your household to use it for any reason. Even if it is your personal device and you are allowed to use it for work—such as through a bring-your-own-device (BYOD) policy—giving others access to it could violate that policy.

A worst-case scenario would be if someone has physical access to your devices and has an intentional and malicious desire to compromise your data. Such a person could install software or hardware to spy on and log all activity on the computer. It could be a software program that records all activity, all key strokes, all things on the screen, or allows remote access to your computer at will. This is sometimes accomplished with a simple hardware device, like a USB memory stick inserted into a USB port, perhaps out of sight on the back of the computer. This device would log everything you do and either store it or transmit it to the malefactor. Allowing physical access to your network devices—such as your router, modem, and cables—can result in a compromise through the installation of a network "sniffer" that captures and copies the data passing through that network point. A wireless network without a password can allow this same access to your data, which is transmitted through the air for anyone to capture.

Hopefully you have already enabled a password on all your devices. But for most devices, even if they require a password to access them, that doesn't mean the files are protected, unless "full disk encryption" has been implemented. We talk more about encryption later in this chapter, as well as in Chapters 8 and 9, and the pros and cons of implementation.

For now, let's assume you have enabled a password on your laptop or desktop, but not any form of encryption. The password, without any form of encryption, will only stop the most casual of thieves—it's like locking the screen door on your house, but leaving the regular door wide open. A casual thief will tug on the screen door and, finding it locked, move on; but a more determined thief will cut the screen, open the door, and walk right in. With a password but no encryption, a determined person with physical access to your desktop or laptop computer can still get access to the data inside. He or she could boot the computer to a different operating system to bypass the password and simply copy your files, or disassemble the computer, remove the hard drive, copy it, and reassemble it. At a later point, the copy of your computer hard drive could be analyzed for every bit of information on it, finding out everything you have done and stored on that computer. Thus, it is crucial to control physical access to your devices. With physical access, anyone can easily compromise a phone, tablet, or computer, either by getting the data from it or inserting something that records your activity and transmits it.

Within your home, the risk of someone targeting you for sophisticated cybercrime or espionage may seem low, but it should still be considered, especially if you have work data, or you access work data, from home. You need not be paranoid, but should nonetheless be aware of the range of risks and threats so you can evaluate the dangers and decide on the appropriate level of protection for your situation. If you are the potential target of a prankster, an angry former significant other, a stalker, or industrial or government spy, you should be aware of what is possible. With this knowledge, you can evaluate the risks and act accordingly. After you have evaluated and secured the risks in the home, you will revisit the analysis and apply similar principles to your travel and office in Chapters 12 and 13.

C. CONFIDENTIALITY

Confidentiality is a cornerstone of both information security and the legal profession. Chapter 14 covers the attorney's professional duty of confidentiality, and this section covers the information security aspects. Storing sensitive private data and information means securing it appropriately, so that you share it only with the people with whom you intend, and keep it otherwise private. One way to achieve confidentiality is by securing access to the data through passwords and other methods of authentication designed to grant access only to authorized individuals. Another method to help achieve confidentiality is through encryption.

1. Authentication

Authentication, often done through passwords, is the process in which a computer system identifies a user and grants access. Through this process, the computer system identifies the user as the person authorized to sign in and view or change certain data. The three general methods to authenticate users, in ascending degrees of security, are:

1. Using something you *know,* such as a password
2. Using something you *have,* such as a digital token or smartphone
3. Using something you *are,* such as your physical characteristics, like your fingerprint, retina, facial features, and more

Each of these is a "factor" that can be used to authenticate the user. Thus, "single-factor" authentication is typically something you know, like your username and password. "Multi-factor," "two-factor," or "two-step" authentication generally means a username and password, plus something additional, like something you have (e.g., a smartphone that you use to receive a one-time code, key fob, smart card) or something you are (e.g., your fingerprint, retinal pattern, etc.).

Many vendors claim to have solved authentication-related problems and offer a perfect solution that provides both security and convenience. But remember, the world of cybersecurity is constantly evolving. There is a continuing battle between those who try to invent better locks—and then try to sell them to you—and those who continually work to break or circumvent those solutions. This tension is similar to the history of fortification techniques and tunnel warfare between the builders of castle forts and the breachers of forts, such as miners, sappers, and siege engines like trebuchets. As the royal engineers of old found ways to make castle walls stronger, the attackers developed machines to hurl bigger or better projectiles at them, or learned how to dig deeper to bypass or collapse the walls. In the modern cyber version of this story, however, it's not only the king's castle under attack. Now, even the home user is part of this escalating battle for safety from criminal hacker attacks.

a. Passwords—Something You Know

For the past twenty years or so, we have relied upon passwords to protect the confidentiality of our data and systems. To log in to an account, we enter our username (which is usually not a secret, and perhaps is publicly known, like an e-mail address), and then we enter our "secret" password. We may believe that no one else knows our secret password, but in many cases this is not true. Passwords have a lot of inherent weaknesses, some of which stem from our human imperfections, as well as the near impossibility of complying with all of the accepted password best practices guidance. Many of us use simple passwords that are easy for others to guess (such as our names or the word "password"), or reuse the same password across multiple devices and services, or never change them at all. Cybercriminals have many ways to defeat passwords, which we introduced in Chapter 2 and will discuss more below. Cybercriminals want to break into our password-protected areas and they have special knowledge and tools to help them. Accordingly, using only a password as the sole protection and authentication method to keep criminals out is often insufficient.

There are some accepted principles for improving our passwords that many people ignore, and some password advice is very difficult—perhaps impossible—to follow. Different rules by different account administrators can further complicate things, some accounts might require long passwords, while others restrict the length; some mandate that you use special characters (such as %, #, *, etc.), while others prohibit such characters.

Password guidance frequently suggests a litany of steps for creating a strong password, all of which can leave one wondering if it is even possible to follow these recommendations:

- Have a long password.
- Don't include regular words.
- Include special characters.
- Use both uppercase and lowercase letters.
- Don't reuse a password across two or more accounts.
- Change your password frequently.
- Don't write it down.

Together, these seem like impossible requirements, especially for busy people with dozens of work and personal accounts to juggle, and that's why some vendors offer "password manager" software, which will be analyzed later. Ideally, every account and device would have a unique password that is complex and long, not recorded anywhere, and changed periodically. It's a tall order unless you have a fantastic natural memory, or significant training as an intelligence operative.

As with all things in this book, passwords are a matter of compromise and risk management. If you were to create a complex, lengthy, and unique password on every device and Internet account, you might find yourself crippled, conducting password reset requests incessantly until you gave up and reverted to a password of "123456." Nevertheless, using a simple password on an important cloud account—such as your e-mail account or cloud document storage—is highly risky because anyone in the world can try to break in and with a simple password, some will succeed. A simple password on your physical device might not be as risky, because someone must first have physical access to your device in order to even try to break the password. A simple password might be sufficient to thwart the casual thief or trespasser, and that might be the main risk you face.

It's also important to note the interaction between passwords and encryption. If you hold sensitive data and have enabled encryption on your device, then the encryption is only as good as the complexity of your password. There is little point in encrypting your device if your password to decrypt it is going to be "password" or "123." Your data is still vulnerable because the encryption password is so easy to guess. Thus, *always* use a password or pass phrase of appropriate length and complexity.

Here are some basic, recommended, and *manageable* password principles:

- *Always* change the default password initially given to you by the provider when you set up the account.
- Longer is better, no matter what the characters.
- Regular words are weaker since they are subject to a "dictionary attack" (cybercriminals running every word in the dictionary against your password).
- Don't reuse the same password across multiple cloud/Internet accounts. If a hacker gets into one account, he or she will try the same password on your other accounts.
- Assess risks and increase the password security on your important accounts (e-mail, cloud storage, financial) compared to less important accounts (shopping).
- Change passwords periodically, but not so frequently that it frustrates you and makes them impossible to remember.

- Change your password if you think you were tricked by a bogus e-mail or other phishing attempt.
- Change your password if you think you typed in your password while using an infected computer.
- Consider using a password manager to store and enter your passwords. (Note that this method surrenders some control over your password process, and presents a single point of failure for all of your passwords if the password manager itself is ever compromised.)
- Ensure your password recovery and account recovery information is accurate and up to date. While this gives your provider more information about you, perhaps surrendering some privacy, it increases your chances of recovering the account.
- For important accounts (e-mail, cloud, and financial), augment passwords with a second factor of authentication.

There are a number of ways that criminals can obtain or guess a password, which we discussed in Chapter 2. These include brute force, trying every possible combination; guessing with popular passwords, words, and combinations; obtaining the password through phishing or other social engineering; or obtaining the password through malware that was installed on a computer.

For each technique, there are many tools available for cybercriminals. To "brute force" guess a password, the tool tries every possible combination of letters and numbers until the right match is found. Then there are tools that combine brute force aspects with more targeted password guessing, including trying out the common passwords that people use (like "password" and "password123"). Software and services try to protect against password guessing by locking the account after a certain number of failed attempts to log in, and by using "CAPTCHA" challenges to try ensure the user is a human. However, these defenses are not impenetrable. Criminals can try "password spraying," where they try to log into 100,000 different accounts by trying one popular password against all of them, rather than trying 100,000 times to log in to a single account. Chances are good that they will gain access to at least one of them.

Another technique is called "password cracking," which involves using password "hashes" that have been hacked from a company, as the publicized hacks of LinkedIn and Yahoo illustrated. The provider does not store your actual password, but rather information derived from your password, the hash, which is a digital fingerprint of the password stored as a long string of numbers. It is obtained through a one-way encryption method, so when you enter your password to log in, the site doesn't know what your actual password is, but runs the one-way hash algorithm on it, and checks to see if the resulting hash is the same as the hash it has on file. If so, you are authenticated and it lets you in. When the criminals obtain a database of hacked password hashes, they can use their own computer and software to make guesses until they figure out your password. Once they've learned your password, they can then go to the provider's website and log in as if they were you.

The password problem and the inadequacy of many people's passwords is illustrated by the LinkedIn data breach in 2012. The well-known professional networking social media site suffered a breach of 117 million password hashes. Again, it was not the passwords themselves that were stolen, but the hashes of the passwords ("password representations"). Criminals know how to leverage this information, as do cybersecurity researchers. The first lesson is that because these passwords were hacked, criminals could have used them to commit social engineering type fraud via LinkedIn, and to branch out from there to further victimize the users by trying to hack the users' e-mail accounts. The second lesson is the poor password practices of many people, including these LinkedIn professionals. Cybersecurity researchers were able to analyze popular passwords, which included "123456," "LinkedIn," "password," and similarly simple passwords. The five most popular passwords were used in about one percent of the accounts. Chances are good that these LinkedIn passwords are representative of what users might use for their other online accounts. Thus, a hacked LinkedIn account could be used to gain access to an e-mail account, and then perhaps even to financial accounts.

Let's extend this analysis further. If a criminal had access to a list of 100,000 accounts for a particular online provider, and the criminal tried the top five most common passwords for each of the 100,000 accounts ("123456," "password," etc.), the criminal might gain access to one percent of the them, or about 1,000 accounts. When viewed in this context, the odds greatly favor the criminal, and if telemarketers had odds this good, they would be quite content.

Because many of us cannot remember all of our passwords and frequently forget them, companies have a "forgot password" option. This tool saves us from being locked out of our data and accounts, but it also creates another vulnerability, because a thief could use this function to take over your account. Sometimes, the "forgot password" feature requires you to answer questions that supposedly only you would know, such as your first car, your first pet, favorite movie, or other information that you would be less likely to forget. The problem with this approach, however, is twofold. First, it assumes that you already have given this personal information to the provider, which means that if the provider is breached this personal information could be exposed. Second, more and more data about us is readily available, between the information we voluntarily post to the world, the information that is gathered about us, and the information that has been hacked throughout the years from retailers, governments, or ourselves. All of this could be floating out in the cybercrime black market. If a cybercriminal really wanted to get into your account, it is conceivable that he could figure out your answers to these "security" questions.

b. Password Managers

Password managers can present a solution to the password problem by using a single software program to keep track of all of the user's passwords. The password manager can generate strong and unique passwords for each online account, as well as stores and automatically enter the respective passwords so the user can access a desired site. Thus, the user only needs to remember a single password, that of the password manager, and does not have to remember dozens of different passwords.

But this convenience comes with risks, because a password manager provides a single point of failure and places considerable reliance on a single software vendor. It puts all of your eggs in one security basket. A password manager might be a fine solution, but only as long as it is very secure and easy to use.

An additional important note about the vulnerability of password managers is that if you use the password manager on a computer that is infected (and a large percentage of computers are, indeed, infected), you are exposing your data. The malware infecting the computer may well be capable of capturing the password you enter to get to the password manager, thereby making all of your passwords available to cybercriminals. There is also some risk that the password manager software itself might be hacked. In 2015, a password manager company was hacked, and the hashed (encrypted) master passwords for all their customers were stolen. This company indicated that it would be very difficult for thieves to crack these passwords because of the strength of the hashes, but still recommended that all users change their passwords and enable two-step authentication.

In sum, passwords are "something you know"—a single factor of authentication. As a sole method of authentication, they present a number of problems in terms of how they are created, used, and stored. Relying on passwords as a single line of security means your data and online accounts are vulnerable—an important concern when they are the barrier to any kind of sensitive or confidential information. Next, we will talk about the pros and cons of two-factor authentication.

c. Two-Factor Authentication, Also Known as Two-Step Login

Two-factor authentication is an important step towards mitigating the "single factor" password problem. Two-factor authentication generally means security based upon something you know (a password) plus something you possess. All of us already use two-factor authentication with our ATM card and PIN. The card is something you have, and the PIN is something you know.

Many cloud service providers allow you to implement two-factor authentication for your e-mail and cloud data accounts, including Google's Gmail and Drive, Microsoft's Hotmail/Outlook and OneDrive, and Apple's iCloud. These services obtain information about you and your devices, so they can recognize devices that have been used to access an account before. When two-factor authentication is implemented, and you attempt to sign in from a new computer, in addition to providing your username and password, you will need to enter a code that is sent to your smartphone. Thus, even if a criminal has learned or guessed your password to an online account—or has learned other information about you and is trying to reset your password—he cannot access your account because he doesn't have your smartphone to access the one-time code being sent to you. Hopefully, you have already implemented two-step login for your important accounts.

One downside of two-factor or multifactor authentication is that if your smartphone is lost or stolen, you may have a very hard time getting back into your account. You might be able to find the backup codes you were supposed to print out when you first enabled two-factor authentication, or you might need to wait until you get your phone replaced. Another downside of two-step login is that it takes a little bit of time to set up and a little bit of ongoing work. Lastly, you are giving the provider additional information about you—your cell phone number—which may have advertising value to them.[1] But, if you have sensitive communications or information within your cloud account, you should implement two-factor authentication.

Of course, criminals will seek ways to circumvent two-factor authentication, or attempt to trick account holders and providers into letting them into the account. Because people lose their phones, and then need access to their accounts, cloud providers have established recovery methods, and hackers inevitably will attempt to exploit those methods to get into accounts. One sneaky technique used by criminals when they attempt to sign in to your account—but are thwarted because they need the code that was sent to your smartphone, is to call you on your phone and ask you for the code that was just sent to you, making up a reason why you should provide it to them. This type of con-artistry is an example of social engineering. The criminal is trying to re-engineer his way into your account by contacting you and tricking you to do something that you shouldn't.

---

1. Methods of implementing two-factor authentication include receiving single-use codes by text message to a cell phone number, or through an "authenticator" application running on your smartphone. It is possible that the text message could be intercepted by a sophisticated hacker, but everything has vulnerabilities. Two-factor authentication, including through the receipt of text messages to a cell phone, remains an essential part of your cybersecurity.

2. Encryption

Passwords and other authentication mechanisms are like closing and locking our front doors with locks. We open the door with our key, and the bad guy tries to pick the lock. The more locks on the door, the more he has to pick to get in. But there are other ways a criminal can get into a house, including a proverbial "back door" that might not be as securely locked. Or perhaps the offender is incredibly brazen and drives a tank through the wall and carries away your filing cabinets with all of your documents. Encryption provides protection against any level of thief who manages to steal your data because encryption causes your files to be unreadable—even if they are stolen—unless the thief has the proper key to decrypt them.

Two main concepts for encryption are encrypting data at rest (where it is stored) and encrypting data in transit (when it travels from one point to another). When encrypting data at rest, such as on your laptop's hard drive, encryption can be applied to selected files (file level encryption) or the entire disk (full disk encryption). Similarly, encryption can be applied to data that is being transmitted, including with a website, through e-mail, or within a network.

Encryption is an area where confidentiality and availability intersect at cross-purposes. Encryption is designed to improve confidentiality by trying to ensure that others cannot read your data. While not foolproof, encryption greatly increases the chances your data will remain private. But encryption comes with costs. For example, it could slow things down, because now your system needs to do the work of encrypting and decrypting your data. Encryption also presents the risk of making your data unavailable even to you; if you forget your password and lose your recovery key, the data is gone. And since it's a process designed to render your data unreadable, if it fails just a little bit, that might make all the data completely unreadable. Even without encryption, we've all had files become corrupted and unreadable—some may have even had entire hard drives crash and become unusable. By adding a process on top of the normal file storage mechanisms, there is an added layer of complexity that might hinder our access to our data at some point. Thus, encryption is another example of how confidentiality and availability might collide.

Encryption is a powerful tool to protect the privacy and confidentiality of data. But, it is only as good as your password, and is not uniformly a seamless process, though Apple's encryption implementation with its mobile devices is a laudable example of a flawless experience. Our data has become increasingly vulnerable to cybercriminals and identity thieves, who face little fear of apprehension; part of the solution to protect ourselves will be to develop and employ encryption methods that are default, seamless, stable, and robust. We'll talk more about encryption in later chapters.

D. AVAILABILITY

Availability means that data is available to you when you need it. For most of us, the main risk to availability is that our computers and devices stop working for a non-malicious reason. You can't access your e-mail, your laptop or tablet stops communicating with your Wi-Fi router, cloud data becomes unavailable, or some other technical issues occur. Information technology (IT) sometimes "just doesn't work," and sometimes we have no idea why. The IT helpdesk's first troubleshooting step is to have you reboot the computer, so that the electronic gremlins can dissipate and go somewhere else, and that's a testament to unexplainable issues. Sometimes, things stop working and we have no idea why, but when devices restart, everything is reset and it starts working again. Sometimes, though, it takes a little more effort to get things going again. Throughout these issues, we merely want things to work, and to be able to access our data.

1. "If It Ain't Broke, Don't Fix It." But Maybe It Is Broken After All?

Concern about availability is the main reason companies often fail to evaluate their security posture properly, or why they fail to implement reasonable security measures. A company might reason that its IT system is "working," so why mess with it? Security measures can seem daunting and there's a fear that if additional security measures are implemented, IT systems will become difficult to use. Any change might result in a loss of function, "less availability," or even total unavailability. Many also fear the costs and loss of control, because implementing security features might require paying a vendor, plus investing in people to administer them.

For the home user, there is no financial cost to implementing the security measures that this book recommends. There is an investment of time, and there is a chance your availability will be impacted somewhat, just as if you were to add a lock to your front door. But the benefits of preserving your data's confidentiality and integrity far outweigh any cost of reduced availability.

If you are worried about introducing a security feature, you might consider the possible outcomes. The best-case scenario is that your IT system continues to work, and your data and services are safer, while remaining just as available. In the worst-case scenario, it doesn't work, and you must troubleshoot what went wrong. While you might spend some more time getting everything working properly, the problem can usually be solved fairly quickly. So what is the right decision—spending some time to tighten security or leaving your system the way it is and hoping for the best?

The answer depends on first making an honest assessment of the risks, and then making a rational decision based on this risk, possible rewards (improved security), and your capabilities to implement and deal with possible problems. The honest assessment of risk should not rely upon the old saying "if it ain't broke, don't fix it." That notion is frequently misused when it comes to IT and cybersecurity, because sometimes the user doesn't know enough to realize that it *is broken*. The door may be broken, it won't lock, or it won't even shut, and criminals can come in. For the unaware, it might seem like their IT "works," but they are carelessly unaware of the real and ongoing risks.

Perhaps your devices, network, and Internet usage seem to be functioning and safe, but you will gain knowledge and then be able to make an honest assessment about how secure they really are. Ensuring the availability of your data should always be a parallel concern, and that is why I recommend you take incremental steps. In choosing the security approach that works for you, evaluate the entire risk spectrum. Consider the risk of both criminal activity directed against you and locking yourself out of your own data. As you take incremental steps to protect yourself and learn more about your computer systems, you will empower yourself without sacrificing availability.

2. Availability, Authentication, and Confidentiality

Always keep in mind the tug of war between availability and confidentiality. Improving confidentiality with stronger security can mean the availability of your data is negatively affected. Security features can lock you out, whether it is a forgotten password, a lost smart phone, encryption gone wrong, or something that is just not working. On the other hand, improving the availability of your data typically makes it less secure/confidential. Features that make things available for you also make them available for the bad guys. If you like storing your data in the cloud because it makes your data available for you, no matter where you are in the world, remember that it also makes your data available to a hacker, no matter where he or she is in the world. This is not to say the cloud is more dangerous than storing the data on your desktop or laptop, since many factors go into this evaluation. If you store all your data on your local computer, which is then destroyed by fire or stolen, you would still have an availability problem.

3. Availability and Ransomware and Other Malicious Destruction

Availability can be affected by cybercriminals who encrypt your data for ransom, or otherwise deliberately destroy or tamper with your data. Ransomware perfectly demonstrates the importance of your data's availability to you, and the adaptability and ingenuity of cybercriminals. Whether your data has value to cybercriminals or not, they realize that it has value to you, and that you might pay to get it back. From their perspective, it is more lucrative and easier to deploy malware that encrypts your data and then collect a ransom, than to analyze the data and attempt to exploit it for profit. Of course, nothing prevents the criminals from doing both, but the immediate scheme is to encrypt your data, make it unreadable to you, and convince you to pay ransom for the decryption key. Understandably, many people are willing to pay to get their data back.

As a reminder, if the criminals were able to insert ransom malware onto your computer and encrypt your data, then they could have monitored your computer's activities, harvested your passwords, and copied all your data from your computer and cloud accounts. This data has value, and can be stored indefinitely and analyzed. However, copying data out and analyzing it is resource-intensive, and ransomware is a perfect business solution for cyber-criminals—the first and easiest way to monetize you as a cybercrime victim.

The best way to protect against ransomware is to keep your computer from getting infected in the first place. The next step toward mitigating the risk of ransomware is to have a back-up of your data in a separate, *disconnected* storage device. There are various ways to try and clean your computer once it is infected, and from there you can restore data from your previous backup. Be aware that if the backup storage is connected to your main system, it can be infected and encrypted by the same malware, rendering it equally unusable.

4. Availability and Backup

It is important to back up your data periodically. Consider how much data you can afford to lose, and how long you could go without access to your online accounts or devices. If your laptop computer crashed today, how much data would be lost forever? When was the last backup you made, and how much data was backed up at that time? If a malicious cybercriminal hacked your e-mail accounts and deleted all of your e-mails and contacts, do you have a backup of them somewhere, and how long ago was it made?

Backups present their own tradeoff. Every time you back up your data, you have protected yourself from loss of availability of your data, but you have also created a greater risk in the "confidentiality" sphere, since there are more copies of your private data out there, creating more exposure if not securely stored. Backups that are encrypted mitigate the risks of theft.

5. Business Continuity and Disaster Recovery Planning

Business continuity planning and disaster recovery planning are important information security and business planning principles. Plan ahead, so that if bad things happen you can get your systems and data restored and running promptly. Part of this planning for a business is determining the amount of data the business can afford to lose, or the amount of time the systems can be down, which might be measured in minutes, hours, or days.

For a business, the threats are diverse—power outages, natural disasters, man-made disasters, terrorist threats, serious crimes, and more—and may require different responses. In planning for these threats, the business evaluates how to protect people, property, and data, and how to get things going again after such an incident. Some businesses even have other sites where they can quickly move their processing, data, and personnel. Companies have faced some extreme situations, and those who planned in advance were best suited to survive the disaster and minimize the business impact.

A power outage is a common broad-scale threat businesses face regarding data access. Computers and servers cannot afford to have a sudden power loss as that would cause computer activity to stop suddenly and data would be lost. Thus, they need a battery backup, such as an uninterruptible power supply (UPS) that will power the computers from the instant the power fails for a limited time period, until either the power is restored, the backup generator kicks in, or the systems can be shut down properly. A UPS is a relatively inexpensive investment and easy to set up. For extended power outages, a solution might be installation of an automatic generator for the building, a significant investment that requires careful thought and continuing maintenance. Even with a generator, the business still needs a UPS solution, since it takes a few minutes for the generator to warm up and generate adequate power.

Power outages are an important concern for the home user as well. Many of your devices, such as laptops and phones, are battery powered. But your desktop computer and router are not, so it may be worthwhile to invest in a UPS that would provide electricity even if the power goes out, and also mitigate power surges and drops. Depending on where you live, there may be the potential for extended power outages and Internet outages. Never before have we been so reliant upon the Internet, electricity, and being able to communicate instantly with family and friends, so planning ahead for power disruptions is a prudent step.

Consider the likely scenarios that your home faces in a power outage and what your home and family will need. If there is no electricity, how will your systems be affected, and what will you do when the batteries on your devices drain? Do you have a generator for your house, or a car in the driveway, that you can use to recharge your devices?

Here are a few other scenarios to think about, where some planning can make an enormous difference for your family should bad events occur:

1. If your house is destroyed by a fire, or all of your electronics are stolen by a thief, will you have a backup of your data stored somewhere offsite?
2. If you lose Internet and cell phone service, do you have a method of contacting your family and others?
3. If you lose your cell phone, or lose access to your contacts in the cloud, would you know how to contact anyone? Once upon a time, we had to memorize phone numbers, or physically carry them with us. Nowadays, phone numbers are rarely in our mind, but stored in our smartphones or in the cloud.

4. If your family is separated and can't communicate, is there a plan about who to contact or where to meet?

Consider that a disastrous event, or even the simple loss of a cell phone, might make the usual instant communication impossible. Not long ago, we were able to get by without constant communication. An appointment was made days or weeks in advance, and we showed up and waited for the other person to appear. There was no text messaging ("on my way"), or a cell phone to call, or e-mail. So, as you are securing your home from cyber threats, it is worth doing some general disaster planning for your family. This planning might simply include having a hard copy of contact information to reach family and close friends, and having designated safe rally points or message points, if point-to-point communication is impossible.

E. INTEGRITY

Integrity is an information security concept of preventing your data and information from being manipulated, tampered with, or accidentally changed. For the home user, data integrity is not as significant a concern, because we expect our systems will perform as they should, and we know that if there's a problem, it's likely going to be a big problem that is readily apparent to us, such as a disk crash or a file becomes corrupted and unreadable. To protect against the possibility of a crash or disk error, it is important to keep current backups of your data. Microsoft provides File History and Apple provides Time Machine for this purpose. These are applications that take "snapshots" of files over time, allowing you to go back to a version of the file before it was corrupted. When you start securing your office, data integrity becomes a greater concern.

Better Call Saul[2]

The television series *Better Call Saul* illustrated the type of harm that inadequate information security integrity can cause, juxtaposing this with a lack of personal integrity. Chuck and Jimmy McGill are brothers and attorneys. Chuck is a respected attorney who helped found a prominent firm, while Jimmy is a former conman who recently passed the bar.

---

2. *Better Call Saul* (AMC Season 2, 2016).

Chuck was working on a matter for his firm's client, the bank Mesa Verde. Mesa Verde sought to expand and open a new branch, so Chuck was preparing a regulatory filing to obtain this approval, and had several boxes of client files at his home office. Jimmy is angry at Chuck because he felt that Chuck's firm had stolen the client from Jimmy's friend Kim, and sought to correct the perceived wrong using skills he learned in his previous career as a conman. Jimmy tampered with the Mesa Verde files, performed old-fashioned forgery on critical documents, transposing the numbers on the address of the proposed branch. Chuck relied on these forged documents while preparing his filing and thus his filing listed an incorrect address, making it appear that he sloppily transposed the numbers. The regulatory agency is annoyed and their approval is delayed, Chuck is embarrassed, and Mesa Verde is outraged and fires Chuck's firm and returns to Kim.

This show gives us an example of what happens when paper-file integrity is compromised. With electronic data ubiquitous today, the consequences of tampering with electronic files could be more severe.

Consider what would happen if a malicious person gained access to your electronic files, and then selectively tampered with your data. The potential negative consequences for your clients, colleagues, and contacts are enormous, and your professional reputation might be irreversibly damaged. Consider if—instead of tampering with your data—a criminal gained control over your computers and e-mail accounts and then proceeded to assume your identity and act as you. The results would be devastating.

Think of the companies you advise and what criminals could do if they were able to tamper with and alter those companies' data. Data integrity is of special concern for financial institutions, since criminals are highly motivated to tamper with account balances and transactions. These institutions must ensure that the data is recorded and kept accurately, and that there is no fraud or tampering.

The Law, Business Records, and Data Integrity

Electronic data integrity is just an extension of what lawyers are already familiar with. Consider the business records exception to the hearsay rule, and how it aligns with the information security concept of integrity.

The hearsay rule holds that a witness in court can only testify about his first-hand knowledge, and about what he or she saw or did, not about events that someone else told him about, and not about events he or she doesn't remember. The hearsay rule would generally preclude testimony about transactions referenced in business records, since these records are often created by multiple workers who would have no memory of what they witnessed or recorded long ago.

Without the business records hearsay exception, certain evidence might never be admissible about transactions contained within business records. But with the exception, the records can come into evidence after it is established that the records were made and kept according to a business duty to do so accurately. This exception is long-standing and firmly established in our jurisprudence, providing a legal mechanism to get such records into evidence. Once in evidence, it is up to the fact-finder to determine the weight and credibility to be afforded those records.

This legal concept evolved from the time when records were kept in paper ledgers, hand-recorded by employees. Today, business records are usually kept and maintained within computer systems. These systems are something of a hybrid, recording actions performed by people while also performing many tasks automatically. It is equally important for today's electronic records to be reliable and trustworthy.

> Thus, the information security concept of "integrity" is closely connected to concepts lawyers are already familiar with. Think of it as placing a "business duty" upon the electronic data systems to make and keep records accurately, just as that duty has traditionally been imposed on employees.

F. THE PRINCIPLE OF "LEAST PRIVILEGE" AND "NEED TO KNOW"

An important information security principle is "least privilege," which is similar to the concept of "need to know." This means the user should only have the access needed to accomplish his tasks, but no more. By limiting access to what is needed, the user is prevented from accessing and damaging information or programs that he has no need to access. It also means that if the user's account is taken over or hacked by a cybercriminal, the cybercriminal's access has been limited. The principle of least privilege is illustrated through two areas: data access and administrator rights.

1. Data Access

In the workplace, access to data is frequently segmented. Documents and data maintained by Human Resources are not accessible to members of other departments because of confidentiality and because most employees don't need access to that data to do their jobs. In the home, you might consider similar segmentation. If your child doesn't need access to your documents, then consider segmenting access through separate user accounts. Even if you trust your child with your documents, by segmenting access, if your child's account is compromised, the hacker will not have access to your documents.

2. Administrator Rights and Accounts

Operating systems and software typically provide for different types of accounts: regular user accounts and administrator accounts. Administrator accounts can do many things to the computer that regular user accounts cannot, and we don't need to use administrator accounts for most of our computer activity. Even administrators of a large network should not use their administrator account for general computer use. Unfortunately, the general practice by many is to use an administrator account all of the time, and this violates the principle of least privilege. By using the administrator account, we are using more privileges than we need and are exposing the account to compromise, which would give the hacker full administrator privileges and the capability to control the computer forever. In contrast, if the hacker compromises a standard user account, that means lower privileges and less opportunity to compromise the computer.

G. INFORMATION CLASSIFICATION

In business or government, there are often regulations about how you store and access certain types of data, based on the principle that not all data and information get treated or accessed equally. In government, top secret information can only be maintained on systems with appropriate security features, and access must be restricted to users with the appropriate clearance and "need to know" authorization. In private and public business, financial, health, or personal information needs to be treated with an appropriate level of security. However, a lot of data is not sensitive, including publicly available information like a cafeteria's lunch menu.

You should think about how you might classify your own data. In doing so, consider the consequences (i) if the data were stolen and released to the public and (ii) if it were destroyed and no longer available to you. Depending on the type of data (e.g., your grocery shopping list, family photos, or client's trade secrets), each event has different consequences that affect how you will treat it.

If you are holding personal information of customers or clients—such as their names, birthdates, financial information, and legally privileged secrets—then it would be serious if it were stolen. On the other hand, if your computer hard drive was destroyed and the information became unavailable, you could restore a backup or even ask the client to provide the information again. It might be embarrassing, but no serious harm would be done. This is an instance where confidentiality is a greater concern than availability, because the exposure of confidential secrets would be disastrous, while the destruction of one copy of the data would merely be embarrassing.

Conversely, if you were writing a book, it might not be serious if a hacker obtained a copy of your drafts. The hacker is unlikely to publish your work, and the information was destined to be public eventually—though it might be embarrassing for people to see how rough the early drafts were. On the other hand, if your hard drive was destroyed or encrypted by malware—and you had no backup—that could be calamitous. This is an example of availability being more important than confidentiality, since it is more essential that you have a copy of the data available to you.

H. CONCLUSION

This chapter has covered the basic principles of information security and cybersecurity, principles that apply to large entities such as governments, corporations, and large law firms, but also to small businesses, solo practitioners, homes, families, and individuals. Now that you know the basics of information security, and understand the cybercrime and privacy threats you face, you have foundational knowledge that will aid you as you progress through the book and secure your home, family, law firm, and practice.

There is increasing regulation and litigation surrounding cybersecurity, and professionals are subject to rules about how they use and store work-related data, whether they are at the office or at home. In many ways, this trend results in better cybersecurity practices; however, the fear of litigation can also result in an overemphasis on "paper compliance," and not enough focus on conducting honest assessments and making meaningful changes to improve one's cybersecurity posture. To avoid a reactive mindset, keep in mind the information security principles discussed in this chapter, and the threats you face to your security and privacy.

CHAPTER 5

Basic Computer Principles

A. INTRODUCTION

This chapter will summarize and explain how computers work. If computers make you apprehensive, this chapter will put you at ease, give you a better understanding of their operation, and enable you to fix issues yourself that you previously might not have attempted. You may start to realize that you have left some electronic doors open that you didn't know about. By understanding how a computer works, you are better able to protect yourself from intruders, and your computing experience will be more enjoyable. By knowing more about computers, and being able to troubleshoot them, you will be able to tell the difference between a technical support issue and a cybercrime attack. In addition, you will be able to have an intelligent conversation with a technical support engineer.

We will review the various devices most of us use for computing and related purposes, such as desktop computers, laptops, tablets, smartphones, and external hard drives. As you proceed through this chapter, consider visiting CybersecurityHomeAndOffice.com, find the webpages that parallel this chapter and view the photographs of the various computer components as they are discussed.

In the next chapter, we will discuss how different computers talk to each other through networking and the Internet, and cover related hardware items like modems and routers. First, let's briefly discuss the basics of computing and its history.

B. THE EVOLUTION OF COMPUTING

Though today's era of connected computers is unprecedented, computers in some form have been around a long time. The abacus (a counting frame) qualifies as a computing device, and is over four thousand years old. It seems like a really simple device, the operations it performs are fairly basic, but people can use it to keep track of numbers and perform calculations that would be impossible for most of us using the mind alone. Today's modern computers, at their most elemental level, perform extremely simple tasks. These

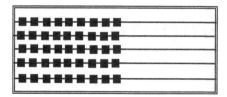

FIGURE 5.1 Base 10 abacus showing value of zero.

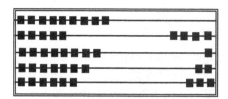

FIGURE 5.2 Base 10 abacus showing value of 4,123.

simple tasks, when combined together in great numbers and at high speed, are capable of extraordinary things.

Abacuses come in many configurations, but usually are made up of several rows of wire with beads strung on them (Figures 5.1 and 5.2). Each wire might represent a particular factor of ten (e.g. the bottom wire is the "ones" position, the next wire is the "tens," then the "hundreds," "thousands," etc.). The position of the bead on each wire determines the value in that position, and together all of the wires and bead positions determine the value that is being stored. Addition and subtraction can be performed using the abacus; it merely requires a person with some understanding of how the abacus works to manipulate the beads. If the person is adding, they move the required number of beads, and if a particular position exceeds 9 beads they reset the value of that position to zero and "carry the one" to the row above by moving a bead one position. As we'll see later, the position of the bead on the abacus is very similar to how computers store values using magnetism and electrical charge. Instead of a human moving beads, the computer processor performs the calculation and changes the output value.

1. Storing Information

Computers work in a similar fashion to store values, but instead of using beads on a wire to keep track of values, they use magnetic charges or electrical charges to store values and count and calculate. An individual bead on an abacus is either "left" or "right," and thus it can only have one of two possible values. The bead position on an abacus is essentially a binary system, and computers use a similar binary system.

Binary	Decimal
0000	0
0001	1
0010	2
0011	3
0100	4
0101	5

FIGURE 5.3 Binary to decimal conversion.

A computer stores these "on/off" designations for information as a positive magnetic charge or a negative charge, or a positive voltage or a negative voltage. Regardless of how complex the ultimate work of a computer is, it all starts with the simple binary "bits" of information, which are tracked by the computer as either "on" or "off," "0" or "1." Thus, we could use binary digits to count from zero to five as indicated in Figure 5.3.

Knowing this fundamental basis of computer counting will help you understand the joke: "There are 10 types of people in the world, those that know binary, and those that don't." After all, "10" is the binary representation of the decimal number "2." Using this method of counting, multiple bits of information can be grouped together to form any sized number. They can also be used to represent any letter, character, or symbol, and put together to form words, documents, books, and more. In the next chapter we will discuss computer counting a little more, and Appendix 5 has even more detail on this.

2. Processing Information

Now that you have seen how a computer stores information, let's cover the basics of how a computer processes information. In the simplest terms, a computer takes the information that it has stored and manipulates it as directed by human input. Computer processing is essentially performing some very simple tasks, such as checking if two values are equal, adding or subtracting values, and returning a result. From these tasks, more complicated math is possible, starting with multiplication and division, up to the most sophisticated calculations, algorithms, and programs. A software program is really just a set of directions written by people to a computer, telling the computer processor what functions to perform and where to get the information inputs. The processor acts upon the inputs as directed and provides an output.

The abacus requires considerable human input, whereas computers have evolved to perform extensive operations independent of human input. Computer capabilities have expanded exponentially in terms of processing power, storage, and memory, while their physical size has decreased. During the 1960s, NASA built and placed the cutting edge of mobile computing in the Apollo program's spacecrafts, but today, the smartphone in your pocket has far more computing power, memory, speed, and storage.

Few predicted or imagined where we would be today. When our current computer and network infrastructure was being built, very few imagined there would be an industry of criminals, not to mention the resources and commitment of nation states, devoted to breaking into computer systems and stealing data. The Internet and our computers were built to share information and were not designed with security in mind. Few can predict or imagine where we will be tomorrow, but it is clear that our planning must provide for the security of our data and computing devices.

C. COMPUTER HARDWARE

You probably have many types of computing devices in your home. A smartphone, a tablet, a laptop computer, and perhaps a desktop computer. You also have devices that interact with your computing devices, such as printers, scanners, external hard drives, and modems and routers. Each computing device is made up of hardware components, and each device runs software that allows you to use the hardware.

Take a look at your computers and the gadgets around them. If someone else set up your system for you, there may be devices you don't recognize, so take a moment to identify them. Years ago, it was easier to tell what equipment was part of your system, since everything was connected by cables. Today, wireless networking and the "Internet of Things" (IoT) makes an inventory of your system harder to complete, since many devices are invisibly connected to each other. IoT is covered in greater detail in the next chapter—it is essentially the phenomenon of previously stand-alone devices that today are connected to your network, the cloud, and other people. IoT devices in your home may include televisions, stereo systems, lightbulbs, locks, thermostats, security cameras, refrigerators, and children's toys, all with mini-computers in them. All these devices can connect to your home network, thus the Internet, and may be transmitting data across it to the manufacturer, among other places.

As we discuss the various hardware components of a computer, it is easiest to focus first on the desktop PC. The term "PC" stands for "personal computer" but is generally understood to mean computers other than

Apple's line of Mac computers. Desktop PCs have larger components which are accessible to the user. One can open the case and see the components inside, parts can be replaced, and there is room to work. PCs usually run on the Microsoft Windows operating system, a massive collection of software programs that provide the underlying instructions for all the computer functions we've come to expect. A PC can also run other operating systems—such as Linux—and is nearly infinitely customizable in terms of parts, drivers, and software.

Macintosh computers, or Macs, are loved by many and run Apple's operating system, currently OS X, pronounced "oh ess ten." Many Mac desktops are "all in one" computers, the computer hardware is integrated with the monitor, making for a very compact, dense space, and many PC makers have emulated this configuration. Macs are much less customizable, as Apple exercises a great deal of control over the computer, parts, and software. Except for some very basic operations like upgrading the computer's memory, a user is not supposed to open up their Mac.

Whether you are a die-hard Mac or PC fan, or don't even own a desktop computer, the following section will familiarize you with the basic parts of a computer. Once you understand them, you will see how computers can be scaled up for a data center, or down to the size of a laptop, tablet, smartphone, or IoT device.

As computers get smaller, the parts are packed together tighter, with less tolerance and less opportunity for the user to open the device to see, upgrade, or change the parts. For many devices, such as Apple products and many smartphones, only a trained and certified technician should open the device, otherwise it might void the warranty or violate the terms of the end user licensing agreement.

Though computers have evolved rapidly and there is a wide diversity of computing devices, they all share the same basic components. Here's a list of basic parts from simple to complex:

- Case to protect the device, and keep the environment out
- Power supply (power converter with fan or heat sink)
- Display (monitor, screen)
- Ports (USB, parallel, serial, DVI, HDMI, DP, etc.)
- Input devices (mouse, keyboard, microphone, camera, etc.)
- Methods to communicate with other devices (network interface card, Ethernet network card, Wi-Fi network card)
- Processor that does the calculations
- Temporary memory to aid the processor as it calculates (RAM)
- Motherboard (where most of the sub-components mount)

- Internal storage: Permanent memory to store the user's data and operating system and applications (spinning hard drive or solid state drive, also known as flash storage)
- External storage (removable media)
- External devices (scanner, printer)
- Software: Computer programs that help operate the computer, from BIOS to operating systems and applications

1. Case

The computer case serves an important purpose of protecting the delicate electronics inside from physical damage. For desktop computers, the case can serve as a monitor stand. The case also plays a role in cooling; components generate heat, and the case has vent holes to passively circulate air and to aid fans that start automatically when the temperature gets too high. You should keep the vent holes clear of dust and debris for better cooling and operation. For smartphones, tablets, and laptops, the case allows you to stuff the device in your pocket, purse, or bag without damaging the components, although there is little or no provision for air circulation within them. It is an engineering challenge for designers to pack all of that computing into a tiny case, and have it withstand the stresses of movement, heat, and shock.

Cases also have holes for ports so you can connect external devices to the computer, such as a monitor, keyboard, mouse, audio, USB cables, or a network cable. The case also allows wireless transmissions to go through it or sometimes acts as the antenna, so that the device can connect wirelessly to the Internet or other computers or devices.

2. Power Supply

A desktop computer needs continual power supplied from an external source in order to run. The power cord you plug into the power strip or wall outlet runs to the desktop, where it connects to the desktop's power supply unit. This unit acts as a transformer and converts the power from the outlet—110 to 120 volts alternating current (AC)—to 12 volts direct current (DC). The power supply unit also has a fan to cool itself and the computer, and may be able to condition the power slightly if it surges.

In the previous chapter on information security basics, we discussed the importance of continual power for data availability. If the power were suddenly removed, you could lose data, and if the power surged, you might not only might you lose data, but your computer could be damaged or destroyed. To protect against power surges, there should be a surge suppressor between your computer and your electricity supply. Even better is to have an uninterruptable power supply (UPS) device that has a battery backup, a surge suppressor, and a power conditioner within it. Thus, if the power suddenly increases, decreases, or shuts off all together, your computer and data will be protected until power returns or you shut down the computer in a controlled manner.

A desktop computer has an internal battery, but it is tiny. Its sole purpose is to keep track of the time and a few other basic pieces of data. Thanks to this battery, when you unplug your desktop, it can still keep track of the time and remember some basic settings.

A laptop computer, tablet, or smartphone has an internal power supply—the battery. We can recharge the device, as well as power it, through the power cord. The power cord for your mobile device also has a transformer within it, converting the electrical outlet's 120/110 volts AC to the proper 12 volts DC that your device needs, ensuring that your device gets the proper amount of current (amperage).

3. Display

The display is the primary method the computer uses to send information to the user, so we can see and interact with it and each other. Some computers have a built-in display, like the Mac "all in one" design, laptop computers, and tablets and smartphones. For a desktop PC, there is an immense selection of monitors from which to choose, from small to giant, basic screen resolution to ultra-high definition.

Displays can be for viewing only but they can also act as an input device—for example, touch screens. Touch screens not only display images, but can tell when and where someone is touching, and process that touch as input, as if the user had clicked with a mouse. We have touch screens on smartphones and tablets, and they are also available for laptops and desktops. Touch screens aren't perfect as input devices—but nothing is. As people become more accustomed to touch screens, it's amusing when they try to use a view-only screen as a touch screen.

a. Video Cable

The physical connection between an external monitor and the computer is by cable, and there are many different cable connections, depending on the computer's video capabilities and the type of monitor. Some common cable connections include:

- DP: DisplayPort
- HDMI: High-Definition Multimedia Interface
- DVI: Digital Visual Interface, of which there are several types
- VGA: Video Graphics Array

Video standards and connectors are continually evolving, so it can be a challenge to maintain compatible connectors across devices, especially laptops, tablets, and smartphones.

b. Video Card

The video cable connects from the monitor to the computer's video card. There are a wide variety of video card types, but essentially the video card is a mini-computer dedicated to providing visual output to the monitor. The video card has connections to the main computer, where it gets instructions about what should be sent to the monitor, and it has a port that the video cable is plugged into though which it transmits data to the monitor. Once it receives these instructions, it transmits data to the monitor through the port, into which the display cable is inserted.

Video cards are also called display cards or graphics cards. It takes a lot of computer power to display detailed and fast-moving graphics, so a powerful graphics card performs this function without putting undue demands upon the computer's main processor. The PC desktop user has a choice of many different types of video cards to suit the user's needs, from budget-conscious users who simply do word processing and Internet surfing, to video gamers looking for the most demanding graphics.

c. Video Driver

The video driver is the computer software that allows the computer to speak with the monitor—it tells the video card how to interpret the input it receives to display it properly on the monitor. The video driver essentially allows the computer, video card, and display to communicate with each other. A video driver is just one type of device driver, and each hardware component the computer communicates with needs a device driver, including the hard disk drive, monitor, mouse, printer, network card, and more.

4. Ports: USB, Parallel, Serial, VGA, DVI, HDMI, DP

Computers commonly communicate with other devices through ports. USB (universal serial bus) ports are the most universal type of port and provide a standardization that allows for "plug and play." Just plug your device into the USB port, the computer will figure out how to communicate with the device (including automatically installing a device driver if needed), and you are ready to go. USB ports can transfer data and also provide a certain amount of electrical power from the computer to an attached device, eliminating the need to have a separate power cord.

USB ports on a computer are physically standardized, though some have different capabilities. The typical USB port on the computer is a USB Type A socket, and the end of the USB cable that plugs into it is the Type

A plug. However, not all Type A sockets are created equal; newer sockets are capable of receiving and sending data at faster rates. At the other end of the USB cable is a connector, which could be one of many types, such as Micro-B, Mini-B, Type B, the new Type C, and for Apple, the new Lightning connector or older 30-pin connector. These connectors attach to the USB device, like a smartphone, tablet, external hard disk, or printer.

Older computers commonly had serial ports and parallel ports, but these are becoming obsolete for the home user. These ports and connectors had multiple sockets and pins that allowed a cable with multiple wires to be plugged into it. Parallel ports (traditionally with twenty-five pins or wires, like the DB-25 connector) were used for printers, and allowed the data to be transmitted along the twenty-five wires simultaneously (e.g. in parallel). Parallel ports are now essentially obsolete, thanks to USB technology. Serial ports allow data to be transmitted one bit at a time in a stream, and are also becoming obsolete for the home user due to USB technology.

5. Input Devices (Keyboard, Mouse, Microphone, Camera, and More)

Input devices allow people to provide information to the computer, so that the computer can act on it. Notable examples include your keyboard, mouse, microphone, camera, and touch screen. On a desktop computer, your keyboard, mouse, and microphone are likely connected by USB cable, though your mouse or keyboard might connect wirelessly. With an older computer, these input devices might connect by a serial-type cable. However they are connected, data is transmitted from the keyboard, mouse, or microphone to the computer, and the computer reacts to the input.

The keyboard and mouse are relatively slow ways of introducing data to the computer—even if one is an expert typist. Consider that there was a time when we didn't have computer monitors or keyboards, and the method for humans to communicate directly with the computer was through punch cards. Voice input is continually improving, but since a person can only speak so many words a minute, it is still a relatively slow input method. Researchers are working on ways that a computer might read a human's mind—that would be a fascinating type of input device.

6. Network Interface Controller

The network interface controller (NIC) connects the computer to a network. You might also hear it called a network interface card or network adapter. It used to be a separate "card" within the computer—thus it's still commonly called a network interface card—but now is usually built into the main motherboard. There are two main types of network cards, an Ethernet card for a wired network, or a Wi-Fi card for a wireless network. If it's a network card for a wired network, your computer probably has an RJ-45 port for an Ethernet-type cable connector; it looks like a phone line connector but is bigger. If it's a network card for a wireless network, there's an antenna inside the computer's case that you cannot see, but that can receive and transmit data wirelessly.

The network interface controller has a unique serial number assigned by the manufacturer, called a MAC (media access control) address. The MAC address is used within a network as an address to send and receive data. Think of it as the phone number of the interface card. In normal usage, the network interface controller ignores all data sent through the network unless it is addressed to its own particular MAC address. It's like politely ignoring conversations that are not addressed to you, when you are in a crowded room. However, if the NIC is set to "promiscuous" mode, then it will receive all data sent through the network, and forward all this data to its computer. This means that any computer can be configured to receive all data transmitted on a local network, thereby eavesdropping on other computers in that same local network. We'll discuss networking and the Internet in detail in the next chapter.

Wi-Fi is one type of wireless technology, and Bluetooth is another type. Most laptops now come with a Bluetooth wireless adapter, which can be used to connect wirelessly with other devices.

7. Processor (Central Processing Unit, Microprocessor)

The computer has one or more central processing units (CPUs), which are the brain and calculator of the computer. The processor performs the calculations and operations that enable the operating system, software applications, the Internet, and all the things you do on your computing device. If you are listening to music, composing an e-mail, writing a document, or viewing or editing a photo or spreadsheet, it is because the processor is doing something that allows that application to run. As indicated previously, the individual operations performed by the CPU are quite basic, but in the aggregate, they are extremely powerful.

Within the CPU are memory registers that temporarily store data for immediate use by the CPU. Traditionally, these registers are like Pez dispensers, in that they store data sequentially so that it can be accessed one block at a time, in the reverse order that the data was added to the register. This system is inefficient for storing a lot of data, which is why the computer has a separate form of short-term memory, called random access memory, or RAM, which will be discussed next.

8. Random Access Memory

Random access memory (RAM), is a temporary or volatile way of storing information that disappears when the power is turned off. RAM is where data is held when the computer needs to rapidly access and reference it repeatedly and generally work on it. The storage space in RAM is limited, so the computer needs to carefully manage what data is stored in RAM, and offload data that is not immediately needed in RAM. For example, when you open an application like Word, the program is loaded (copied) into RAM, and then, when you open a document, that too is loaded into RAM. From there, Word can tell the CPU to perform calculations and generate output, and keyboard inputs cause the document to be changed, and the change to be displayed on the screen. RAM is not where your final changes will be stored, it is just the temporary holding area where your document is loaded while you are doing the work. When you save your work, it is written to the hard disk for long-term storage.

At its most basic level, RAM is like an abacus, storing bits of information as either a "0" or a "1," or a positive voltage or negative voltage. These bits of information are combined into bytes (eight bits), then larger groupings like kilobytes, megabytes, and gigabytes. Instead of the abacus analogy, you can imagine a huge sheet of graph paper, with each square representing a single "bit" of data, and inside the box can only be one of two possible binary values, 0 or 1 (Figure 5.4). The computer processor is continually reading from RAM, and writing to it, but it is simply storing values needed by the computer processor. The values might be a software program, like Word, or it might be a document, like your legal brief. RAM is temporary and requires continual power, so if one were to turn the computer power off, the electrical charge would be lost, and so would the value of each bit of information.

Since RAM is limited, the computer needs to manage what is stored in RAM. Users like to have many applications and documents open at one time, which demands more RAM than the computer has. The solution for this is virtual RAM, where the computer takes some of the data in RAM and stores it on your hard disk drive temporarily. Thus, virtual RAM acts like a slower version of RAM, but it isn't really RAM. The computer tries to anticipate your needs and the needs of your applications, to ensure that it is using available RAM and virtual RAM efficiently. Virtual RAM means some of your data

	Bit position within byte							
	1	2	3	4	5	6	7	8
1st byte	0	1	1	0	1	0	1	0
2nd byte	0	1	1	0	1	1	1	1
3rd byte	0	1	1	0	1	0	0	0
4th byte	0	1	1	0	1	1	1	0

FIGURE 5.4 RAM storage in each memory bit.

is written to the hard drive, where it takes on a degree of permanence even though you didn't knowingly save it to your hard drive. This can present a confidentiality issue because someone with sufficient technical knowledge and access to your computer could recover data from virtual RAM whereas data in RAM disappears when the computer is turned off.

9. Motherboard (System Board)

The motherboard is the name for the large, often green, plastic circuit board to which many of the computer's important parts are attached or connected, including the CPU, RAM, video card, ports, and more. It's called a "printed" circuit board because the board has electrical connections embedded into it, so that various components, once they are plugged into their respective places, are automatically properly wired and electrically connected. For example, once a chip is plugged into its proper spot, the inputs and outputs for data, control, and power are all properly connected, through the printing of the electrical circuits by the manufacturer at the time the motherboard was built. The motherboard has places where external devices plug in, like USB ports, video ports, and network ports (Figure 5.5). It also has places where internal devices plug in, such as internal hard drives, which we'll talk about next.

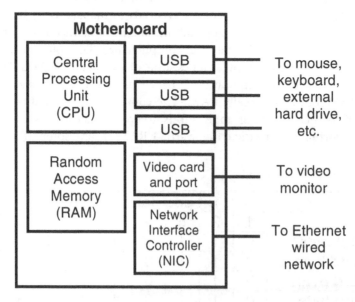

FIGURE 5.5 Motherboard.

10. Internal Data Storage

Internal storage holds data even when the computer is turned off, and is in the form of hard disk drives with moving parts, or the newer solid state drives that have no moving parts.

a. Hard Disk Drives

Hard disk drives (HDD) contain spinning magnetic platters that store data in the form of a magnetic charge. These platters are divided into millions of bits, each of which can have either a positive or negative magnetic charge. Once it is assigned a charge to record a piece of data, it maintains that charge until it is rewritten—even if the power is turned off. Some hard drives have multiple platters—like multiple layers of a cake—and each platter is divided into pizza-slice-shaped sectors. To write and read the data on the magnetic platter, the drive has an arm with a head at the end of it. The arm can traverse from the inside of the platter to the outside like a record player needle or the laser on a CD or DVD player. The platter rotates, allowing the head to access any portion of the platter, and the head can read from the platter even as it rotates at tremendous speeds. If the drive has multiple platters, it has multiple heads, to simultaneously read from each of the platters.

For information security and computer forensics purposes, it's important to understand what physically happens on the hard disk when you delete a file. When you "delete" a file, you are not actually deleting the data from your computer. Instead, you are merely telling the computer that the place where the file used to be is now free, and available to be rewritten. However, until that space on the hard drive is actually rewritten with new data, the old, "deleted" data still exists there and can still be recovered. Sometimes the user can recover "deleted" data by going to the recycle bin or trash bin. Even more can be recovered by someone with some training and forensic tools. We'll discuss this concept in later chapters, including ways to securely decommission your devices so that you are not inadvertently leaving your data behind when you sell or recycle the device. Until then, remember that a hard drive sitting in storage can retain data indefinitely.

Usually and ideally, the data for a particular file or application is stored sequentially, all next to each other on the magnetic platters in the hard drive. But sometimes the hard drive starts writing a file in a particular sector, but the sector fills up, and the computer has to find the next available sector to continue writing the file. Thus, the file is not stored in continuous sectors, but has been fragmented. File fragmentation can slow down access to files, which is why operating systems have utilities to defragment files—rearrange them and copy them so that they are stored sequentially next to each other. This is also one reason why fragments of data can be found in multiple places on the hard drive.

b. Solid State Drives

Solid state drives (SSD) are a newer technology that is faster, more durable, and uses less electricity than a hard disk drive, however they are more expensive per the amount of data they hold. SSDs don't have moving parts, nor a spinning platter, and data is stored in a similar manner as RAM, except that the data is permanent, rather than volatile. Think of an SSD as similar to your flash drive, or thumb drive, except it is internal to the computer and holds more data. Whereas hard disk drives store the data as magnetic charges, SSDs store it as electrical charges, and the electrical charge stays even when the device is powered off.

Solid state drives are extremely reliable but also relatively new. It is conceivable that a worn SSD drive that is left disconnected from any power source could experience some leakage of the electrical charge, resulting in a loss of data. This emphasizes the lesson that applies to all electronic storage: digital data left untouched for many years may end up being unrecoverable.

c. Hybrid Drives

Manufacturers also provide hybrid drive technology using both a hard disk drive and a solid state drive working together, to offer the best of both worlds for the user. A copy of the data that the user is using currently can be stored in the SSD drive, while the HDD is used for longer-term storage. This concept is similar to the way RAM and virtual RAM work together.

There are other ways a computer can internally store and access data, including removable media drives, like DVD and CD drives, which are becoming outmoded. There have also been a host of other technologies that are now essentially obsolete, including floppy disk drives, zip drives, and other removable storage media. As discussed next, flash storage, removable flash drives and external hard drives have become popular, fast, and inexpensive storage methods.

11. External Data Storage

Nearly any type of storage device that could be internal to the computer can also be connected externally to the computer, especially with USB "plug and play" connections. There are a number of ways to store data that are external to the computer: external hard disk drives, external flash drives (including thumb drives), external DVD/CD media, and a host of other technologies. External storage can be attached directly to your computer (such as via a USB cable), or it can be attached to the network and potentially made available to multiple computers on that network, which is called network attached storage (NAS).

An external hard disk drive is similar to the hard drive inside the typical computer, except they are designed for portability. It has the same type of spinning platter inside, relying upon the same magnetic storage technology. Many external hard drives, especially the smaller ones, are powered through the USB cable that connects to your computer, which removes the necessity of having a separate power cord. You should have an external hard drive to periodically back up your important data, and store it in a safe location when not in use. External flash drives (including thumb drives) use flash storage technology to store the data. They are small and fast, and we've all used them by plugging them into the USB port and using them like a mini hard drive.

In your home, your data storage needs might be minimal. Your computer's internal storage, plus an external hard drive for periodic backup, may be sufficient to store all of your data. An external hard drive is also helpful to store voluminous data that you don't access regularly. Some users need more speed, reliability, or storage than a single external hard drive can provide. Enter the RAID configuration, which stands for redundant array of independent (or inexpensive) disks. To the user, a RAID array appears to be a single hard drive, but behind the scenes it is really two or more hard disk drives working together to provide enhanced reliability and speed. In most configurations, RAID can provide redundancy, so that if one disk should fail, the user is alerted to the bad disk, the system continues to work until the bad disk gets replaced, and no data is lost.

There are many computer storage types that have become obsolete, in the relatively short history of computing. Further, we have limited experience regarding how long certain storage technologies can hold their data. We know that paper documents and paintings have lasted hundreds, even thousands of years, but digital storage has had only a short existence thus far. Many specific types of digital storage have quickly become obsolete. If you have any 5 ¼ -inch or 3 ½ -inch floppy disks left over from 10 to 20 years ago, you probably will have a hard time finding what you need to read them, and you may find the data has been damaged. Chapter 9 will discuss ways to store your data and protect it from obsolescence and accidental destruction.

12. External Devices Such as Scanners and Printers
Your home computer is probably connected to a printer, scanner, and/or fax machine. If that connection is through a USB cable, then it's a relatively direct communication between computer and device. However, printers, scanners, and fax machines that are connected to your computer can also be connected with other computers on the network, and there is the possibility of connecting the printer directly to the network via Ethernet cable or Wi-Fi. As we will discuss in following chapters, devices that are networked and communicating with each other can present security vulnerabilities.

D. PROGRAMS THAT RUN ON YOUR COMPUTER: BIOS, OPERATING SYSTEM, APPLICATIONS

Now let's discuss the various types of software that tell the hardware how to operate, and that interface between the hardware and the user. Normally we use the term "software" to refer to programs that we use, like Word, Excel, or Safari; in this section we use it to refer to any computer program running on the computer.

1. BIOS

BIOS stands for basic input output system and is the most basic level of software in a computer. It provides instructions for how the computer communicates with both the outside world and with its internal devices. This software sets forth how the computer reads input from the mouse, keyboard, and storage devices. When your computer boots up, the first thing it starts loading into memory is BIOS, since without the BIOS, the computer can't proceed through the next steps, which include loading the operating system and receiving input from the user.

2. Operating System

Next, the computer needs to load the operating system. The operating system is the middle layer between the software applications that you run and the computer's basic functioning. There are three main operating systems in use today for home computers: Microsoft's Windows, Linux, an open-source operating system based on the Unix operating system, and Apple's operating system for the Mac called OS X, which is based on Free BSD, which is somewhat related to Unix. Most home users are running a Windows or Mac operating system, so that's what this book focuses on.

A Mac computer can generally run only Apple's operating system. That said, it is possible for one operating system to "virtually" run one or more other operating systems. Thus, a Mac user could run Microsoft Windows or Linux on a Mac by running it "on top of" the Mac operating system. Put another way, the Mac computer hardware is running the Mac operating system, and then the Mac operating system is running a "virtual" Microsoft Windows operating system, which can then run Windows-based applications. A Windows user could also virtualize various operating systems.

Mobile devices also need operating systems, and examples of these include Apple's iOS, Google's Android, Microsoft's Windows 10 Mobile, and Blackberry 10. As of this writing, Apple's iOS and Google's Android control 99% of the mobile market.[1]

---

1. *Global Mobile OS Market Share in Sales to End Users from 1st Quarter 2009 to 1st Quarter 2016,* STATISTA, https://www.statista.com/statistics/266136/global-market-share-held-by-smartphone-operating -systems (citing statistics from third quarter 2016).

3. File System

The operating system needs a file system to store data and access it. If you are transferring data among different operating systems (e.g. Mac to Windows, vice-versa, or an older operating system to a newer one), one issue you might encounter is related to different file systems. Every device that stores data, whether it's your internal hard drive or external thumb drive, needs to use a particular file system. For your reference, here are some lists of common file systems over the years.

Microsoft's file systems:

- FAT: File Allocation Table
- FAT32: a newer version
- NTFS: New Technology File System (for larger files and increased security)
- exFAT: extended File Allocation Table (works with flash drives, can handle large file sizes, and is more compatible with Mac and other devices)

Apple's file systems:

- HFS: Hierarchical File System
- HFS+: Hierarchical File System Plus
- APFS: Apple File System

4. Applications (Software)

Applications are the software programs that we regularly use on our computers to accomplish tasks. Most operating systems come preloaded with many built-in applications, and there are millions of additional applications that can be obtained. Popular applications include the suite of Microsoft Office business applications (Word, Excel, PowerPoint, etc.), Apple's Pages, Numbers, Keynote, and more. As we transition to the cloud, our reliance on web-browser-based applications increases. Web browsers include Google's Chrome, Microsoft's Edge and Internet Explorer, Apple's Safari, and Mozilla Firefox. Our increased reliance upon the web browser makes its security critical.

Years ago, you might have purchased software in a store, carried it home on a CD, and then installed it onto a single computer. Today, many users want to access their software and data from anywhere, on any computer, and software providers want to keep better track of their users, retain them, and prevent piracy. Today most software makers distribute their products through downloads over the Internet, and have you use the software by interacting with them through the Internet. Many software packages are by subscription, which includes cloud applications or storage, and this keeps the user and software provider connected constantly, allowing the software provider to prevent piracy, learn more about the user, and to try sell the user more products.

5. Virtual Ports

Earlier, we covered the computer's hardware ports—holes in the case where you plug cables to connect other hardware to your computer. Consider that there are also "virtual ports," an addressing system created by computer software, and they facilitate communication between different devices and applications. Usually they are simply called "ports," making it easy to forget they are a manifestation of computer programming. For now, just be aware of the difference between a physical and virtual port, and that virtual ports are an addressing mechanism. In the next chapter we will discuss how ports are used for networking.

E. FROM DESKTOP TO MINIATURE: LAPTOP, NOTEBOOK, TABLET, SMARTPHONE, SMARTWATCH, IOT

We covered the main computer parts from the perspective of a desktop computer, enabling us to disassemble the device and visualize each component. As computing devices get smaller and more mobile, the functional design principles remain the same, but the technology and capabilities change in order to shrink the device and make it lighter and more portable. A smartphone is not going to use a spinning hard disk drive for storage, but rather the more compact flash storage technology. No matter the size, the device needs a processor, temporary volatile memory, permanent storage for when the device is powered off, methods to communicate with the user and other computers, and software. Thus, the principles remain similar across devices of all size, including security vulnerabilities. As our devices become more and more interconnected, it's important to recognize how a security flaw in one device can affect other connected devices.

F. COMPUTERS ON STEROIDS: THE CLOUD AND DATA CENTERS

Both at work and at home, cloud data storage has become commonplace, and cloud providers try to entice and encourage us to keep our data—in all its various forms—with them. Some people don't even realize that some or much of their data is stored in the cloud, but the test is pretty simple. If you can access data from any computer device, and from any Internet connection, then it is probably stored on the cloud. This data could include your e-mail, contacts, calendar, documents, and more.

The "cloud" seems an ambiguous term, and that is fitting. What is the cloud? Think of it as someone else's computer that you are allowed to use. We know our data is out there "somewhere," it remains available continually, but we never see the physical location where it is actually kept. The cloud is a storage system that keeps massive amounts of data within enormous data centers. Data centers are locations that have been scouted, built, and maintained with special considerations, such as good connectivity to fiber optic Internet highways, strong and secure buildings, good electricity supply with backup generators and fuel, specialized cooling and ventilation, lots of hardware, computers, and software, plus highly trained people to watch over it (Figure 5.6). Data centers have massive computing and storage capabilities, plus mechanisms to keep it running without interruption. They might be located anywhere in the world, but if you are in the United States, it is likely the data center holding your data is also in the United States. Many cloud services offered to us are ultimately hosted in a data center somewhere. Companies who offer cloud services directly to the public include Google, Amazon (AWS), Microsoft (Azure), and many others.

The data centers are like an army of high-performance computers. Whereas your desktop might have one internal hard drive, a data center has thousands of hard drives running and storing data. If one hard drive goes bad, there is no interruption as your data is seamlessly accessed and stored on another drive. Your desktop has a case with a single internal fan, whereas data centers have rows upon rows of hardware, with expensive ventilation systems designed to keep cool air flowing across the servers.

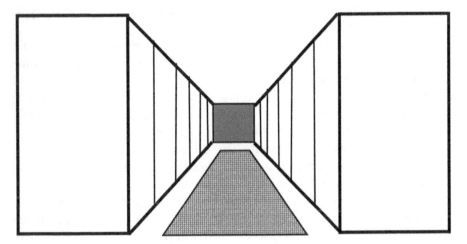

FIGURE 5.6 Data center: Long rows of server racks filled with computers. Needs lots of Internet connectivity, electricity, and cooling (note the air-conditioning grates on the floor).

These data centers allow for an economy of scale. Before cloud services were available, we had to store our own data on our own equipment, in our own home or business. For home users, our data generally resided on our desktop computer. For businesses, data storage required an investment in computer hardware and people to keep it running. The cloud offers amazing possibilities and access to data and software, managed better than most individuals and businesses can do on their own. But it also means we are giving up some control, and that cybercriminals can try to access our data via the cloud—just like we do.

Hopefully you have enabled two-step login (two-factor authentication) on your important cloud data. If you haven't, remember that anyone—anywhere in the world—who learns your password can probably access your data. Remember all of the ways we have discussed that criminals can learn your password.

G. ENCRYPTION OF DATA AT REST

In the previous chapter, we introduced encryption as an information security principle; now, let's briefly discuss how it applies to basic computing principles. If a computer is not using any encryption, then files and documents saved within internal storage—such as a hard disk drive or solid state drive—are readable as needed, without requiring a secret key to decipher them. Encryption is the process of disguising data written to the hard drive, so that it can only be decrypted with the secret key. Consider two types of encryption, file level and full disk encryption; file level encryption encrypts only specific files when they are saved to the drive, whereas full disk encryption encrypts all data written to the drive.

A weakness of file level encryption exists because normal operation of a computer creates multiple "temporary" copies of a file or document on the drive. The computer uses the drive like a "scratch pad" with virtual RAM and other processes, and creates "temporary" copies that can remain for a long time. With file level encryption, these temporary copies are not encrypted, and can be recoverable, even if the file itself is stored in encrypted form. In contrast, full disk encryption means that all data written to the disk, even "temporary" data, is encrypted and protected. File level encryption has many uses, but you need to understand the vulnerabilities associated with it.

The next chapter will discuss encryption of data in transit—when your computer sends or receives data to or from another computer. Chapter 8 will discuss implementation of encryption on your devices.

H. CONCLUSION

We've covered the basics of how a computer works, whether it is a desktop, smartphone, or something smaller, and this information can empower you to take a more active role in setting up your system and diagnosing any technical support issues. Most importantly, it allows you to take a more active role in securing your systems. The next chapter will take you through the basics of how computers talk to each other via networking and the Internet.

CHAPTER 6

Basic Networking and the Internet

A. INTRODUCTION

This chapter provides an understanding of the Internet and networking principles and how computers talk to each other. If a cybercriminal is attempting to victimize you, it will most likely be through the Internet, with his computer interacting with your computer—or his computer interacting with a series of intermediary computers, then interacting with your computer. With traditional street crime like burglary, the criminal has to go to the house physically to commit the crime, but with cybercrime, all that is necessary is for the victim and the criminal to have an Internet connection. Thus, your cybersecurity is aided by knowledge of how networking works.

As we assess the hardware devices in your home used for networking, we'll review various devices used to access the Internet and your local network, such as routers and modems. Then we'll talk about how these work together to provide you with Internet access and the potential security risks that result.

B. NETWORK INTERFACE CONTROLLER

In the previous chapter, we introduced you to the network interface controller (NIC; also known as network interface card or network adapter), the component within a computing device that connects to a network. There are wired and wireless network controllers; a wired network controller has a physical port to plug a network cable into, and a wireless network controller has an antenna to receive and transmit data wirelessly. Your network controller has a unique serial number assigned by the manufacturer, called a MAC address (media access control) because it's used as an address, or identifier, when communicating with other devices on a local network. There's another type of networking address we'll talk about later, the Internet Protocol (IP) address.

Network controllers have two modes: normal operation—which we will call "polite" mode—and "promiscuous" mode (which is the actual technical name for it). In normal (polite) operation, the network controller only listens to communication across the network that is specifically addressed to the MAC address of that network card. When the network controller "hears" communication addressed to it, it forwards the information to the computer (CPU); when there is communication addressed to someone else on the network, it politely ignores it, and does not pass it along to the CPU. However, when set to "promiscuous" mode, the network card listens to all data on the network, no matter who it is addressed to, and it forwards everything to the CPU.

Setting the NIC to promiscuous mode, and reviewing all of the data it captures, can be a way for someone to eavesdrop on all communication within a local network. This is commonly called using a "sniffer" or "sniffing the network." This has significant implications that are not fully appreciated by many people, and which this book explores further in Chapter 10 and Appendix 8. Thus, you must be careful about what networks you join, and whether your communications are encrypted when you use that local network to access a distant website through the Internet. We'll discuss more on encryption in transit towards the end of this chapter.

When going online, your computer's network interface card, with its MAC address, typically accesses a local network, and uses this local network to share resources, including Internet access. We will discuss the components of a local network soon, but first we will review the Internet.

C. INTERNET

Internet access is now ubiquitous and essential. Today, our devices are constantly connected to the Internet and each other, and that means we need a consistent Internet connection, and a way to share this Internet connection with our many computing devices. As the era of the "Internet of things" comes upon us, this could mean there are dozens—and perhaps will be hundreds—of devices within our homes that need to communicate with each other and the outside world. Not long ago, our computers were connected merely by the "sneaker net," meaning that in order to transfer data from one computer to another one we needed to use a removable media device, like a floppy disk, and then walk it over to the next device. Over time, telecommunications companies that were already providing telecom services started to offer us Internet connectivity, using existing technologies and evolving new technology. Thus, phone lines, cable lines, and cell towers were adapted and improved to provide Internet service, in addition to existing voice and television service.

To get Internet access within your home, you are probably paying a company, whether it is a cable company, telephone company, cellular phone company, or even satellite company. This company providing Internet access is known as an Internet service provider (ISP). When it provides you with Internet access, it assigns you an Internet Protocol (IP) address, which is how data is routed to you through the Internet; it is your Internet "return address." Your IP address might be static—remaining stationary as long as you stay with the same ISP, or dynamic—changing periodically depending on the needs of the ISP. Even a dynamic IP address can stay the same for an extended period of time—days, weeks, and months—but if you turn your cable modem off at some point, the company might reassign that IP address to another customer, and when you turn your modem back on, you might get a new IP address.

1. Dial-up

Dial-up was the first type of Internet access for the public, and a relatively small number of people still use it. Dial-up means using a standard phone line to make a phone call to the Internet service provider and, when the connection is made, data is transmitted back and forth through the phone line. Dial-up may be the only access available in a very rural area, it may be more cost effective for some, or perhaps some people are resistant to change. America Online (AOL), founded in 1985 and one of the early Internet and e-mail providers, reported in 2015 that there were still about two million people using AOL dial-up to connect to the Internet.[1]

To dial-up to the Internet, you need a telephone modem, which in the early days was a separate, external device. Later, the telephone modem was typically installed inside the computer, and today they are rare because they are slow and obsolete for the home user. The phone line is connected to the modem, and the computer tells the modem to dial the proper phone number for the Internet service provider (such as AOL), thereby connecting to them and establishing Internet access. When you are done using the Internet, you hang up, and the Internet connection is gone. From a cybersecurity perspective, disconnecting from the Internet when you aren't using it is a valuable security feature. It prevents cybercriminals from breaking through your electronic doors—conceptually replacing the doors with a solid wall. However, using a dial-up connection has proved inconvenient, and has been surpassed by technology. Dial-up requires dedicated use of a phone line while accessing the Internet, forcing many frequent Internet users to obtain a second phone line, and it is inherently slow. Our Internet experience requires more speed to view the websites we want to visit, with all of their pictures and videos, and even to view all the advertisements that we would rather not see. It is no coincidence that our computing experience has evolved to require more

---

1. *See* Jose Pagliery, *OMG: 2.1 Million People Still Use AOL Dial-Up,* CNN Money (May 8, 2015), http://money.cnn.com/2015/05/08/technology/aol-dial-up.

bandwidth to download data, and more space to store data, requiring us to spend more money to accommodate this expanding process.

2. Cable Internet (Broadband)

The next evolution in connectivity was cable Internet, also called broadband, which most of us are using today. We were already paying the cable company for our cable television service, and our homes were already wired with coaxial cables for this TV service. It was no surprise that the cable companies found a way to provide and sell Internet connectivity through these existing cables.

The term coaxial cable means a cable with wires wrapped around the same center. First is a center copper wire which transmits the signals and data, then a layer of insulation, and then a wire around the insulation, which is grounded and acts to shield the first wire from electrical and magnetic interference. Finally, there is insulation around the grounding wire.

Today, the term "broadband" Internet can refer to any type of Internet access that is fast and always on. In the context of cable Internet, "broadband" described the technology developed by cable companies to transmit dozens of different television channels through the same cable at the same time. Each channel used a different signal frequency, all of which were continually flowing through the wire, and the cable box could distinguish among the many frequencies and channels to show the channel selected for viewing. Cable companies found a way to allow that same cable to transmit and receive data for your Internet usage while simultaneously receiving the TV programs. The cable technology can move data at a much faster rate than dial-up, and the Internet connection is always present.

Over time, the cable company technology has evolved from transmitting data in analog form—relying upon a continuous spectrum of wavelengths to transmit information that describes the picture and sound you receive—to digital, which relies on binary bits of information to describe the picture and sound. Broadband helps describe a large bandwidth of data that can be transmitted to and from the consumer. With the advent of digital cable connections, and the use of phone services over the Internet (e.g. VOIP, or voice over Internet Protocol), cable companies now can offer a bundling of services for television, Internet, and phone—perhaps marketed as a "triple play" service.

The components of your cable Internet service within your home start with internal wiring (with RG6 coaxial cable, or possibly the smaller RG59 coaxial cable), which exits your walls at a wall jack. Then, there is a connection from the wall jack to your cable modem via coaxial cable, and then to your router; we'll cover those devices shortly. The other end of the cable travels to your cable company with its computers and servers and connection to the Internet.

3. Phone Company Internet (DSL, FiOS)

The telephone companies experienced a boom when the Internet first began, because customers were using dial-up to access the Internet, paying the extra telephone charges, and installing secondary phone lines. Then, the cable companies started winning Internet customers through cable broadband, which was much faster. With voice over Internet capabilities, cable companies were able to provide phone service as well, so some customers left their phone companies completely. It was only a matter of time before the telephone companies started to develop methods for delivering fast Internet service as well as television content to their remaining telephone customers.

Telephone companies started developing technologies to deliver more data through existing phone lines and through upgrading other infrastructure. A digital subscriber line (DSL) is one such technology that allows phone company customers to have fast and always-on Internet connections using the traditional phone lines. However, DSL and the phone wiring in our homes have limitations in speed and bandwidth, as well as distance limitations from the phone company's central office. Phone companies and Google have developed technology and methods—such as Verizon FiOS and Google fiber optic service—which provide not only phone and Internet, but also television content. Fiber optic service means that the digital data is being transmitted through light pulses through special fiber optic cables, instead of using traditional copper wires to transmit the data through electrical pulses. Fiber optic cables can transmit much more data, much faster than traditional copper.

If you have fiber optic Internet, the provider (e.g. Verizon, Google, etc.) created a special connection between their new fiber optic cables and your home's internal wiring. Traditional home telephone wiring can't handle all of that data, but home coaxial cable wiring can, so this external fiber optic service gets connected to this internal coaxial cable. Outside your home, the data travels through speed-of-light fast fiber optic cables, while inside your home the data either uses Ethernet or the same coaxial cables that it used when you had regular cable service. Ethernet or coaxial cables are more than adequate for speed and bandwidth inside your home, and they have the added value of being inexpensive, easy to work with, and resistant to damage when they are bent.

With fiber optic technology, phone companies can now offer a "triple play" of voice, Internet, and television. Thus, the line between traditional "telephone companies" and "cable television" or entertainment companies has blurred, as both can offer all three services to the consumer.

4. Cellular Company Internet

Another popular method of accessing the Internet is through cellular phone providers. This is another example of the telecom industry adding Internet capability to a service it was already providing to us. We already had cellular voice service, they added the ability to access the Internet, check our e-mail, and surf the Internet. Usually, cellular Internet access means purchase of a "data" plan from the provider, in addition to the traditional voice plan. In sum, the cell phone has an antenna that is continually communicating with the cell towers of the cell phone company, and these communications not only allow you to make and receive phone calls and text messages, but also allow you to transmit and receive data for Internet communication.

The cell phone companies also offer wireless Internet access through devices such as an "air card" or a mobile "hot spot." An air card is a device with a cellular wireless antenna capable of communicating with the cell tower to send and receive data to and from the Internet. The air card plugs into the computer and—assuming you have paid for the Internet service and there is cellular coverage where you are—your computer has Internet access. A cellular mobile hot spot is similar to an air card, but it also has a router-type function that creates a Wi-Fi network you can connect to, making the Internet connection available for multiple devices. Most smartphones also have the capability to be a cellular mobile "hot spot," such as iPhone's "personal hotspot" option. In Chapter 12 we'll discuss how using your cellular phone as a personal hotspot can be useful to avoid having to connect to a public Wi-Fi network.

5. Satellite Internet

It is also possible to access the Internet through a satellite connection, although this method is less common. It is used mostly in rural areas to obtain faster Internet service than a dial-up connection, or for travelers in locations with no access to phone lines or cell towers. The user has a satellite dish pointed at the appropriate satellite above the earth, and the dish and satellite communicate back and forth. After the satellite receives data from the user, it relays the data to the Internet provider on Earth, then the Internet provider relays it to the website the user requested to visit, receives the data from the website, transmits it up to the satellite, and then it goes down to the user. That's a lot of steps, and the data is travelling a long distance, into space and back several times, which takes time even at the speed of light. Just as there is a delay when the overseas news correspondent reports live via satellite, there is a delay for other types of data travelling via satellite. Delay in the network is called latency, and that is one problem with satellite Internet. The other problem is cost, since it is expensive to launch and maintain the satellites, and those costs get passed down to the consumer.

If you are wondering how a satellite dish on a house can stay pointed at a space satellite that is whizzing around the earth, it's because this type of satellite is in geosynchronous orbit—orbiting around the earth at the same rate that the earth is spinning. That keeps the satellite above the same point on earth continuously, as the earth and satellite rotate together.

D. MODEM

When the Internet comes from the outside world to your home through cables it first passes through your modem, which acts as a translator between the Internet service provider and your computer. The Internet service provider uses one language, or communication protocol, along its networks, and your computer uses another language. The modem is the middle man and translator.

The term "modem" derives from the words "modulator" and "demodulator," and originated in the days when telephone dial-up was the main way to access the Internet. During the dial-up Internet days, the data was transmitted along phone lines as a range of audible tones, which were in the form of analog—rather than digital—signals. The modem translated the tones into bits of digital data that the computer could understand, and vice-versa when the computer was sending information.

With a cable modem, the cable connected to the modem is carrying your cable television content as well as your Internet traffic. The modem ignores all of the data that relates to the television channels, and looks only at the data relating to your Internet traffic, and converts it into a language your computing devices can understand. It then sends the data directly to your router or computer device. More frequently, the modem and router are combined within a single unit, but discussing their functions separately aids understanding.

E. ROUTER

A main purpose of our home router is to allow multiple devices to use the same Internet connection. The modem is connected to the router, and the router connects to all the other local devices on the network. Although the modem and router are sometimes combined within a single unit, we are focusing on the router function in this section. The router allows multiple computers to independently send and receive data to and from the Internet. To do this, the router needs to keep track of which device is sending and receiving what data, and with whom on the Internet. The home router also is the basis for your home network; it establishes the home network (also known as a local network) and acts as the gatekeeper (or gateway) both within the home network and to other routers and devices outside of the home network.

Routers can be wired, wireless, or both. Most homes have a wireless router, since most of us want to connect our multitude of mobile computing devices that all require an Internet connection. A wireless connection is often much more convenient than running a cable to a device, but they can be subject to interference. We may not be aware of all the wireless connections in our house, and they can present security vulnerabilities.

Connecting a device to a router could be as simple as plugging an Ethernet cable between your device and the router. Or, to connect to the wireless network, you may need to find the router's wireless signal, called an SSID (service set identifier), and connect to it wirelessly. The wireless signal should be encrypted and accessible only by someone who knows the password. That's covered in Chapter 10. Just as your computer needs protection from power surges, drops, and outages, your router and modem do too. Consider plugging them into the same surge suppressor and uninterruptable power supply used by your computer.

The router is an important device and when you start to secure it, you'll want to be familiar with how it works. Here's a quick summary that the next section will build upon. The router creates a local area network (LAN) and provides local IP addresses to your devices on the network, such as your desktop, laptop, and tablets. These local IP addresses are typically in the network range of 192.168.0.0 and slightly above that, and these are called "private" IP addresses since they are used only on private, local networks. Then, your Internet service provider (ISP) provides you with Internet access and a "public" IP address (e.g. 72.224.166.225). When your devices access the Internet, your router "translates" that public IP address to each of the "private" IP addresses of each of your devices on your local network—a process called network address translation (NAT). The router uses virtual ports to help with addressing and keeping track of each device's Internet traffic. This whole process allows each of your devices to share a single Internet connection to access the Internet.

Chapter 10 will help you secure your router, which should require a unique and complex password to access its administration portal, and its firmware should be kept updated. Too many routers are running with default and generic usernames and passwords, or running old and vulnerable firmware, making it easy for hackers to get in.

F. INTERNET COMMUNICATION 101

Now we will discuss how devices communicate through the Internet.

1. IP Addresses on the Internet

We connect to the Internet thanks to our Internet service provider, which assigns an IP address to our home router that we then use to communicate with other computers on the Internet. Our IP address is simply our address on the Internet. When we send data, our IP address is included as a "return address," which is how others know where to respond to, so that we get their reply. We can check our IP address by visiting a variety of reputable free sites, such as ipchicken.com, whatsmyip.org, or by searching "what's my IP" and selecting a reputable site. When we are at our home, using our laptop, desktop, or any mobile device connected to our Wi-Fi, then all data to and from the Internet uses the same external IP to access the Internet. However, each device will have a unique IP address within the local area network. A smartphone could communicate through the Wi-Fi network or through the cellular signal. If it is not connected to the Wi-Fi network, it will not have an internal IP address on the local network, and it will use the external IP address of the cellular provider.

A public IP address might be something like 72.224.166.225, which is IPv4, or Internet Protocol addressing version 4. It is four sets of numbers, each ranging from 0 to 255. For those of us accustomed to a decimal world, where things are based on ten, this range seems random. But in a binary world of computers, the range of 0 to 255 represents 256 possible values, which is the number of possible values that can be stored by a byte (8 bits). Thus, an IPv4 address is made up of 4 bytes, or 32 bits. This has proved to be insufficient for the number of companies, people, and devices wanting to use the Internet. Already, the Internet is transitioning to IPv6, or Internet Protocol addressing version 6, which uses 16 bytes, or 128 bits, to store the address, allowing for exponentially more possible IP addresses. Since it would be cumbersome and confusing to write these addresses in the same format of IPv4, with a sequence of numbers from 0 to 255, they have chosen to represent IPv6 addresses in hexadecimal, meaning a series of digits from 0 to 9 and then from A to F. For more information about binary, hexadecimal, and how computers count, see Appendix 5.

Every computer on the Internet needs an IP address, including the websites you visit. When you visit a website, whether it is a news site or your online banking site, you are both sending and receiving data from the website. Your computer needs to know the IP address of the website in order to get there, which is handled by the domain name system (DNS). You know that you want to go to CybersecurityHomeAndOffice.com, so you type that into your web browser's address bar and hit return. The domain name system looks up this name to see the IP address where the website is hosted, and redirects you to that IP address. Once you access the website, your computer asks to download information to load the webpage, and that data is sent from the website to the home IP address. Then the web browser loads the pictures and text into the computer's memory and it is displayed on the screen.

That's the basics of how it works. It gets slightly more complicated because often a single IP address could be shared by hundreds of different websites—there are not enough IPv4 addresses available for each website to have a unique address. Thus, the web hosting company routes the Internet user to the proper website within that IP address. In contrast, some websites are global and with millions of visitors (such as google.com or cnn.com) and for those a single IP address would be insufficient, thus they will have multiple IP addresses and Internet traffic will be routed to optimize the user's experience and reduce overload on certain web servers.

2. IP Addresses on Your Local Network: Network Address Translation

For communication to be routed between computers on the Internet, each device needs to know the other's IP address. In a sense, a home IP address is like a mailing address; house number, street name, and apartment number (if one is in an apartment building). When a device connects with a website and asks to load the home page, the website responds by sending the data to the device's IP address.

Not long ago, it was common for a home's Internet connection to connect directly with a single computer—the only computer in the house. When the sole computer in the home was connected to the modem, any and all Internet communication to and from that house was for that computer, and only that computer. That would be like a home with one person living in it—it is not necessary to specify the occupant's name, the address alone is sufficient, either to receive data, or when providing a return address while sending data. Any mail gets delivered to the apartment, and is opened by the single resident; there's no issue about who it's for.

Today, most homes have multiple devices connected to the Internet, which is accomplished through the use of a Wi-Fi router. This situation is like having multiple people living together in a home, and each computing device is a different person. The router acts as a gateway between the user and the Internet, and creates a local network (or local area network, or LAN) for the devices in the home. Through this process, Internet activity is directed to and from a particular device using your home network. While you are looking at and downloading work e-mail on your laptop, your spouse can post pictures from a smartphone to a social media website without the data transmissions ending up on each other's device. Without this routing and address translation, it would be like getting piles of mail that didn't have the proper name or apartment number on it—they would get lost or returned to sender.

We gave a brief introduction to NAT in the preceding section. The home router creates a LAN, which typically is on the private IP network range of 192.168.0.0 and slightly above that. For computers on this LAN, the router assigns itself an IP address (e.g. 192.168.1.1), assigns all computing devices on the local network their own IP address (e.g. 192.168.1.2, and so forth), and

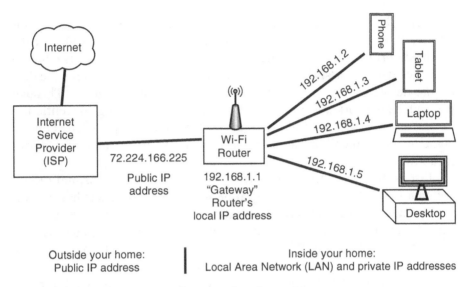

FIGURE 6.1 NAT, public, and private (local) IP addresses.

keeps track of the MAC address of each computer's network card. The ISP (Internet service provider) has provided you with a public IP address (e.g. 72.224.166.225), and each device can use this public IP address to access the Internet thanks to the router and NAT. Figure 6.1 indicates how this works.

The router needs to keep track of each device's communication with the outside world, and to do this, it assigns port numbers for each communication to the Internet, and when the website on the Internet responds, it references that same port number. The router then knows which device to forward it to.

3. Ports: Virtual Router Ports and Computer Ports

The router performs this addressing and routing function, like a mailroom worker putting letters into the correct boxes. It does this through assigning each device on the local area network its own local IP address, thereby keeping track of all devices and who they are communicating with. A device on the local area network isn't tracked by its name (e.g. "John"), but by its local IP address, which the router assigns. When the device requests to load the website CybersecurityHomeAndOffice.com, for example, it does so via the router. The router relays this request through the Internet to the website, and when it sends the request, the router provides the home's external IP address as a return address, but also appends additional address information so that the router knows who requested the data. This additional information is a port number. When the website responds with the requested website data, it sends it to the IP address that was specified as the return address, appended by the specified port number. When the router gets this data, it checks its tables to see which device is associated with that port number, and forwards the data to that device via the local area network, at its local IP address. Through the router's network address translation and port addressing convention, it can act as the mailroom and intermediary between multiple devices on the home network and all of the places on the Internet with which each device is communicating.

Just as the router provides a mailroom function in sending and receiving data for each device on the local network, each computer has its own mailroom for all the applications simultaneously sending and receiving data with the Internet. One device may be sending and receiving data relating to multiple applications at a time. You may have many Google Chrome tabs open; one tab is connecting with a news site, one with Gmail, one with iCloud, and many other applications also connect to the Internet. Your network controller is sending and receiving data constantly, and your computer needs to know where to route the data it receives. Like the router, your computer does this through port addressing. When data is sent, it is appended with the port number, which is typically standardized for various applications. When data is received, it typically is addressed to a particular port, and that helps the data get routed within your computer to the particular application.

4. TCP/UDP Internet Protocols (Language)

There are two main Internet connection protocols: transmission control protocol (TCP) and user datagram protocol (UDP). Think of them as two different languages for sending and receiving data. TCP is a protocol that is designed to ensure that each packet of data is properly received, like having a radio conversation and after each transmission, the speaker asks if this listener heard and understood, and waits for the listener to respond affirmatively with "Roger!" or "10-4!" If the listener didn't hear it, then the speaker repeats the sentence—the data is re-sent. TCP is used when it's important that every bit of data is received properly and accurately. UDP is like a lecturer who keeps talking no matter what, even if students are nodding off. UDP is faster than TCP, and is used when it's important for the data to flow without interruption, and if a little bit of data is lost, it's not a big deal, such as when streaming music or a movie. If you are watching a movie and a few pixels weren't received properly, you won't notice it, so it's preferable to keep watching without interruption.

Computer Ports

When you start securing your devices and home network, enabling firewalls or checking Internet firewalls or traffic, you will see references to particular computer port numbers and connection protocols. These are just conventions designed to allow traffic to flow smoothly using common language and addressing. Hackers are trying to sneak in and out, and firewalls try to detect suspicious Internet traffic through unusual ports.

There are many ports, over 65,000 of them for both TCP and UDP. Some ports are standardized to carry certain communication by default, but users can change that. Some common port numbers that your computer uses by default for addressing to common applications are:

- Port 80: Regular, unencrypted Internet traffic for your web browser (HTTP, Hypertext Transfer Protocol)
- Port 443: Encrypted Internet traffic for your web browser (HTTP over SSL/TSL, Hypertext Transfer Protocol over Secure Sockets Layer/Transport Layer Security; see later in this chapter)
- Ports 20/21: File Transfer Protocol (FTP)
- Port 22: Secure Shell (SSH)
- Port 25: E-mail routing between mail servers (SMTP, Simple Mail Transfer Protocol)
- Port 110: Some types of e-mail download on this port (POP3, Post Office Protocol 3)
- Port 995: Encrypted POP3 e-mail download

A list of all the common ports can be found at https://en.wikipedia.org/wiki/List_of_TCP_and_UDP_port_numbers.

5. Network Layers

Data flows through many network layers as it communicates and traverses from the wires and cables outside the home, inside the home, to the computer, and finally to the application being used by the user. There are two main models for network layers, the OSI (Open Systems Interconnection) model and the simpler TCP/IP (Transmission Control Protocol/Internet Protocol) model. Just remember that data traverses multiple layers as it goes from a device through the Internet and to another device.

Network Layers

This is kind of technical, so read the following details only if you are interested.

Data travels in encapsulated packets up and down a stack of layers. Within each layer protocols are defined that specify how the data is to be used. Under the OSI model, the seven conceptual layers can be remembered through the phrase "Please Do Not Throw Sausage Pizza Away."

Physical layer (the cable, wire, or fiber)
Data link layer
Network layer
Transport layer
Session layer
Presentation layer
Application layer (e.g. your web browser, Google Chrome)

Under the TCP/IP model, the four conceptual layers are:

Link layer
Internet layer
Transport layer
Application layer

Our computers are connected to the Internet most of the time, and have many applications continually running, accessing places on the Internet that we may not be aware of. If you have a web browser open at a webpage like a news site, it is probably sending data back and forth even if you are not actively clicking on anything. If you have web e-mail open (e.g. Gmail or Hotmail), it is probably actively sending data back and forth, periodically checking if you have new mail, or responding to your mouse movements. Software that you have installed on your computer may have an update agent, something that is always running and periodically checking with the software manufacturer to see if an update is available, and possibly providing other information to the manufacturer. Any of your software that stores your data or licensing information on the cloud might be consistently in contact with the software manufacturer. Your operating system (Windows 10, Apple OS X or iOS, Android, etc.) is regularly connecting also, to check if it's licensed, to check for updates, and more.

Check Programs Running and Accessing the Internet on Your Computer

It is worth familiarizing yourself with some of the programs running on your computer and accessing the Internet. Realize that it's nearly impossible to figure out every single application and process, so keep your goals modest.

In the previous chapter, we covered accessing the list of the applications running on your computer, and we'll run through that again here since that's how you get to see the network traffic.

Windows

Task Manager

- Open the Task Manager through one of these methods:
    Method 1: Control–Alt–Delete and select Task Manager

Method 2: Control–Shift–Escape
Method 3: Search for "Task Manager" or
"taskmgr.exe"

- Select the "Processes" tab, and review the "Network" column
- Select the "Performance" tab and review network activity

Resource Monitor

- Open the Resource Monitor through one of these methods:
  Method 1: From the Windows 10 Task Manager, go to the "Performance" tab, at the bottom, click on "Open Resource Monitor"
  Method 2: Search for "Resource Monitor" or "perfmon.exe"
- Within Resource Monitor, select the "Network" tab

Mac

- Open Activity Manager and click the tabs labeled CPU, Memory, Energy, Disk, or Network to get more detail on activity

G. WIRED NETWORKING

Wired networking simply means that the local area network is connected by a cable—what looks like a supersized phone line with Category 5 or 6 cable (CAT5 or CAT6) and an RG45 connector. These are commonly called Ethernet cables because that's the typical communication protocol (language) on a local wired network. Some routers are designed only for wired connections, and most wireless routers also permit wired connections. If a device is connected by wire to a router establishing the local area network, typically the device is automatically included on the network, and no additional authentication or password is required.

The best connection and security will always be provided via a wired connection. A wired connection can generally only be tampered with by having physical access to the wire. In contrast, a wireless connection can suffer from environmental or deliberate interference and is vulnerable to attack, even from people outside your home.

H. WIRELESS NETWORKING

A wireless connection can be very convenient—no wires need to be connected, and no one is physically tethered to a connection. A wireless (or Wi-Fi) network transfers data through the air, not through a cable. This feature gives the user freedom of movement, subject to the strength of the signal and any signal-blocking obstacles.

Wi-Fi presents many security risks, and because the risks are "out of sight," they are "out of mind" for many. Consider if you ran an Ethernet connection out of your home, to the lobby of your apartment building or out to the street, so that anyone could connect to your network. You would feel uneasy about this arrangement because you would have no idea who was plugging into your network, or what they were doing while using your Internet connection. In effect, your wireless network is similar, because the signal extends outside of your home. Early on, few people protected their wireless networks at all, and they were open to attack and misuse by people with laptops or smartphones sitting outside a home or office and using their Wi-Fi and Internet service. Today, many wireless networks still are vulnerable, primarily because they don't require a password to connect.

The most important aspect for wireless networking is that it should be configured so that a password is required to join the wireless network and so that communications within the wireless network are encrypted. Otherwise, the network and data are accessible to anyone and information is transmitted through the air for capture. Also, some of the older encryption methods are not secure. We'll discuss this in more detail in Chapter 10.

Interestingly, a device that was once connected to a wireless network might be constantly looking for that wireless network, and not just passively; it might actually be calling out for it. We'll cover this more in Chapter 12, but you should be aware that when you leave your home, if your smartphone's Wi-Fi adapter is on, it might be constantly calling out for your home network, with security and privacy implications.

Because wireless networks are hampered by physical objects like walls, by distance, and interference from other devices, the range can be improved by using better Wi-Fi antennas, by transmitting at increased power, and by adding Wi-Fi extenders or access points. A Wi-Fi extender acts as a repeater, relaying Wi-Fi signals between the user and the Wi-Fi router. A Wi-Fi access point can be placed to optimize the Wi-Fi signal, and then is connected to the Wi-Fi router by cable.

I. ENCRYPTION IN TRANSIT

Encryption of data in transit is an important concept, and an important method to keep your communications secure and protected from eavesdroppers and hackers. When you use your web browser to visit a website that encrypts its communications with you, you typically will see a green lock at the beginning of the URL address bar, and you will see that the website address begins with HTTPS instead of HTTP. The "S" in HTTPS stands for secure, and it means the data being transmitted to you is done so in an encrypted fashion. Usually, that encrypted fashion is through Secure Sockets Layer/Transport Layer Security (SSL/TLS). This protocol provides you with considerable protection, even if you are sharing a network with strangers at a coffee shop or on a train—which hopefully you do not do regularly. When you visit a website where important information is being transmitted and received, the site should be in HTTPS mode. Make sure to check for an HTTPS connection when you are using your online banking site, when you are paying at an online merchant's site, or when you are working with e-mail or cloud documents.

Websites Connecting with HTTP vs. HTTPS

Web browsers (such as Chrome, Safari, Edge, and others) try to alert you about the security level of the websites you visit, including whether they are HTTP or HTTPS, and if the security certificate is valid. Here are some examples:

> 🔒 Secure | https://cybersecurityhomeandoffice.com

Website transmitting encrypted webpage data via HTTPS with a valid "certificate."

> ⓘ www.bandlerlaw.com

Website transmitting data in plain text via HTTP. The data sent between user and the website is not private.

> **🔒 Secure | https://www.bandlerlaw.com**
>
> The same website that has a valid "certificate" and is transmitting encrypted data via HTTPS.
>
> **⚠ Not Secure | ~~https~~://www.bandlergroup.com**
>
> This could be a dangerous website, or simply a website with an expired certificate. Either way, it is not secure. Here, the security certificates were being transferred, resulting in a temporarily invalid certificate.
>
> **🔒 Secure | https://www.bandlergroup.com**
>
> The same website after the new security certificate was recognized.
>
> We talked about ports earlier. When your web browser communicates with a website, it will generally use your computer's port 443 if the communication with the website is encrypted (HTTPS), and port 80 if it is not encrypted (HTTP).

Another way to encrypt data in transit is to use a VPN, or virtual private network. This creates an encrypted tunnel through which your data can be transmitted via the Internet between your device and the VPN server. The VPN server then acts as an intermediary and sends and receives data on your behalf with the Internet. Using a VPN can provide you with considerable protection if you are on an untrustworthy local network and Internet connection. However, using a VPN means all of your Internet traffic is routed through that VPN provider, meaning the VPN provider should be trustworthy in order to keep your traffic secure and private.

Asymmetric Cryptography

Encryption in transit is typically done with public key infrastructure encryption, or PKI. This is also known as asymmetric cryptography because two different keys are used to lock (encrypt) and unlock (decrypt) the data. Some cryptography uses a single key to both lock and unlock the data—that's symmetric cryptography. With PKI, one key is called a public key because the encryptor gives that out to the public, and the other key is the private key which the encryptor keeps private. This type of two-key encryption is an ingenious way to keep data confidential without worrying that a single, secret key might be stolen or hacked. It not only keeps criminals from eavesdropping on the data being exchanged between the user and the website, it keeps criminals from impersonating the site or tampering with it.

Suppose you go to your bank's website for online banking. Your bank has both a public and a private key to secure the website. The bank keeps the private key secret, and gives you the public key. When the bank first sends you data, it is encrypted with its private key, which only the public key can decrypt, and this helps you know you are dealing with the bank, not an imposter. Then your web browser sends data to the bank, which is encrypted with the bank's public key, which can only be decrypted by the bank's private key. This helps keep the data you send to the bank confidential.

While using this secure communication channel to establish initial communications between you and the bank, the bank sends you another unique encryption key which is used to encrypt the rest of your website session. This unique encryption key can use symmetric cryptography, because you are able to receive this encryption key secretly and securely during this initial process. This initial communication is known as a networking "handshake." After this SSL/TLS handshake, your browser displays the lock icon, and you can submit your username and password and know that they will be encrypted, along with all of the subsequent financial information that is transmitted.

HTTPS and many other forms of encryption use PKI. This important method of securing website communications is for more than just bank websites now, and helps protect your security and privacy.

J. CONCLUSION

Cybercriminals may try to attack you through the Internet and break into your local area network, so this chapter provided important knowledge of how local networking and the Internet work. Chapter 10 will provide the details on how to secure your network and Internet activity. Meanwhile, you have completed the first part of the book, which provided you with underlying knowledge on a variety of fronts that will help you to secure yourself. It is now time to start improving your cybersecurity.

CHAPTER 7

Start Securing Yourself

A. INTRODUCTION

This chapter starts the work of assessing yourself and your systems and making security improvements. Perhaps, while reading through the previous chapters, you have already implemented some of the suggestions, in which case this chapter will simply affirm what you have already done. This chapter also asks you to revisit the question of where your "cybersecurity dial" is now, and where you want to adjust it to.

The previous half of this book has given you an understanding of the threats and risks you face, basic information security principles, and how computers and networks work. This background knowledge means you can make informed decisions about where to set your "security dial," and find a security vs. risk level that is appropriate for you. Every cybersecurity precaution represents a choice between security and convenience.

It also helps you address the biggest security risk, which is you, the human. Remember, it doesn't matter how strong your locks and doors are if the malefactor is able to deceive you so that you willingly open the door and invite him in. Many cyberattacks rely upon human fallibility to do just this, usually through some form of social engineering. Armed with the information in this book, you are now better equipped to be a skeptical computer user and successfully recognize these ploys.

B. SET YOUR CYBERSECURITY DIAL

You decide where you want to set your security dial. If you are reading this book, you probably have security concerns, and if you are a lawyer or other professional, you have professional responsibilities to others. Every person needs to secure themselves and their family, however, it is not a "one size fits all" solution for cybersecurity. You have developed personal preferences in your use of computing devices, and you should consider both accommodating your preferences as well as rethinking them. Take some time to consider how these choices affect security, access, and efficiency.

Pick a path that you can stick with, a path where you have a consistent security posture, perhaps one you can gradually increase over time as you learn. Don't go from zero to eleven all at once, only to frustrate yourself, give up, and go back to zero. Don't let cybersecurity be like a fad diet that you try for a few months and then abandon, or like an impulsive New Year's resolution that you can't sustain. Decide what you can live with, make a small change, and see how it goes. Incremental change works, and will keep you from getting frustrated. Steps you take to protect against cyber threats might make your computing experience somewhat more cumbersome—at least initially. Therefore, you should be methodical and incremental as you develop good habits that eventually will become second nature.

Being methodical and incremental is also important because one change might affect another area. If you add a password to your desktop computer, which is shared by the family, that step affects other users. If you change your password for your e-mail account or add two-step login, it will require some adjustments to your smartphone, tablet, and laptop. Try for a step-by-step approach to both learning and implementing proper cybersecurity features and consider taking notes as you do it. If you are doing something for the first time, it might be confusing. Don't make multiple changes at once, and don't make changes late at night, when you are frustrated, or right before an important deadline or trip. Instead, start with a small change when you are not rushed, and test it out to see how it works.

Start with the "low-hanging fruit"—the changes that can most improve your security with the least amount of effort. This process means making some changes now, but putting off others for a later date. Each time you review your devices, data, and networks, you will understand them better, and be able to make more advanced changes.

For the short term, you might simply decide that you want to make your security a "little bit" better by making some simple improvements. For the longer term, consider what your threats and risks are, and prioritize the improvements that should be made to best reduce those risks and avoid the threats in the future.

Take another look at Appendix 3, which was first referenced in Chapter 1. You should have a general idea of where your cybersecurity dial (Figure 7.1) was set before you started reading this book, where it is now, and where you want to be in the future.

Zero is essentially "off," meaning you don't care at all about your data and devices, anyone is free to steal it, post it to WikiLeaks, or destroy it. If you are handling client confidences, then zero is below the professional and ethical standards that are required. None of us want our dial to be at zero, however some of us are unintentionally at zero, or just slightly above it. All of

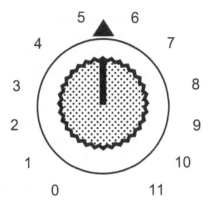

FIGURE 7.1 Your security dial. Decide where to set it. Don't turn it up too fast.

us are targets for cybercriminals and identity thieves, whether we realize it or not, and if we have never evaluated our cybersecurity, we simply don't know where our dial is set.

Ten wasn't high enough, so the dial goes to eleven,[1] above the traditional scale and thus suitable for people who need that extra level of security. Eleven is aspirational and extreme, and might mean disconnecting from the Internet entirely, or having some really burdensome security measures. Zero isn't reasonable, and eleven isn't realistic, so conceptually think of a happy medium in between those extremes.

C. TURNING UP YOUR SECURITY DIAL IS AN INVESTMENT

You are making an investment in your own learning, security, and efficiency. Direct costs are quite low, because this book doesn't recommend that you buy anything to improve your security posture. There will be an investment of time, but the skills you gain will be rewarding, and this will actually save you time and grief in the long run. You will be more efficient in your use of information technology, and you may well prevent a catastrophic loss of data, data breach, or other issue that would cost you time, stress, possible embarrassment, and money.

---

1. *See e.g.,* THIS IS SPINAL TAP (Embassy Pictures 1984).

There will be some up-front work, and a continuing commitment which will soon become second nature. If you are already in the habit of putting on a seatbelt when you get in a car, or locking your doors at night, you do it automatically and it requires no real work or thought. You can build similar good habits with cybersecurity. If you intuitively know not to take a night-time shortcut down a dark alley, you can apply this same risk reduction principle to cybersecurity. Since it is a continual process, it is not about setting the dial and forgetting about it. Everyone, including corporations, can fall into this trap, thinking that cybersecurity can be implemented with a one-time investment with an expensive security tool. Instead, cybersecurity requires a thoughtful, long-term investment, not just in tools, but in training people, mindset, and process.

Of all the things to spend time on, cybersecurity should be a high priority, because it will protect yourself, your family, and your home. While you protect yourself and your family, you are investing in your own education and knowledge, which will help you reap dividends personally and professionally. Nearly every security improvement you implement in your home and personal life can then be translated to your firm, business, and clients.

D. THERE IS NO PERFECT PRODUCT OR SOLUTION

If only there was a perfect cybersecurity and privacy tool that solved all of your problems, worked seamlessly, and required almost no work on your part. It sounds too good to be true, yet some companies seem to advance this claim. There are many paid products that work well and give great value, but the tools or resources recommended here are free, effective methods and products. Some highly regarded information technology and information security instructors highlight the capability of free tools, including more advanced "freeware" that can be used by security experts working in companies with limited cybersecurity budgets.

Some argue that with free products, "you get what you pay for." Remember that any product—free or paid—can have vulnerabilities, which are being discovered daily. Security software is no exception, though we might want to think it is more secure. In 2016, we learned that a major security software company had vulnerabilities in nearly all of its security software, which was used by millions of paying individuals and corporations. Security experts commented that security software is written just as poorly and insecurely as other types of software. Because the software is written poorly, it is vulnerable to attack, and the attacker can use the flaws in the software to take control of the entire computer. We give security software extensive power over our systems, and a vulnerability in the software can expose the computer to compromise.

This illustrates two principles: first, every piece of software your devices run could expose your device and you to vulnerabilities, and second, you can't blindly trust software just because it is sold by a security company. Perhaps an analogy is the home security or locksmith company that has a corrupt employee. You paid the company to help secure you, but you unwittingly allowed a criminal to learn about you and your residence, and they now have inside access that could enable a crime. That's the exception rather than the rule, but you get the picture.

There are reputable websites that test and rate various security software, such as:

- How-To Geek, howtogeek.com
- ZDNet, zdnet.com
- c/net, cnet.com
- PCMag, pcmag.com
- Consumer Reports, consumerreports.org

If you find security software that is well rated by reputable reviewers, you can download it directly from the software maker's website. There are many reputable download sites as well, but there are also some that are not reputable, or that bundle other programs into the download, like "adware" that is of limited use to you but displays advertising or tracks you.

E. LET'S GET STARTED (IF YOU HAVEN'T ALREADY)

This section gets you started, and addresses low-cost but high-value changes you should implement to get your dial at or above 3. They will be covered in more detail in Chapters 8, 9, and 10, so if you are wary of technology and hesitant about some of these changes, wait to implement them until you read about them in those chapters. Reading about them here will provide you with an introduction of what you need to do.

1. Put a Password on All of Your Computing Devices

Every computing device you use should require a password to use it (access it), and the device should automatically lock after a period of inactivity. Put a password on all of your computing devices such as smartphones, tablets, laptops, and desktops (see Chapter 8, Secure Your Devices). Pick a password you can remember—it doesn't have to be extremely long or complex. But don't pick a password that every casual thief will guess, such as "password" or "1234."

You can also enable fingerprint unlocking of your device if it is so configured—for example, iPhone's Touch ID and Android's Fingerprint ID. However, you should also get used to entering your password and learn it by heart—you will need it in certain circumstances. Don't lock yourself out. If you think you might, you can ease into this process:

- Write down the password and store it in a secure location.
- It could be acceptable to reuse the same password across your devices, as long as that is not also a cloud account password.
- So long as the device remains in a secure location like your home, and only for a short period of time, you could tape the password to the device until you memorize it. Once you are comfortable with this security measure, remove it.

2. Enable the "Auto Lock" Feature

All of your computing devices should lock after a period of inactivity (see Chapter 8, Secure Your Devices). You can pick the amount of time that needs to elapse, from thirty seconds to several minutes or longer. Plus, try and get used to locking it affirmatively when you are done using the device, if you have to walk away from it momentarily, or even when you put it in your pocket.

3. Run an Anti-Malware Scan on Your Laptop and Desktop

Periodically, you should have an anti-malware program run a full scan of the hard drive of your laptop and desktop computers (see Chapter 8, Secure Your Devices). These devices should also have an anti-malware program running continually, in "real-time," to catch malicious downloads before they take hold.

Malwarebytes offers a good free anti-virus and anti-malware program for Windows or Mac that will scan your computer. If you have never run a scan on your computer, you might be surprised at what you find. It might find a serious infection or it might find some unwanted programs that are not dangerous. A surprising number of computers connected to the Internet are infected with serious malware, some of it detectable, some not. You can download Malwarebytes at: https://www.malwarebytes.com. See Chapter 8 and Chapter 15 about what to do if you have a serious malware infection.

Some other options for free anti-malware software include:

- Sophos (free version)
- AVG (free version)
- Avast (free version)
- Spybot Search and Destroy (free version)
- Bitdefender (free version)
- Windows Defender (free)
- Other free software that is reputable and has been positively rated by trusted technology websites

Remember, you don't need to pay or provide a credit card number. Select a custom installation option so you install only the tools you need, not additional tools they might offer. You may be asked to upgrade to the premium (paid) version but you need not do this. Beware of malware masquerading as security software, and avoid unknown, unvetted applications, sticking to the above list if you are not sure.

4. Disconnect from the Internet When You Don't Need It

Every moment that your device is connected to the Internet is a moment that it is exposed to criminals who are literally scanning the Internet for vulnerable devices, or even actively trying to break into one. Perhaps your computer is already infected, and the malware inside of it might be trying to communicate out to criminals on the Internet. Because of all these possibilities, consider turning your computer off when you don't need it, or at least turning off its Internet connection at night and when you aren't using it (see Chapter 10, Secure Your Network and Internet Use). Depending on the device, the Internet connection can be turned off by disabling the Wi-Fi adapter, or putting it into airplane mode. If you reduce the amount of time your device is exposed to the Internet from 24 hours a day to 12 hours a day, you have, in theory, halved your threat exposure. You also may be doing your brain a favor, by giving it a break from your devices.

5. Use Complex and Unique Passwords

For your important online accounts like e-mail, cloud, and financial accounts, you need complex, unique passwords or passphrases (see Chapter 9, Secure Your Data). Not simple passwords such as "password," "123456," "hummingbird," or something equally easy to guess. If you have passwords that are not complex, you need to update them. Don't reuse the same password across multiple important Internet-based accounts, such as e-mail, work, and financial accounts. Come up with a system that works for you. Write down the passwords in a safe place so that you don't forget them. A longer password is always preferable to a shorter password, and add complexity with special characters and capitalization.

6. Enable "Two-Step" Login

Enable the two-factor authentication option (or "two-step" login) in your e-mail and other important cloud accounts (see Chapter 9, Secure Your Data). To do this, you'll need to use your web browser, sign in to your cloud account, and check your security settings. The e-mail or cloud service will send you a confirmation code to your cell phone, either via text message or via a special authenticator application, and you will need to enter that code to access your account. When you sign in to your account from a new laptop or desktop computer—or perhaps every month—you will receive a new code to your phone that you will need to enter. In order for your smartphone and tablet to access your e-mail, they might require a special password that is generated by your cloud provider through the settings section. Two-factor authentication is one of the single most effective measures you can implement to protect your accounts.

7. Ensure That Your Home Wi-Fi Network Is Password Protected

We'll review all of your router's settings in Chapter 10 (Secure Your Network) and it's a higher degree of difficulty, so plan accordingly. If you've never accessed your router's configuration pages, wait until Chapter 10 to do so.

Your home Wi-Fi network should require a reasonably complex password or passphrase to log in to it. If your Wi-Fi network displays with a lock symbol, it is probably password protected and encrypted. Today, nearly all Wi-Fi routers ship with password protection on by default, so chances are good that your Wi-Fi network requires a password. Once upon a time, Wi-Fi routers shipped with default settings that did not require passwords, and this created great opportunities for criminals and identity thieves to borrow a stranger's Internet service to commit crimes, or to hack into home networks.

Don't panic if your devices automatically connect to your Wi-Fi network without requiring you to enter a password. Though you might not remember ever using a password to access your Wi-Fi network, it still might be password protected. Your devices can save passwords for "known" Wi-Fi networks, so perhaps you connected your device to the network years ago, entered the password back then, and never had to enter the password again.

Your router itself should also require a password to access the administration settings, and it should not be a default generic password set initially by the manufacturer or your Internet service provider. Default generic username and password combinations such as "admin/admin" and "admin/password" make you extremely vulnerable to hackers.

F. CONCLUSION

This is only a start, yet addressing these risks quickly puts you in a much better security posture. The following chapters go into greater detail, outlining a plan and methods to systematically secure yourself, first by securing your devices, then your data, and then your network.

CHAPTER 8

Secure Your Devices

A. INTRODUCTION

This chapter focuses on the devices that you touch and use daily to communicate, access the Internet, for your applications, and to send, receive, and store data. In other words, your smartphone, tablet, laptop, and desktop. Our devices are enormously important to us and this is where cybersecurity starts.

We will review the devices you are using for your computing needs, how they are configured, and what software is on them, and then move on to securing them. Computers store massive amounts of your data, but they are also gateways to even more data that may be stored in the cloud or at your workplace. We cover securing your data in detail in the next chapter, but it's important to realize that devices are not only storage media, but gateways to even more information storage.

The main takeaways from this chapter are:

- Secure your mobile devices and keep them from getting lost, stolen, or damaged.
- Ensure your devices require a password to access, and automatically lock after a brief period of inactivity.
- Keep your computing devices malware-free.
- Disconnect from the Internet (or power down) when not needed.

Securing your devices is the highest priority for your cybersecurity. This approach also tracks the recommendations of the twenty Critical Security Controls, a security framework we will cover in Chapter 14. This chapter will not discuss "Internet of Things" (IoT) type devices (security cameras, thermostats, toys, etc.), or other electronics that are connected to your network—we'll cover those in Chapter 10. This chapter will focus on the computing devices you physically put your hands on to use—your desktop, laptop, tablet, and smartphone.

B. MENTALLY ASSESS YOUR DEVICES

For this section, relax and conduct a quick mental inventory of the computing devices you use in your home, and how they are configured. This section is a tremendously scaled-down version of what a business should do—an assessment and audit of computer hardware and basic policies and procedures. Think of this section as an outline of what is to come, and a way to mentally review each category:

- Device inventory: What computing devices do you use or possess within your home? Try to think of everything, whether it is a desktop computer, laptop, tablet, smartphone, or something in between, whether it is used daily or stuffed in a closet. Your highest security priority will be the devices you use daily.
- Device description: Can you adequately describe and identify each device, if you needed to get technical support or report it lost or stolen to the police?
- Ownership and expectation of privacy: Who owns each device, who uses it, and who has an expectation of privacy when they use it?
- Physical access: Who has physical access to the device and could steal it or tamper with it?
- Electronic access (technical): If someone gets physical access, how do they gain electronic access to the data and applications? For example, is there a password requirement?
- Usage and user accounts: Who uses the device, and for what purpose? How does each user log on to the device? Is there a single user account that all people share, or does each person log in to their own account? Do users have standard user accounts, or are they using administrator accounts?
- Operating system: What operating system is on the device, is it updated, and what are the security and privacy settings?
- Applications (software): What software is installed on the device, what is its purpose, is it trustworthy, is it updated and patched for vulnerabilities, when does it run, and is it configured appropriately?
- Data stored on the device: What data is stored on each device? Is the data sensitive, and what would be the consequences if it were lost, destroyed, or stolen? Is any or all of the data on the device encrypted? When was it backed up last?
- Data the device can access (e.g. cloud data): What data can the device access that is stored in the "cloud"? Does the device automatically synchronize with cloud data such as e-mails, contacts, calendar, documents, and photos? Is the device "signed in" to websites or cloud data so that anyone who accesses the device can also access this cloud data?

- Anti-malware: If the device is a laptop or desktop, is anti-malware software running continually, and are full scans run periodically?
- Internet access: How does the device access the Internet? Cellular data plan? Wi-Fi within the home? Cable Internet, DSL, FiOS, dial up? How can you disconnect the device from the Internet if needed?
- Firewall: If the device is a laptop or desktop, does it have a software firewall running on it?
- Decommissioning: If the device is no longer in use, or no longer being used for its original use, has it been properly decommissioned? Have stored passwords, stored data, and residual data been securely cleaned from the device?

C. GETTING STARTED

Now, on to securing your devices. Depending on your comfort level, time, and energy, you don't have to do everything at once, nor do you have to dive into the most technically challenging area. You can decide whether to fix simple security issues as you find them on each device, or whether you want to first do a general assessment of all your devices and then set about fixing the highest priority issues. Any changes should be done methodically, systematically, and incrementally, and some changes will affect multiple users or devices. Consider taking notes as you go, especially when adding or changing a password and also to keep track of the security alterations you make. To help you with these notes and organization, use the forms available in Appendices 10 and 11.

D. DEVICE INVENTORY (SCAVENGER HUNT)

Quick tips:
- Appendix 10, Home Device Inventory, is a form to help you record what devices are being used in your home, regardless of by whom. Adapt it to *your own* use, and be as general or specific in filling it out as you choose.
- Appendix 11, Personal Device and Data Summary, helps you keep track of *your own* primary devices and cloud accounts. For now, only the top part of the form is relevant and pertains to your most-used devices. In the next chapter, you will review your cloud data and complete the bottom part of the form.
- These forms are available for download at CybersecurityHome AndOffice.com.

Your highest priority should be the computing devices you use most frequently, perhaps your smartphone, laptop, and desktop. Eventually, you will need to identify all computing devices that you use, that your family uses, or that are otherwise in your home. Even your old obsolete devices stuffed in a closet or drawer should ultimately be reviewed. Just because you stopped using a device doesn't mean you can forget about it, since it still may have data on it, or provide access to data. For these disused devices, see the section on secure decommissioning towards the end of this chapter. Again, here we are dealing with desktops, laptops, tablets, smartphones, and everything in between, but not IoT-type devices.

1. Device Description

For each device, you should become generally familiar with the following characteristics:

- Date of purchase/manufacture
- Manufacturer (Apple, Dell, Samsung, LG, etc.)
- Type of device (desktop, laptop, all-in-one, tablet, smartphone)
- Operating system type (Windows 10, OS X, Linux, iOS, Android)
- Model
- Serial number

Appendix 10 can help you keep track of this information. The date of purchase is helpful because it lets you know the existing warranty and life span of the device—all computer hardware eventually becomes obsolete. The manufacturer, model, and operating system are important to know for technical support issues, as this knowledge puts you in a better position to either resolve technical issues yourself, or get assistance from others. The serial number is useful to record for certain technical support issues and in case the device is lost or stolen.

2. Ownership and Expectation of Privacy

With each device, it is important to consider who owns the physical device and the data on it, as well as whether the user has a personal expectation of privacy. If the device was issued by your company, you should be aware of your company policy. Chances are good that the company policy states that you have no expectation of privacy for the device, and the company can do anything they want in terms of monitoring use on the device, taking all data on the device, or erasing all data on it.

If you own the device, but you also use it for work purposes according to a company policy, be aware of what this "bring your own device" (BYOD) policy states. Your employer might have the legal authority and the technical capability to monitor and record your activities, record the contents of your device, and even to remotely wipe all data from your device. You may even have work-imposed obligations for ensuring the security of this device and reporting any loss or theft.

It might seem draconian that the company asserts rights over your entire phone and all of its usage and contents merely because you use your phone for company e-mail. Company policies often have provisions designed to address their worst-case scenarios, such as a corrupt or larcenous employee. Even if employers are fair and reasonable in enforcing these policies, the fact that they have these rights is significant. These company policies may also apply when you use a personal computer to access corporate e-mail or servers.

This concept translates to your household members. Consider what expectation of privacy exists within your home, among family members. For adult household members, it would be rude and invasive to sift through another adult's Internet browsing history, e-mails, or documents. But parents may have a responsibility to keep their children safe, to monitor them, and to educate them about the perils of the Internet and the world. This responsibility might include inspecting children's cell phones and Internet usage regularly and asking with whom they are communicating with and about what. We cover this subject in Chapter 11.

E. ACCESS: PHYSICAL CONTROL

Quick tips:

- Keep the device from being lost, stolen, damaged, or tampered with.
- Maintaining physical control is especially important for smartphones or tablets that you are using for two-step authentication.

With physical access, the question is who can pick up the device and walk away with it, open it up, or otherwise tamper with it. One of the greatest security improvements you can achieve is proper physical control of your devices. Theft or loss is less likely within the safety of your home, but security is still an important concept. It becomes more critical when you travel outside the home, as we cover in Chapter 12. If you can keep control over your devices, and keep them from being lost, stolen, or damaged, you have eliminated a great number of risks. We've all heard personal stories from friends or family about lost cell phones and laptops, and read news reports about the lost or stolen laptop computer that contained sensitive customer data on it. Losing these things means that not only can bad guys get your data, but also that you don't have access to it. This cybersecurity tip is low-tech but important.

Inside your home, you may want to mentally evaluate the risk that a burglar or guest will steal a laptop, smartphone, tablet, or external hard drive. What are the chances someone might tamper with your device, for example put a key-logger on it that records every key pressed by the user? You have risks if you frequently host parties attended by many strangers, or if a family member has a substance abuse problem. If your "significant other" has a stalker-type personality, or if you are heading towards a nasty breakup, those are all risks. If you or a client might be the target of national espionage or corporate espionage, that creates a danger. Your client, or even your firm, might spend a lot of money to secure the workplace, and malefactors might realize that your home computers are vulnerable to attack. Whether these scenarios seem realistic or outlandish is for you to evaluate, so that you can determine what level of precautions to take.

For each device, consider the consequences if you lost the device, it became unusable because of an unexplained software crash, or if it was dropped on the floor or even into the tub. Smartphones and tablets are going to get dropped or have things spilled on them, so an external case that absorbs impact or repels water can help increase their chances of survival when these things happen.

As good as your habits may be to keep physical control of your devices, remember that there will likely come a time when you will voluntarily relinquish physical control by giving it to your children, donating, selling, or recycling it. Before you pass the device on, make sure that you have decommissioned it properly as discussed towards the end of this chapter.

F. ACCESS: ELECTRONIC (TECHNICAL)

Quick tips:
- Each device should require a password to access it (or fingerprint or retinal scan).
- The password should not be too easy to guess.
- Each device should automatically lock after a reasonably short period of inactivity.
- You should make a habit of affirmatively locking the device when you are done using it.

With electronic, or "technical" access, the key question is, if someone else gets their hands on your device, can it be turned on and used by them, or is there some type of mechanism—like a password and possibly encryption—that restricts access? If you don't have a log on and screen lock password on your desktop, laptop, tablet, or smartphone, you should implement one now. Every device you use should require a password to access it, and should lock after a certain period of inactivity. These simple steps will increase your security level.[1]

Every time you power on a device, it should require a password or fingerprint before you can start using it. Even if you pick a fairly simple password, and even if you reuse the same password across all of your devices (not ideal), you will improve your security and possibly thwart a casual thief or trespasser from accessing your device and its data. Depending on the device, a simple password might even stop more substantial threats. If your device is an Apple iPhone with a newer operating system, for example, enabling a password means the contents of your device are encrypted, and it would take a determined attacker with significant resources to break in. If your device is a Windows laptop or desktop, and you have *not* enabled any encryption options, then this password can be bypassed by someone with mild technical skills, but it will still stop the casual thief.

1. Device Password Complexity

As a general rule, your device password does not have to be as complex as the passwords for your cloud accounts. For a thief to start guessing your device password, he first needs to get physical possession of it, and that's a hurdle that limits the pool of possible attackers. In contrast, for a cybercriminal to start guessing your cloud account passwords, all he needs is Internet access—which means many criminals can try to break in and some might get lucky. Thus, for your personal devices, it is acceptable to use simpler passwords that are easier for you to remember, and it is acceptable to reuse the same password across multiple devices. After you get comfortable with this you could increase the complexity of the password, and you could consider having unique passwords for each device.

There are a few exceptions to this general rule that simple device passwords are acceptable. The first is if you have chosen to sign in to your device using your cloud account, rather than creating an account local to the device. Microsoft Windows and Apple OS X both offer this option. In Windows, you can choose to have your device account linked to your Microsoft cloud account, so that when you sign into your device, you are simultaneously signing into your Microsoft cloud account, so that your data and settings automatically synchronize. Apple allows the user to do the same with their iCloud account, and if your device automatically synchronizes to a corporate

---

1. One exception to this device password rule might be if there is an impediment that makes entering a password very difficult. For example, someone with Parkinson's disease might have a lot of trouble having to reenter the password frequently. In a case like this, work to provide adequate physical security that limits physical access to the device.

enterprise type network, a similar risk exists.[2] In these cases, you are effectively signing into your cloud account, using your cloud password, and that password should be complex and unique.

Another exception to the rule that device passwords can be simple is if you have sensitive data on the device, or if you have taken the time and trouble to enable encryption on your device. Remember that the encryption is only as good as the complexity of your password, and if someone is able to guess your password, they are able to decrypt the contents of your device.

2. Auto Lock Feature and Affirmatively Locking Your Device

After you implement a good device logon password, the next step is to configure the device so that it locks after a period of inactivity. Depending on your usage, the device, and where you want to set your "cybersecurity dial," this period could be thirty seconds, a few minutes, or an hour. If it's a desktop computer in the safety of your home, an hour might be fine. If it's a smartphone that you take outside the house and may leave on a restaurant table, you might want it to lock automatically after thirty seconds of inactivity.

Regardless of your automatic lock setting, try to make it a habit to manually lock the phone when you are done using it, if you are not in the safety of your home. Lock it when you put it down within the grab area of thieves, or before you put it into your pocket or purse. If nothing else, this will prevent you from accidentally "pocket dialing" others.

One of the early cybersecurity consultations I did after leaving government work was for an attorney who initially insisted his security was satisfactory. I persisted, and the first thing I asked was whether his iPhone required a password—it did not. I explained the potential ramifications, including that if the phone was lost or stolen, the thief would have access to all of his business and personal e-mails, and be able to read them, including e-mails with clients. The thief would be able to send e-mails from the stolen phone as if he were that lawyer, have access to all the contacts, and everything the device stored or could access. After we discussed this security risk, he set a password, and also configured the phone to lock after few minutes of inactivity. When I asked later if this had been inconvenient, he reported it had been a smooth transition, and his habits had changed without incident. The added bonus was that he no longer needed to charge the phone constantly—it got a much longer battery life, since his phone was automatically locking and going into sleep mode.

---

2. If your computer user account is part of an "active directory" on a corporate Windows network where active directory authentication is integrated with online applications and databases, then a clever hacker with access to your device may be able to access e-mail and other corporate resources remotely.

The Pocket Dial

I was at an evening reception as part of an information security conference, and I stepped outside the venue to call home, then put the phone in my pocket. Normally, I lock the phone before putting it in my pocket, but not this time for some reason. My brother later reported he got about a half dozen FaceTime calls from me, each time with a dark screen and he couldn't hear anything. Fortunately, no harm was done. But imagine the potential consequences: if a client were to be called, the client would not be impressed; if opposing counsel were accidentally called, the adversary might be able to listen in on a confidential conversation. So make it a habit to lock your smartphone or tablet before stowing it in your pocket or purse. You'll save your battery and potentially avoid embarrassment or revealing private information.

Note that one doesn't need to be physically present to gain electronic access, because there are many remote access software tools that can be used to access a computer from great distances. When you get to the sections in this chapter on applications and anti-malware, remember that remote access tools can be in the form of applications that you installed, or malware that has infected your computer. Every remote access tool creates a portal to enter your computer that could be exploited, so you need to review the settings, and if you have such an application installed but no need for it, uninstall it.

G. USER ACCOUNTS: USAGE BY WHOM AND FOR WHAT PURPOSES?

Quick tip:
- Reconfiguring user accounts can be a significant time investment. Thus, the beginner might want to address other areas first.

There are two main things to consider with respect to the people using your computers and devices. First, evaluate if members of the household are using administrator accounts on the device for general computer activity—which is not a good practice. Second, consider which users share a local account on the computer. Switching an account from administrator to standard user is relatively simple, but other readjustments of user accounts on a computer can take some work, so you may want to put this off until you have corrected other issues first, or until you purchase a new computer and are setting up new accounts anyway.

Windows and Mac operating systems allow computers to have separate compartments in them—called "user accounts"—so that multiple users can keep their own data private and customize their settings for the operating system and applications. Consider who uses each desktop or laptop, and for what purpose. Does each user sign into a unique user account, or do several people share user accounts? Is the use for personal purposes, work, or both? Does it involve sensitive, confidential, or financial data? Some usage may be more sensitive or more risky than others. Certain parts of the Internet are relatively safe, and certain parts of the Internet are more dangerous and risky, and likely to subject you and your computer to attack and infection. Consider the three methods shown in Figure 8.1 for configuring local user accounts on your computer.

In the left and riskiest configuration, the family has a single user account with administrator privileges, shared by all family members. In the middle, the family shares an account, but it has standard user privileges, rather than admin privileges, and only the parents know the password for the admin account. In the right, the family has segregated their accounts between

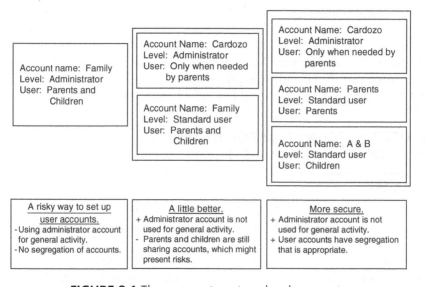

FIGURE 8.1 Three ways to set up local accounts.

parents and children, making it harder for the child to access or modify the parents' data. Windows also allows users to sign in to their device with a cloud account, rather than creating an account local and specific to the device, however this creates some security vulnerabilities.

1. Administrator Accounts vs. User Accounts

Quick tip:

- General computer usage on laptops and desktops should be with a standard user account, not an administrator account.

Device accounts come in different levels of capability; administrator accounts have elevated powers and privileges to affect the computer's settings, and standard user accounts only have power to control things relating to that account, and less power over the computer. If you have only one account on your Windows-based computer, it is probably an administrator account and you are taking risks using it for general computer usage because malware or an attacker can take advantage of those privileges to compromise the entire computer.

The best practice is to have a standard user account for your general computing needs, whether it is surfing the Internet, checking e-mail, word processing, playing games, or working. You should not use an administrator account for these tasks, and should reserve use of an administrator account only for administrator-type tasks, such as configuring your computer, installing new software, adding new external devices, and more. Use of an administrator account for all computer usage violates the information security principle of "least privilege" we covered in Chapter 4. This principle dictates that you use only the privileges you need to accomplish a task, and no more. From this perspective, using administrator privileges to surf the web or check e-mail is overkill which exposes you to greater risk should your computer be attacked and compromised. Remember, if your account is compromised, the attacker gets all the access and privileges that you have. If you are running a regular user account without administrator privileges, then the attacker only has access to user-level information, and cannot control the entire computer and all of its data. However, if an attacker gains control of an administrator account, the attacker can control and change your entire computer, install malware that controls your entire computer, and access all of the data stored in your computer. The computer can be permanently affected.

Because of this risk, your laptop or desktop should have a minimum of two accounts: the administrator account, which you will almost never use—though you may need to enter the password for this account periodically to authorize certain actions on the computer, and a user account, which you use for all of your computing needs. Each account needs to have a password. Reusing the same password across accounts is better than having no password at all, and it is not the ultimate in security sins. One benefit of having separate passwords is it prevents you from accidentally signing in to the wrong account.

You should check if the account you use on your laptop or desktop is a standard user account, or an administrator account. If you currently use an administrator account for regular computer activity this presents risks and is not the "best practice." This may not be your first cybersecurity priority to correct if you merely want to raise your security level one notch, but remember it is vital to return to this task at a later time.

Transitioning from Regular Use of Administrator Accounts

If you currently use an administrator (admin) account for general computer activity, and want to stop this practice, it's easy, and no data transfer is required, though some continuing effort will be required since you will periodically have to provide administrator authorization for various computer tasks. On occasion, you may need to log in to the administrator account to perform certain actions, or learn how to run certain operating system applications with administrator rights.

Your computer needs to have at least one account that has administrator privileges. If your current account is the only one with administrator rights, you will need to create another local user account and give it administrator privileges. Then, reduce the privileges on your original account to that of a regular user. You're done! Breaking it out into individual steps goes like this:

1. Navigate to the user account settings interface.

   Windows 7/8/10: Control Panel → User Account

   Windows 10: Settings → Accounts

   Apple OS X: Apple menu → System Preferences → Users & Groups

2. (If needed) Create a new administrator account. Try to avoid naming it "Admin" or "Administrator." Ensure it is password-protected. Don't use this account for anything except tasks that require an administrator account.

3. Change the privileges on your current user account so that it is no longer an account with administrator privileges. Make it a "standard" or "non-admin" account.

4. Continue your normal computer usage with your standard user account.

    a. When the computer requires administrator level approval, you will be prompted to enter your administrator password.

    b. Malware that attempts to take over your computer while you are using a local user account will not be able to do so automatically. It will be forced to request permission from you.

2. Segregation of User Accounts

Quick tips:

- Users with very different needs or skills should have separate user accounts.
- Users who need their own privacy and customized settings should have separate user accounts.

Laptops and desktops can be configured to have multiple user accounts, so that each user can keep their data private, and customize his or her settings. Traditionally user accounts were unique to the device, but now they also can be associated with a cloud account from a cloud provider such as Apple iCloud or Microsoft Outlook.

This discussion of multiple user accounts is largely limited to desktop and laptop computers. If you are using a tablet or smartphone, these mobile devices are set up to be used with a single user account, and they don't have the capability to have separate user accounts unless you install special software. Thus, anyone who has the device password can generally access all of the applications and data on the device. Though there is the capability to have separate e-mail accounts and other separate Internet accounts on your device, there isn't the capability to keep each user's activity compartmentalized within the device. A rare exception is a dual-partitioned mobile device, which might be found in large companies who have implemented this solution to segregate the user's work use and personal use.

How and whether to segregate members of your household into separate user accounts is a matter that requires a balancing of security, privacy, sharing, and convenience. Whatever your configuration is now, know that changing it will involve some work and migration of data. If you are not prepared to do that yet, consider staying with the status quo until you have first addressed other security issues, or until you perform your next device upgrade.

From a cybersecurity perspective, it is preferable for each user to maintain a separate user account. This approach keeps each person's data private and compartmentalized in case another user's account is compromised. Many users stay "logged in" indefinitely to most Internet and cloud accounts, thus anyone with access to the user account on the device would have access to these cloud accounts. Though segregation is good from a cybersecurity lens, it can be cumbersome from a sharing and convenience viewpoint. Sometimes household members share a computer and software, and collaborate on games, projects, and documents, and it could be annoying and frustrating to have to repeatedly switch between accounts.

As we've discussed, deciding what to do is a matter of finding compromise between convenience and security. In many areas, the line is clear. If one member of the family is performing sensitive and confidential work on the computer, no other family member should have access to private, confidential data. If a family member is working on important information, teenagers or young children shouldn't have access to that data, nor the opportunity to expose that data to compromise. That means either supervising the computer use or segregating the user accounts. Of course, if you have work data, or access to work data, on your home computer, then you have a professional responsibility to guard that data and access. Separate user accounts are one mechanism to guard access and protect privacy.

In general, each additional account means additional work, since each account needs to be separately configured. Data may need to be migrated, if it was initially shared by all, but now will be restricted to certain users. Thus, you don't want to create more accounts than you really need, as this can mean extra work and possible frustration. Perhaps spouses can share an account, since they share a lot of information and data, and collaborate on many things. Perhaps children can share an account, since their privacy needs and computing activities are similar. Remember that there are many ways to share data and documents among different user accounts, such as via a shared or public folder.

Needless to say, each user account should have a password, and the passwords for each user should be different. The child should not know the password for the parent's account or the administrator account, but the parent should know the password for the child's account. The child's password should be as complex as is practical, or it could be a passphrase that is meaningful to them. It's never too early to start instilling good computer security practices. If you want to get your child started with a simple but useful password, consider using your phone number, which will allow them to learn it and memorize it.[3]

When you are ready to start creating additional user accounts, you will find this in the same place where you adjusted the account privileges:

- Windows 7/8/10: Control Panel → User Accounts
- Windows 10: Settings → Accounts
- Apple OS X: Apple menu → System Preferences → Users & Groups

Aside from having multiple users on a single laptop or desktop, an alternative might be for children to have their own laptop or desktop, perhaps a hand-me-down from the parent. As covered later in the decommissioning section, certain steps need to be taken when the device is transferred from parent to child.

Chapter 11 provides more detail about keeping your family and children safe with their devices, data, and on the Internet. For now, remember that the device is the gateway to the Internet and the rest of the world—to anyone with an Internet connection—as scary and amazing as that may be. Parents should play a role in securing devices, monitoring children's usage, and educating their children. There are settings that can help prevent your children from accessing risky sites or using certain applications, which might be helpful while the child is very young or to avoid accidental exposure to certain content. Explore, and consider implementing the built-in parental controls that come with Windows and Mac OS. Ultimately, these parental controls will not be enough—children will need to learn about the threats, and learn to make responsible decisions when using computers and the Internet.

---

3. Yes, it's controversial to use a phone number as a password, but this is a device password, not a cloud password, and it's for a child, not an adult. You're accomplishing a few things—the device has a long password, which is more secure than a short password, and your child learns to use and memorize not only a password but your phone number.

H. OPERATING SYSTEM

Quick tip:

- Know what your operating system is, keep it updated, and learn the basic settings.

Your device has an operating system that comes with many applications, and these have many settings that affect your security and privacy. As we covered in Chapter 5, your operating system is a complex software program that sits between your hardware and your applications. For laptops and desktops, the main operating systems in use are Microsoft's Windows and Apple's OS X, with a small percentage of users who run the open source Linux, while with smartphones and tablets, the main operating systems are Google's Android and Apple's iOS.[4]

Operating systems are so complex that they contain many lurking vulnerabilities that can put your device at risk for compromise and infection. Every day, computer experts identify new vulnerabilities which the operating system manufacturer (Microsoft, Apple) attempts to patch by periodically sending out updates. Every so often they come out with a new and improved operating system designed to utilize new hardware, and makes things better, faster, more efficient, and more secure for the user. Of course, issuing a new version of the operating system may enable them to learn more about you, or perhaps even charge you more money.

You should check to see what operating system you are running on your device, and you should check that automatic updates are turned on, and that the operating system has been recently updated.[5] Periodically, check to confirm that your operating system is updated. Your operating system also has many configuration options for various security and privacy settings. You should review these settings periodically. Some sample areas to check are indicated below for Windows 10 and Apple OS X.

---

4. For desktops, Windows has about ninety percent of the world's market share, Mac is about five percent, and Linux has less than three percent. Within the United States, Windows has under seventy percent and Mac takes most of the market share that Windows loses. With smartphones, Google's Android has over eighty percent global market share, with Apple's iOS at a little over ten percent, while within the United States, Apple is more popular than it is worldwide, and its iOS and iPhones comprise about forty percent of the smartphone market share. *See, e.g.,* STATISTA, statista.com, and NETMARKETSHARE, netmarketshare.com.

5. Are you running Windows XP on any of your laptops or desktops? Microsoft stopped supporting it, so it does not get updates, and its unpatched vulnerabilities make that very dangerous. A Windows XP computer should not be connected to the Internet, and should probably be decommissioned.

Review Operating System Privacy and Security Settings

Review your operating system's security and privacy settings periodically. You will learn more each time you review them, and new updates may make automatic changes that you should be aware of and prepared to undo. Within these settings you will encounter options relating to firewalls and anti-malware detection—we will cover those topics shortly, but for now realize where you can find them.

Windows 10

Settings → Update and security

- Operating system should update periodically.
- Windows Defender is a solid anti-malware option that comes with Windows. This will be covered later in this chapter.
- Backup and recovery—do you have an automatic or manual process to back up your important data? This will be covered in Chapter 9.

Windows Firewall

- Windows firewall is a capable option. We'll cover that later in this chapter.

Settings → Privacy

- These settings determine which applications have access to your data and input devices, including your location, microphone, and camera.

- Turn off any access that is not needed. Don't give an application (app) access to information unless you really need that app to have access. Don't let apps run in the background unless you need them to. For example, if you don't use the Windows "Store" app at all, then you should not allow it to access your microphone, camera, and it should not be allowed to run in the background.
- Some of the apps to check include: Location, Camera, Microphone, Speech, Account Info, Contacts, Calendar, Call History, E-mail, Messaging, Radios, Other Devices, Feedback, Background Apps, etc.
- Review these settings periodically—a new update to the operating system sometimes means access has been enabled automatically.

You might need to use the microphone and camera on your laptop for a variety of activities. However, they also present a risk, because a hacker could take control of your microphone and camera, allowing him to listen and watch what is happening in your home or office. The more programs that are authorized to access the microphone and camera, the larger the "attack surface" for an attacker trying to listen in, or look in on what you are doing. Thus, if you can limit the applications that have access, you are reducing your attack surface. If you have no need of the microphone and camera, then you should disable the software and drivers for the microphone and camera, and also tape over them for good measure.

For Apple and Android products, the principles are the same. Here are some details on how to find the basic settings.

Apple/Mac OS X

System Preferences → Security & Privacy

- General tab: Select "disable automatic login" and "require a password" after sleep or screen saver activates.
- Privacy tab: As with Windows 10, decide which apps can access your various data, by reviewing the settings for location, contacts, calendars, accessibility, and more. If you don't use an app, don't grant it access to the data. Similarly, if the app doesn't need access to the data, don't grant it.

iPhone/iPad

- Settings → Privacy
- Settings → Touch ID & Passcode
- Settings → Control Center
- Settings → (review other settings)

Android

- Settings → Security
- Settings → Security → Screen Lock
- Settings → Security → Automatically Lock
- Google Settings

I. APPLICATIONS (SOFTWARE)

Quick tips:
- Install and run only reliable software, and keep it updated (patched).
- Give software access only to data or functions that the software needs.
- Don't let software run automatically unless it really must.
- Uninstall software that you will never use.

- When installing new software, select "custom" installation option, and don't install add-on components that you don't really need, such as browser toolbars.

Applications are the programs that you run and use on your devices. Many come pre-installed on the device, either with the operating system or by the device manufacturer. Other applications are loaded onto the device by you or other users of the device. While some applications run only when you explicitly launch them, some run automatically when your device is turned on. You should periodically review the software that has been installed—but doesn't necessarily run—as well as the software that is regularly running on your device. It may be unrealistic to learn every single application and process, but improving your knowledge a little bit at a time will be helpful.

Every application presents a security risk, because even those from reputable software companies can have vulnerabilities. Software vulnerabilities, like operating system flaws, are being discovered every day and these vulnerabilities could allow an attacker or malware to compromise and exploit your device. When reputable software companies learn of new vulnerabilities in their products, they attempt to plug the holes, and push the patches (updates) to their customers. Many software products also collect or track data about you, and even legitimate and well-intentioned software companies want to know about you and your usage habits, and there are some that don't play by the rules and use deceptive or illegal practices in how they collect and use data. Simply put, the more software you run, the more risks you introduce that can affect your security and privacy. Every application on your computer is like a skylight in your roof—if it's built and installed perfectly, it will probably never leak—but if something about it isn't exact, it will be the first place that your roof leaks.

Because of all these risks associated with software, you should take stock of what applications are running on your computer, and you should evaluate all new software before you install it. If there are applications that you don't need, consider removing them, or at least configuring them so they don't automatically run unless needed. If there is software that isn't trusted, it should be removed. Software needs to be obtained from a reputable source, and kept updated and patched. Aside from being a security risk, every application that runs automatically consumes resources from your computer that are limited. If you are running applications you don't need, then you are unnecessarily slowing the computer down, and for mobile devices, draining the battery.

A review of your device's privacy settings is a first step in seeing how your data is being accessed by your software, such as your location, camera, microphone, contacts, and more. You can restrict the applications' access to this data, and see if you notice any ill effects. The next step would be uninstalling applications that you know are not needed.

Every time you install software on your computer, pay attention throughout the process. Select the "custom" installation option rather than the "default" option, so that you can decide what gets installed. Frequently, the default installation option installs additional software and features that you really do not need, such as adware or spyware that bloats your computer and could compromise your privacy or security.

Review Running and Installed Programs

When you are feeling ambitious and want to learn more about what applications are on your computer, use the operating system's built-in method to view this.

Windows 10 (Task Manager)

View running programs, programs that launch automatically on startup:

1. Access "Task Manager," review processes, app history, startup.
   Method 1: Press Control-Alt-Delete, then select "Task Manager"
   Method 2: Press Control-Shift-Escape keys simultaneously
   Method 3: Type "taskmgr.exe" in the search bar to locate and run the program
2. View installed programs:
   Method 1: Settings → System → Apps and Features
   Method 2: Control Panel → Programs and Features
   Sort by install date to see what programs were recently installed or updated. Sort by name to see what is there.

Don't uninstall programs just because you don't immediately recognize them. Make sure you know what the program is and that you don't need it before you uninstall it.

3. View operating system privacy settings (as in prior section), by navigating to Settings → Privacy.

Mac OS X (Activity Monitor)

View running programs, programs that launch automatically on startup:

- Open Activity Monitor
    - Method 1: Applications → Utilities → Activity Monitor
    - Method 2: Use Spotlight (Command-Space) and search for "Activity Monitor"
    - Method 3: View the "Force Quit Applications" window, which shows what is running; use Command-Option-Escape

Mac iOS

Review icons of installed apps:

- Settings → scroll down
- Settings → Battery (see what apps run and use battery power)

Android

- Settings → Apps

J. DATA STORED ON DEVICE

Quick tips:
- Sensitive data should be encrypted.
- Your data should be backed up periodically.

The next chapter covers all things "data" in greater detail, but for now remember that that your device stores data on it, and there's a fundamental difference between data that is stored on your device, and data that your device accesses from elsewhere, such as the cloud. For the data on your device, you can mentally evaluate the following issues:

- Type of data
  - Data you affirmatively store vs. what is automatically stored by the device
  - Personal vs. work data
  - Sensitive or confidential data vs. public data
- Harm if access to the data is lost
- Harm if data is stolen by criminals or competitors
- Whether or not your data is encrypted
  - If not, can it or should it be encrypted?

If the data relates to your employer, or a client or customer, you have a fiduciary and professional responsibility to safeguard it. If it is sensitive, confidential, privileged, or financial, you are required to treat it accordingly. If it is your personal information, documents, photographs, and contacts, then these may be irreplaceable. There may also be data stored on the device that you don't realize is there, perhaps several years' worth of your Internet browsing habits, or remnants of documents or communications that you thought were removed.

Evaluate what data you are storing on your device, and consider whether you can improve its security. The two principal risks are that your data will become inaccessible to you (loss of availability), or that someone else might access it or steal it (loss of confidentiality). You can reduce the risk of loss of confidentiality by keeping physical control of your device, using strong passwords, and through encryption.

To protect against loss of availability, you can back up your data. But remember that any time you make a backup of your data, you may also increase the risk of theft, since you now have two (or more) copies of the data that you need to safeguard. There are many companies that try to solve this problem for you by offering software and cloud storage so that your device data is automatically and securely backed up into their cloud. Evaluate the security issues surrounding this cloud storage, look for encryption in transit and at rest, and ensure this cloud account is secured with two-step authentication.

Sometimes, needs are transient, so you should try to make the risks temporary as well. If you need to copy sensitive data onto your laptop for the purpose of traveling to meet a customer or client, you should consider removing and securely deleting the data once the need has passed. Encryption of data that is stored on your device is one way to keep the data safe, even if your device is lost or stolen. However, there are different types of encryption, with different levels of security, and encryption is only as good as the password or key. The next chapter covers encryption of data at rest in greater detail.

K. DATA THE DEVICE CAN ACCESS (CLOUD DATA)

Devices are the gateway to cloud data, whether they automatically synchronize and display our e-mails, contacts, calendar, or documents, whether we use a web browser to access cloud data, or whether our folders automatically synchronize with the cloud. Thus, securing a device is an important step towards securing data that we store in the cloud.

We'll cover cloud data in the next chapter, but regarding your device, consider the consequences of losing your device as to availability and confidentiality. If you lost your device, would you still be able to log into your cloud accounts? If a criminal stole your device, would he or she be able to access your cloud accounts? These issues are interrelated, and the scenario of a lost or stolen device is addressed in Chapter 15.

L. ANTI-MALWARE

Quick tips:
- You should have software running continually on your laptops and desktops that actively scans for malware.
- You should periodically (monthly) scan your laptop or desktop for malware using a different type of anti-malware software.

Anti-malware software is essential for your desktops and laptops. By anti-malware, we mean security software designed to protect against bad, malicious software. "Malicious software" means malware, virus, rootkit, worm, or any other name for software that tries to compromise your computer. Smartphones and tablets require a slightly different approach. For Apple iOS, there are no real anti-malware solutions. Apple has attempted to build the iPhone securely, partly by taking steps to ensure that only vetted applications can be installed on the iPhone and only through Apple's App Store, though this is far from a guarantee of security. For Android, mobile malware is more common, and thus there are some anti-malware solutions available. The main key to avoiding malware on your mobile device rests with you. As we discussed in the section on applications, ensure that you install only reputable software, and not malware disguised as legitimate software. You should not "jail break" or otherwise modify your phone in order to install unapproved software.

For your desktop and laptop, evaluate whether you have software running continuously that scans for malicious software and activity. Windows 10 comes with Windows Defender, which is a capable solution, and there are also quality free products you can download and use. Aside from this continuous monitoring, consider the last time anti-malware software scanned the contents of your computer's storage devices, and consider the last time you got a "second opinion" by running a second malware detection software from a different provider.

Many Mac users are under the mistaken impression that Macs are completely secure and they don't need to be concerned about malware. Though one could make the argument that Macs are indeed more secure, or at least less prone to infection, they are definitely not impervious. Macs have benefited from being a relatively small percentage of all computers used in the world, and with less than ten percent of the world running Mac computers, criminals generally have devoted more resources towards exploiting Windows operating systems. That doesn't mean it will always stay that way, and as Apple's market share increases, they become a more profitable target for cybercriminals.

Some recommended free anti-malware solutions are listed below. Some offer versions for different operating systems, and some only offer it for a single operating system, so download the free version that is right for you.

- Windows Defender (comes with Windows for free)
- Malwarebytes (free)
- AVG (free)
- ClamAV (free)
- ClamWin (free)
- ClamXav (free for Mac OS X)
- HitmanPro (free)
- Avast (free)
- Sophos (free)
- Bitdefender (free)
- Kaspersky (free)

With each of these solutions, select "custom" installation, and install only the anti-malware software, not additional programs like toolbars or search optimizers. The program may repeatedly encourage you to upgrade to a paid version, but you don't need to buy anything to obtain and use the free anti-malware software.

The Paid Anti-Malware That Didn't Work

Just because it's free, doesn't mean it's bad, and just because you pay for it, doesn't mean it's great. In the summer of 2016 we learned that a major anti-malware software company had used poor software coding and security practices, resulting in a vulnerability in all of its software, which many individuals and corporations were paying for and using.

I used to pay for an anti-virus and firewall (we'll cover firewall software soon) for myself from a respected vendor whose product got great reviews, and every year, I paid the subscription fee. Then, my home computer became infected with "scareware," a malicious software that pretends it is helping you, but tells you that you are infected and you need to pay a subscription fee to the scareware entity to remove the supposed infection. This scareware took over my computer—despite the anti-malware protection I had paid for.

I tried many things to remove the infection, but my anti-malware software couldn't touch it, nor could others, and I ended up having to reinstall the operating system. This expensive security product didn't protect me, which was frustrating enough, but to add insult to injury, even though I canceled the subscription, the company continued to bill me for it, causing further headache. After this incident, my inclination was to use free software, rather than to pay for anti-malware services.

There are certainly some excellent paid anti-virus tools available. Just be realistic about the advertising pitches made by some of these companies.

M. INTERNET ACCESS

Quick tips:
- Know how your device accesses the Internet, and how to turn access off.
- Disconnect from the Internet when you don't need it.

Consider how each of your devices accesses the Internet from within your home. Remember that this is a two-way street—your path to the Internet is how the Internet sends data back to you, and also how an attacker might try to get in. For now, just consider how your devices access the Internet from within your home, and in Chapter 10 we will get into greater detail.

As we covered in Chapter 6, your devices ultimately connect to the Internet through an Internet service provider (ISP), which could be your cable company, residential phone company, cellular phone company, or even a satellite provider. Each of your devices might have slightly different ways of getting to your ISP and the Internet. Your desktop may be connected by an Ethernet cable to your router, then to your cable modem, then to your cable Internet provider. Your laptop computer might connect to your Wi-Fi network, which is established by your router, and then proceeds to your cable modem and then to your cable Internet provider. Your smartphone can connect through cellular signals to the cell towers managed by your cell company, but it can also connect to your home Wi-Fi network, and thus may have two different methods for reaching the Internet.

It is also possible to "tether" devices, using the Internet access of one device to give a second device access to the Internet. Your smartphone might access the Internet through its cellular signal, and you could connect your laptop (or tablet) to the smartphone to gain Internet access. This connection between smartphone and a second device could be via wireless connection (like Wi-Fi or Bluetooth) or even through a wired connection. Conversely, if your smartphone gets poor cellular service in your house, it can connect to your Wi-Fi network, and phone calls can go through your Wi-Fi Internet access, rather than through the cell towers.

The longer your device remains connected to the Internet, the more it is exposed to attack by the seemingly infinite number of criminals roaming the Internet and constantly scanning for available and vulnerable devices. When your device is connected to the Internet, you are exposed to attack, and criminals could try to hack into your device or infect it. It's not a matter of whether there is a hacker specifically targeting you; cybercriminals have an array of automated tools scanning the entire Internet looking for devices and vulnerabilities. Also, consider that your device may already be infected—like millions of other infected computers in the world—and may be transmitting data about you and your usage, or being used for another purpose by a botmaster.

Taking your device offline, even for a short time, protects your device from attack and prevents it from being used by a botmaster while it is off the Internet. You can turn the device off, or you could disconnect it from the Internet by putting it into "airplane mode," turning off the Wi-Fi and Bluetooth, or disabling the network adapter. There are some software firewalls that also allow you to block all Internet traffic, but these can sometimes interfere with other device activity. Cybersecurity threats aside, our mental health is improved by periodic disconnection from the Internet and our devices.

Chapter 10 covers more details about securing your home network, and Chapter 12 discusses securing yourself when you travel outside the home. For now, a brief mention of two concepts that relate to the device:

- It's OK if your device automatically connects to "known" and trusted Wi-Fi networks, like your home or office. However, it should not automatically connect with unknown networks.
- The names of Wi-Fi networks your device has connected to in the past are stored within the device, and may be "advertised" by the device when you travel.

N. FIREWALL

Quick tip:
- Use the operating system's software firewall for your laptop or desktop computer.

Your laptop or desktop computer should have a software firewall implemented—an application that monitors data flowing to and from your computer and blocks unauthorized or malicious traffic. Windows comes with a built-in firewall that has received good reviews, and does not significantly interfere with your use of the computer. Any firewall product can create issues, because sometimes it blocks connections that you don't want blocked, but a software firewall native to the operating system will be least disruptive. Note that for smartphones and tablets, there is no reliable firewall product yet.

Some third-party firewalls also perform the function of being able to shut the device off from the Internet when desired, a helpful feature. Unfortunately, sometimes these third-party firewalls interfere with the operating system and home networking features. Thus, to disconnect a device from the Internet, it is simplest to disconnect from the Wi-Fi network, disable the relevant network adapter, or put the device in "airplane mode." As we will cover in Chapter 10, routers also have a firewall function which can help protect you by blocking traffic before it gets to your devices.

Implementing a Software Firewall

Windows 10

1. Access "Windows Firewall" settings
   Method 1: Control Panel → Windows Firewall
   Method 2: Settings → Network & Internet →
        Windows Firewall
   Method 3: In the search bar, type "Firewall" or
        "Windows Firewall"
   Make sure the firewall is "on" and review the
   settings.
2. Access "Windows Firewall with Advanced Security"
   settings
   Method 1: In the search bar, type "Windows
   Firewall with Advanced Security"
   Method 2: From Windows Firewall, click on the
   "Advanced Settings" link

Apple Mac OS X

1. System Preferences → Security & Privacy → Firewall tab

O. DECOMMISSIONING YOUR DEVICE

Quick tips:
- Your device accumulates a lot of data when you use it, and stores this data in many places.
- Your device has access to a lot of cloud data.

Early in this chapter we covered the importance of retaining physical control of your devices. But consider what happens when you voluntarily give up control. Whether you are selling, donating, or recycling an older device, you need to take specific steps to protect your data. If certain precautions are not taken, others who obtain your device could access either your cloud data or the data remaining on your device. Decommissioning is the process of converting a device from your own use to another use, whether it is for another family member, sale, donation, or recycling. Secure decommissioning is our focus.

If you just bought a new computer device for yourself, you are not going to use the old device in the same manner as before, so it should be securely decommissioned. Don't wait until you forget to do it, and don't leave old devices lying around that haven't been decommissioned. The decommissioning process gives you an opportunity to review your security, privacy, and data practices, improve them for your new device, and put old electronics to a proper use.

The general goal is to make sure that the device can no longer access your cloud data, including e-mail accounts, cloud documents, and Internet accounts, and also ensure that you have securely erased data stored on the device so that it cannot be recovered by anyone. How you decommission the device depends upon what you stored on it, how you used it, what you will do with it, and where your "security dial" is set.

For smartphones and tablets, the device has a convenient and simple to use "reset" or "erase" feature, and that may be completely sufficient, especially for devices that are encrypted (as most Apple iPhones and iPads are by default). For laptops and desktops, there are some methods and tools to clean the contents, and Windows 10 also has a simple "reset your PC" feature. Recognize that nothing is perfect, so it's a matter of how much time you are willing to spend, and whether you are willing to take a hammer and nail (literally) to your devices.

Appendices 6 and 7 have more detailed checklists you can use to decommission your devices, but some basic steps are below which may be suitable if the device does not contain, and cannot access, sensitive or confidential data. In sum, you will first make sure your new device is working and can access all of your data properly, including data copied from the old device. Then, manually review the old device and delete your data. You might find data you forgot to copy out, and also learn more about all the apps and data you have accumulated over the years. Once you've done that manual review, then you can use some automatic features to delete the data.

1. Basic Decommissioning Steps

1. Ensure the new device is working, and that all data is transferred and accessible. Use the new device for several days.
2. Evaluate any reasons to preserve data on the old device (e.g. business, legal, and ethical obligations to preserve data).
3. Consider the future use of the old device (family member, friend, stranger, trash, recycle). If it's for a trusted family member or friend, you may want to preserve certain applications and access and not delete everything on the device.

4. For laptops and desktops, download a free secure erase tool, such as CCleaner (free version) by Piriform (https://www.piriform.com/ccleaner/download).
5. Disconnect the old device from the Internet (but be prepared to reconnect temporarily if needed).
6. Clear all Internet history and cookies in all web browsers and delete all stored passwords in web browsers.
7. Delete all passwords and all references to your cloud accounts.
8. Manually search for your data on the device and delete it.
9. Uninstall unneeded apps/applications/software on the device.
10. For laptops and desktops, delete the existing user accounts.
11. For laptops and desktops, use CCleaner to securely delete data and to wipe free space.
12. Use the device's erase settings/data feature, and consider using the device's reset device/erase device feature (Windows 10 and most smartphones and tablets have these features).

P. CONCLUSION

This chapter provided details about securing devices, which are important because we use them constantly, they store our data, and they allow us to access the Internet and our data stored in the cloud. Securing our devices is the foundational step towards cybersecurity. Start with a device password and good physical control habits for all your devices, and work from there. If this chapter seemed like too much information to digest or implement at once, don't be concerned. Start small, periodically review all of the settings on your device, and make improvements as you become more comfortable.

CHAPTER 9

Secure Your Data

A. INTRODUCTION

This chapter focuses on your data, on learning and understanding what you have, where it is stored, how it is accessed, and how to protect it. There are two main goals when it comes to protecting your data: to make sure it remains available to you when you need it, and to make sure it is not stolen by others. These goals invoke the principles of availability and confidentiality, which require both data backups and adequate security. Like the rest of this book, this chapter takes an incremental approach toward improving your data security, to ensure you don't lock yourself out of your data, and to help you gradually improve your knowledge and skills so that you can create and maintain control. You should take an especially careful and methodical approach when making changes to how and where your data is stored, as it might be difficult to undo changes, or in some cases, impossible.

The previous chapter focused on securing the computing devices you use. That's an important first step, because devices store some of your data, and are also the mechanism to access your data that is stored in the cloud. In this chapter, the focus is your data, what you have and where it is stored. You will do a home version of what corporations are supposed to do when assessing their own cybersecurity status, looking at privacy, e-discovery, and business continuity practices. You will evaluate data, what it is, where it is stored, and then decide whether to retain it and if so, how to protect it.

As with each activity in this book, you will not only improve your security posture, but also your work efficiency. For example, if you don't fully understand where your data is being stored, it can be time consuming to locate what you need when you need it. Our devices synchronize so seamlessly with the cloud that we sometimes don't realize how much of our data is stored off the device. When you don't know where your data is, it can be confusing when you try to locate it.

Where's Your Data?

As I was upgrading my wife's iPhone years ago and migrating her cloud storage, I learned that she had two separate ways of storing contacts: one address book that stored contacts locally to the device, and another address book that synchronized with the cloud. By consolidating her address book, I greatly improved her efficiency and ability to find contacts, and to keep them current.

On another occasion, I worked with someone who believed that an attacker was stalking, hacking, monitoring, and deleting data from his iPhone address book. However, investigation revealed that he had simply disconnected the device from the cloud accounts, resulting in contact information disappearing, so it was simply confusion over where data was stored and how it was accessed. By understanding where our data is, not only can we secure it and back it up appropriately, but we know where to find it when we need it.

With your home cybersecurity, as well as for companies for which you work or advise, assessing the "what" and the "where" of your data is the start of cybersecurity and e-discovery planning. If your company or client is involved in a lawsuit, there will be discovery—disclosure of evidence in their possession—and much of that evidence will be stored in electronic form. Companies need to know what data they are storing, and where, or else they may face discovery sanctions. The best time to figure out what is being stored is *before* a lawsuit, so that smart decisions can be made about what to store. From a cybersecurity perspective, not all data is equal—some needs to be protected more than others, so a review of the data is important for that purpose as well. This is commonly called "data classification." Not all data needs to be encrypted, and not all accounts need two-factor authentication. But if a review of your data reveals that unneeded, sensitive data is being stored in the dusty forgotten storage space of some old laptop, it is better to discover that situation before the laptop is lost or stolen.

B. MENTALLY ASSESS YOUR DATA AND WHAT IT MEANS TO YOU

Take a moment to reflect upon what data you have, and where and how you store it. Before computers and the cloud, it was easy for us to know where we stored our information, because it was tangible, such as an address book, calendar, or a filing cabinet. Now, our data is stored in many places, including places we can't see or touch. We have so much data that it's easy to lose track of it, or feel overwhelmed by the thought of dealing with it.

It's also worth considering how the way we think has changed with the growing use of technology, and how the amount of data stored in our heads may have actually decreased. For example, once upon a time, we memorized many of our most important phone numbers, and this memory was reinforced each time we dialed the phone. Today, phone numbers are stored electronically in our contacts database, and our devices automatically dial the numbers for us. This makes us less reliant upon our brains and more reliant upon the electronic data we have stored, which arguably increases our vulnerability to cyber threats.

All the data stored by you and about you comes with differing concerns and levels of importance. Family photos may be priceless to you, so you need to keep them "available" to you.[1] If a copy of a photo is stolen, it might not concern you, so long as you still have another copy available. With the criminal innovation of ransomware, cybercriminals profit from your need to maintain access to your data by remotely locking up your data and demanding money to unlock it. Other data may be highly sensitive or confidential, requiring protection from being stolen or copied, and thus you are worried about maintaining confidentiality. This could include client materials stored on your computer, in the cloud, or in an e-mail account. E-mail can present interesting complexities as some types of e-mail software download your mail, while others let you view it on the e-mail server, located on a company server or in the cloud.

In assessing what you have, you may realize that you have a lot of data you just don't need, like a lot of junk in your attic, basement, garage, or storage unit. You may find that you are storing data that is dangerous or unnecessary to hold on to, like customers' personal or financial information from a business you had many years ago. Storing this unneeded sensitive data is like having old ammunition or firearms hidden and forgotten in an attic. People really do that with old ammunition, firearms, and even hand grenades— stashed and forgotten for years and decades, only to be discovered much later. It is time to identify your unneeded data and securely delete it.

---

1. Remember the information security triad of CIA: confidentiality, integrity, and availability, as we covered in Chapter 4.

For each piece of data, ask yourself what you would do if it were lost or destroyed and no longer available to you. Ask what the consequences would be if you were the victim of a data breach and it was stolen. By going through this thought process, you will help evaluate the level of care with which to treat the different types of data you are storing. If the data were lost or destroyed, would you try to replace, recreate, or restore it? If not, consider deleting it, since you may not need it after all.

Though this book focuses upon data stored in electronic format, remember that information is stored in many formats, including paper and in your brain. Notwithstanding some of the trends to "go paperless" and the convenience of electronic document storage, don't discount traditional paper storage for certain documents. History shows that paper documents can last hundreds, even thousands of years, and they can always be read by the human eye—no special hardware or software is required. On the other hand, data storage technology changes rapidly, so our data storage mechanism of today may not be readily accessible in a decade. Further, there is less research about how long certain storage devices and media last. Do not assume that data copied onto a floppy disk drive, zip drive, DVD, flash drive, or external hard drive will survive intact for decades, and be readily readable in the future.

Your data assessment will consist of mentally reviewing information about yourself and your data in four basic ways:

1. Your own skills and memory
2. Data type
3. Data importance
4. Storage location

By inventorying and assessing your data and where it is stored, you are doing what law firms, professional firms, and businesses are supposed to do—but frequently neglect. Unless you assess, you don't know what you have, you don't know the risks, and you don't know how and what to protect.

While reading Chapter 8 you may have filled out the top of Appendix 11 (Personal Device and Data Summary), where you listed the devices you use regularly. In this chapter, you can fill out the bottom half of that form to summarize your important cloud accounts, such as iCloud, Gmail, Outlook, or Dropbox, to name a few.

1. Assess Your Own Skills and Memory

Remember, whatever your current skill level, you can learn more, and you will be well served to gradually improve your skills and knowledge, allowing you to take control of your data. If you don't already have basic computer skills that allow you to search for files, copy them, move them, and organize them, then you should develop these skills. They can be learned by anyone, even if you have a self-imposed mental block.

That said, your current skill level will determine how quickly you should proceed to organize your data, because there is the potential to unintentionally do quite a bit of damage. It's good to learn and try new things, but when it comes to your data, it's important to be methodical and incremental. If you are not familiar with moving and copying files, you should improve your skills and experience before you embark upon a large data reorganization. When you copy or move files, don't assume that everything worked perfectly—you need to verify that everything copied properly before you move on to another action.

If you are not comfortable with the techniques required to copy, create, and organize files and folders, then an automatic backup solution might be of extra benefit for you. Some experts suggest that many computer users are best served by surrendering control to an automated tool. Keep in mind that tools are fallible too, and sometimes are only as good as the person configuring them and monitoring them. Without having the underlying knowledge, and conducting a periodic review of these automated tools, there is no way to ensure that the tool is working properly. By conducting backups manually and periodically, you will gradually improve your knowledge and skills. Practice restoring individual files, directories, and full systems so that you know it works properly, and so you could do it in an emergency.

In sum, let an honest assessment of your own skill level be your guide, but resolve to improve your skill level continually so that you will eventually take control of your own data.

2. Assess by Data Type

Here, you want to conduct a simple, mental review of some of the basic categories of information that you are storing, whether it is on the cloud, a local device, an external storage device, on paper, or in your brain. Where is the primary copy of the data (which is read and modified), and where is the backup copy of the data (which you access only if something happens to the primary copy)? Information types to consider include:

- Passwords. If passwords to your e-mail accounts are stored in your device and automatically entered by the device to access your e-mail, and you lost your device, would you be able to remember your passwords and access your e-mail?
- E-mail.
- Contacts.
- Calendar.

- Tasks, reminders, etc.
- Documents, spreadsheets, PDFs, etc.
- Photos, videos, and music.
- Personal information about you and your family, like birthdate, Social Security number, financial information, and medical information.
- Personal information about clients or customers.
- Customer/client files.
- Social media–related data: contacts, messages, photos, etc. (e.g. LinkedIn, Facebook, Twitter).
- Online accounts: shopping (Amazon, eBay), etc.
- Data specific to certain software, like accounting, personal finance, etc. In other words, is there any software that you use and enter data into, and that stores this data either locally or in the cloud?
- Software that accesses a cloud account (e.g. some cloud versions of Microsoft Office, Google Docs, Adobe, practice management software, etc.).
- Backups of the above data.

3. Assess by Data Importance and Risk

For each of the above types of data, mentally assess the relative importance of the data, and the likelihood of harm if it became unavailable to you or stolen. Assess how secure the storage of each type of data is, what protections are in place, and how often you access each type of data.

What if your entire computer crashed, and all of the data on it was unrecoverable? Would you have a backup? If a hacker takes over your e-mail account, or social media account, and you can't recover it, or he deletes all the data in it, how would that impact you or your operations? What if the hacker used information within your e-mail account for a criminal or malicious purpose? How often have you forgotten your passwords and had to reset them?

For each data type, there are also important questions around who it belongs to or impacts, so consider:

- Who owns the data?
- Who is the subject of the data?
- What duties do you owe to others with respect to the safeguarding of the data?
- Do you possess or access work-related data from your home or personal devices?
- What is your professional and legal duty to protect data and information relating to clients and customers?

- Does the data relate to personal or financial information (your family's names, birthdates, Social Security numbers, bank information, etc.)?

As for protections in place and planning for potential disaster recovery or business continuity, consider:

- Whether you have a backup, and when your device was last backed up
- The strength and uniqueness of your password
- Whether two-step authentication is in place
- Whether encryption is in place

4. Assess by Data Storage Location and Provider

Mentally inventory and assess the various places where you store information and data (Figure 9.1). There may be more places than you would think. You store information in many places, including:

- Your brain (certain passwords, phone numbers, contacts, calendar, etc.)
- Paper
- Local devices (locally on a computer, smartphone, etc.)
  - Data you have affirmatively stored
  - Residual data you may not be aware of that is still stored on the device
- Network storage (data storage device accessible to your local network)
- External storage (a data storage device that is detachable, like an external hard drive, thumb drive, DVD, etc.)
  - Data you have affirmatively stored
  - Residual data
- Cloud storage (cloud provider, e-mail, documents, etc.)
  - E-mail and related cloud providers: Gmail, Hotmail/Outlook, Yahoo, AOL, etc.
  - Social media: LinkedIn, Twitter, Facebook, Instagram, Pinterest, etc.
  - Other software as a service provider
- Internet accounts, shopping sites
  - Amazon, eBay, e-commerce sites, etc.

We covered the "cloud" in Chapter 5. It's an all-encompassing term which is perceived as a brand new invention but actually has been used by many of us, especially for e-mail, for many years. Once you started accessing your e-mail through a web browser (using providers like AOL, Yahoo, or Gmail,

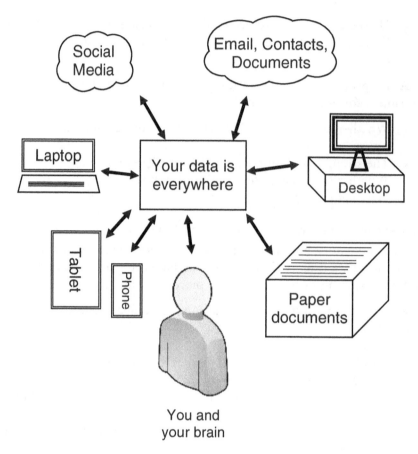

FIGURE 9.1 Assess where your data is.

for example), you were using the "cloud" to store your e-mails and associated contacts. In other words, the e-mail was not stored on your local machine, but was stored on the servers of your e-mail provider. E-mail providers have greatly expanded the cloud services they offer, to include calendar, tasks, document storage, and more. These services—often accessed through your web browser—use "cloud" storage, in that they store your e-mail, appointments, contacts, and other data on their servers. This "cloud" storage of data is extremely convenient and keeps things available to us independent of the device used to access the account, but it comes with security risks we have previously discussed. Any time you can access your data remotely, through the Internet, it means a criminal can try to access your data remotely as well.

5. Assessment Wrap-Up

You may feel that you are embarking upon an enormous undertaking, but don't feel overwhelmed. You need not achieve perfection, but merely improve your understanding about your data, where it is stored, how it is backed up, and how it is secured.

C. GETTING STARTED

Quick tip:
- Appendix 11 (Personal Device and Data Summary) has a place you can write information about your important cloud accounts.

Now on to securing your data. The main steps we will cover include:

- Secure your devices (encore).
- Back up your data.
- Secure your cloud data with strong passwords and two-factor authentication.
- Consider encryption of your data at rest.
- Organize your data.

D. SECURE YOUR DEVICES (ENCORE)

Again, you must properly secure your devices in order to secure your data. There is data stored within your devices, and your devices are the gateway to access data stored in the cloud and in online accounts. Not only should you secure your own devices, you should avoid using devices if you do not know their level of security and who else uses them. The device could be compromised, putting both your passwords and cloud-stored data at risk.

Let's restate the basic principles to secure your devices:

- Your devices should require a password to access them and should automatically lock after inactivity.
- Be aware of all software on your devices, including remote access software.
- Keep your devices malware-free.
- Protect your devices from loss, theft, or damage, especially your smartphone.
- Disconnect from the Internet (or power off) when not in use.

E. BACK UP YOUR DATA

Securing your data starts with backing it up. Backing up your data should be your highest priority, and it is also fairly simple to do. It will cause you no disruption, requires minimal work, and will put you on a path towards greater awareness, knowledge, and skill, let alone improved business continuity in a disaster.

Many problems that the home user faces concern the loss of access to data, not just from a theft, fire, or flood, but often from a crashed hard drive, or a lost or corrupted document. Often, this type of event seems to happen at the worst possible time, like when you are working on a project with a short deadline and something happens that causes you to lose all of your work. Even before cybercrime was a booming industry, we were victims of this problem, but now it happens even more, thanks to malicious people and software, including ransomware.

For the home user, backups can save you from a devastating loss of data, and from having to re-create important work. For a law firm or business, maintaining availability of data is critical to survival. Businesses invest considerable funds to minimize the potential for loss of data. Depending on the business need, the acceptable data loss and down time may be zero, or measured in seconds, minutes, or days. You should decide how much data loss is acceptable, and invest the time and effort necessary to protect yourself to this degree. Your financial investment is minimal—you just need storage—and this is relatively inexpensive.

This section offers a number of techniques to protect your data, and you can decide which to employ, and how often. The methods include:

1. Periodic, manual backup of your documents, photos, etc. to an external hard drive.
2. Periodic incremental backups of your most important works-in-progress.
3. Operating system backup application.
4. Periodic, manual backup of your cloud data to a local device—and from a local device to a cloud. Research your cloud provider's backup and restoration abilities.

Redundancy can be valuable in some situations, so if the data is currently stored in the cloud, consider having a backup that is stored locally, and vice versa. This belt-and-suspenders approach is not necessary for all data types, but can be useful for some business continuity and disaster recovery needs.

Remember that backing up your data represents a compromise between availability and confidentiality. Backing up your data is insurance to maintain availability of your data, even if one copy of your data is destroyed. However, creating a backup can slightly raise confidentiality risks, because each copy of the data needs to be properly secured. The more copies of it that you make, the more copies are available for malefactors to steal. In cybersecurity lingo, you have increased your "attack surface." One way to help maintain confidentiality of these many copies of your data is through encryption, which is covered later.

Backups and the Laptop in a Burning House

The importance of data backups is highlighted by a news story about a novelist who ran into his burning home to rescue a most valued possession—his laptop.[2] No doubt he had years of work stored in that laptop, which would be destroyed if it wasn't saved from the fire. Our data can be our livelihood, representing days, months, and years' worth of our work, sweat, and intellectual capital.

Instead of finding yourself in a situation like this novelist did, you should recognize now—before the fire or theft—that you have data and information that is very important to you, and back up this important information periodically. Of course, you should never risk your life in order to retrieve or save personal property—it's not worth it.

In writing this book, I spent hundreds of hours creating data, stored electronically on my computer. But I made many backups of the book as it was in progress to protect against calamities. The master copy was on my desktop, but I had copies on my laptop, copies in cloud storage, and every time I e-mailed a draft to my editors and reviewers, that left a copy in both my e-mail account and theirs, albeit a copy of an older version of the chapter. If something bad like a hard drive crash or ransomware infection occurred, these older versions would have been available—it would have been disruptive to lose the original—but the situation would not have been catastrophic.

---

2. Matt Sledge, *Man Dashes into House to Save Laptop, 2 Completed Novels from Fire in New Orleans' Broadmoor Neighborhood*, THE NEW ORLEANS ADVOCATE (Sept. 15, 2016), http://www.theadvocate.com/new_orleans/news/crime_police/article_62593cd4-7b61-11e6-a9b6-971ab1e197c9.html.

1. Manually Back Up Data to an External Hard Drive

Quick tips:

- Ensure you have an external hard drive to make a backup of your data (USB "plug and play").
- Do it—make a backup periodically. Then disconnect the external hard drive from the computer and turn the external hard drive off.

You need to have an external hard drive available to back up your data. I recommend a small, portable, USB-powered drive from a reliable manufacturer, such as My Passport from Western Digital or Backup Plus portable drives from Seagate (or other well-reviewed manufacturers). You will need to manually copy files from one hard drive to another, so if that is beyond your current comfort zone, then this is the opportunity to learn. It will be a skill that will aid you for all your computer usage.

You need to store this drive in a safe place, disconnected from the computer, perhaps in a different room, or even a different house or safe deposit box. Periodically, you will connect it to the computer to manually copy certain files. Some external hard drives come preloaded with software that asks to automatically back up your data, and we address automatic backup solutions in the next section. This section is about manually copying files to the external hard drive.

You should find a reasonable backup interval that works for you. The time period should be somewhere between daily and never. A daily manual data backup might use too much of your time, so if daily backup is essential, you should find an automated solution. Never doing a backup means risking catastrophic loss of all of your data. Somewhere in the middle is a happy compromise that balances the burden and your risk. You might find it acceptable to risk a loss of three months' worth of family photos and personal data, but it might be unacceptable to lose more than a week's worth of work on a critical project. You decide how much time you want to invest in backing up your data and what level of risk you want to assume.

A business may invest heavily in systems to ensure redundancy, so that they don't lose any data, or lose only a small amount of data. For example, financial firms processing transactions cannot afford to lose data on a single transaction. An e-commerce site taking new orders every second will lose business and customers if any of those orders are lost. For the home user, your needs are different, and you balance time and expense with the amount of data you are generating and how much you can afford to lose. It might be acceptable to lose a month's worth of general data. If you are working on a special, important project, there are ways you can back that up more frequently, as discussed in the next section.

Your external hard drive needs to be in a safe spot. You don't want to keep it connected to the computer constantly, as that defeats the purpose of having a separate backup, since it can be destroyed in the same fire, stolen by the same thief, or infected by the same malware. Once you make a backup, you need to secure this copy of your data. One way to secure it is through encryption, but you will need to remember the encryption password, and there is always the very slight chance that the encryption doesn't work as intended. Another way to secure your external hard drive backup is in a physically secure space, a bank's safe deposit box, your own locked safe, or a safe at a family member's house.

Based on the assessment of your needs, decide the interval of backup to an external hard drive, whether it is monthly, quarterly, or annually. Consider having one external hard drive that you store in your house for quarterly backup, and one external hard drive that you store offsite (in a safe deposit box or family member's house) that you update with a new backup annually. Perhaps you employ another solution to back up certain documents at a more frequent rate. Not every backup should be saved forever, and you don't need to perform a full backup every time. Having a system that meets your needs can prevent you from a catastrophic loss to a theft, flood, fire, or hard drive crash.

2. Make Incremental Backups of Your Most Important Documents

If you are working on important documents, you can periodically back them up using a variety of techniques. It is important to develop a system that enables you to keep track of which copy is the original or master version, and which is the backup. Thus, good file naming and storage practices are important, which we cover in section H below. Here are some creative ways you can make backups of individual documents.

a. E-mail a Copy of the Document

When you e-mail a copy of the document, you are storing a copy of it within your e-mail account (as a sent e-mail), and in the e-mail account of the recipient. If you are using a cloud-based e-mail service (as most people are), by e-mailing the document you effectively have stored a backup of the document in your e-mail account's cloud. If you are collaborating with others and sharing the document by e-mail, you are also, in effect, backing up the document. If you are not collaborating with anyone else, then you can simply e-mail yourself a copy of the document periodically. Creating a draft in Gmail and attaching the document, but never sending it, also serves a similar purpose.

As with any form of backup, creating another copy of the document within your e-mail account (or the recipient's e-mail account) means that if the e-mail account is compromised, so is that document. The best way to prevent such a compromise is to make sure your e-mail accounts are secured with a strong password and two-step authentication.

b. Save a Copy on Your Local Drive

Sometimes documents become corrupted, or through user error the information within the document gets deleted or altered. For example, spreadsheets are powerful tools to analyze and store data, but a mistake can make the information within them useless, and you might not detect the error until it is too late. To guard against this problem, you should make periodic backups of all your important documents.

You can do this with either the "save as" or "copy" commands, where you make a duplicate copy of the current file. Give the copy a helpful filename—such as putting a "z" in front of the backup's name—to distinguish it from your master (working) copy. We'll cover this process more in section H.

c. Back Up Important or Active Folders

If you are working on an important client matter, you might back up only that client's electronic files and folders to another location. You can also search for files and folders on your computer that were recently created or modified (e.g. within the last week or month) and copy only those to your backup location.

3. Manually Back Up Data from Your Cloud Accounts to a Local Device or External Hard Drive

You probably have a lot of data in your cloud accounts, and this data should be periodically backed up to your local device or an external hard drive. This mitigates the damage in case you lose access to your cloud account or the data there is deleted by accident or by a malicious hacker. If you are storing documents in the cloud (e.g. Google's Drive, Microsoft's OneDrive, or Apple's iCloud Drive) then you may want to copy them into a folder on your local drive. The folder name could be something like "zGoogle Drive backup 2017-1-24." The "z" in front tells you it is a backup that you don't need to touch unless you need to restore data.

4. Backup Using Your Operating System's Native Backup Application

Your operating system comes with its own backup and restore utilities which can be set to operate automatically. However, these utilities may not always be effective, so don't forget to verify them occasionally. The Windows 10 backup function is called "File History" and prior Windows versions called it "Backup and Restore." Apple's backup function is called "Time Machine." Navigate to the backup configuration panel, and you can set it to backup certain files, at a certain time interval, and to a certain location.

5. Automatic Backup vs. Manual Backup

As indicated above, your operating system probably comes with automatic backup software. There are also many applications and services that will automatically back up your data to your external hard drive or to their cloud. You should consider a cloud backup solution as it provides off-site redundancy of your data, guarding against a local disaster like fire or flood. Even if you choose to use an automatic solution, you should periodically manually back up your data because it gives you control over the process, and each time you do it, you get better at it. A downside of manual backups is that often people forget to do them, or don't do them properly.

Automatic backups have downsides too, because it can be unclear what is being backed up or how the data can be restored. A main principle of any backup procedure is to periodically verify that the backup process works—by doing a test restore to ensure that the proper data was backed up and is recoverable. The wrong time to discover that a backup system isn't working is after a hard disk has failed or been encrypted by ransomware. Corporations with dedicated IT departments are supposed to do these test restorations of backed up data, but this is an area of habitual deficiency even for corporations. Without testing that you can successfully restore, there is no way to know for sure if the automatic backup is working properly. For all these reasons, a simple, manual backup process can be an ideal method to help you build awareness and skills regarding your data, and take control over it.

F. SECURE YOUR CLOUD DATA AND INTERNET ACCOUNTS (AND BACK THEM UP)

From a data security standpoint, certain Internet-based accounts are more important, and certain accounts less. Important accounts include your e-mail accounts, which often come with additional services like contacts, calendar, document storage, etc. Providers of these services include Apple's iCloud, Google, Microsoft, Yahoo, and more. Important online accounts also include your financial accounts, for your bank and credit card companies, as well as your social media accounts, like LinkedIn, Facebook, Twitter, and more. Every few months, you should spend a bit of time reviewing these accounts and your various settings relating to security and privacy, and backing up important data from these accounts to a local computer.

Some Internet-based accounts are less important and more difficult to secure, such as the accounts you use for Internet shopping with various e-commerce sites. You may have dozens of these, and there is probably very little that you can do to secure yourself regarding these accounts, other than to limit the amount of information that you give to them and let them store.

1. Secure Your Important Online Accounts

Quick tips:

- For your e-mail accounts and important Internet accounts, enable two-factor authentication and ensure you have strong, unique passwords.
- Review your account settings, including security, recovery, and privacy.
- Continue to review account settings periodically, every few months.

Now (and periodically), you should review all of your account settings for your e-mail, cloud, financial, and social media accounts. To do this, you need to log in to your cloud account from a web browser, and navigate through the service's various settings menus. Remember, this is different from adjusting the settings on your device. You need to go to the provider's website, log in, and use their interface. If you have never reviewed the various settings and options, it may seem confusing and overwhelming at first, which is one reason you should do this review of the settings periodically. Each time you review them, you will increase your knowledge, slowly take control of your security and privacy, and keep yourself aware of recent changes in the services and settings. As features are added or changed, your privacy can be negatively affected. It is vital to keep on top of this evolution.

Remember that your cloud accounts not only contain your important data, but they are important tools that you use for social and business purposes. Losing access to these tools can cause great inconvenience and embarrassment. If criminals get access to your accounts, they can use them to impersonate you and others and commit fraud.

You can give the provider information about you to secure your account and help recover it should it be hacked. Providing accurate information helps ensure recovery and your ability to prove you are the rightful owner of it. Two-factor authentication is a very important security measure to keep control of the account, and by giving the provider your mobile phone number, you have enabled one of the most effective ways to secure your account. At the same time, giving this information to the provider also gives them helpful marketing and tracking information, and cell phone numbers are becoming increasingly important for tracking people. Thus, there is a tradeoff between keeping some of your information private, and securing your accounts. I believe that you are better served by providing a reputable online provider with your mobile phone number in order to enable two-factor authentication because the security gain outweighs the privacy loss. Some basic things to check in your cloud account settings are:

- Account access settings.
  - Enable two-factor authentication (also known as two-step login) to require not only a password, but also a single use code sent to your cell phone (or an authenticator application).
  - Ensure that you have a strong password in place (that you can remember).
  - Don't reuse the same password across multiple important accounts.
  - If you make a change to your password or add two-factor authentication, you should promptly sign on to your account with all of your primary devices (smartphone, tablet, laptop, desktop) to verify that you can get access.
  - Periodically, but not too often, change your password. A complex password is better than a weak, regularly changed password.
  - Take notes of any changes and changed passwords and store them in a secure location.
- Account recovery settings. These settings set forth how you would regain access to the account if it was hacked or if you forgot your password or otherwise lost access.
  - Recovering an account with a lost or forgotten logon or password requires proving to the e-mail provider that this is your account. Have you provided your true name and contact information to the provider? By doing this, you are giving up a little bit of your privacy to the provider, but you are increasing your ability to recover the account if it is hacked.
  - Do you have a recovery phone number listed?
  - Have you shared secrets with the provider for account recovery?
  - Do you have an alternate e-mail account listed? This could be your second e-mail account, or a trusted family member's account. This alternate e-mail account should be secured properly as well.
- Recent access, and all devices and applications that have access to your cloud data. See if there is anything out of the ordinary. Chances are everything is fine, but familiarizing yourself with this gives you a baseline so you can identify if something is out of the ordinary.
- Privacy settings.
  - Check what the provider is tracking and storing, and whether there is a way to turn this off, or to delete data the provider has already stored. By default, the provider is probably tracking and storing a lot of information about you.
    — For Google, this could include your search history, websites visited, YouTube videos viewed, and more. Fortunately,

Google allows you to stop (or "pause") the storing of this information and allows you to view it and delete what has been stored.

- Review what information you are making public.
- Review who can view what information about you. Everyone? Friends/contacts? Friends of friends/contacts of contacts?
  — Cybercriminals and identity thieves can research your profile and contacts in order to conduct more believable scams and social engineering attempts against you.
  — Remember that some sharing is out of your direct control, such as if your friends or contacts post information or photos about you.
  — Check if you know who your online contacts and "friends" really are.
- Back up your cloud data to your local device.
  - Your e-mails, contacts, personal settings, calendar, documents, and more can be backed up or archived, and you should do this periodically. Most services have a function for this, but each service requires a slightly different method.
  - If you have files stored in the cloud, you can simply copy ("drag") them to your local device.

2. Secure Your "Unimportant Accounts" as Best You Can

Quick tips:

- Don't give your bank account information to "unimportant" e-commerce sites.
- Don't give your debit card information.
- If payment card information is required, just give your credit card information.
- Don't reuse passwords from unimportant accounts on important accounts.

Unimportant accounts include various e-commerce sites where you have created accounts in order to shop. Other accounts that fall within this category include the Internet accounts you create to access websites or e-mail newsletters. Accounts like eBay and Amazon might be "important" (and fall under the previous section) since they contain a lot of information about you and your buying habits, and even your reputation. Unfortunately, there is not a lot you can do to secure these "unimportant" accounts. These companies may not devote significant time, money, or resources into securing customer data and accounts.

It is worth assuming that these sites are insecure and easily hacked, and that your data, including your e-mail address and password, will be compromised. That's one reason why you should never use one of your sensitive passwords on these kinds of accounts. Also, these sites may not have consumer-friendly privacy policies, or they might not follow whatever policy they have, so you don't know how they store and share your information.

There is certain information you have to provide to the e-commerce site, such as your name, billing address, shipping address, and a payment method. For the payment method, you should provide credit card information, and not debit card or bank account information. If the online merchant's customer database is hacked, and your information is exposed, the criminals will only have your credit card information. Hacked credit card information is far less damaging than hacked debit card or checking account information. If your credit card is used without authorization, you have the right to decline to pay the charge, you will not be held responsible for the fraudulent charges, you will be issued a new card, and you will not lose money. In contrast, if you provide a payment method that comes directly out of your bank account, and if this information is hacked, the criminals will steal funds directly from your account. Once you identify this fraud, you will have to notify the bank and ask them to refund the charges. In some cases, the bank will not cover the fraudulent debits from your bank account if they cannot recover the money. In the meantime, you have no access to the funds, and your other payments could result in insufficient funds charges and fees.

When you sign up for e-mail newsletters, they may ask you for a host of personal information. They may want this information for marketing purposes, but they don't really need it in order to send you the newsletter by e-mail. You should consider what information about yourself you provide. Consider having two e-mail addresses, one e-mail address that you provide to merchants and use for shopping and newsletters, and another e-mail address you use for family, friends, and people and businesses that you trust. The e-mail address you provide to online merchants may be sold, shared, or stolen, so you may receive more spam there. All of your e-mail accounts should be secured appropriately, including with two-factor authentication.

Again, your passwords for your unimportant accounts (like e-commerce shopping sites) don't have to be quite as strong as for your important accounts, and you should never reuse passwords to an unimportant account with an important account—that makes it too easy for a hacker to expand their attack.

Some E-Commerce Sites May Not Be Concerned About Your Data and Account Security

A lot of e-commerce sites and websites are not secure and you can't trust them. One organization I belong to set the online password as the member number, and didn't allow the user to change their password! That practice is extremely insecure. They fixed this problem when their new website was launched.

I used to buy from a particular e-commerce site that sells computer equipment, and I had an account with them. In December of 2015, I received an account notification e-mail from them that the e-mail address associated with my account had been changed. I tried to log in to my account, but I no longer could access it. Multiple attempts to contact the merchant proved fruitless, their customer service was terrible, and they advised me that I would not be able to access the old account. They suggested I could create a new account with a different e-mail address but, of course, I was not interested in buying from that merchant again.

My account had been hacked, and the hacker had changed the password to lock me out of it, and changed the e-mail address so I would no longer receive notifications about it. Instead of trying to return the customer account to the rightful customer, the merchant essentially gave up. Since I hadn't used this account in years, I don't think I was to blame for the hack. I believe the merchant was breached, or otherwise had poor security, allowing hackers to take over customer accounts. Whatever the hacker did with my account, I don't know, and the merchant never gave me any information. But surely the hacker obtained the stored information about me, and probably tried to make charges on the stored credit card information.

A different e-commerce site once sent me a notice that I had items left in my shopping cart, suggesting that perhaps I wanted to log back in to complete my purchase. This notice was a surprise, since I hadn't used that site in years either. I logged in and saw that someone else had gained access to my account and added a new shipping address—which turned out to be a shipping and mail receiving business in Oregon. The hacker had tried repeatedly to purchase electronics with my stored credit card information, to be shipped to the new address, but the credit card company declined to authorize these purchases.

None of the businesses involved seemed appropriately concerned about the hack of the e-commerce account, nor would they provide any information to me about the fraud. These hacks and data breaches happen a lot. Sometimes you learn about them, often you don't, and many companies don't care as much as they should about your personal information and fraud.

G. CONSIDER ENCRYPTION TO SECURE DATA ON YOUR LOCAL DEVICE

Quick tips:
- If you encrypt, ensure the password is complex but something you can remember. Also, write it down and store it in a safe place.
- Don't lose or forget your password!
- If you encrypt, also print out the decryption recovery key and put it in a safe place.
- Your operating system's built-in encryption application will provide a relatively seamless experience.

Encryption is an essential tool to keep your data confidential if the device is stolen, but it generally does not provide security against intrusion or access while the device is running and a user is logged in. Remember that securing data has two parts: keeping it confidential, and keeping it available. Encryption is essential to ensure maximum confidentiality—if you need that. However, while encryption methods are getting better, they are not always seamless, they may require some effort, and encrypting your data creates a chance that you might lock yourself out of it.

As we mentioned in Chapters 4 and 5, the main encryption methods for data at rest are file-level encryption and full disk encryption. Now we'll talk about the nuts and bolts of using these encryption methods to secure data.

1. To Encrypt or Not to Encrypt? That Is the Question

Let's start with looking at whether to encrypt data that's stored on your device or in the cloud. Remember this type of data is "at rest." Depending on your device, enabling an encryption solution for the data stored on it can be seamless, efficient, and can even occur without your input (by default). Apple's iOS mobile operating system—which is running on iPhones and iPads—offers seamless encryption operation by default so long as you have enabled a password. For other devices and operating systems, encryption might require you to affirmatively configure an option within your operating system, or you might need to obtain an encryption application. These options will entail varying degrees of complexity.

Encryption should not be the first cybersecurity measure you implement, and it should be done with careful thought beforehand. If you consider yourself a beginner with technology, or have problems remembering passwords, don't start implementing encryption until your skills and knowledge have improved. As we'll discuss shortly, if passwords and keys to encrypted data are lost, the data cannot ever be recovered. Encryption of data at rest has a number of pros and cons, as shown in Figure 9.2.

FIGURE 9.2 Encrypting data at rest: pros and cons.

Pros ➕	+ To prevent data theft.
	+ To protect sensitive data.
	+ To carry sensitive data when traveling.
Cons ➖	− It requires a strong password to be effective.
	− It locks you out permanently if you forget the password.
	− It could fail and the data could be lost to you.

2. Encryption by the Application

Many applications allow you to password-protect individual documents, and creating a password generally encrypts the file. Microsoft Word, Excel, and Apple's suites of software, and many others, allow you to save a document with a password, which is then required to open the document. The document is encrypted and needs the password to decrypt and unlock it. This is a good solution if you have a few documents that you need to keep more securely. For example, if you have an electronic file on your computer that contains some of your passwords, a list of your financial accounts, or a journal with your most personal thoughts, those files could be encrypted by the application itself. The rest of your files and data would remain unencrypted.

This type of encryption has some weaknesses because the sensitive data in the file you encrypted can probably still be recovered from your device—if someone gets access to your device. That's because when you open and work with a document, it may be copied to many places on your hard disk without you being aware of it. Those copies would remain unencrypted, even if you created a password and encrypted the original file. Of course, it's up to you to assess the likelihood that someone might be examining your device with the level of expertise required to recover this type of data. Later, we will discuss full disk encryption, which keeps all data on your device secure, making it difficult, perhaps impossible, to recover any of the data you store unless the password is obtained.

Encryption by the application is also a good technique if you want a level of security while e-mailing the document to a client. If you encrypt the document you are e-mailing, the data will be much more secure should the e-mail be misdirected, accidentally forwarded, or if an e-mail account is hacked. Only the intended recipient can open and read that file, using the password you have separately provided.

The password should be something that you previously agreed upon with the client, or that you share by phone or text message, not send with the document. Of course, you should not share the password via e-mail, since the encryption will be of little use if the e-mail account is ever hacked. Adding a password and file-level encryption may cause a little bit of frustration on each end, as there may be difficulties opening the file, forgetting the password, or a typo in writing the password. Sometimes different applications and operating systems don't handle this encryption and decryption well. But, overall, this type of encryption can protect against a host of common harms, including a misdirected e-mail, hacked e-mail account, and hacked computer. As with everything in security, it has positives and negatives, as shown in Figure 9.3.

FIGURE 9.3 File-level encryption by the application: pros and cons.

Pros **+**	+ Provides security for individual documents. + Contents of the file won't be indexed for search. + Even if a hacker gains access into your computer and is reading and copying files out, he can't open this file without the password, or without doing forensic analysis.
Cons —	– It slows things down as you manually enter a password each time you open the file. – It can be cumbersome to keep track of different passwords. – It is only as strong as your password. – Contents of the file won't be indexed for searching. – Unencrypted copies of your file may be automatically copied and stored elsewhere on the device, and could be recoverable.

Implementing Application-Level Encryption

Here we'll discuss how to save a file with a password (and encrypt it) using the application's native capabilities.

Microsoft Office (Word, Excel, etc.)

Open the document, and select:
File → Save As → Tools → General Options → and enter "Password to Open"

Apple iWork (Pages, Numbers, etc.)

Open the document, and select:
File → Set Password, and then enter the desired password

For your particular software, review your software's "save as" options, review help files, and conduct a search of the Internet for reputable sites for instructions on how to encrypt a file using the application (if possible).

3. File and Folder Encryption by the Operating System

Windows' encrypting file system (EFS) is an encryption method offered by Windows that allows you to encrypt only certain folders or files. It is applied easily by changing the properties of the file or folder, and it is seamless to the user, with the file decrypted automatically when the user logs in to his or her Windows user account (Figure 9.4).

FIGURE 9.4 File- and folder-level encryption by the operating system: pros and cons.

Pros ✚	+ It is more secure than doing nothing.
	+ It allows you to encrypt certain files and folders, which are automatically unlocked when you log in to your user account and access the files.
	+ It is secure because it is unlikely someone will be using forensic tools on your device.
Cons ▬	− It is only as strong as your password.
	− If you forget your password you will be locked out.
	− There can be unencrypted copies of your file stored on the device, available with forensic analysis.
	− If a hacker is in your computer while you are logged in, these files are readable.

Some experts emphasize that the EFS file- and folder-level encryption system is vulnerable and not worth using, especially since Windows BitLocker full disk encryption is a ready alternative for most Windows users (see the next section). EFS has the same weakness as application-level encryption—the underlying data may copied and left in many places on your hard drive and be recoverable with analysis. The acts of previewing a document, opening it, and working with it cause copies of it to be stored in various places on the device, in an unencrypted state.

With EFS, all of the Internet activity logged by your web browser may be stored in an unencrypted state. Thus, a trained person with the right tools and access to your device could recover a lot of information about you and your computer usage. Another limitation in using EFS is that it is protected only with the device user login password. It is for you to decide where your security dial is set, and if you wish to have additional security, you should consider full disk encryption. Only with full disk encryption are all of the background workings of your computer and data storage encrypted.

Implementing File- and Folder-Level Encryption by the Operating System

Windows EFS (Encrypting File System)

Use the Windows file explorer and select the file or folder you want to encrypt and view its properties. In the "General" tab, select "Advanced" and then select "encrypt contents to secure data."

Apple: Open Disk Utility (within Applications/Utilities)

Click the "New Image" button, or select File → New → Disk Image from Folder. Select the folder you want to encrypt, and pick your encryption method and a password. You can also use this feature to create a "Blank Disk Image" which is a place that you can copy files to in order to encrypt the files.

4. Full Disk Encryption

Full disk encryption (sometimes called whole disk encryption) means that all data on your hard drive is encrypted, including documents, pictures, Internet history, temporary files, and more (Figure 9.5). Full disk encryption is

FIGURE 9.5 Full disk encryption: pros and cons.

Pros ➕	+ It is the strongest method of securing data on your device.
	+ It encrypts everything on the device, not just some data.
	+ It is secure even from forensic analysis.
	+ It is seamless, once configured, and you log in to your device.
Cons ➖	− It is only as strong as your password.
	− If you forget your password, and lose your recovery key, you are locked out of all your data.
	− If a hacker is in your computer while you are logged in, he or she can still read and copy out these encrypted files.
	− A small software or hardware problem could potentially make everything unrecoverable.

necessary if you travel with a laptop computer that is used to store or access sensitive, confidential information—it is a safeguard against data loss in the event of physical theft of the device. Methods of implementing full disk encryption vary by device type.

Encryption, Security, and Law Enforcement

The default encryption approach has sparked considerable debate between government, technology companies, and security and cryptography researchers. Widespread use of encryption affects the ability of law enforcement to gather evidence. Law enforcement seizes a criminal's device, obtains a search warrant, yet still can't view the data because of encryption, and that's frustrating. Apple's iPhone is a popular product that many people use, but it's far from the only encryption available.

Encryption is a tool that anyone who wants confidentiality should use. Our government uses it and mandates that corporations use it, and other countries use it too. Unfortunately, so do terrorists and criminals. It would be nice if there could be a secret master key that only the "good guys" had, but it's not that simple.

Security and privacy should be everyone's concern, and encryption has essential benefits in these areas. Encryption is not as simple as it sounds, and not every encryption solution works perfectly. With Apple and their iPhone, they have enabled this encryption by default when a password is implemented, and it works so effectively and seamlessly that most users don't even realize it's enabled. That's no small feat. Whatever your view on this debate and the nuances of it, Apple should be recognized for providing this security and privacy feature for consumers that is effective and causes no impediments to use.

Encryption is a fantastic tool to protect confidentiality that is almost impossible to break unless someone knows or guesses your password, or uses your finger to unlock the device. There may be a few companies or governments that can defeat this security, if they are willing to spend the time to do so. The FBI was able to hire a company to do this in the San Bernardino case that gathered significant press attention.

This is a compelling issue with many facets and implications, and there is room for extensive debate and reasonable disagreement. Whatever the solution, rest assured it is not as simple as building a "back door" into the encryption, mandating encryption standards, or banning encryption solutions.

Full disk encryption is a seamless experience with the Apple iPhone and iPad devices. The Apple iPhone comes fully encrypted by default if a password is enabled, and this encryption works efficiently without any user intervention required. Apple's File Vault encryption for Mac OS X also works relatively seamlessly. Microsoft's Windows BitLocker encryption also works reliably, though it is not available with every version of Windows operating systems, and there may be some quirks. An encryption tool that is native to your operating system (like File Vault or BitLocker) will probably provide the most seamless experience. There are also many other options offered by independent software providers to enable full disk encryption.

Remember, encryption is a powerful tool. If you lose the password or decryption key, your data will be lost. You should print a copy of the decryption key and keep it in a safe place, and consider storing an electronic copy of it somewhere safe—not on the device with the data on it.

Implementing Full Disk Encryption

Windows BitLocker (not available on Windows 10 Home)

1. Navigate to BitLocker control panel

   Method 1: Control Panel → BitLocker Drive Encryption

   Method 2: Search for "Manage BitLocker"

2. Select "Turn on BitLocker"

Apple File Vault

1. Navigate to: System Preferences → Security & Privacy → File Vault tab

2. Select "Turn On File Vault..."

There are also many other providers of full disk encryption software.

---

5. Encryption Summary

It is easy to say that data should be encrypted, but implementation is not always completely painless. There are few perfect encryption solutions, and each remedy affects the availability of your data due to slower retrieval times or additional passwords. Each encryption solution is only as good as its password.

Keep in mind that not all encryption solutions are created equal, and each has vulnerabilities that a sophisticated attacker could exploit. If you are the potential target of nation-state attacks, then this book is only a starting point for you, because you need a carefully selected encryption solution and more. For most of us, the real concern is thwarting attacks by the criminal economy, and in our homes with our personal data, encrypting our personal data remains a choice for us. Encryption becomes more important when we evaluate how to store sensitive or confidential client materials.

H. ORGANIZE YOUR DATA—YOUR FILES AND FOLDERS

This section covers house cleaning and reorganization of your data. Good file and folder organization is beneficial to your efficiency and also helps ensure that backups are done properly. As you periodically back up your data, you'll have a chance to review how your data is organized and where it is stored. It's like periodically going through your filing cabinets, closets, attic, and basement, and seeing what you no longer need. Spring cleaning for your computer. It may not be a favorite task, but it's something we should do periodically and not procrastinate too long.

No one can tell you exactly how to organize your data, just as you wouldn't want someone telling you how to organize your office files or dresser drawers. You should develop a system that works for you that you control, leveraging the built-in file management features of your operating system. There are software products designed to help you organize and track your documents and files, but they will require an investment of time to learn to use them properly. What works well today may not work well years from now, especially if the software you buy today ends up discontinued or altered in the future. Your computer's operating system, and your own brain and file naming conventions, have great capabilities to organize your data, so invest some time periodically to learn about how best to use what's already available to you.

You Can Organize Your Data with the Tools You Already Have

I spent many years working on a complex cybercrime case, which involved enormous amounts of diverse data and evidence. A lot of this evidence was in electronic form, and included everything from photos, spreadsheets, and documents, to PDFs and data in much more complicated formats. This data was stored in traditional network folders, and we evolved skills and methods to organize it, using a consistent naming and folder structure. As trial approached, we reviewed various software products that were designed to make presentation of evidence in court simpler, and each software brand purported to make the extremely complex process effortless. However, I realized that this software required training and practice, even if it was advertised as easy to learn. After the training, there would be a learning curve, and then a significant investment of time to get the data into the software. We worried what might happen if different computers weren't properly loaded with this proprietary software, or if the paralegal trained to operate the software was sick one day, or left the office.

In the end, we created, managed, and organized our files with the tools that come with Windows and Microsoft Office, and we chose not to invest time in learning and conforming to a particular software product. We developed a common-sense system for naming and organizing our files and folders, and we all became skilled at using the operating system and standard applications. The methods we employed worked out really well.

The lesson here is that you can organize yourself with existing tools, and you do not have to buy any special product to help you organize your data, documents, and photos. It's not that those special tools are totally unnecessary, or that they don't have valuable uses; it's that you can make some enormous improvements and do a really good job with the tools you already have.

Every reader can learn how to organize his or her data, but you should assess your skills and capabilities before taking on more than you can handle. If you have never created, renamed, or moved a folder, then you need to start small, get some experienced help, and begin by testing on less important files. Better to make mistakes while you learn with less valuable data, not your favorite photos or important business documents.

1. Basic File Organization Concepts

Here we will cover some basic concepts to help you navigate through your files, and develop a system to organize and store them, including:

- File and folder naming.
- Folder structure: Create logical categories. Also, your desktop is not for storing files; instead, place *shortcuts* to the files on the desktop.
- Searching for files.
- Understanding basic metadata and file properties (metadata, or data about your data).

There are many methods and systems to organize and store your files, these are merely a few suggestions.

a. File and Folder Naming and Structure

You should give names to your files and folders that are meaningful and searchable. Sometimes your software suggests a filename for you, but you are under no obligation to accept the suggestion, especially if the suggestion is "Document 5" or the first few words of the document. You don't want the filename to be too short because then it won't be descriptive enough, but you don't want it to be too long either, because that can cause other problems. For example, Windows has a limitation on how long the filename and file path are, and generally that limitation is 256 characters. That may sound like a lot, but if you have a document stored many folders deep, and the folder names and document names are all long, you can exceed that limitation quickly.

Organizing your electronic data is very similar to how you would organize paper documents within folders, cabinet drawers, cabinets, and different offices. The more documents you have, the harder it is to find the document you want, so you need a system to divide documents among different folders and to name them. You also need to become adept at using your computer's search features. Of course, you should organize your data in a way that works for you and makes sense for you, and there is no "one size fits all." Some concepts that might assist you as you refine your data organization are:

- Ensure filenames are meaningful.
  - The name could include what the file pertains to, and what type of file it is.
  - A date in the filename can be helpful, even if it is just the year.
    - Letter to Joe Smith 2017-1-3
    - ABC Co Annual Report 2017-4
    - If you write dates in the format YYYY-MM-DD, then they will sort chronologically.

- As with filenames, ensure folder names are meaningful. Folder names define your categories and how you will group files together.
- Group related files together.
- Group related folders together.
- The first characters of the file or folder name determine how it will sort alphanumerically, and this sorting can be a helpful organization method.
  - You can "force" a certain sort order by putting a number at the front of your file or folder name. You can even create your own "Dewey Decimal System." For example, you could name folders like this:
    — "1 Correspondence"
    — "2 Motions"
    — "3 Discovery"
  - You can clearly indicate something is a backup file by putting a "z" at the front of the name. It will sort alphanumerically to the bottom, and you'll know it is not an original or working copy.
- Version control: Have a system to keep track of what is the current, working file, and what is a backup.

b. Document Version Control

You need a system to keep track of document versions, and doing this is known as "version control." Such a process will save time, frustration, and possibly embarrassment if, for example, you were to file or deliver the wrong version of a motion or letter. Good file naming practices help with version control. If the document is a backup, you want the filename to reflect that fact, so you don't accidentally open the backup and work on it. It is frustrating to have to redo work you have already done, or spend time figuring out which document is the current version. Putting a "z" in front of the folder or filename, and putting the backup date at the end of the name is one way to help with this problem. Putting a notation within the document can also be helpful, since that will remain visible within the document if it is printed to paper or if the filename is changed.

For example, if your document name is "Important Article.docx," then a periodic backup of this file might be called "zImportant Article backup 2017-1-24.docx." Putting the "z" in front of the backup's filename ensures that you can easily tell that it is a backup file, not a master or working copy. This "z" in front is especially helpful if you search your computer and find multiple search hits with similar names. Backups are easy to spot with this early "z," even if you cannot see and read the whole filename, and when they are sorted alphabetically, all of the "z" files (the backups) will be at the end of the list, instead of cluttering the list of files you might need regularly. Putting the date at the end helps you identify the date of the backup, without having to review the document's metadata, and ensures that each backup has a unique filename.

c. Hidden Data in Your Files

Each file on your computer has metadata attached to it, which can help you manage your data, but which can also unintentionally provide information to others that you don't mean to provide. Metadata is data about the file itself, such as when it was created and accessed, or when it was last saved. Operating systems store this information about each document, photo, e-mail, and other forms of data we create and store. Doing so helps the operating system function within its organizational structure, and helps the user keep track of his or her data.

If you ever need to restore backed up data, the metadata associated with the files can be very helpful. For example, by looking at a file's modified date, accessed date, and creation date, you can identify the correct version to restore. However, it's not always obvious what these dates mean. If the file was copied from one disk to another, you might see dates pertaining to the creation of the copy, rather than the creation of the original document.

There is other meta information within an electronic file that is not visible to the casual observer, including file properties such as author, last saved by, revision number, version number, total editing time, version number, and more. The document may also contain data that includes edits and comments, which can be hidden from casual view depending on how the word processing application is configured. If the "track changes" feature is enabled, the document is storing all changes made to a document, which may include confidential information that you don't want others to know. Awareness of this hidden data allows you to make proper choices about the data you want to share and the data you want to keep private.

Remove Hidden Data

There are various ways to remove hidden data from files, including the following.

Windows 10

Through Windows file explorer: Right click on the document, select "File Properties," navigate to the "Details" tab, and select the link "Remove properties and personal information."

Microsoft Office Applications

- Use the "Document Inspector" tool, by selecting "inspect document" from the file menu.

Converting a document to PDF (portable document file) may also remove large amounts of hidden data and metadata. When you are in your document, do a "save as" and then select a PDF file type, or save it by printing it to a PDF file.

Still, PDF files can also contain large amounts of hidden data and metadata. So, use a tool that can inspect and remove this hidden data from PDF files, such as Adobe's paid version of Acrobat.

d. Searching for Files

Your operating system comes with some powerful tools to find files and folders, and you will be well served to learn these tools. Searching for files is part science and part art. Your search needs to be broad enough to find the file you want, but narrow enough that your search doesn't find an overwhelming number of irrelevant files that you need to sift through. Your search can be tailored based upon:

- Filename (characters or words within the filename)
- File contents (characters or words within the contents of the file)
- File location (within a certain part of the computer or certain folder, to narrow down the search results)
- File modification date
- File type (word processing document, spreadsheet, photo, video, application, etc.)
- File size

There are other applications that you can download for free or purchase that can help you search for files, but start by learning the details of your operating system's capabilities, which will probably be sufficient for your needs.

2. Storage Location

Organizing your data means storing your primary copy of the data in an appropriate location, and a backup copy in a separate location. There is no "right" answer about the best place to store your data, and it's hard to state definitively that one place is more secure than another. Whether you store it in the cloud, or locally on a device in your home, or on a piece of paper, there are positives and negatives to each. Depending on the data, your skills, and your needs for convenience, availability, and confidentiality, one method may be preferable to another as a primary method of storage. Let's look at the pros and cons of the various options.

a. Cloud vs. Local Device

As access to cloud storage becomes more and more commonplace, we find ourselves having to decide whether to store data in the cloud or maintain it directly on our device. Your needs and your own assessment will help you determine what documents, if any, you should store in the cloud. Some factors to include in your assessment are your job and related client or fiduciary duties, the type of data you wish to store, and the risk of compromise (loss of confidentiality) along with the risk of loss or destruction (unavailability). Don't assume that local or cloud always wins any of these risk reduction contests (Figure 9.6).

FIGURE 9.6 Local storage versus cloud storage: pros and cons.

	Local Storage	Cloud Storage
Pros ✚	+ Harder for hackers to access. + You control your data.	+ Accessible from anywhere with an internet connection. + Can be secured with two-factor authentication. + Cloud provider devotes significant resources towards ensuring availability and protecting confidentiality.
Cons ▬	− Data can be lost or destroyed due to malware infection, crash, fire, theft. − If your computer is hacked or infected, the data can be stolen or encrypted. − Less availability.	− Data can be lost or destroyed by hacking. − Any hacker with an internet connection can try to access it. − You can't access it without an internet connection (unless using a hybrid type solution that synchronizes your changes).

Your cloud provider has probably invested a lot of resources and expertise into keeping that cloud data secure and available, and they probably do these things extremely well. If your house burns down or your laptop is stolen, your data remains safe and secure in the cloud. The great thing about the cloud is that you can access your data from anywhere in the world, as long as you have Internet access. But that very benefit is also the scary thing about the cloud—anyone in the world can try to access your data, and if successful, can distribute it, delete it, or alter it.

The great thing about having documents on your local device (like your desktop or laptop) is that you can work with them without an Internet connection. The data stays there, and is in some ways more difficult to steal (assuming no one hacks into your computer or burglarizes your house). But if your house burns down, the hard drive crashes, or your laptop is stolen, you risk losing the data.

Many services provide a hybrid solution, where documents you access on your device are automatically synchronized with the cloud. More and more, this process is seamless, and the folder looks just like a regular folder on your local device. You might not even realize where a document, photo, or other piece of data is stored. Sometimes the dual storage process is not quite so seamless.

Software companies have an incentive to get you to use their cloud, because having your data in their storage system tethers you to them. Not only does it encourage you to stay with them, and buy more services from them, but they may gain valuable information about you as a person and customer, which can be monetized. To get you to sign up, many cloud providers offer a small amount of cloud service for free. It is no surprise that most people quickly run out of the free space, and then need to pay for additional space now that their data is already with that provider.

b. Network Storage

If you have a home network, there are also storage options that allow data stored in one place to be accessible from multiple devices. One option is to use networking features of your operating system, such as Windows Home-Group, which allow you to share data among different devices, and share printers. Another option is network attached storage (NAS), a separate storage device that can be connected to your home network and accessed throughout your home, regardless of which device you are using.

Another form of network attached storage is a RAID-type device, which is basically a piece of hardware with multiple connected hard drives in it that provides additional redundancy over a single drive for storing and retrieving your data. Even with the redundancy that a RAID device provides, it still needs to be backed up, in case the entire device should fail.

c. Storing Information on Paper and in Your Brain

Some data, even if it is a backup copy of certain data, should be stored on paper, and some should be stored in your brain. Today, we take for granted that we will have immediate access to our smartphones, with their contact databases, instant contact methods, and Internet search capabilities. This reliance upon our devices makes us vulnerable to sophisticated, malicious hackers, and to Internet or power outages.

You needn't abandon the "storage capabilities" of paper and your brain just because we have devices around us 24/7. Paper is a tried-and-true storage method that has worked through the ages, whereas electronic storage is in its relative infancy. Today's industry of computer forensics and electronic discovery is a testament to the fact that retrieving data from electronic storage can be time consuming and expensive. The rapid obsolescence of certain computer hardware and software can be mitigated through proper data storage and migration, but paper has none of those issues. Paper storage takes a lot of physical space, and it can be cumbersome to find and share specific documents, but paper still should play a role in your data storage plan.

Consider the college essay you submitted in paper form, that your professor commented on, graded, and returned, and which has been stored in a box all these years. You pull your paper out and look at it, and it is as readable as it was long ago. If your writing assignment was stored electronically on a floppy disk, reading it will not be so simple. You will need a working floppy disk reader to determine whether the data is still readable, and getting your modern computer to communicate with that floppy disk reader and make sense of the data will be a significant challenge. Twenty years from now, we will have similar challenges with today's digital storage devices.

Your brain should also play a role in your data storage plan. Consider your mind as the ultimate backup storage if all other things fail, the power goes out, your devices are lost or stolen, or a fire burns up all your paper and electronic files. You should memorize some essential information, such as emergency phone numbers and procedures, and addresses or routes to important places. You should also memorize certain simple passwords, and memorize a "base" of other passwords, since passwords are a key that unlocks your other data.

As to passwords, remembering them is an important way your brain can help with your cybersecurity and efficiency. If you need to look up every password every time you need it, you will become frustrated. It's better to come up with a method that makes it easier to remember your passwords. One method is to create a base password that you memorize, plus a system for filling in the rest of the password. The more the base password is memorable for you, and the more meaningful the system to you, the better it works. We discussed passwords in Chapter 4, and the sidebar has some practical tips.

Password Tips

Here are some password tips that can help you.

Simple Base Password

This is a six or more character password that you memorize, which could be the base of the passwords for your devices, as well as for any specific files that you've encrypted with application-level encryption. You could then modify the password for specific uses by appending or prepending the password with a unique character or set of characters for each device.

Example of a base password: Cithao2017

That's from the unforgettable passphrase, Cybersecurity in the home and office, plus the year of publication, and it's reasonably complex.

If we're getting started with security, we can reuse that password across devices. If we want unique passwords, we could add characters at the front or end of the base for each device, such as:

iPhone: jqiCithao2017
iPad: jqbCithao2017
Laptop: mbqCithao2017

For this example, I used a very simple encryption method to prepend the base, a "Caesar" or "shift" cipher, where an "a" becomes a "b," an "i" becomes a "j," and so forth. You pick a system that works for you.

Important Internet Account Password Base and Supplement

This is another base password that you could reuse, with additions, across multiple Internet accounts such as e-mail, cloud, or financial. Note that you are not reusing the entire password, just the base portion of it.

For simplicity's sake, let's reuse our base from above: Cithao2017

Then, you can prepend or append the base password with a supplement, and the supplement could change for each account according to your own system.

LinkedIn: mjoCithao2017
Yahoo: zbiCithao2017
Facebook: gbdCithao2017

Unimportant Internet Account Password

This is a password you reuse across multiple Internet accounts that are not important to you, such as news site registrations and certain e-commerce sites.

One important caveat. By using a password system, and by picking characters or combinations that have meaning to you, you are introducing weakness into your passwords by making it easier for someone to fig- ure out your passwords. This problem is a good exam- ple of the tradeoff we face with cybersecurity: setting the dial in the spot that makes things available enough for you, but still secure enough to provide protections from most of the bad guys. The point here is to find a middle ground between passwords like "123456" that hackers will try first, and random generated passwords like "9T\P^9<pU$e5V'9M" which are near impossible to remember and that you would need a password man- ager to use.

d. This Is Your Brain—This Is Your Brain on Devices

There is a tendency for some people to become enmeshed with their electronic devices constantly, even when they are walking and driving. This behavior can be dangerous and we've all seen it. Someone so engrossed in their electronic world that they are unaware of their surroundings, unaware of traffic while they are crossing the street, unaware of the thief who might snatch their smartphone from their hand. Sometimes, New York City might seem like an episode of *The Walking Dead,* streets crowded with individuals glued to their smartphones, oblivious to what's happening around them. When we are not preoccupied with our smartphone, sometimes we absentmindedly put it down somewhere and forget about it, making it susceptible to loss or theft. The most important way your brain can protect you is by being aware and mindful of your surroundings and your devices, to avoid their theft or loss.

Perhaps we should think how our brains might be changing through constant reliance upon devices. Will we become less skilled in navigating and learning our surroundings if we rely upon our phone to direct us from Point A to Point B? Will our memories become weaker if we become dependent on devices to retain important information?

Some argue that constant connection to our devices could be harmful to our well-being and health and relationships, especially for children. Sometimes it is important to disconnect. Be aware of what is around you and the interesting things one might see, and communicate face-to-face with those in your proximity. Perhaps there is no need to instantly respond to the latest message or e-mail. Chapter 11 emphasizes the need to reduce screen time for children. In sum, your brain is the most important part of your cybersecurity plan, holding not only data and knowledge, but common sense to protect you from threats, so don't neglect it or discount it.

e. Data Migration

If you have data in a place that it shouldn't be, or you now realize it should be moved from one location to another, then you will need to migrate that data. If you are storing any data on obsolete or soon-to-be-obsolete devices, that data should be migrated. The best way to maintain your data is on a desktop computer in your home with an external hard drive. External hard drives are easy to use and inexpensive to purchase. It is best to continually and gradually migrate your data as you upgrade devices, because gradual migrations are easier to perform and keep up with. In contrast, if you forget about your data for twenty years and then try to get it off an old device, you're in for a time-consuming, complicated undertaking.

Signs that you need to migrate your data include:

- You have highly sensitive work or personal data stored without encryption on your laptop.
- You find that it is extremely inconvenient for you to access certain data, wherever it is currently stored.
- You are holding onto obsolete devices because you want to hold onto the data inside them.
- You have access to highly sensitive or personal data of others and you don't need that access.
- Others have access they don't need to highly sensitive data of yours.
- You have highly personal data stored in a work device or environment where you have no expectation of privacy.
- You believe your data is vulnerable—for any reason—where it is stored.

Migrating the data is a matter of copying it to where it needs to go, and deleting it from where it is no longer supposed to be. While you are migrating data, and copying it once, it never hurts to make a second backup copy also. When you make a copy of your data, you should ensure that the copy is made properly and completely by comparing the "properties" of the copied files to those of the original files. Doing so will ensure that the total number of files are the same between the original location and the new location.

When you have verified that the copy was performed accurately, you need to delete the data from the place where it is no longer supposed to be. When you delete data, you need to be aware of residual data, and take steps to ensure the original data is not recoverable. This may involve some of the steps of device decommissioning as covered in Chapter 8 and Appendices 6 and 7, such as using a software tool to "wipe" the free space of the drive.

If others use the data that you have moved, they need to be alerted to the change, and taught the new location for accessing and storing data. Making sure everyone is aware of the storage changes will avoid the frustration of not being able to find the data, and avoid people accidentally saving data to the old location.

I. CONCLUSION

Your data is important to you, perhaps so important you might consider running into a burning house to save it, and may be valuable to criminals who want to steal it. Criminals know how important your data is to you, so they may try to encrypt it, lock you out of it, and extort a ransom from you. Technology and people have always been fallible, even before there were cybercriminals trying to disrupt the world we live in and threatening to damage your data. The fundamental security principles of availability and confidentiality play against each other, and the steps you take to increase your data's availability to you may decrease the security, and vice versa. Find an appropriate compromise based upon where your security dial is set.

By now you should have a better sense of where your data is, and you can gradually improve the way it is stored, and how you access it, back it up, and secure it. The improvements you make with your personal data habits and the knowledge you gain will pay dividends for your firm and the companies you advise. Firms and companies need to have sound data management practices—it is important for their cybersecurity, e-discovery, and disaster planning.

CHAPTER 10

Secure Your Network and Internet Use

A. INTRODUCTION

In this chapter, we look at devices in your home that transmit data amongst themselves, and to other people and places on the Internet. In today's typical home, data is always flowing, and devices are frequently—perhaps constantly—connected to each other and the Internet. It's great to always be connected, but as we've discussed, it also means that your devices can be reached by cybercriminals through the Internet. It's like having your electronic "doors" visible to cybercriminals, who can try turning the handle to see if the door is open. If your door is open, they may walk right in, and if it's locked, they can try to pick the lock. Since many of your home's devices are connected, and constantly talking to each other, a small compromise in one device can lead to full control over that device and then to other computers on that network. This hacker technique is known as "pivoting." The attacker exploits a current position within one compromised device to attack other parts of your network. Thus, your network connectivity and Internet connection is a two-way street which can be traveled not just by you to get out to the Internet, but by cybercriminals anywhere in the world to get into your systems.

In Chapter 6 you learned the basics of how home networks work, then you learned how to secure your devices and then your data, and now it is time to secure your home network. This chapter starts with a quick mental assessment of your network, then helps you make improvements on a prioritized basis. You don't have to become an expert all at once, and you should be cautious about trying to boost your skill level too fast. Instead, changes should be made methodically. After you make one change, make sure your system is still working normally, your network still functioning, and your device still has Internet access.

B. MENTALLY ASSESS YOUR HOME NETWORK

Review the basics of your home network and see if you understand its components and settings. If you have never seen—or don't remember—your router's administration settings, that is something you will learn about shortly. If you don't know which device is your router, this is the time to learn. Don't let what might feel like a lack of knowledge, or perhaps a mental block, prevent you from learning how to secure your system. You know how to shut and lock your front door to protect yourself from burglars, so now it's time to learn how to do the same with the electronic devices that connect you to the Internet.

The items you should mentally assess are:

1. Basic network setup.
2. Internet access. How do you get Internet? Is it by cable, DSL, FiOS, cellular, satellite, dial-up?
3. Modem.
4. Router and Wi-Fi. Do you know how to configure your router? Is it properly and securely configured?
5. Software firewall (for your laptops and desktops).
6. Software that accesses the Internet. How many applications are on your devices that are constantly accessing the Internet?
7. Data transfer to the Internet. When is the data that you transmit and receive sent as "clear text," and when is it encrypted?
8. Devices on your network—what is connected?
9. Internet of Things (IoT) and smart home issues.

C. IDENTIFY PARTS OF YOUR HOME NETWORK

Quick tips:
- As you proceed through this chapter, fill in Appendix 13, Home Network and Internet Summary.
- This form is available for download at CybersecurityHomeAndOffice.com.

Now it's time to roll up our sleeves and dig in, and get a basic understanding of how your home network is set up (Figure 10.1). Appendix 13 has a form you can fill out which will be of assistance as you continue through this chapter. A typical home network has basic components as indicated in the diagram. Note that your cellular phone might have two paths to the Internet, one through your home's Wi-Fi network, and one through the cellular tower.

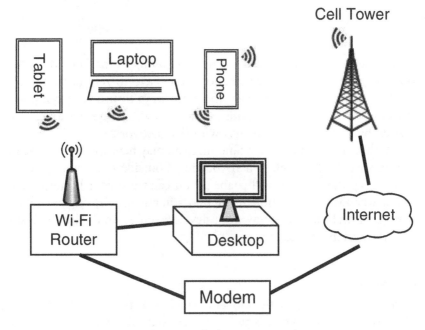

FIGURE 10.1 Sample home network.

As we go along, if you newly discover the purpose and name of a piece of equipment, consider labeling it for future reference. While you are making a label for the device itself, make a second label for the power cord, to place near the electrical outlet plug. This will help you if you are ever underneath the desk trying to identify a certain cord, and will keep you from accidentally unplugging the wrong equipment. If you have Luddites or parents whom you help with technical support, these labels are especially useful. There's nothing more convenient than being able to say: "Do you see the modem? It's the thing on the desk with a label reading 'MODEM.'"

D. INTERNET CONNECTION

Within your home, you probably have two ways of connecting to the Internet: through an Internet broadband provider such as your cable company or phone company, and through your cell phone company. Some people still use dial-up connections and some even use satellite connections. Those with inadequate or no cellular service reception within their home should be aware that most modern smartphones have a setting that allows the phone's voice and text data to be routed through the home Wi-Fi network. By using this setting, the phone can use your Wi-Fi signal and Internet rather than relying solely upon the nearest cell tower to send the data.

If you have an emergency, storm, or equipment malfunction, you might lose one of your Internet connections and have to rely upon the other. If you lose access to cable Internet, there are ways to use your cell phone as a "hotspot," so that your cell phone's data provides Internet access to other devices, by essentially creating its own Wi-Fi network.

Within your home, understand that you may have more than one method of accessing the Internet. When you travel outside the home, your method of accessing the Internet will change. You can't use your home's broadband service when you travel, though you may still rely heavily on your cellular service. For now, be aware of how your devices connect to the Internet, and we'll discuss travel in Chapter 12.

E. MODEM

As covered in Chapter 6, the modem, which is sometimes integrated with the Wi-Fi router, is the device between the coaxial cable and your Wi-Fi router. Depending on your equipment, the modem is either a standalone device, or is integrated into a single unit with a Wi-Fi router, called a modem-router device. If your cable or phone company provides you with a "triple play" type service that includes Internet, phone service, as well as television content, then you may have a modem-router combined with phone jacks for the phone service. Whether you have a standalone modem or a modem combined with other features such as a router, this section focuses only on the modem function, and the next section addresses the router and Wi-Fi functions.

Figure out where your modem is, and write down the make and model using the form in Appendix 13. If this is your first time locating your modem, know that it is a device located between your Internet connection and your router, and if you are likely to forget what it is in a year, put a label on it. The modem itself usually won't have a username or password, or any method to access settings, because they don't have options the user can configure. It might have a power switch or a standby switch.

There's not much for the home user to do with the modem, except recognize its role when troubleshooting, and power it off occasionally. If you cannot access the Internet, sometimes that could be a modem issue, and sometimes that can be solved by resetting the modem. To do this, you turn off your modem, perhaps even unplug it for about ten seconds (to ensure all electricity within it dissipates and the flash memory is erased), and perhaps even unplug the cables that deliver the signal from the cable company, and then turn it back on. If this doesn't work, you could contact the cable company; they can check your service and even send a signal to test and reset the modem. Chapter 15 has some troubleshooting tips.

Unplugging the modem, especially when this is done for a longer period of time, can reset one's IP address. We covered Internet Protocol (IP) addresses in Chapter 6, and most home users have "dynamic" IP addresses, meaning they are assigned a changeable IP address when the modem is powered up and connected to the Internet service provider (ISP). Though technically "dynamic," it tends to remain constant until the modem is cut off from the ISP, such as when disconnected or turned off. When a modem is disconnected, and then reconnected, it might be assigned a different IP address.

If you leave home for vacation, and have no need to leave the modem on when you are gone, consider unplugging it. The one sure way to ensure hackers are not scanning your Internet presence, and are not trying to get in, is to turn your modem off, thereby affirmatively disconnecting devices in your home from the Internet. However, if your home has phone service through the Internet (VOIP), or "smart" home type features like home security or temperature or flood monitoring, understand that you may be disconnecting and disabling all of these features.

F. ROUTER AND WI-FI

Whether your router is integrated with your modem, or is a standalone device, this section covers configuring and securing the router and Wi-Fi functions of the device.

1. Learn About Basic Wi-Fi Routing

As you learned in Chapter 6, a router allows multiple devices on a network to communicate with one another, share files and printers, and also to share the same Internet connection. Without a router in your home, you would need a separate Internet connection for each device. A Wi-Fi router produces a wireless signal and allows multiple devices within your home to connect wirelessly to it, and thus utilize these connections and Internet access without using a cable.

You should identify your router, and write down the make and model using Appendix 13. Your router probably also has the default username and password written on the label, so write that down too. If the default username and password are generic, such as "admin," and they have not been changed, this creates a significant risk of compromise. You will need to change that later—but not quite yet.

The router is extremely important for your home network security because it is the center of your home network. It routes data and Internet traffic into and out of your home, keeping track of various devices and their communications with other devices within your network and on the Internet.

Typical home networks have one of the following configurations with respect to the router and Wi-Fi devices, starting with the most common:

a. Wi-Fi router connected to a separate cable modem
b. Integrated modem router: a Wi-Fi router and cable modem within a single unit
c. Two or more Wi-Fi routers connected to each other, one of which is connected to a cable modem
d. Router (without Wi-Fi) connected to Wi-Fi access points

No matter what your network configuration, the basic principles for securing your Wi-Fi network, home network, and router are the same.

a. Wi-Fi Router Connected to a Separate Cable Modem

This used to be the most common configuration, but is becoming less so because some Internet providers often supply the router and modem as an integrated cable unit. Where the Wi-Fi router is a separate device, it's conceptually simple to identify the router and envision accessing that device to adjust the settings.

b. Integrated Modem Router

Here, the Wi-Fi router is integrated in a unit that also contains the cable modem. The combined unit allows the user to adjust the settings on the Wi-Fi router portion of this device.

c. Two or More Wi-Fi Routers Connected to Each Other

Some networks have two or more router devices, one of which is connected to a cable modem. If so, both need to be secured and configured appropriately. Here's how a home network might end up having two Wi-Fi router devices. The home network is originally configured with a Wi-Fi router and separate modem, and then the cable company comes and upgrades the old modem with a new integrated modem and Wi-Fi router device, but leaves the old Wi-Fi router in place. Now, the network has two routers. Leaving the old Wi-Fi router in place saved having to reconfigure the Wi-Fi network, and perhaps reconfiguring your devices. If you have two Wi-Fi routers through this method, you need to ensure that the new Wi-Fi router is properly configured. Check that the new router is set to "bridge mode," a setting that instructs the new router not to issue local IP addresses to the next router or your devices. "Bridge mode" should also ensure the new router does not broadcast Wi-Fi signals, but you should verify this and all of the other settings in this new router.

Another way you might wind up with two Wi-Fi router devices is if you have a large home, and a single Wi-Fi router is insufficient to provide a wireless signal to the far reaches of the house. A second Wi-Fi router device can be added and configured to retransmit ("repeat") the signal to boost the range. There are other repeater type devices that can extend wireless signals within a house, by repeating the wireless signal, by using a wired connection, or even using existing electrical power cables to transmit the signal. You should check all the settings of any router or repeater device in your home to ensure they are secure.

d. Router (Without Wi-Fi) Connected to One or More Wi-Fi Access Points

This involves a standalone router which is connected by cable to one or more Wi-Fi access points. Although having a Wi-Fi and router combined into a single unit is convenient for many homes, it has limitations. By separating the functions of router and Wi-Fi access points into separate units, the router can be located conveniently (or locked securely in a closet) and connected by cable to one or more Wi-Fi access points. The Wi-Fi access points can be placed in optimal locations to provide the best signal coverage within your home or office, but minimal broadcast outside. This configuration is more common in offices than homes. In this case, there are separate settings for the router and for each Wi-Fi access point, each has their own IP address on your local network, each should have a unique administrative password, and all settings should be reviewed and secured.

2. Log In to Your Router Administration Portal

Quick tips:
- Log in to your router's administration portal several times per year.
- Review whether the firmware needs updating, devices that are connected, and various settings.

You should log in to your router administration portal several times a year to check settings, check if firmware updates are available and install them, and to gain familiarity with the interface and settings. As you proceed through this section, take notes, and fill in Appendix 13. In this section, you will merely log in to your router, not make any changes. Thus, nothing we do in this section will affect anyone using your home network.

If you have never reviewed your router settings, and you didn't set it up in the first place, this is your opportunity to learn about the settings. This task may seem intimidating for the first-timer, but it is essential that you get familiar with the settings and how to access them. First, if possible, try to check with the person who set up the router because he or she might remember, or have documented, how it was set up. Many times, home networks are set up in a hurry, perhaps by the cable technician, a friend, or a family member. When setting up networks, often the urge is to do it quickly and get it to "work," and security might not be a concern. Once the network is established and things are "working," many people never review the setup again to determine if it is secure. Remember that just because you "have Internet" doesn't mean the router really is working properly. Access is different from security. Returning to our analogy of the front door, we can enter or leave the house if the door doesn't lock, but we wouldn't consider the door to be working properly unless the lock works and door latches. Thus, if your router has a default generic username and password such as "admin/admin," then it's like having a front door to the Internet without a lock.

   If you are unable to find the username and password for your router, first try the default passwords, and if that doesn't work you may need to reset the router to the default settings. Doing so will restore the default username and password so that you can log in. Be aware that if you have to reset the modem, it *will* affect all users of the network, and you may have to reconfigure the network and devices on it. Basic steps to log in to your router are summarized in the text box, and can be found online at a reputable website such as the manufacturer's website.

Log In to Your Router's Administrator Portal

Here are some basic steps to access your router's administrator settings.

1. Ensure your device (laptop or desktop) is connected to your home network. A wired connection directly to the router is preferred, but you can also use a wireless connection.
2. Open your web browser (Chrome, Safari, Internet Explorer, Firefox, etc.).
3. In the address bar of your web browser, type the router's IP address, meaning the router's local IP address on your local network. Sometimes this is called the "default gateway." This will take you to the router's administration login page.
   - Two common router addresses are 192.168.1.1 and 192.168.0.1.
   - There are many other possibilities, such as 192.168.2.1 or 10.0.1.1.

- Each router make and model has its own default address. Any administrative user can change this default address when configuring the network.
- There are several ways to learn (for sure) your router's local IP address:

Windows

- Method 1: Navigate to Settings → Network and Internet → View Your Network Properties. Check "default gateway."
- Method 2: Navigate to Control Panel → Network and Sharing Center → Local Area Connection Status and click the details link to see the "default gateway."
- Method 3: Windows command prompt: Type the command "ipconfig." The IP address listed for "default gateway" is your router's IP address.

iPhone

- Settings → Wi-Fi, select your network, select the information icon, and it will tell you the router's IP address.

Mac

- Network Preferences → Advanced → TCP/IP tab. Look for "Router."

4. Enter your router administration username and password to log in (make sure you have navigated to the router's login webpage at the IP address above).
   - If you don't know your router's username and password, check the router for a label, check with the person who set up the network, or try looking up the default usernames and passwords for that router.

- If you cannot find the username and passwords, you will need to reset the router to the default settings in order to log in. This action will reset all of your router settings, making your home network unavailable for your devices until you re-establish your network and re-link your devices to the network. This process may require considerable work to get things running again.
5. Write down your router IP address, username, and password in Appendix 13.
6. If you need additional details or assistance, conduct an Internet search for specific instructions or for screenshots pertaining to your router.

Once logged in, review your various router settings and the devices that are connecting to your home network. Each router administration interface is different, and there may be many tabs and links to navigate through. Don't make any changes yet, just familiarize yourself. In the following sections, we'll start making changes.

3. Secure Your Router Administration Username and Password

Quick tips:
- Your router administration password should be strong. Do not use a default generic username/password like "admin/admin."
- If you change the username and password, write it down in Appendix 13 and your personal notes.
- It can be helpful to write your username and password on a label on the router itself (assuming you trust those in your home).

This section secures access to the administration features of your router, and does not affect how you access your Wi-Fi network. Thus, changing the router administration username and password will not cause any network users to lose access to the network or the Internet.

It's extremely risky to leave the username and password as generic defaults from the factory because hackers (and their automated tools) will try these defaults and will be able to log in and take control of your router and network. If you are using a generic default username and password (such as "admin/password" for username and password) then you should change it immediately. When the cable company technician set up our new cable modem router phone device, he left the generic default username and password in place, meaning an attacker could have easily entered the administration portal of the router. Some routers ship with usernames and passwords that are unique to that device, and this information is printed on a label affixed to the router. These usernames and passwords are probably safer to continue to use, but a best practice is to change them.

You should ensure your password is reasonably long and complex, and write it down somewhere, including in Appendix 13. If you are bad at keeping track of your passwords, it's OK to label the router itself with your username, password, and the router IP address. The main risk is the cybercriminal, hacking through your network to gain control over your router, and that cybercriminal won't be able to see the label taped onto your router box.

4. Update Router Firmware

Quick tip:

- Ensure your router is updated (patched).

Routers have software called firmware that controls how they operate, and acts like their operating system. Firmware vulnerabilities are routinely being discovered, and these vulnerabilities could allow criminals to compromise your router and network from afar. Periodically, you need to check and update your router firmware.

To update your router firmware, you need to be logged in to the router's administration portal, as discussed in section F.2. Then, navigate to the firmware upgrade area, find the option to check for upgrades, and download and install the firmware upgrade. Each router manufacturer has a different interface for this process and you should get to know yours. While upgrading the firmware, you will have a momentary loss of network and Internet connectivity, and after the upgrade, check your settings. The upgrade may come with new or changed features, and it may have slightly altered some of your settings.

Write down the date you updated or checked the firmware in Appendix 13. Try to check for firmware updates several times a year, monthly if possible. Recognizing that many people fail to upgrade their routers, some manufacturers now create routers that automatically keep themselves updated—Google's Wifi and OnHub devices are examples of such devices.

5. Secure the Wi-Fi Network Password and Ensure the Network Is Encrypted

Quick tip:

- Use a strong password to access your Wi-Fi network.

Caution:

- If you change your Wi-Fi password or network name, every device that has "remembered" your Wi-Fi network will need to update its settings to reflect the new password.

This section addresses the password that users are required to enter in order to access your Wi-Fi network, which in turn allows them to access the Internet and other network services. This is different from accessing the router administration interface, which we covered in section F.2. Do not use the same password for your Wi-Fi network that you used to access the router's administration interface.

You should require a strong (complex) password in order for devices to gain access to your Wi-Fi network. Though many devices connecting to your Wi-Fi network simply want access to the Internet, they also may have considerable access across the network that could be exploited. A rogue or hacked device attached to your network may be able to eavesdrop on all network traffic by all devices, and could gain access to other devices on the network. Thus, a strong password is required. Using a strong password isn't much more inconvenient than a weak password, since most devices "remember" Wi-Fi networks they have connected to. You will only have to enter this Wi-Fi password one time per device to connect, and then once each time you change the Wi-Fi password.

Consider changing your Wi-Fi password periodically, perhaps annually. Changing the Wi-Fi password means you will need to update this password setting for every device that accesses your network, including your laptops, tablets, smartphones, smart TVs, and any other IoT devices. This periodic change is worth the effort, because it will help you to identify all of your devices that access your network, including some you may have forgotten about but that are nevertheless communicating with other devices inside and outside your network. Changing the password will also remove access for people who know your password, but shouldn't have continuing access.

You should ensure your Wi-Fi network is properly encrypted. With a modern router, it is probably encrypted by default, but navigate through the interface to be sure, checking settings such as "Authentication Method" and "Encryption." Not all encryption is equal, so you want to be using encryption such as WPA2 (Wi-Fi Protected Access version 2) or whatever the most current encryption standard is. You do not want to be using the obsolete and weak form of wireless encryption called WEP, a misnomer that stands for Wired Equivalent Privacy. Networks using WEP encryption are so insecure that even a novice could hack them.

If your router has the capability, consider having separate Wi-Fi networks, one for guests to access the Internet, and one for members of your home who need greater access to your network, to share files, or use the printer. The guest network could allow access only to the Internet, and—like your regular network—should be password-protected and encrypted. Since the guest network only allows Internet access, you could post the password on a bulletin board or refrigerator so that guests have easy access to it. The home network could grant access to the rest of your network, including printer, files, music, and more, and you should guard that password more closely.

6. Evaluate Your Wi-Fi Network Name

Quick tip:

- Consider changing your network name to something innocuous which does not identify you.

Caution:

- If you change your Wi-Fi network name, every device that currently logs in to your Wi-Fi network will need to update its settings.

Your Wi-Fi network name, also called the subscriber set identification (SSID), might say a lot about you and even your router. If you live in a densely populated area such as an apartment building, your Wi-Fi network name might allow others in the building to easily identify which Wi-Fi network is yours, or to identify your router type in order to tailor an attack specific to that router's vulnerabilities. For example, when I use my device to review available Wi-Fi networks from my home, I can see about a dozen Wi-Fi networks belonging to my neighbors. Some indicate first names, others indicate a router model. This information about the router gives helpful intelligence to a potential hacker, including what network to hack, and how to hack it. When the cable technician set up our new cable modem router, he enabled a Wi-Fi network that we didn't need since we already had a Wi-Fi router in place. He didn't tell us he did that, and he also named the network after the new device's model number, and he left the default username and password in place. This makes it too easy for a hacker. The remedy to such a poor installation and configuration is for the user to review all settings.

The SSID has other privacy considerations. Your smartphones and laptops may continue broadcasting the network names of "known" networks when you leave your home, because the devices are trying to find these known networks and connect to them. It's like searching for someone in the woods, calling out the person's name again and again. That might not seem awkward, but consider whether you would call out someone's name at a crowded cocktail party. When our devices broadcast the names of known networks, this has privacy implications because it tells others about us, and it has security implications because a hacker could impersonate our network and connect to our device. Although there are ways to tell your device to forget certain networks, you don't want your device to forget your home network. You can stop your smartphone from calling out for remembered networks by turning your device's Wi-Fi adapter off every time you leave the house. This is a good practice, but most of us will forget to do that occasionally. Thus, it is worth considering whether your Wi-Fi network name is appropriate and consistent with what you want neighbors and those around you—even when you leave the house—to learn about you. Many people prefer to choose an innocuous name or number, but it's up to you what you want to reveal to others.

Wi-Fi Network Names

We vacationed to the shore two years in a row, and each time, it was amusing to see a neighbor's Wi-Fi network named "FBI Cutter Offshore." Clearly this resident was making a joke, and enjoyed the thought of dozens of vacationers seeing this SSID while searching for a Wi-Fi network, and perhaps imagining law enforcement sitting in a boat conducting surveillance.

Someday, if not already, there will be a legal dispute about the propriety of the SSID name that someone has broadcast. It could be a name like "John Doe is a jerk," "People who like ice cream are idiots," "Dewey, Cheatem, & Howe should all be disbarred," or something inflammatory that I will leave to your imagination. Anyone in the local area searching for a Wi-Fi network would see this network name, and feel enraged, insulted, harassed, or defamed. Consider the SSID name an electronic lawn sign, with similar free speech issues, in addition to the privacy considerations.

Things to avoid in a Wi-Fi network name:

- Your name or address
- Your router's make or model name
- Anything about you that you don't want broadcast to your neighbors, or to people around you when you travel

7. Disable Wi-Fi Protected Setup

WPS, or Wi-Fi Protected Setup, is an unnecessary feature that compromises your security—so you should disable it within your router administration interface. WPS is designed to make connecting to your Wi-Fi network easy by pushing a button on the router, which saves you from remembering your network name and typing in the network password in order to connect. The WPS feature assumes that anyone with physical access to the router is trusted, and that you are too hurried, too disorganized, or just too lazy to remember the Wi-Fi password. This feature puts availability so far before security and your learning that it exposes you to vulnerabilities that make it easier to hack your router and network. If you are able to read this book, if you know your Wi-Fi network name and password, then you have no need for WPS. Any feature has vulnerabilities, but here is an unnecessary feature which outweighs any benefit. The WPS vulnerability is significant, because it relies on the use of a code number which an attacker could guess. Thus, you should disable the WPS feature within the router administration settings.

8. Disable Remote Access Features You Don't Need

Your router may have a feature that allows you to remotely access the router, as well as your files on your computers or storage devices, even while you are traveling. Sometimes this is called a "private cloud" capability. If you will not be using this remote access feature, then disable it so that a hacker cannot attempt to use it. If such a feature is enabled, then a hacker could try to use it, to try to enter this virtual door into your network and files. Review your router administration interface to find this setting, if it exists.

9. Enable Your Router's Firewall (If Available)

Your router may have a firewall function that helps protect your network from attacks from the Internet. Review your administration interface to look for this feature and review any options. Like any security feature, it may not be perfect, but you should take advantage of the protective qualities it can provide.

10. Disable Universal Plug and Play If You Don't Need It

Universal Plug and Play (UPnP) is a router feature that automatically allows devices on a network to get to know each other and communicate with each other. It automates the process of opening firewall ports and forwarding network traffic from one port to where it needs to go. Some programs, like video games, phone-and-video applications (e.g. Skype), and webcams might run better if UPnP is enabled, or even require it to be enabled. But malware and hackers can also take advantage of UPnP. Thus, if you don't need this feature, disable it though the router administration interface.

11. Run Your Router's Security Self-Assessment Function (If Available)

Navigate through your router settings and look for a security assessment feature, and if it has one, run it. Evaluate each of the suggested changes and consider implementing them to improve your security. You don't have to be an expert on each setting, but perhaps every month or quarter that you log in to check it, take the time to learn about some of the settings. Your router manufacturer's help or support pages may help explain what they mean.

12. Enable a Guest Network on Your Router (If Available)

As we touched upon earlier, some routers have the capability to have two separate wireless networks, one for the home resident, and a guest network for—you guessed it—guests. When we have visitors in our home, hospitality often means providing Wi-Fi access. Who can live without constant Internet access?

Here we see an application of the principle of "least privilege"—we want to give guests the least amount of privileges that they need. We want to give them access to the Internet, but we don't need to give them access to other parts of our network or to other devices. "Least privilege" isn't about whether we trust the person or not, it's about minimizing potential harm. Even if you trust the visitor, they shouldn't have access to data or parts of the network that they don't need to access, because if—unknown to your guest—their device is infected by malware, their device could copy your data out, or try to spread the malware in your network.

In sum, a router's guest network is a way to give people or devices access to the Internet, and not to other devices on the network. Of course, your guest network should also be encrypted, and require a password of decent strength which is different from your home network password.

13. Check Your Router's Physical Security

Your router's physical security is important too. Normally, physical security would be the first issue to consider, but we are starting in your home, and this book assumes your home is reasonably secure. Anyone with physical access to your router could also simply plug in to one of the ports, and then enter your network. Hopefully you have disabled WPS (Wi-Fi Protected Setup) based on its vulnerability to hacking. If WPS is enabled, then anyone with physical access to your router can connect to your Wi-Fi network—even if they don't know the password. WPS allows network connection with a push of a button on the router.

Assuming that your home and router location is secure, it's acceptable to tape onto your router its administration username and password. This will make it easier for you to periodically log in and check your settings.

14. Learn About Additional Router and Wi-Fi Security Features

There are some additional security steps you may hear mentioned elsewhere but which are not recommended in the home. They don't provide a great security benefit in the home and they will interfere with your access to your systems. You need not implement them now, but you should read about them and what they do. When you get to Chapter 13, you will see that some of these measures might be appropriate in your office.

a. Don't Hide the Broadcast of Your Network Name

Some routers offer the option of hiding the network name (SSID). Hiding the broadcast of the network name might stop the casual neighbor or snoop from seeing the network displayed while checking for available Wi-Fi networks. Unhidden, the router is basically shouting out for all to see about its presence and what the network name is. Hiding the network name conceals the Wi-Fi network from casual attackers, such as a neighbor who sees the network, then tries to log in by guessing the Wi-Fi network password (perhaps without realizing the seriousness of this act). However, hiding the SSID does not make the network invisible—a sophisticated attacker can use readily available software tools to see hidden SSIDs. Hiding the SSID makes it harder for you and your guests to connect to your Wi-Fi network, because you need to type in the SSID name—without errors—rather than simply clicking on an SSID that is displayed as being available. In other words, hiding the SSID creates extra work for you without substantially improving your security. That's why I don't recommend it when it comes to your home network.

b. Don't Implement MAC Address Filtering

MAC filtering is a feature most routers can employ, which allows one to specify the MAC addresses that are allowed to connect to a network. It is a type of network access control (NAC). Remember from Chapter 4 that a MAC (media access control) address is the unique address for the network interface controller (NIC) within each of your devices. In theory, every computer has its own, unique MAC address, and if you were to enable MAC address filtering, you could ensure that only specified computers are allowed to connect to your network. It is a method to lock down your network, since even if an attacker knew your Wi-Fi password, or even if the attacker plugged in to your router with an Ethernet cable, he or she wouldn't be able to connect to the network since his or her computer's unique MAC address would not be authorized to be on your network.

That's the theory, but in practice, criminals can defeat MAC address filtering simply by pretending to be an authorized MAC address. They can eavesdrop on the addressing portion of the wireless traffic—which is not encrypted—and learn which MAC addresses are authorized to be on the network. Then they can pretend to be the authorized MAC address and attempt to connect to the router. All of this trickery can be done easily by a sophisticated hacker.

Also, enabling MAC address filtering can lock you or a guest out of your own Wi-Fi network. Suppose you enable MAC address filtering today, and then a year from now you get a new smartphone or laptop. You try to connect the new device to the network, you enter the Wi-Fi password, time and again, and can't figure out why you are not granted access to the network. Finally, you realize that your router is denying access to the unrecognized MAC address, so you access the router administration interface, and change the setting to allow the new device to access your network.

For these reasons, you probably shouldn't enable MAC address filtering as a security feature in your home, as it will take a lot of your time for a limited security benefit. Instead of enabling MAC filtering in the home, you can periodically check your router interface to see if any unrecognized devices have logged in to your network. When we start looking at your office in Chapter 13, it might be worthwhile to implement either MAC filtering or another type of network access control.

c. Don't Limit the Power of Your Wi-Fi Transmission Broadcast

One important security principle to keep in mind is not to blast your Wi-Fi signal further than is necessary. You want to maximize the strength of the Wi-Fi signal in places where you need it, and minimize the signal strength where you don't need it. You need a strong signal inside your house, but you probably don't need it outside your house. Most Wi-Fi routers allow you to decrease the strength of their broadcast signal. If your home is relatively small, and your Wi-Fi router is powerful, you don't need to blast your Wi-Fi transmission signal to the greater metro area. By limiting the range of your Wi-Fi, you reduce its visibility, and make it harder for a hacker, who must get closer and be more exposed to detection. If you are on the tenth floor of an apartment building, your Wi-Fi signal needn't be so strong that a hacker parked on the street can receive it and try to log in to your network.

However, like Captain Kirk and Scotty, we usually need more power, not less, and especially in our home, where we may expect a single Wi-Fi router to give us coverage throughout. Few people complain that their Wi-Fi signal is too strong, so in the home it is probably best to keep your Wi-Fi signal at maximum power. That said, you can adjust the router and antenna location to optimize where it goes. Solid walls and distance weaken the Wi-Fi signal, whereas windows are relatively porous. All things being equal, it's better to have your Wi-Fi router near the middle of your home, rather than by a window. If the router needs to be near an edge of the home, it's better to have it against a solid wall, rather than a window, so that the wall blocks the signal from escaping the home.

For your firm and clients, this is a matter of greater concern because that Wi-Fi network might provide access to the firms' network and client files. If you are blasting the Wi-Fi signal to the parking lot, a hacker sitting in a parked car could patiently hack your network and steal sensitive client information. We'll cover that problem in Chapter 13, along with an example of a hacker who specialized in this type of wireless network hacking.

15. Wi-Fi Router Conclusion

Your router has a number of features that might either assist in your security or aid in your convenience. Disable any convenience features that you are not using; we specifically covered a few of these features, such as a remote access or "private cloud" capability. If you aren't using them, these features are simply vulnerabilities that can be exploited by criminals.

Your router may have additional security features, including a feature that tries to prevent you from connecting to malicious websites. Unfortunately, nothing is perfect. The many security products we use sometimes cause "false positives" that disallow access we want, and any feature can have undiscovered vulnerabilities. Technology and cybersecurity are not perfect, and few things work seamlessly, and that can be very frustrating. On the bright side, it is nice to know that sometimes we are not to blame when things don't work.

False Positives

An example of a false positive occurred for me when suddenly one day, I could not access my own website because my router was blocking it as a "malicious site." Of course, there was nothing malicious about my site, it was a very simple website I had created for my business a year earlier. I scanned the website to be sure it was safe, had others scan it, and confirmed nothing malicious or dangerous had infected it. The problem was my router, and its security feature called "malicious site blocking" that was designed to protect the user from going to websites containing malicious code.

Supposedly, their process detected whether a website was safe or malicious, and it was particularly suspicious of newly created websites. However, my website wasn't new, it wasn't malicious, and they had never even scanned it. Thus, this feature should never have blocked access to my website. I followed the process to "appeal" this blocking, provided some information, and access was granted. Cybersecurity products are supposed to lock the door against the criminals, but they are fallible and sometimes they lock the door when you want it to open. Frustrating, but a fact of life.

G. SOFTWARE FIREWALLS (ENCORE FOR YOUR LAPTOPS AND DESKTOPS)

We covered the importance of having a software firewall on your laptop or desktop in Chapter 8, but it's worth repeating here. To protect yourself from network and Internet threats, your laptops and desktops should be running some sort of a firewall.

For Windows, the operating system comes with Windows Firewall, which is adequate and will give you decent protection with a minimal amount of difficulty. It includes a lot of detailed settings you can become familiar with, if you are so inclined. For Mac OS X, the operating system comes with a firewall, but you have to enable it yourself if you want it on. Navigate to "Security and Privacy," then to the "Firewall" tab, and turn it on.

There are also some free third-party software firewalls with which you can experiment, and which can help you get a feel for the many applications on your computer that are sending and receiving data to the outside world. There will be a learning curve with these third-party firewalls, and sometimes they will block Internet activity that you don't want blocked.

H. REVIEW DEVICE SOFTWARE THAT ACCESSES THE INTERNET (ENCORE FOR WHAT IS PHONING HOME)

Your computing device has many applications that access the Internet, often without you being aware of it. Chapter 8 covered this, but as a reminder it's unrealistic to try and learn about every piece of software running on your computer. However, it is worthwhile to periodically review the software on your smartphones, tablets, laptops, and desktops and see what is on it, and what accesses the Internet. If there is software you definitely don't need, and you see it has access to the Internet, then you should consider limiting this access, or even uninstalling the software.

Remember that all software has the potential to be exploited by a hacker, and hackers are looking for methods to communicate with and to compromise your device. Software manufacturers want to improve the functionality and security of their products, so there are legitimate reasons for much of this constant communication. They also want to learn more about you and your habits, so sometimes this continuing communication is about tracking you and your activities.

I. HOW YOUR DATA IS TRANSMITTED

You should be aware of whether the data you send and receive on your home network and through the Internet is transmitted in clear text (plain readable form) or if it's encrypted. We covered encryption in transit in Chapter 6, but think of the data you send through your network and the Internet as being written on a postcard, available for anyone to read if they wanted. If you've written that postcard in plain English, anyone can understand your message. But if you've written that postcard in a very complicated code that no one can figure out, then you have protected the confidentiality of the message. That's what encryption in transit does.

Be cognizant of whether a website that you visit encrypts their communications with you. Websites that use plain HTTP (Hypertext Transfer Protocol) are not encrypting the data going back and forth, but websites that use HTTPS (where the "S" stands for Secure) are encrypting the data. HTTPS used to be less common, used only when you were transacting with a bank website to view your financial information or to make a payment with a credit card. Today, more and more website administrators recognize that the user's privacy is at risk if website traffic is unencrypted. With unencrypted website traffic, a malicious actor could snoop upon all of the user's Internet activity, including website searches, articles viewed, and more. Also, malicious actors could compromise the website, and use the website to attack visitors.

Encrypting the site through HTTPS provides a layer of protection against these possibilities.

Be aware of each site you visit, and how your web browser displays the web page address in the address bar. A lock (or green lock) with "HTTPS" in front of the address lets you know the site is more secure than if it does not have the lock, or if the address starts only with HTTP.

Consider whether your e-mail provider encrypts communications between you and the provider. All major e-mail providers now do this. If you are logging in to your e-mail via a web browser (like Chrome, Edge, or Safari), be aware of what is displayed in the address bar (e.g. HTTPS vs. HTTP). You should send confidential e-mails via HTTPS, not HTTP. If you are connecting to e-mail via another method, it's good to know if it is transmitted with encryption or not. Remember, this encryption is just for the communication between your device and your e-mail provider, and does not secure it at other points in the journey, or where it is stored. It is not "end to end" encryption. When you travel and use unfamiliar local networks, you should also consider whether your data is encrypted in transit, as we will cover in Chapter 12.

J. EQUIPMENT ON THE NETWORK

Get to know the various pieces of equipment connected to your home network, including computing devices like desktops, laptops, and tablets, and other devices like smart TVs, video games, home security cameras, sensors, and more. We'll cover IoT type devices in greater detail in the next section.

The best way to see what equipment is currently on your network is to enter your router's administration interface and view the current and saved list of clients or connected devices. Section F.2 covered how to view your router's administration interface, but to summarize: open your web browser, and in the address bar, enter your router's IP address on the local network to access the router login screen, then enter your router's username and password.

From your device (without logging in to the router), you might also be able to see certain other equipment connected to your network. There may be graphical interfaces through which you can view other computers on your network, as well as printers. In Windows and OS X, this is done by viewing "Network," "Printers & Scanners," "Connected Devices" and other settings. There are also some commands, discussed in sections M.5 and M.6, that you can run on your computer to determine what devices are currently connected to your network.

1. Printers, Scanners, Fax Machines, All-in-Ones, and More

Printers, scanners, and fax machines need a brief review. These devices can be connected to a network, but it's more secure to plug them directly into a particular computer, such as with a USB connection. If the device has a password, change the default password to something unique and complex. Update the firmware or device drivers periodically, and before decommissioning the device ensure any stored data is erased.

2. Network Attached Storage

Network attached storage (NAS) makes storage space available to users on the network. You should review all of the settings, and disable any features that you do not need. Administrator passwords should be complex and unique, not the default password. Individual user passwords should also be strong. Guest access should be disabled, and where available two-factor authentication should be enabled, unneeded ports closed, and HTTPS enabled.

K. THE "INTERNET OF THINGS" AND SMART HOMES

The term "Internet of Things" (IoT) was coined some time ago by someone in charge of managing his company's supply chain with radio frequency identification (RFID) tracking of parts. Today, IoT is a common buzzword that refers to the networking of all sorts of physical objects. In theory, if all things are networked and tracked, if sensors are collecting data and reporting it, and if that data is analyzed properly, systems can run at maximum efficiency. In terms of supply parts or merchandise, a complete network and tracking system will ensure that consumers, stores, and warehouses have the inventory that they need, exactly when they need it, without storing excess inventory, and without waiting for merchandise to be delivered. In the example of the power grid, all customers get the power they want when they need it, and the power company generates only the power that is needed, without waste. The IoT concept has amazing potential.

In the home, this type of ultra-networking can mean connecting and tracking of things like your refrigerator, laundry machine, coffee maker, and all the products that go in them. It could mean maximizing your energy efficiency and comfort through optimized temperature control, and adjusting, even remotely, your house's lights, shades, temperature, and music from a single control. It could mean never having to worry about losing your keys and calling a locksmith, and it could mean enhanced security. Some are plagued by a dark unsettling fear that they might run out of milk, eggs, coffee, or laundry detergent, and IoT could enable these supplies to be monitored and automatically ordered.

However, it also means many security vulnerabilities and risks. First, remember that every device, every operating system, and every application is imperfect, and all have vulnerabilities in the coding and operation that criminals can exploit. This has always been a significant problem, even before IoT, but IoT exponentially increases the number of devices, while decreasing the planning and maintenance of their security.

We know that most people already fail to implement patches that are developed for the vulnerabilities in their traditional devices, and that the average hack involves a vulnerability that was discovered a year prior, yet the victim failed to implement an available patch for it. Now, IoT increases the problem exponentially. There are more IoT devices than traditional computers, and the software within them is less sophisticated and less secure. Patches are released less often—if at all—and implementing the patches is difficult or forgotten about. Some manufacturers for newer IoT devices do not have established mechanisms for discovering vulnerabilities and pushing out patches to the consumer. Some manufacturers are pushing out a product quickly at a low price and don't consider security. Some go out of business, or are sold, and then there is no support for their IoT devices, which remain in use within homes.

Without a doubt, IoT creates a large attack surface, meaning there are more areas that the malefactor can try to attack. If the refrigerator, smart TV, security camera, light bulb, or child's toy has vulnerabilities and is not patched, the attacker could hack into the device, monitor it, or use it to "pivot" onto another device in the network. The attacker could make that device a part of his botnet and use it to launch a cybercrime attack on someone else. This has led to the rise of distributed denial of service (DDoS) attacks that are even more crippling than before due to the number of bots an attacker can muster.

The rise of IoT also means increased privacy risks. Utility companies may want to install sensors to monitor, in real time, your use of electricity, water, gas, or other resources. Private companies may want you to use their IoT devices not only because it becomes easier for customers to buy things from them, but also because they find it easier to learn more about consumer habits, which is useful for marketing. These devices are able to track, store, and transmit an enormous amount of data, and this data could reveal things about you that you don't want others to know. Perhaps the companies receiving this data have good privacy policies, and perhaps they follow them, but maybe not. Compounding the problem, every company that stores data about customers is susceptible to being hacked.

It seems amazing that a device can listen and respond to your wishes, get to know your voice and speaking manner, and learn about you. Personal assistants like Apple's Siri, Microsoft's Cortana, Amazon Echo's Alexa, Goggle's On Hub, and more offer these services. Who needs to fiddle with buttons and menus if a device can just hear you and respond? However, devices that listen to you, and respond to you, are always listening.

In a way, millions of people are voluntarily installing listening devices in their homes. Of course, the device is not supposed to eavesdrop, record, or transmit your conversations, but it does need to listen to function. The company running the device is eager to improve response to voice commands, so it may analyze your voice for this purpose. For example, companies like Apple, Google, Microsoft, and Amazon may want to analyze whether consumers are repeating certain words because the device isn't responding, or what questions consumers are asking the device. This is done in order to improve features, for general marketing purposes, or to target marketing. If the device can listen, then, in theory, a hacker could hack the device and listen as well.

There are many devices we can purchase and connect to our home network that listen, see, and collect data, and we need to be cautious, or at least conscious, when purchasing and installing this equipment.

Security Risks of IoT Devices in the Home

IoT devices present many cybersecurity issues, because many of these new and networked devices have very poor security features. People connect "smart" systems, appliances, and gadgets to their home network, and these devices begin to automatically communicate with other devices and companies inside and outside the home. These IoT devices could be wireless cameras, thermostats, security apps, toasters, refrigerators, and kids' toys. Your car—with features like GPS navigation, satellite radio, and emergency notification systems—has also become linked to the Internet and cloud.

Some IoT devices use antiquated and insecure configurations that most IT professionals stopped using decades ago. They may be poorly designed, and cheaply and hastily assembled and sold, all with no thought to security, and no thought to patching or updating them after they are sold. Such devices are vulnerable to hacking through several techniques.

Bringing an insecure IoT device into your home exposes you to threats, since it has vulnerabilities that may never be patched. This exposure could mean cybercriminals taking over your IoT devices and eavesdropping on or surveilling your family, whether through video cameras, toys, or the immense amount of data that the devices are transmitting. A cybercriminal could even interact with your child, yell "Hey baby, wake up" through the baby monitor, or "Johnny, open the front door" or "Johnny, turn on the stove" through the interactive child's toy. They could enlist the hacked devices into their botnet, and use them to attack other computers through distributed denial of service (DDoS) attacks.

The lesson is that all of these IoT devices can affect your security and privacy. As a consumer, decide which of these types of devices you really need. If you decide to buy one, try to select a device from a company that has demonstrated a commitment to security and privacy, then use caution and connect it securely to your network. Throughout the lifetime of the device, be aware and proactive to see if it can be updated to protect against newly discovered vulnerabilities.

Beyond devices, we are also in the age of the "smart home." This term describes a home where various systems can be controlled remotely, such as by an app on your smartphone, meaning these systems are connected to your home's network and electronically controlled. "Smart home" systems could control your lighting, entertainment systems, heating and cooling, security—including door locks and cameras—and more.

With smart homes and IoT devices, it is especially important that you develop a solid foundation of cybersecurity in the home. Smart homes mean you should turn your "security dial" much higher than it otherwise might be. Imagine that your entire home was "smart" and networked, and you could monitor and control almost anything in your home from your smartphone, tablet, and laptop computer. Imagine any of these scenarios:

- Your smartphone or laptop is lost or stolen, and in the hands of a malicious individual.
- Your laptop has serious malware in it, and a malicious cybercriminal gains control of the laptop, and decides to explore what he can do with it.
- Someone near your home gains access to your Wi-Fi network.

In these scenarios, if you have not properly secured your devices (Chapter 8), your data (Chapter 9), and your networks (this chapter), the criminal could have the literal keys to your kingdom. He or she could lock and unlock your doors, turn the lights on and off, change the music volume and station, turn your heat off in the winter or turn it up to a dangerous temperature, or eavesdrop on events captured by your security cameras.

Buying or Selling a "Smart Home"

If you are the buyer or seller of a smart home, you should consider the data and systems involved. Even though you'll have a lot to think about during the sale as a buyer or seller, it's worth thinking about the data involved and security of the systems. If you are the buyer of a smart home, it might be unrealistic to learn about all aspects of the smart home at once. Your first priority would be to ensure you have access to all the systems, and that means having passwords to them. Think of that step as getting custody of the physical keys at the time of closing.

When you move in, you may be confronted with a mass of new technology that you don't yet understand. Your first instinct may be "It works, and if it ain't broke, don't fix it." But as we mentioned previously, it might not really "work" if the prior homeowner configured it insecurely, if the electronic doors are wide open and don't lock, or if the prior owner still has access. Even if the prior owner is trustworthy, if he or she still has access and is hacked, then the hacker could use that access in order to monitor or control your house. Similarly, the prior contractor who installed and maintained the system may still have access, as would some of their current and perhaps former employees. Thus, you should take the time to investigate the system, and if it's not secure, you should fix it. Change the passwords, review the settings, and take notes as you do so.

If you are selling the home, you'll be equally busy, but you still need to protect your privacy and also ensure the systems are working for the new owner. Consider having a knowledgeable person assist you with the review. You may need to undertake a decommissioning process, as discussed in Chapter 8. Your smart home may have dozens of devices that have stored data about you and have your passwords stored in them. You will want to clear this data and reset the passwords before the sale. You'll want to make a note of the new passwords for the new owner, as well as how the owner can change those passwords.

Battlestar Galactica and the Internet of Things

Battlestar Galactica is a science fiction television series that first appeared in 1978, was reimagined in 2003, and contains an imaginative and interesting plotline, set in a time of advanced technology. Humans created robots, the robots evolved, and then there was a war for survival between humans and robots. Eventually, there is a truce, and the robots lull the humans into a sense of security and complacency over many years, but then suddenly launch a devastating attack, not only through traditional missiles and bombs, but through infecting their networks and computers.

The namesake of the series was a very old space battleship—Battlestar Galactica—which was about to be decommissioned when the attack came. It was the only Battlestar to survive, ironically because it was so old. Because it did not have the latest networking technology, it was not affected by the computerized network attack launched by the robots.

The time when robots might attack us is far in the future, but there's a lesson for us here. We are installing and connecting IoT type computers into our networks without fully comprehending the potential consequences. These devices can be hacked and infected and used by criminals or nation-states. If compromised, they allow a hacker to do something through the Internet that has a physical, "brick and mortar" effect upon us in our home.

L. REDUCE YOUR ATTACK SURFACE: DISCONNECT WHEN NOT NEEDED

Every hour your device is turned off, or disconnected from the Internet, is an hour that the device cannot be attacked, compromised, or used as a tool of a cybercriminal. Of course, if it's off, you can't use it, and if it's disconnected from the Internet, that limits what you can do with it. It's a balance between availability of your data to you and confidentiality of your data from criminals.

If you leave your desktop or laptop computer on and connected to the Internet constantly, 24/7, you are providing 24/7 opportunities for criminals. If you can reduce the time these devices are connected to the Internet, you will reduce the amount of time criminals have to attack you. If your computer is already compromised and has malware in it, when you disconnect it, at least you will reduce the time that criminals can make use of your device. When you go on vacation, consider turning off devices in the home, including your modem and router. If you don't need them to do anything while you are gone, why leave them on and connected to the world? That said, more and more homes now require constant Internet connection to operate—for phone service, monitoring, security cameras, alarms, and more. If that's the case for your home, disconnecting the modem and router may not be an option.

Wake on LAN

Network interface cards within desktop computers and laptops have a feature called "Wake on LAN" which can be enabled or disabled. If this feature is enabled, it's possible to send a signal through the network to a sleeping or off computer to tell it to wake up and power itself on. This feature is designed for large companies, allowing the IT department to turn the computers on remotely so they can send updates to them, and so that a worker doesn't have to visit each computer to manually turn it on.

Hackers might try this "Wake on LAN" technique for your computer, so if you do not need this feature, it shouldn't be enabled. Whatever your "Wake on LAN" configuration, rest assured that hackers have no method of getting a computer to plug itself in, either with the power cord or the Ethernet cable.

M. MORE ABOUT NETWORKS FOR THE VERY CURIOUS

If you feel you have read enough about networks to last you a while, skip this section. If you are excited and want to learn more about them and the data being transmitted to and from your devices, this section explores additional details.

1. Windows Task Manager

Windows Task Manager allows you to check what's running on your computer and what is using the network.

- Open the Windows Task Manager:
  - Method 1: Control – Shift – Escape (press and hold all three keys).
  - Method 2: Search for "Task Manager" or run application "taskmgr.exe."
- Review the "Processes" tab; sort by "Network" to see which processes are transmitting across the network.
- Review the "Performance" tab; click on Ethernet or Wi-Fi Tab.

2. Windows Resource Monitor

This is a way to get another look at processes and network activity.

- Open the Windows Resource Monitor:
  - Method 1: Search for "Resource Monitor."
  - Method 2: Run application "perfmon.exe."
- Review the "Network" tab.

3. Windows Firewall

These are basic firewall settings you may have already reviewed.

- Open the Windows Firewall window:
  - Method 1: Navigate to the control panel, then to "Firewall."
  - Method 2: Search for "Windows Firewall."
- Review the simple settings available here.
- Click on the "Advanced Settings" link to take you to the next step.

4. Windows Firewall with Advanced Security

- Open the "Windows Firewall with Advanced Security" window:
  - Method 1: From Windows Firewall (above) click on "Advanced Settings."
  - Method 2: Search for "Windows Firewall with Advanced Security" or run application "WF.msc" (must be run as an administrator).
- Review the many firewall settings ("rules") for every application and service on your computer. Do not change the settings unless you know what you are doing.

5. Windows Commands Regarding Network Activity

Windows provides two methods of entering commands, the "command line" and through the "PowerShell." Whichever you use, run them with administrator privileges, rather than regular user privileges.

- Open a "Command line" or "Command prompt" window:
  - Method 1: Search for "Command Prompt" application.
  - Method 2: Run application "cmd.exe."
  - For either method, make sure you run it with administrator privileges.
- Open a PowerShell window:
  - Method 1: Search for "Windows PowerShell."
  - Method 2: Run application "PowerShell.exe."
- Enter various commands (each command has options that alter how it is run):
  - ipconfig   Learn your router's address and basic information
  - ipconfig /all   View detailed information including your MAC address
  - net view   Displays a list of resources being shared on a computer
  - arp -a   Displays list of devices on the network with their IP address and MAC address
  - netstat   Displays current network connections from the computer
  - netstat -a   Displays all connections and listening ports
  - netstat -r   Displays the routing table

6. Mac Applications and Commands Regarding Network Activity

- Review the Mac Activity Monitor:
  - Finder → Applications → Utilities → Activity Monitor
- Open a command shell (bash shell):
  - Finder → Applications → Utilities → Terminal
- Enter various commands:
  - ifconfig   Learn your router's address and basic information
  - arp-a   Displays list of devices on the network with their IP address and MAC address
  - netstat -a   Displays all connections/ports
  - netstat -nr   Displays routing table
- Review the Mac Console:
  - Finder → Applications → Utilities → Console

7. Install a Free Software Firewall

You could install a free software firewall on your laptop or desktop, and configure it to log certain activities and alert you to others. Some free software firewalls to consider:

- Zone Alarm Free Firewall
- Privatefirewall (free version)
- Little Snitch for Mac (free version)

Be aware that use of these applications might be time consuming, and may interfere with the trouble-free usage of other applications. The firewall might occasionally block traffic that you don't want blocked, and interfere with use of the computer.

N. CONCLUSION

This chapter covered a lot of ground, and was the most technical and hands-on part of this book. You have crested the hill and it's all downhill coasting from here, applying your technical and information security knowledge to other areas, including your family, travel, and workplace. Learning about your devices, data, and networks is a process—especially networks—so don't feel discouraged if you didn't master everything in the first sitting. If you enjoyed this chapter, including the technical aspects of the preceding section, then see Appendix 8 and the tools you can use to view the data traveling on your network.

CHAPTER 11

Secure Your Family, Children, and Seniors

A. INTRODUCTION

The information in this chapter will help keep your family, children, and seniors safe. It builds on past chapters, and focuses on aspects that are unique to your household members and family. Through the prior chapters, you have gained knowledge and insights on how to secure your computer devices, data, and network, and to protect your privacy. You already have secured your home quite a bit, and probably have a list of things you want to do in the future to make it even safer.

Children and seniors are especially susceptible to certain cybercrime threats. Children may be trusting and unaware of threats, and seniors may not understand the technology. A trusting or unsophisticated computer user can make mistakes that might allow cybercriminals to gain control of the device, data, and network. Further, technology and the Internet bring many concerns that relate to a child's well-being, development, and safety.

B. CHILDREN

There are special concerns with children. Studies indicate that children are doing risky or harmful things with their devices and on the Internet, overusing and misusing the technology. Overuse includes spending too many hours a day on their devices, hours when they should be studying, communicating face to face with others, playing outdoors, and sleeping. One-quarter of teenagers indicate they are constantly connected to the Internet, and one-half indicate they are addicted to their phones.[1] Some studies suggest that excessive video gaming, Internet, and computer use can be linked to emotional problems.[2] Misuse risks include communicating with dangerous strangers, or accessing adult topics and inappropriate materials. Children and teens can be vulnerable

---

1. Yolanda (Linda) Reid Chassiakos, Jenny Radesky, Dimitri Christakis, Megan A. Moreno, & Corinn Cross, *Children and Adolescents and Digital Media*, 138 PEDIATRICS 5 (Nov. 2016), https://pediatrics.aappublications.org/content/pediatrics/early/2016/10/19/peds.2016-2593.full.pdf.

2. DIAGNOSTIC AND STATISTICAL MANUAL OF MENTAL DISORDERS (5th ed. 2013).

to different types of criminals, such as pedophiles, sex traffickers, hate groups, and terrorist groups.[3] Studies also indicate that parents are not as vigilant in monitoring and reviewing their children's activity as they could be.[4]

There are also developmental, educational, and welfare aspects for children. The Internet makes things possible today that were impossible before the Internet existed. Children today have instant access to content that we did not when we were growing up. In many ways, that is good, because they have access to a wide range of facts, information, and knowledge. But in many ways this can be bad, because the Internet provides a gateway to pornography, hate speech, falsehoods that masquerade as truth, and information that "educates" the viewer about drugs and criminality. Our parents might have been able to postpone discussing and educating us about certain topics. Today, if a child is curious, the child can simply ask Google or Siri and then see what results are available.

Aside from the information available on the Internet, computer devices and video games can become all-engrossing. Teens can become addicted to their devices as well as the constant communication it demands, and this can detract from in-person communication. Friends and even family members can become enmeshed in their devices, even while together, and even at dinner. Habits like these increase the developmental risks that the Internet and devices can pose for children.

These risks present opportunities for families to increase their interaction and communication among one another. First, parents can use their own increasing knowledge about cybersecurity to educate their children about the positives and risks of the technology, to discuss security, privacy, and safety on the Internet, and to gradually start discussions about some of the bad things that exist in the world. These conversations can offer opportunities to discuss ways to think critically, to evaluate statements and separate fact from fiction, and to assess differing views and credibility. Exploring these topics also allows parents to learn more about their children, learn what their children are doing on the Internet and with whom, and also to learn from their children about the technology and how it works. Chances are good that with any new technology, the child knows how to use it before the parent, and can show the parent how to use the device or software. The parent can teach the child that using technology properly means using it safely, with careful thinking about security and privacy, as well as being responsible and considerate towards others. These parent-child communications are true teaching moments.

---

3. *See e.g.,* Kate Briquelet, *Dad Saves Daughter from Snapchat Sex Traffickers,* THE DAILY BEAST (Oct. 10, 2016), http://www.thedailybeast.com/articles/2016/10/10/dad-saves-daughter-from-snapchat-sex-traffickers.html.

4. CENTER FOR CYBER SAFETY AND EDUCATION, *Children's Internet Usage Study* (Apr. 4, 2016), https://safeandsecureonline.org/wp-content/uploads/2016/03/Childrens-Internet-Usage-Study-DETAILED.pptx.

1. Assessment

This is the most personal self-assessment of the book because it involves your family. There is no "one size fits all" for cybersecurity, and there certainly isn't for parenting. Whatever the strengths and weaknesses within your family, finding more ways to interact with and communicate with your children is beneficial, as is learning more about what your children are doing. Your efforts to improve your cybersecurity can be a wonderful means of connecting with your children on a topic of interest to all of you. Don't be intimidated—it's a learning opportunity for everyone.

Some initial questions for you to ponder and think about are:

- Do you know your child's "real world" friends and acquaintances, and do you know their parents?
- What about your child's online friends and acquaintances? Do you know who they really are?
- What is the understanding between you and your child about whether you can (or will) review his or her online activity?
- Do you know what your child is doing while on a smartphone or computer?
- When was the last time you reviewed your child's smartphone, tablet, and/or computer, including their online activity and communications?
- Do you know how much time your child spends on a smartphone (or other device) each day?

Consider what steps you have taken to educate yourself on various issues, including through websites such as:

- SafeAndSecureOnline.org
- HealthyChildren.org
- StaySafeOnline.org

2. Your Parental "Privacy Policy"

It might seem odd to talk about a "privacy policy" in the home, but this is a book from and for lawyers, and cybersecurity principles and analogies extend from the workplace to the home and vice versa. Just as corporations should have privacy policies about how they collect, use, and share customer information, perhaps you and your children should have an understanding about how you monitor them and their Internet usage. It needn't be a written policy posted in your home, but rather a mutual understanding with general ground rules. This way, children know what is expected and know that their parents are watching. Having a clear understanding helps to set up better communication for the future.

When a minor child is living in the home, and the parent is paying for the child's device and Internet service, it is reasonable for the parent to be able to review the contents of the device, including the child's contacts, data, and online communications. In essence, this is saying the child has "no expectation of privacy" within the device, just like you probably have no expectation of privacy in your usage of an employer's computer systems. Of course, this review should be done with tactfulness and respect. Your child should have some privacy, but it may also be beneficial for the child to know that the parent is monitoring things, especially within devices. By reviewing your child's devices periodically, learning how and when a device is being used, and who is being contacted and why, you will learn about what is going on in your child's world. This process can bring you closer to your child, and you will be in a better position to detect if your child is having issues at school or with friends, being bullied, bullying others, accessing inappropriate material, or is in contact with strangers or potentially dangerous people.

Sample Parental Privacy Policy

A visit to some close friends years ago provided a great demonstration of one such "privacy policy." The two children had smartphones and the mother requested to see them—she put out her hand and said, "Hand it over." The kids did so good-naturedly. She looked through the phones, checked the text messages and e-mails, asked who this person was, how that child was doing, how the parents were doing, what this text message was about, and more. Though similar in some respects to a military inspection or police interrogation, it was also a friendly interaction that the children were accustomed to, and a method to catch up on what the children were doing. The boys knew this was a condition of having the phones, needed them to communicate with the parents about pickup times, and most of their peers in school had smartphones. By periodically inspecting the phones and discussing the contents, these parents helped mitigate the potential threats, and were guiding their children towards eventual unsupervised Internet access.

3. Educating Your Child to Make Good Decisions

Eventually, children will grow up. They will walk to school on their own, get involved with summer or after-school jobs or activities, travel on their own and eventually live on their own. Sooner or later, they will have full access to everything out on the Internet, which, as we all know, includes some nasty things and people. Of course, there are good things there, too, but the point here is to educate your children so that they can grow up and make sound decisions and take proper actions on their own to guard against the threats. The goal should be that—long after you are gone—your child will have the knowledge and experience to make thoughtful, safe decisions affecting cyber-security, privacy, and other issues.

Our parents taught us some basic safety rules that had little to do with the Internet, but still hold valuable analogies. Initially, parents shepherded us everywhere, decided for us when to cross the street, and held our hands. Then they taught us to cross the street only when the signal says "walk," look both ways, and to walk through safe neighborhoods, and in lighted streets. They also taught us to avoid suspicious looking people, not to talk to strangers, and to never go anywhere with a stranger for any reason. Eventually, we went to school or the store alone for the first time, and our parents were nervous, maybe they even followed and watched from a distance to make sure we were safe, and making good decisions. There were other rules, too. Keep the front door locked, don't tell callers your address or personal information. Our parents probably kept an eye on who we were hanging out with, which then involved in-person visits or phone calls on a shared phone line, providing parents with opportunities to learn what we were doing and with whom. We want to teach those same lessons to our children, but the lessons now apply not only to the physical world, but the digital world as well.

The world has always had dangers and bad people. But it is only recently—with the Internet—that a child or teenager can interact with anyone, anywhere in the world. Now, predators and criminals aren't limited to their immediate geographic neighborhoods. Now you have the responsibility to educate your children about keeping themselves safe in the Information Age. You still need to teach about "real world" threats—the physical bullies, muggers, and predators. But you also need to teach them to keep safe on the Internet and from the people they might meet through the Internet. There are many places on the Internet that are like that dark alley, places that can either compromise the computer, or expose the user to inappropriate content. There are manipulative and twisted individuals and groups, including child predators, pedophiles, sex traffickers, terrorists, and hate crime groups, who may try to get to know your children and "groom" or recruit them. There are many online habits and behaviors that can be damaging to children, whether it is digital addiction, pornography, sexting (taking or sharing of inappropriate photos), cyberbullying, and more.

It might seem tempting to keep your child off the Internet, and restrict what your child can access. That may work for a period of time, and may last up to a certain age, but it will not be possible forever. Your child will eventually find unrestricted access to the Internet, and will eventually be more technologically sophisticated than you are. It might seem tempting to relinquish oversight, and let your children have free reign with devices and the Internet, trusting their good judgment and the odds. That approach may work, but it also opens up many risks. You need to find a middle ground that works for you. Part of protecting a child is teaching him or her how to make good decisions about using devices and the Internet, about what is safe and proper, and what is not.

Before the Internet, only a select few could get their words edited and published to the masses. This process reduced the writing available for consumption, undoubtedly censoring some valuable writing, but also enforcing some standards, whether one agreed with the standards or not. Now, anyone can publish anything to the Internet. The massive amount of information already online and growing daily at an exponential rate includes both facts and disinformation. It is magical to be able to "ask the Internet" any question, using Google or another search engine. The Internet has democratized information, and made it instantly available to anyone, but it has also created a free-for-all for disseminating false, biased, and unverified information. It is important to teach our children critical thinking skills, which will help not only with security, but also in many other parts of their lives. Now, more than ever, it is important for people to assess information, the source, and the underlying basis for knowledge, and to evaluate its accuracy. From an anti-fraud perspective, common sense and critical thinking can help the user detect whether an e-mail that just came in is a phishing or fraud scam, or if it contains malicious links or attachments. From a broader perspective, this critical thinking can help determine if that chain e-mail or blog post is a joke, a hoax, fake news, or a wild and unsupported conspiracy theory.

Every day, children will be faced with more and more decisions about how they use their devices and the Internet, and how they communicate with others. As parents we can help educate them so that they make the right decisions as often as possible, and learn from their mistakes as much as possible.

4. Reviewing Your Child's Devices and Computer Usage

Securing your home means securing all of your family's devices and data as well. When you read Chapter 8, you should have reviewed *all* devices in your home, including those used by your children, and when you read Chapter 9, you should have reviewed all online accounts and profiles, even your children's. But when you conducted those reviews, you were looking at these topics from a more general perspective.

This chapter presents an opportunity to revisit your children's devices and data, while paying special attention to areas applicable to child safety and well-being. It is an opportunity to not only discuss and review security, privacy, and safety issues with your child, but also to discuss your child's activities and friends, and see with whom he or she is communicating and about what, even if the technology seems daunting. You don't need to pretend to be a technology master; this can be the child's opportunity to show you and teach you.

You should review three basic areas concerning your child: first is a review of devices, second is a review of data, and the third is a more general review of your child's contacts and communications. This last review transcends the traditional cybersecurity framework, recognizing your broader parental role in your child's social interactions. Some of the technical review of devices and data should be done with your child present so that you can discuss and learn things together. There will be other circumstances when you may need more time and may want to conduct a review out of the presence of your child—perhaps with your spouse.

a. Device Review

With your child, review all electronic devices your child uses, including smartphone, tablet, laptop, desktop, and video games. Your child is probably an expert on using the features of these devices, so he or she can walk you through all of the settings, apps, and data on them. Make sure your child becomes an expert on the security and privacy features as well.

1. Review device settings. The child's device should be reviewed for basic settings that affect operation and security of the device, including a good password that isn't shared with anyone except the parent. Configure proper privacy and security settings.
2. Review installed apps. Have your child explain any apps you don't recognize and ask what they do. For any apps that include communication with others, review those communications as indicated below.
3. Review communications with others. Review who your child is communicating with and ask who they are and what the communication is about. Review phone calls, text messages, e-mails, and other apps that allow communication too.
4. If there are apps that do not store the communications for later review (e.g. Snapchat), consider removing them.
5. Review photos and ask who the people are. Are the photos appropriate?
6. Review contacts, calendars, and notes.
7. Review Internet history (e.g. web browser history).

b. Data and Online Profile Review

With your child, log in to all online accounts he or she uses. Again, your child is probably great at using the features, but make sure she is an expert on the security and privacy settings. Review all data stored there—photos, communications, and contacts.

1. Discuss security and privacy with your child and have your child log in to their accounts so you can review the settings.
2. Do the accounts have a strong password and do they know not to share it with anyone except the parent? Remind children to never share passwords with friends.
3. What personal information is available to the public? You don't want strangers to be able to access your child's social media account profile, nor should they be able to contact your child online, or by using information posted online.
4. Review photos, ask who the people are.
5. Review and discuss your child's "digital footprint." Your child should act as if anything communicated electronically or posted to social media will be available publicly and permanently.

c. Overall Review of Communications, Contacts, and Apps

When you review your child's devices and online accounts, you will learn about what they are doing, with whom, how they are communicating, and how they are spending their time. Some of this data may be stored on the device, and some on their social media accounts, e-mail accounts, or elsewhere. Where it is stored is not important—you are trying to ensure your child's activities and friends are healthy and appropriate. You can begin to assess this by evaluating the following questions:

1. What websites are they accessing?
2. What are they posting, texting, and e-mailing, and is it appropriate?
3. Are there any signs of bullying or inappropriate writings or images (e.g. "sexting" or pornography)?
4. Are they exposing too much personal information to the world?
5. What are their friends and contacts saying and posting online, especially about your child? Review their friends' social media accounts. Ask your child who the friends are, and how he or she met them.
6. Does your child have contacts he or she met through the Internet? Do you know who these people really are?
   a. What can you do to verify the age, name, and identity of this stranger?

b. Malicious individuals often will assume a fake persona to gain the trust of a child or teenager. An older male might pretend to be a teenager. A younger female or male might recruit victims on behalf of older men.

7. Is anyone, especially an older person, and including a person in a position of trust, taking an unusual or inappropriate interest in your child?

8. How much time, and at what hours, are your children using devices/ Internet?

   a. Are they spending appropriate time on other pursuits, including play, exercise, homework, and sleep?

   b. Do they have time to "wind down" before bedtime that does not involve device usage?

   c. Dangers of excessive device usage can include lack of sleep, school problems, obesity, addiction, and more.

Cyberbullying and the Lori Drew Case

Few things are harder for a parent than to learn their child is being mistreated or bullied. The parental instinct to protect a child can be powerful and sometimes override rationality. However, you should not directly contact other minors who are communicating with your child, except after considerable thought. If you feel you have to do this, be very mindful of the manner in how you do it. You do not want to overreact, and you do not want to do something that another child's parent will become angry about, or perceive as bullying. Instead, discuss the problem with your child and come up with a plan, and involve the school, law enforcement, and the parents of the minor as appropriate.

One such case taken to the extreme was the case of Lori Drew. Lori Drew, a mother, felt that a teenage neighbor (Megan Meier) was spreading gossip about Lori's teenage daughter. So Lori created a fake social media account under the made-up name of "Josh" to interact with Megan, and others. Lori communicated with Megan for a month, the whole time posing as "Josh," and Megan developed feelings for "Josh." Ultimately, Lori as "Josh" told Megan the world would be better without her, and Megan eventually committed suicide.

Clearly, Lori's actions were the wrong way to handle that dispute. This terrible story shows that there can be real-life consequences to what happens online, and we need to teach our children not only how to handle cyberbullying, but avoid the actions that can be perceived as bullying.

5. Sample Guidelines or Rules of Conduct

All of the above information told you what to review, and what to look for, but it didn't tell you what rules to impose and how to do it. There's no simple answer to that question—so much depends on your child, your concerns, and your parenting priorities and style. This section does not pretend to tell you what to do. However, it will give you some potential guidelines and rules to choose from and adapt as needed.

If you've reviewed your child's device and Internet usage, you have an idea of how much time your child spends on his or her devices and on the Internet. Addiction is a threat, whether it's addiction to the device itself, or to the things the device can access, so usage should be limited to some extent. Besides, your child needs to develop skills independent of devices, whether it is math without a calculator, spelling without spell check, handwriting with a pen, or navigating without GPS. These guidelines are merely samples for you to pick and choose from, and adapt as you see fit.

1. Time and place of use
    *   No device use for 1 hour (or more) before bedtime to "wind down." No computers in the bedroom, put mobile devices to charge, or in a drawer.
    *   No device use after bedtime (devices left outside the bedroom).

- No device use at meals.
- No device use while walking, biking, driving, etc.
- No device use during class.
- No device use while doing other tasks like homework, family conversation, etc. Multitasking is not a real thing, especially for kids. People need to concentrate on one task at a time.
- No device use in a locker room or anywhere people are changing clothing.
- Other designated "no use" times.
- Younger children may need device use restricted to a family public area (e.g. living room) under general supervision (depending on age).
- Older children may be able to use devices unsupervised, but should not be allowed to delete any data or history, so that the parents can periodically review it.

2. Purpose of use (what devices can be used for)
   - You can limit what a device can be used for, such as phone calls, texting, e-mail, and certain web surfing, and restrict use or installation of other applications.

3. Prohibitions of use (what devices cannot be used for)
   - No pornography, hate speech, researching criminality, etc.
   - No use of certain apps (anonymity type apps, secure/disappearing message type apps, other unapproved or unnecessary apps).
   - No disappearing texts/e-mails (e.g. no Snapchat).
   - No clearing of Internet history or deleting of texts/e-mails.
   - Social media apps: Consider either (i) No use of social media apps, or (ii) no posting to social media apps, or (iii) some limitation or supervision of social media app usage and posting.
   - No selfies, no sexting, no forwarding of photos/sexts.
   - No taking pictures of others without their consent, even otherwise appropriate photos.
   - No video chat with anyone unless supervised. Or, no video chat with anyone unless that person has been approved.
   - Observe school rules (e.g. no phones out in locker rooms, or when any friends are changing, no use of phones in classroom, etc.).

4. General rules of conduct (miscellaneous)
   - Avoid doing stupid, dangerous, or illegal acts.
   - If any of the above are done, they are not something to be proud of, and should not be publicly posted. Sensationalizing such events can lead to serious consequences for the child, and encourages others to do similar foolish acts.

- Treat their social media accounts as permanent, public records. While their current group of friends may find something funny or cute, future friends, colleges, or employers may not.
- Device use should not interfere with other activities.
- No bullying, no harassing, no sexting. The child should report to a parent if these things occur.
- No unauthorized access of accounts or devices of others. No sharing passwords.
- Be good people, good citizens, and good online citizens.

5. Enforcement options
   - By agreement or trust?
   - By periodic monitoring and supervision?
   - By physical controls?
   - By technical controls? (See discussion below.)

The ideal method to enforce rules is through agreement and trust, plus periodic monitoring and supervision. Violations of the agreement and trust should be followed by real consequences. Parents can help ensure compliance with physical controls—removing physical access to the device by requiring the device be placed on a counter, in a drawer, or in the parent's room.

Technical controls are another way parents can enforce rules about devices. These controls could include restrictions on how the devices and applications operate, restrictions on Internet access, and adjusting settings within each child's device and within your home router. However, if your child is determined to circumvent rules and restrictions, don't think that technical controls will solve the problem. It's hard enough to keep a determined hacker from getting into your network; it's harder still to keep a determined child inside your home from reaching the Internet.

Importantly, do not forget to lead by example and practice what you preach. It is easy for the parent to get distracted by devices, which reduces interaction with the child. These moments are not only missed opportunities, but they teach the child a bad lesson. Whatever the demands of work and personal life, resist the impulse to check your phone every few minutes, and try to designate certain periods and places as device-free.

6. Reviewing the Data That Is Posted About Your Children

In this chapter, you reviewed any information your child and your child's friends have posted online. In Chapter 9, you reviewed the information that you have posted online, and now it is time to review your own postings again, but this time with an eye to your child's safety and well-being. It's also time to review what other people might have posted online about your child.

Some people are avid users of social media, and also proud parents who frequently post about their family. Sometimes they post frequently, with no awareness about their privacy settings, or that these postings might be visible to anyone in the world. If this sounds like you, it is time to start considering whether that proud picture of your child, plus other information in the posts, tells strangers on the Internet more information than they should know about your child. Do you want people you don't know—potentially sinister individuals—learning where your son or daughter lives or goes to school?

The first step is to reconsider what you are posting on social media that relates to your children, and evaluate whether it should even be posted at all. At some point, you should involve your children in the conversation, and ask them how they feel about having information about them posted. After all, it is your job to teach them how to make informed decisions about their own privacy and security, and it is hard to teach that concept if you are posting about them without their permission.

The next step is to re-evaluate your own social media privacy and security settings, as you did in Chapter 9. Now, you are looking at it through a different lens, to protect your children, and that may warrant turning up the "security dial" a few notches. Perhaps previously you didn't care if the world saw your postings, or if your account and all its contents were hacked. But now, thinking about the potential implications for your children, you may decide you want to make your settings more private, enable two-factor authentication, or perhaps delete certain posts, communications, or other content that are stored in the account. In other words, when you consider that your child is involved, you may decide your existing "security dial" setting wasn't high enough.

The third step involves broadening your review to online postings by family and friends that might pertain to your children. Suppose your family has chosen to limit or avoid posting anything to social media about your children, but you have relatives or friends who haven't considered it as an issue. Suppose these relatives or friends post photographs or videos about you or your children, and those posts are publicly available for the world to see. One potential guideline is that if one posts materials or photos relating to others, they should obtain appropriate permission. Of course, a written waiver would be excessive, but some type of communication and understanding seems appropriate.

The Birthday Party Video, and Other Facebook Postings

A friend held a large birthday party and many attendees were taking photos and recording videos, especially during the "Happy Birthday" song. However, one attendee immediately posted his videos and photos to Facebook, including videos of the hosts and their young children. The first problem arose when some people viewing his Facebook updates saw this wonderful party and became upset that they weren't invited to it. The next issue was that the attendee posted images and videos of others, especially children, without their permission. The hosts weren't active Facebook users, so these postings might have gone unnoticed forever—except that one person who was not invited to the party was offended enough to complain to the hosts. When the hosts learned about the photos and videos they asked that they be taken down, and they were. Social media creates another issue: some people who should be enjoying a great party are distracted by their devices and posting to social media, and others instantly learn of events they wish they were invited to and feel left out.

Fortunately, this incident resulted in only some hurt feelings and a little annoyance, and no lawsuit was contemplated or filed. In an interesting case, an eighteen-year-old woman sued her parents for posting over 500 pictures of her to their Facebook account without her permission, and for refusing to remove the pictures when requested.[5] There may be more to this situation than Facebook postings, but the lesson is instructive. Parents should lead by example and teach children to make good decisions about what they do online.

---

5. Ann Brenoff, *Woman Sues Her Parents for Posting Her Baby Photos on Facebook*, THE HUFF-INGTON POST (Sept. 16, 2016), http://www.huffingtonpost.com/entry/woman-sues-her-parents-for-posting-her-baby-photos-on-facebook_us_57dc03c3e4b04a1497b3ebdd.

C. SENIORS

Seniors may be especially vulnerable to scams, cons, and thieves who rely upon social engineering. Seniors were not born into this highly technological age and may be easily stumped by new devices. They also may face physical limitations like diminishing eyesight and motor skills. As more and more aspects of daily life move online—from banking to making medical appointments—the older people in our lives are required to navigate the world of technology. Extra care is required to ensure that seniors can maintain access to their devices, data, and the Internet, and, by extension, to connect to the important new benefits these devices bring.

Securing your parents and seniors requires a different focus. With children, we focused a lot of attention on maintaining the confidentiality of their personal information, images, communications, and general data. With seniors, our focus turns more to the "availability" of data and systems—an important information security principle that is highly applicable to their well-being. Age interferes with the ability of seniors to access and use their devices and data, because they may not be as technologically sophisticated, and also may have diminishing eyesight or motor skills. You can help your parents, as well as older relatives, friends, and colleagues, maintain the availability of their devices and data, and keep them connected with others and the outside world, while keeping them safe from cybercrime and fraud. As with your children, discussing technology and Internet safety with elders provides an opportunity to maintain a personal connection with them.

Seniors face different challenges with respect to technology compared to younger generations. Personal computing is a relatively new concept for seniors, a sea-change in everyday living that appeared later in their lives. People born in the 1920s to 1940s grew up and spent most of their lives using paper, pen, and telephones. They got newspapers on their doorstep, saw movies in the theatre, and met people in person. Then, all of a sudden, the personal computer age was upon them, and the changes have been exponential. The ongoing technology explosion has meant big adjustments for everyone, but for seniors, the experience can seem foreign and incomprehensible. Technology also magnifies fraud risks that seniors have traditionally faced.

Seniors are often susceptible to certain social engineering and fraud scams, whether from the Internet, by e-mail, telephone, or a knock on the door. Traditional frauds against seniors typically involved face-to-face con-artistry, like home repair scams where the fraudster pretends to be a reputable contractor, knocks on the door, and purports to sell home repair services. Criminals have preyed upon seniors with scams like these for some time, and today's cybercriminals merely continue that trend with technology. Cybercriminals and other fraudsters typically contact the potential victim by phone or e-mail, and try to convince the victim to provide personal or financial information, to grant access to their computer, to invest in worthless scams, or to pay money for worthless or nonexistent services.

A current scheme preys upon seniors' fear of technology. With this fraud, the scammer makes a phone call to the victim, pretends to be from a legitimate company, claims that the victim's computer is not working properly, and offers to fix the problem right away. It can be a believable scam, especially for seniors who don't understand technology. The scammer convinces the victim to grant access to the victim's computer by directing the victim to a certain website and authorizing access, then performs malicious actions, and convinces the victim to provide financial information or otherwise pay for the "technical support."

Beyond the rampant fraud schemes, older people also face physical challenges, since eyesight and motor coordination diminish with age, and these deteriorations can interfere with using a computer. Whereas you may be concerned that your teenager is using her device too much, your senior family members may lose the ability to use their devices. It is important to routinely evaluate our older relatives' use of devices. Are they able to keep in touch with the outside world, to video chat with family members, correspond by e-mail, surf the Internet, and even do old-fashioned things like write letters? When travel outside the home becomes more difficult, being able to communicate by video or e-mail becomes more valuable.

Also, regardless of age, it is good for anyone to learn new things—yes, it is definitely possible for "an old dog to learn new tricks." Research indicates that learning new skills and information is good for the brain.[6] That said, too many changes can be unnecessary, overwhelming, and frustrating. Seniors might not need a Facebook or LinkedIn account, nor a smartphone, nor the latest device that comes out every two years. But they should have access to the services and communications methods they want or need, including the ability to communicate with others through the Internet.

With seniors, you might focus more on implementing and configuring, rather than educating about how to navigate the online world. They may not have the desire to learn about the dozens of configuration settings on an iPhone, a Gmail account, or a Facebook account, and that is an understandable position. It may fall to you to configure and review the privacy and security of their devices and cloud accounts. The good news is that you have already done this with your own accounts and with your children's accounts, and it becomes much easier each time you do it.

---

6. Denise C. Park, Jennifer Lodi-Smith, Linda Drew, Sara Haber, Andrew Hebrank, Gérard N. Bischof, & Whitley Aamodt, *The Impact of Sustained Engagement on Cognitive Function in Older Adults: The Synapse Project*, 25 PSYCHOLOGICAL SCIENCE 103–112 (2014), http://journals.sagepub.com/doi/pdf/10.1177/0956797613499592.

Tips for protecting your seniors:

- Take an active part in the setup and upkeep of your senior's information technology (IT), cybersecurity, and anti-fraud posture.
- Be the "go to" person for IT issues. If you are the first call they make after a minor issue, you can prevent a more serious issue.
- Configure your own devices and accounts securely, then work on configuring your seniors' (and children's) systems securely.
- Implement systems and tools for your seniors that are similar to what you are using. You probably have a preference for certain services and devices, whether it is Mac or PC, Gmail, Hotmail, or Apple for e-mail. If you and your parent use the same service and product, then technical support is vastly simplified because you already know the technology.
- Consider upgrading equipment for your seniors when you do so for yourself. Your parents may not need a new device every year or two, or every time you get a new device for yourself. But when your parents are ready, it saves much work in purchasing and configuring if you both get similar or identical devices.
- Seniors may need things configured with simpler interfaces, larger screens, and larger fonts. They may have trouble with annoying advertisements. There are ways to configure the settings options to make the device easier for them to use. Some operating systems and applications have "ease of access" or similar settings.
- Consider setting up remote access. When your senior parents live outside of your home, it might be helpful to have a remote access capability so that you can adjust settings on their computer. Remember that remote access is a feature that creates vulnerabilities. Hackers also look for devices with remote access, and they could try to use the remote access tool for their own purposes. You should pick a tool and configuration that requires your senior parent to affirmatively allow the remote access before it is granted.
  - Some web conferencing tools offer screen-sharing features. You and your parents could have a web conference, and your parents could share their screen with you.
  - Operating systems offer remote access options. With Windows, it is Remote Desktop, Remote Access, and Quick Assist. With Mac OS X, there is Screen Sharing.
  - There are many free applications that can allow remote viewing, including Chrome Remote Desktop and TeamViewer free.
- Equipment labels on the senior's computer equipment can help if you are trying to talk them through an issue over the phone.

D. CONCLUSION

Nothing is more important than your family and their safety and well-being. With seniors, we want to keep them safe from cybercrime and fraud, but we also want to help them maintain access to the outside world, which means maintaining access to their data, devices, and the Internet. With our children, it's our role to protect them and teach them to protect themselves by making good decisions in a rapidly changing world. We need to lead by example, and also follow through to ensure rules are sensible and being followed. Additional resources on these topics are found within Appendix 9.

CHAPTER 12

Secure Yourself When You Travel

A. INTRODUCTION

No cybersecurity book would be complete without addressing the issues that arise when traveling outside your home or home office. We all travel and leave our homes, whether it is to work every day, to dinner, for business travel, or vacation. When you leave the home, your environment changes, impacting your cybersecurity in ways you may not be aware of. This chapter provides information about threats that affect you as you travel, and suggested strategies to mitigate them. We are not going to cover new technical ground, as you have already learned about your devices, data, and networks, and how they access the Internet. Instead, this chapter analyzes the changes that occur when you leave your home network, the hazards you face, and ways to reduce the risk of having your devices and data compromised.

We have previously focused on your home and home office, the devices and people in your home, how you access the Internet, and how you control access to your home network. Our homes are generally stable and safe places, where the risk of physical theft is low, and the devices and Internet connection don't change often. We control our home security with the equipment, settings, and security measures we choose and maintain.

Once we leave the home, we lose some of this control, and we are exposed to new threats. Many aspects of our devices change, including our Internet connection and perhaps our paths and methods to access certain data change as well. We will cover those three areas in this chapter, in prioritized order.

Prioritization

Within your home, we prioritized security differently, first covering devices, then data, and finally Internet and networks. That was because your greatest gains were made by first learning about and securing your devices,

---

then your data, the two components of your computing world you already use constantly and have the most
control over. Networks were the most complicated topic
and were reserved for last to give you a chance to learn
the basics first, and because your home Internet connection is very stable and consistent.

In this chapter, we've prioritized things differently.
Devices remain first, still the most important component
of your security, and the one you have the most control over, even when traveling. Your Internet service is
the next most important security concern when traveling, because you can choose whether or not to connect
to the Internet, and you should understand that decision
is important. Data comes next. In Chapter 9 you already
evaluated where and how you store your data, including methods to improve your data practices. This chapter
won't revisit that analysis, but will merely highlight what
changes occur for you and your data when you travel.

B. DEVICES AND TRAVEL

Quick tips for traveling and devices (encore from Chapter 8):

- Avoid device loss or theft. Be mindful of your surroundings and actions, and keep physical control of your devices at all times. If you have enabled two-factor authentication on cloud accounts, losing your smartphone will cause difficulty accessing your data.
- Manually lock your device when you are temporarily done using it, and ensure the auto lock feature is enabled.
- Ensure you've selected a strong password to secure the device.
- If your device stores sensitive information, then it should be encrypted and have a very strong password.
- If your device contains sensitive information, it should be kept on your person at all times.
- Be aware of how and when your device connects to the Internet.
- Be aware of the data on your device and the data that the device accesses.

1. Preventing Loss or Theft

Most of us travel with our smartphone, and might also bring along a tablet or laptop computer—perhaps a really small laptop device like a "notebook" or "netbook." Traveling with these devices raises special concerns because when they leave your home they are at heightened risk for loss, theft, or damage. Traveling, meeting people, and rushing in and out of taxis, trains, and planes are all opportunities for distraction, and thus loss or theft. We need a plan to mitigate those risks.

Don't Be Like This Person Who Lost or Destroyed Many Devices

A close friend, earlier in his life, experienced a number of losses, thefts, and destructions of his personal devices, averaging more than one per year—an extraordinary record. One of the funniest incidents was when he left his smartphone in his pants pocket, and then put the pants in a front loader washing machine. This happened long before water-resistant smartphones. He realized his mistake shortly after starting the cycle, but it was impossible to stop the machine or open the washer door. The phone put up a valiant fight, displaying its lights for several minutes through the initial rinse and wash cycles, but it eventually succumbed to water infiltration and its lights were extinguished forever.

Another time, my friend was bending over a pond and his smartphone fell out of his shirt pocket into the water, gone to sleep forever with the fishes. On another occasion, he was getting out of an elevator and his phone fell from his hand, rebounded along the floor and elevator walls, and then slipped through the gap when the elevator door opened, plummeting through the elevator shaft to its demise in the basement.

Once, working in a war-torn Middle Eastern country, he left his phone in a bar, forgot it, and then had to convince the entire group (with security escort) to return and retrieve it. That phone never made it out of the country because it later fell out of a pocket while he was exiting a car. He didn't notice until much later, and a return to the scene with hours of searching was fruitless. Another phone was forgotten and left in the custody of an unfriendly acquaintance, who held it until his return, and left him with an uneasy feeling that it had been looked into.

One laptop was left on the floor and his young child did some dancing and jumping maneuvers on it, breaking it and rendering the data unrecoverable. Another laptop was left unattended for just a few moments at a busy New York City open-air cafe, and disappeared forever. Other devices met similar demises, disappearing, impacting with pavements, or rendered unusable by coffee or bodies of water.

My friend has improved greatly, and few others may ever accumulate this record of loss and destruction. Nevertheless, loss, theft, and damage of our computer devices remain the number one risk for all of us. Lawyers and other professionals can't afford the loss or theft of our devices, because the consequences are too severe for ourselves and our clients. We also need to advise our clients on how to prevent these avoidable circumstances, and what to do if it happens.

With a little bit of time and effort you can develop good habits to secure your devices, ultimately saving a tremendous amount of time and frustration.

For most of us, our biggest security risk while traveling is losing our devices—our smartphone, laptop, or memory storage device. It's just a fact of life, people lose things, and thieves steal objects that are left unattended. You can significantly reduce threats of loss or theft through good habits, and maintaining physical control of your devices.

These habits might mean always keeping your smartphone in a particular pocket when not using it, preferably an inner pocket or zipper pocket to prevent it from falling out or being stolen by a pickpocket. Consider finding a comfortable bag for carrying your laptop all the time, so you don't feel tempted to check it at the coat check or leave it at a table. Consider choosing a laptop that's small enough for you to comfortably carry everywhere. When you are in a taxi, think about keeping your bag on your lap or your strap around your arm, so that it is impossible to forget it when you exit the cab. Developing these habits means they become automatic, even if you are tired, distracted, confused, or returning from an evening event.

If you remember nothing else about the risks while traveling, take extra care to keep physical control over your devices. Even if your devices are password protected and the data is encrypted, you do not want to lose them. If they disappear, there is the inconvenience of losing access to your e-mail and other cloud accounts and settings, even if this is temporary. Also, devices are expensive and may contain invaluable data that might be lost forever. Losing the device could even violate your duty to keep matters confidential, and could mean you are legally required to notify people about the loss of the data. Later, we will emphasize the importance of encryption to limit the damage in the event your device is lost or stolen.

Some basic tips to protect your devices against loss and theft include:

- Store your smartphone in the same place, every time, on your person (e.g. left, front pants pocket, belt holster, or a specific pouch in your purse).
- If you have your smartphone out but become engaged in another activity, lock the smartphone and return it to its safe place.
- Taxis, trains, and other transportation situations create opportunities to forget your device. Keep the devices on your person, or keep them in a bag that you strap over your shoulder. It's harder to forget something that you are holding.
- Be aware of your surroundings—pay attention and develop situational awareness.
- Don't text or read your smartphone while walking.
- Going through airport-type security is very distracting. Try to have a system so you put all of your valuables in one place, such as in a bag's pocket, before placing them on the conveyor belt.

- If your laptop or device is big or heavy and you hate to lug it around, leave it at home or consider buying a smaller device that you don't mind carrying all the time.
- Be aware of the risk of someone snatching your smartphone out of your hand while you are talking or texting, using it in a subway, etc.
- Don't leave property unattended.

Learning Good Habits Helps

I have learned some relatively good habits for keeping track of property and equipment thanks to the U.S. Army and the N.Y. State Police. Those organizations were not subtle in their disapproval of property ending up lost or stolen. It didn't matter if it were rifles, pistols, night vision goggles, evidence, or even inexpensive items that were nevertheless inventoried. In the Army, we tied certain items to our equipment harness, so that if it were to fall from our pocket or pouch unnoticed it would not be lost.

You don't need to tie your smartphone to you, unless you are crawling through rough terrain, or you are my close friend discussed earlier. However, you can start by developing good habits about where you put your devices. When I was a rookie state trooper, there were a few times that I put objects on the roof of my police car so I could unlock the door and get in—I didn't have enough hands to handle a hot coffee, car keys, and equipment bag. It's easy to get distracted, and the first time I forgot about the object on the roof and drove off it was embarrassing, so I learned that lesson. I also learned that with an open window and the right combination of acceleration and turning, a coffee placed on the roof near the light bar will fall through the open window and onto the driver. In the future, when my hands were full when getting into the car, I placed objects on the hood near the windshield—if I forgot about it before driving off I would see it.

If your habit is to put personal property in a place where you might forget about it, don't be surprised if you end up losing items occasionally. So substitute that habit with a better habit. Remember that good habits make the action easy; once you start making a certain action part of your routine, you'll soon keep doing it without effort or thinking.

Remember to configure your devices to require a password to unlock them. If your device is stolen, and does not require a password, even a casual thief can access nearly all of your data and online accounts. You do not want that to happen. If your devices have sensitive data on them, you must keep physical control over them. Also, they must have strong passwords and be encrypted, as covered more in section D.1.

The risk of theft is also important to guard against, and similar principles apply. Pay attention to your surroundings and keep your devices close. Thieves might not only pick your pocket to steal smartphones and tablets, but they might simply grab them out of your hand. Always be aware of your surroundings. It is better for your safety, and your physical and mental well-being, to put your phone away while you are walking.

This section is all about keeping your devices safe, and whatever data you have chosen to store there. Later, we'll address the choice about what data you are storing on devices you bring outside your home.

Grab Theft

Unfortunately, some thieves are so brazen they will grab a smartphone right out of a person's hand and run. Sometimes, it's not enough just to have your hand on your device; you also need to be aware of your surroundings.

Though most grab thieves are just trying to make a quick buck by selling your electronic device, don't assume that is always the case. Consider pickpocket rings, which are sophisticated, highly trained, and work in teams. With the advent of identity theft, pickpocket rings realized that once a wallet or purse was stolen and the cash removed, the remaining identification, credit cards, and other personal identifying information were useful for committing identity theft. The thieves can sell these materials to an identity thief, or perform frauds themselves.

Similarly, an identity thief could partner with that unsophisticated grab thief, and pay good money for the stolen and unlocked smartphone. An unlocked smartphone device contains and can access a lot of information; for example, there may be payment applications enabled, and the device could be fertile ground for exploitation. Each criminal has different skills, and where money can be made through collaboration, it will be.

2. Using Someone Else's Device

Quick tip:
- Avoid logging in to any of your important accounts on a public computer (such as a hotel or library computer).

Even though we travel with some of our devices, we may sometimes be without them, or find them insufficient, and be tempted to use someone else's computer. Perhaps we want to use a computer in the hotel's business center or in a public library, to log in to an account, or to print something for a meeting or event. Using public computers raises special considerations because sometimes these borrowed devices may not be safe to use for certain purposes, such as accessing important accounts.

By now you understand the importance of keeping your device malware-free and patching vulnerabilities. When you use someone else's device, you don't know how clean it is, what malware may be on it, or if it might be recording your login credentials and the data you view and access. Even if the computer is not infected, by using this device, you will leave traces of yourself and your activity. Someone else using that computer at a later time could find this data and exploit it.

Suppose you are traveling and go to the hotel's business center to use their computer. When using a public computer, consider it to be similar as using a restroom in Grand Central Station or Yankee Stadium—it's not private, it's been used by a lot of people, and it's not as clean as the bathroom in your home. Computers can become infected simply by a user opening an unsafe attachment containing malware, or visiting a malicious website, and chances are good a prior user did something like that.

The biggest risk with a public computer is there might be malware or spyware on it, such as a key logger, which could log the websites you visit, the usernames and passwords you enter, and everything else you type. This data is then transmitted to criminals who compile it for immediate or later use. It is very hard to know if the computer is infected or not without running anti-malware tools on it. Maybe you have the capability to run a quick scan on the computer before you use it, but probably not. If you are using the public computer to simply check the news or weather, you are not at risk of being compromised. Yet if you use the public computer to log in to any of your important accounts, especially your e-mail account or banking account, the risks are high. Before you use that public computer to log into an account, ask yourself if it's really necessary; otherwise, wait until you have access to a known clean computer. If you do access one of your accounts, you should have multi-factor authentication enabled for the account, so that even if the cybercriminal harvests your username and password, he or she would still lack your one-time code to get into your account. You should also consider changing your password once you get back to a safe computer.

When you use a computer, you leave digital trails of what you did within the computer. For example, if you surf to various websites, the computer is downloading files and images and text from these sites, and storing them in the computer, perhaps as "temporary Internet files." The computer is also storing "cookies" from each website that the website uses to identify you and store information about you and your preferences. Text and graphics that are displayed on the computer monitor are temporarily stored somewhere in that computer, as well. If you viewed a confidential e-mail, or viewed a confidential Word document, traces of it may well be stored on that public computer, without your knowledge. Thus, you should not access sensitive information from a device that is not your own.

If it is necessary for you to use a public computer, there are ways to reduce the traces you may leave on it during your use. When you first start a browser session, you can open a "new incognito window" or private browsing session to prevent browsing data from being saved into that computer. Or, if you logged into any of your online accounts (a very risky choice), make sure you have logged out of these accounts, and look for an option to tell the website you visited not to "remember" you on that computer—so that the next user isn't prompted to log in to your account. The computer's Internet browser (e.g. Internet Explorer, Chrome, Firefox) stores a lot of data about your Internet surfing and use, and you can delete that data through various browser functions. You will want to delete the record of the websites you visited, the cookies you acquired, and the temporary Internet files (Internet cache) you downloaded. Elsewhere within the computer there may be options so you can delete temporary files (cache), as well as links and records your computer stored relating to the documents you might have viewed, edited, or printed.

Basic rules when using a public computer are as follows:

- Don't work on sensitive materials.
- When you first start a browser session, open a "new private window" or "new incognito window" if possible.
- Don't log in to any of your important online accounts unless you absolutely must do so. Your username and password will be at greater risk.
- Evaluate if the public computer is maintained well, with a good security policy.
  - If you are using the computer with administrator privileges, or if you can access and modify many computer settings, that means other users and malware can also. It's not a secure computer.
  - If the computer is "locked down" and many settings and features are not available to you, and it is running anti-malware, it may be well secured. You still have no idea who used it before, and who will use it after.
- Check if it is running anti-malware applications and run a scan on it if possible.
- After use, log out of any accounts you logged in to, and tell websites not to remember you.
- Clear browser history, cache, and cookies.

C. INTERNET ACCESS AND TRAVEL

Quick tips:
- Avoid joining public or unknown Wi-Fi networks, if possible.
- Turn off your Wi-Fi adapter if you are outside the home and don't need to connect to a network.
- Turn off your Bluetooth adapter if you don't need it to connect to something.
- Configure your device so it doesn't automatically connect to any available Wi-Fi network without your permission.

- Consider using your smartphone's data plan as a personal hotspot.
- Consider buying a hotspot service from a cellular company so you have a portable Wi-Fi network, instead of using public Wi-Fi. It is much harder for a hacker to compromise your data when you are using your cellular network than when sharing a public Wi-Fi network.

When we leave our homes, we are changing the way we access the Internet. We don't have access to our home Wi-Fi network, so we need to access the Internet in a different manner. Our smartphones have service options from a cellular provider (such as Verizon Wireless, Sprint, AT&T, and others), which probably includes a data plan in addition to the standard cellular voice service. We can use that data plan to access the Internet, and we can even allow other devices to share access to the Internet through our smartphone by "tethering," or using the smartphone's connection as a hotspot.

There are Wi-Fi networks available everywhere when we travel, many for free, although sometimes there is a fee, such as in an airplane or at some hotels. These networks are convenient and allow your devices to access the Internet, but their risks are similar to using a public computer at a library, or the restroom at Grand Central Station. They're probably not clean, and might not be safe. Public Wi-Fi networks may not be configured securely, and you don't know who else is on the network. A cybercriminal could snoop on your communications or it's even possible a criminal is running that network. If even one cybercriminal is logged in to the same Wi-Fi network that you are logged into, he can compromise your security and privacy. An airplane is a good example of a situation that allows a hacker time to play with the devices of unsuspecting public network users. On a plane, the hacker has a captive set of potential victims when dozens of passengers are connected to the same Wi-Fi network, using their devices for hours.

Remember from earlier chapters that users logged in to the same network are like people at a crowded cocktail party. They can choose to be polite and not eavesdrop on other conversations, or they can choose to snoop and listen to any conversation they want. If your conversation is in normal language (e.g. unencrypted plain text), then it can be overheard when you're on a public Wi-Fi network. The only way to protect your communication is by encrypting it, as we'll discuss in the following section.

You should check how your device is configured to connect to both "known" and "unknown" Wi-Fi networks, also referred to as "trusted" and "untrusted." Your device should not be configured so that it automatically connects to unknown or public Wi-Fi networks. That would be like configuring your front door like a supermarket door with an electric eye—that automatically unlocks and opens for every person that approaches it. Connecting to any Wi-Fi network other than your home network is something that you should control, and do only after careful consideration.

Perhaps your device is configured to automatically connect to any "known" Wi-Fi networks. That setting can be very convenient, so that every time you enter your home, or your parents' home, or office, your device can automatically connect to the Wi-Fi network. You just need to be conscious about which Wi-Fi networks are known to your device, and occasionally you should do some housecleaning. As you travel, your device might automatically be connecting to various "known" networks you've used, such as the coffee shop, and that exposes your device and data to threats.

Regarding Wi-Fi networks that are "known" to your device, and stored within your device's settings, consider whether these Wi-Fi network names reveal anything about you that you don't want others to know. For example, if an undercover police officer connected his phone to a police department Wi-Fi network named "NYPD1stPct," he could potentially be broadcasting his affiliation when he brings his device around the criminals he is investigating. Maybe you have clients whose identity you need to keep confidential. If you visit the client and log into their Wi-Fi network, the network name might get stored on your device, and your device might broadcast that affiliation in other places. The name of your home or work Wi-Fi network is stored on your devices and your devices might be broadcasting that name, searching for the network. That's like wearing a nametag or carrying a large sign with your name on it, or even announcing your presence when you enter a room ("Hear ye, hear ye, a device that once connected to "Your_Name_Home_Wi-Fi_Network" is entering").

When your Wi-Fi adapter is on, your device may be looking to automatically connect to known Wi-Fi networks. Your device is calling out for "Your_Name_Home_Wi-Fi_Network" and seeing if anyone answers. This call-out exposes you to a security threat. A criminal can set up a device that listens for your device's call, and pretends to be that network. It tricks your device into connecting to it, and gives the criminal the opportunity to infect your device, steal your data, and monitor your communications. The best protection against all of these threats is to turn your Wi-Fi adapter off when you leave your home, and turn it on only if you need to connect to a Wi-Fi network you trust.

Bluetooth is another wireless data transfer protocol, and operates on similar principles as Wi-Fi. It allows your device to connect and exchange data with other known devices, such as your car's speakers and microphone (for hands-free phone calls), a wireless keyboard, wireless earpiece and microphone, mouse, GPS, and many other devices. Bluetooth devices also call out for each other constantly, and cybercriminals can impersonate your trusted

Bluetooth devices. The protection against this threat also lies with turning off your Bluetooth adapter when you don't need it.

Given how dangerous public Wi-Fi networks can be, a reasonable tactic is avoiding them altogether. You can use your smartphone as a personal hotspot, then connect your laptop or tablet to the Wi-Fi network created by your smartphone, and use that to access the Internet. This means relying upon your cellular data plan more, the download speed will be slower, and it will drain your smartphone battery faster, however it is safer.

If you are frustrated by the slow speed of your smartphone's data stream, you can also purchase a Wi-Fi hotspot. This is essentially a traveling antenna that can provide Internet access to your devices through a cellular data plan. This hotspot provides Internet access by connecting to cell towers, and also creates a private Wi-Fi network that your devices can connect to. Anywhere you travel, so long as you have good access to your provider's cell towers, you can have reasonably fast Internet service using the hotspot's Wi-Fi network. Of course, this hotspot feature costs money. If you decide to purchase this hotspot service, remember to configure this Wi-Fi network securely and according to the principles you've learned in Chapter 10.

Once you have connected to any Wi-Fi network and have access to the Internet, you are sending and receiving a lot of data. The next section covers how to protect this data in transit.

D. DATA AND TRAVEL

Quick tips:
- Don't bring sensitive information with you that you don't need.
- Sensitive data stored (at rest) on your devices should be encrypted.
- Use secure data transfer for important and sensitive work (e.g. HTTPS not HTTP).
- Ensure two-step authentication is enabled for your cloud accounts.

1. Data You Bring (Data at Rest)

Think about the data that you are bringing with you when you travel, notably, the data that resides in your laptop. If you are storing sensitive data on your laptop that doesn't need to be on the laptop, you should securely delete that data.[1] Otherwise, you are creating a risk for no benefit—you are risking the loss or theft of sensitive data when you have no need to carry that data

---

1. As we mentioned in Chapter 8, there are free tools that assist with this, such as CCleaner by Piriform.

around. If your laptop is lost or stolen, you put yourself and your clients at risk for no reason.

Whatever data you are bringing with you on your devices, consider how it is secured within your devices. All of your devices have at least some sensitive information stored in them, including stored usernames and passwords, which allows the devices to automatically access your cloud accounts, e-mail, calendar, and contacts. For these reasons, all of your devices need to be physically secured, and also password protected. If you have sensitive data within your laptop, that laptop computer should be encrypted, with a strong password.

2. Data You Access (Data in Transit)

Most of us store our data in a variety of places, including the cloud, the devices that stay at home, and the devices that travel with us. Your personal preferences and needs inform how and where you store your data. In Chapter 9, you evaluated your data-related habits and customs; now we review them through the travel lens.

For most of us, when we travel, we are still accessing data stored in a public-type cloud, such as your cloud-based e-mail, contacts, calendar, and documents. In many ways, this cloud data remains just as available to you when you travel as when you are at home. That's an amazing benefit of cloud storage. The more you travel, the more the benefits of cloud storage are apparent.

When you travel and access your cloud data, whether it is your e-mails, calendar, contacts, or documents, your device must communicate with the cloud provider, and that might mean connecting your device to a local network and the Internet. You already know the potential dangers of connecting to the Internet through public networks, or any network that has users on it who you don't know or trust. Aside from the dangers near you, when you communicate with another device or person through the Internet, the data you send and receive makes a long trip and passes through many waystations. All along the trip there are opportunities for someone else to eavesdrop on your communications. Think of Internet communication as sending a postcard through the U.S. Mail—anyone who handles that postcard can read what has been written on it.

Fortunately, there are ways to protect your communications from being accessed on public Wi-Fi networks, and while in transit through the Internet. By encrypting the data while it's traveling from your device and across the Internet, you can make the data difficult—or nearly impossible—to decipher. If we consider network and Internet traffic as postcards through the U.S. Mail, there is no privacy if you write the contents of the postcard in regular

English. Without some form of encryption in transit, you are sending data in clear text, and anyone along the way can read it. However, if you send a message written in an encrypted code, it's like sending it in a locked box. You can maintain the confidentiality of that message, and you can decide who should get the key to decrypt and read it.

There are two primary techniques to encrypt data in transit: HTTPS or secure access to a website, and virtual private networks (VPN). More and more websites now transmit their data to the user in an encrypted format called HTTPS, rather than using unencrypted HTTP sites. All of the major e-mail providers (e.g. Gmail, Yahoo, Hotmail, Apple, etc.) offer web access through HTTPS sites, meaning that the e-mails, calendar information, and documents that you are downloading and uploading cannot be read while in transit.

The data is encrypted between the provider (e.g. Gmail) and your device, and is protected all along the route, within your local network, and as it traverses the Internet from your local network to the provider. Using HTTPS is seamless. If the website you choose to visit is hosted as HTTPS, your browser and that website will do everything needed to encrypt and decrypt the communications without any input from you. Someone snooping on your Internet traffic will know that you are connecting to Gmail, but they won't be able to see or read what you are sending or receiving.

A VPN is a connection method via a tool you obtain from an Internet company that offers this service. A VPN connection means direct encrypted access from your device to their server, and their server acts like midpoint or "proxy" between your device and the rest of the Internet. To make use of a VPN connection, you need Internet access and a VPN software application from your VPN provider. You then connect to the VPN server through a virtual encrypted "tunnel" that eavesdroppers can't break into and you send your communication to this proxy server encrypted. The server receives it, decrypts it, and then reroutes it to its final destination on the Internet, such as the website you are visiting. When the recipient of your communication (such as the website) responds, it returns to the VPN provider's proxy server, which encrypts it and sends it back to you—through that same VPN tunnel. This VPN tunnel allows your communication between your device and the VPN proxy server to be secure, and no one can snoop on it because of the encryption. While someone snooping on your traffic may know that you are connecting using a VPN, they can't see the data you are sending or receiving, or even which websites you are contacting.

VPN options are becoming more common for the individual user. Google offers a free VPN service for its Chrome web browser which you could choose to enable. Google's Android Wi-Fi Assistant offers a free service that uses public Wi-Fi networks to connect to Google's VPNs, protecting your communications as they traverse the public network. There are many other VPN services that are available, though you should find one that is reliable, reputable, and with an appropriate privacy policy. It is possible for criminals or a nation state to establish a VPN service in order to eavesdrop on customers' Internet communications. All VPNs come with a downside because they may cost you money, and they can slow down your Internet traffic. Many larger businesses and firms rely on VPNs so that employees can remotely access files.

If your data is stored at home or at work—rather than the cloud—and you want to access it when you travel, there are ways for you to configure some form of remote access. Remote access is like having your own "private cloud," and there are many remote access software solutions. However, setting up such a system is an advanced technique, and you must be extremely careful that you configure it securely. Remember that if you create remote access for yourself, you have also made it possible for hackers to gain this same access to your data. You will need to dedicate special work and maintenance to keep it running, available, and secure, and it is not recommended except for the technologically advanced.

E. MISCELLANEOUS ANTI-FRAUD WHEN YOU TRAVEL

As we have covered, the main fraud risk when you travel is loss or theft of your devices. Don't leave them unattended, and be wary of even putting them down momentarily. But there are other threats from criminals and unethical people when you are outside your home. Someone might "shoulder surf" and look over your shoulder at your laptop screen out of curiosity or in the hopes of learning confidential information that might be of value to them. A privacy screen can help minimize this threat, as can awareness about how your screen is positioned and who can see it. Shoulder surfing threats when traveling are not limited to your device's screen. It's also a concern when you enter your PIN at an ATM machine or store checkout, so be aware of who might be watching when you enter your PIN or password.[2]

Finally, if you should have your wallet and devices stolen when you're traveling, it is good to know, in your brain, some emergency phone numbers to reach your family or work. It is good for your family to have access to certain emergency information or contact information so they can assist

---

2. Note that some identity thieves even install a camera so that they can record your fingers entering the PIN on the keypad. Coupled with an electronic skimmer device that records your card information, they have obtained enough information to steal cash from your bank account. Thus, your awareness should be not just of people but of unusual devices such as cameras and skimmers.

you. This might include data accessible from a tablet you left at home, printed recovery codes for cloud accounts, or a printout of an itinerary or address book.

F. SPECIAL CONSIDERATIONS WHEN TRAVELING TO CERTAIN COUNTRIES

Travel to certain countries puts you at special risk for spying by sophisticated nation-state hackers, or cybercriminals who need not fear law enforcement. For example, advisories warn that travelers to China and Russia may be subjected to espionage attempts, their devices may be hacked or searched, and their Internet traffic may be eavesdropped upon.

That's a very different danger than the constant threat of cybercrime-for-profit. Cyberattack from a sophisticated country is very difficult to defend against. A nation state could eavesdrop on all of your Internet communication, either from the computer you are using, within a local network, or at the Internet level. The nation state could attack and infect your device with sophisticated malware that cannot be detected. Your cybersecurity dial should be elevated when you travel, especially to countries that are the subject of cybersecurity warnings. Some steps that can mitigate these threats are:

- Check with your IT department before traveling. There may be policies and procedures you need to comply with.
- Back up your data before you travel.
- Don't bring devices if possible.
- Consider purchasing temporary devices for exclusive use on that trip.
- Don't do any operating system or software updates while on foreign soil—they might be malicious.
- Follow heightened security procedures, and disable unneeded features.
- Don't bring data or sensitive data you don't need.
- Consider creating a temporary e-mail account for exclusive use on that trip.
- Don't access your sensitive e-mail accounts or data while in that country.
- Temporarily disable all remote access capabilities connecting to your home or office.
- Decommission the device when you return to the United States (e.g. a "full device wipe" and reinstall operating system and applications).
- Change your passwords when you return to the U.S.
- Consider using a VPN for all Internet activity.

G. CONCLUSION

Leaving the safety and security of your home exposes you to cyberthreats and other threats. Protecting yourself starts with keeping custody of your devices, turning your Wi-Fi and Bluetooth adapters off when you don't need them, and avoiding public Wi-Fi networks, public computers, and any computer that might not be trustworthy. Be conscious of the data you are carrying, minimize potential harm, and be aware of what your devices are broadcasting about you.

CHAPTER 13

Secure the Work Office

A. INTRODUCTION

This chapter, like the previous chapter, does not break new technological ground. You already know the basic principles, the technology fundamentals for your devices, data, and networks, and how to secure them in your home and home office. As we turn our focus to securing your office systems, the scale may expand, but you will still be applying the same principles that you applied in your home and home office. Some of the differences we will be considering in the workplace include the type of workspace and location, and if you have employees or coworkers, there will be more devices, more data, and your network will probably be more complex.

The principles of CIA—confidentiality, integrity, and availability—still apply. The principles of securing your devices, data, network, and Internet access still apply. It remains essential to secure yourself, to be knowledgeable, and exercise common sense in the face of cybersecurity and fraud threats. No matter the size of your office, or the size of your client's business, all of these essential elements continue to be important.

It is quite possible that your information technology (IT) systems at work are not much more complicated than your system at home. An "IT system" is just a fancy way of describing the devices, method of storing and sharing data, router, and network. About one-half of all lawyers in private practice are solo practitioners, and another fifteen percent of private practice lawyers are in an office with fewer than five attorneys. This means many attorneys can have IT systems at work that are similar or even identical to what they have at home. Thus, an attorney in a solo or small firm who is capable of handling a home IT system may be able to administer a small work IT system as well.

At a certain point, it becomes too time-consuming or specialized for non-IT professionals to maintain their own systems by themselves. The more attorneys and employees in your office, the more users and devices there are, expanding the volume and complexity of your network, and probably requiring IT specialists to set up and maintain systems. As such, a small firm may wish to hire an outside IT company to handle its needs, whereas a large firm likely will develop an in-house IT department.

Even if someone else runs your computer and data operations, don't abdicate responsibility for having an efficient and secure IT ecosystem. You are now educated and empowered to ask good questions, evaluate the responses, and take charge of shaping your firm's cybersecurity. Regardless of the size of your office and the number of employees, you need to accept responsibility and pay personal attention to information security. If you are running an office and directing IT professionals, you need to emphasize that having a working system also means having a secure system. In other words, part of the IT professionals' job must be security, protecting data and keeping cybercriminals out, not just ensuring that the system "works" for the user. Many IT professionals are focused on keeping things running and available for the users; you need to ensure they also pay attention to keeping things secure and confidential. A "working" IT system is like a working front door—it not only opens to let you in and out, but it can be closed and locked to keep burglars and thieves out.

There are controls your IT team can implement to greatly improve security, such as two-step authentication to access e-mail or document stores. In the home, these changes are pretty simple for you to configure yourself for your own accounts, and hopefully, you have done so. For work, this is even more important. You should evaluate the threats and risks, and consider the potentially devastating financial and reputational costs of a serious breach. Those possible harms outweigh the minor inconveniences involved with implementing security measures. In your home, with personal data and accounts, your cybersecurity choices are mostly personal, and the consequences are mostly personal. In your workplace, a data breach or cyberattack will cost money, lost productivity, and reputational damage, and could even cripple your business.

Each employee adds a human factor, and your employees may not have taken the time to read a book like this one. They may need training to prevent them from becoming an unwitting portal through which you or your firm becomes a victim of cybercrime or fraud. If your employees are trained well and are aware, they can be transformed from a threat vector into a threat sensor to protect your firm.

Improving your cybersecurity posture at work has multiple benefits. When you approach it holistically, it's an opportunity to improve efficiency, productivity, business continuity planning, and anti-fraud measures.

The threats to your office include some of the same dangers that you face in your home and personal life, as well as other significant threats targeting businesses and their interests. The same cybercrime economy we've discussed in earlier chapters, fueling a wide range of frauds against individuals, also creates scams to steal from businesses and their employees. Beyond cyber fraud, there are teenagers or budding hackers out there, who are looking for a conquest—for a Wi-Fi network, business website, or network to hack—but don't care about your business in particular. Then, there's the possibility of a more dedicated adversary, who has targeted your firm or one of your clients. Your job is to employ reasonable security measures in relation to all of these threats, to make it difficult for the criminal to break into your system, and to try to detect the attempt. And of course, there is always traditional theft to worry about—burglars or thieves looking for valuables and electronics.

Lawyers, Professionals, and Their Secrets

The attorney–client privilege and the attorney duty of confidentiality are ethical standards with an important cybersecurity component, as we discuss in the next chapter. Attorneys may be working on highly sensitive matters, entrusted with highly sensitive secrets. Suppose an attorney represents an organized crime member who is a criminal defendant, charged with serious crimes. The defendant's criminal associates may be very concerned that he has turned into an informant, and is cooperating with law enforcement. The associates may brainstorm about how they can find this out, and one method is to look at the attorney's files, whether by breaking in to the attorney's office physically or electronically. Alternatively, an attorney might represent someone on a pending business deal, and inside knowledge of that deal might be worth a lot of money.

Every attorney has secrets and confidences they need to keep, and these confidences create professional obligations. All of this confidential data is an information security risk. Your clients probably have similar responsibilities to keep their information secure, whether they are a psychiatrist or other physician recording medical confidences, a scientist conducting research, an accountant or financial adviser who stores clients' tax records and financial information, and so on. In all these industries, a malicious person might be interested in client files, medical records, personal information, or some other component of these confidential records, providing another critical reason that lawyers and others must provide adequate security for the data in their control.

B. THE WORKPLACE MENTAL ASSESSMENT

Now is the time to mentally assess how your work setup differs from your home setup, and how those differences affect your security. When you evaluate what is different (such as location, and perhaps the number of people), and what is similar (devices, data, and a network), it's easy to see that a number of learned concepts translate nicely to the workplace. A few new factors you need to consider include:

- The security of your office
  - How is access controlled during the day for visitors?
  - How is the office secured at night from break in?
  - How do you secure sensitive materials in the office?
- Your employees
  - Number of employees and coworkers
  - Screening process
  - Training process and awareness of cybercrime and fraud
  - Use of employer-provided IT for work and personal use
  - Use of personal IT for work use
- Devices in the office
  - How many computing devices are in the office?
  - Are work devices used for personal purposes?
  - Do employees take devices home?
  - Do employees use their personal devices for work?
  - Is there an office policy on device usage and privacy?
- Data
  - Where is your data stored?
  - How often is it backed up, and where are the backups stored?
  - What measures are in place to secure sensitive client and employee data?

- Network/Internet
  - Who administers the network and reviews the settings periodically?
  - Do you have a diagram or description of your network?
  - Are the passwords complex and changed periodically?
- Anti-fraud
  - Do employees know the common fraud schemes?
  - Have they been trained on what to do when they encounter suspicious e-mails, links, etc.?
- Business continuity and disaster recovery
  - What is the plan if your office building is destroyed by fire, flood, or other disaster?
- Incident planning and response
  - Do you have a plan if you are hit by a cyber intrusion or ransomware?
  - Do you have a plan if you are the victim of a data breach?
- Cyber insurance
  - Have you evaluated obtaining insurance for various cybercrime events?

C. PHYSICALLY SECURE YOUR OFFICE

Quick tips:
- Consider what measures are in place to prevent and detect burglars and thieves, both during and after business hours.
- Evaluate what sensitive or confidential information might be posted, or left open to view.

When we addressed cybersecurity in your home, we assumed that it was a safe place, occupied by your trusted family, that it wasn't broken into regularly by burglars, and that you were not routinely allowing strangers to come in and out. Given this assumption, we glossed over certain principles related to physical security as they relate to information security.

Now that we have switched focus to your work office, a place of business, that means reexamining physical security. Physical security is important because that's where cybersecurity starts. If you have confidential papers and electronic devices containing confidential information all around the office, a thief, cybercriminal, or spy could simply walk off with your papers, phone, laptop, or server, unless the office is physically secured.

1. Visitor Entry
You should evaluate physical security at two different time periods: during business hours and after business hours. Each workplace is different, with

varying security concerns and vulnerabilities. During the workday, there may be a lot of traffic through the workplace, with many visitors, clients, potential clients, delivery people, and other individuals whom you don't know personally. This traffic can allow thieves to slip in unnoticed and steal. Thievery aside, you don't know the people you do business with as well as you know the people who visit your home. You don't know about their other business dealings, family, and associates, and the possible motivations they carry. Even if they are not tempted to steal anything, they may accidentally see or hear something that was supposed to remain confidential.

After business hours, offices are generally unoccupied, providing a long, undisturbed opportunity for burglars and thieves to sneak in or break in. During off-hours, cleaning personnel and security guards may have access to the premises, which can be a good way to prevent burglars from breaking in; however, if one of these workers is corrupt, then he or she has an opportunity to look around at confidential information and even to steal.

Physical security in the office starts with controlling physical access by thieves, burglars, and spies. Evaluate how access is controlled in your building and office. Some professional offices open directly to the outside, so once the visitor enters the building, they are in the office. For these types of offices, there is only a single layer of screening and defense, but you can retain control with good reception policies at the door, and by ensuring the door is monitored any time it is unlocked.

Some offices are within larger buildings, so a visitor first needs to gain access to the building, then navigate through elevators or halls to the office, where the visitor can be greeted and screened. This type of office setting provides additional layers of security since there may be building security staff, an entry procedure for the building, and possibly building video surveillance. However, the building might not do a good job screening visitors, and a person who slips though security may be free to roam the building unnoticed.

Consider that building security can have an effect on privacy and confidentiality, and you might have no control over the information that the building collects. Security measures can include identification checks, scanning of identification documents, lists of scheduled visitors, video surveillance, and even facial recognition. All of those measures mean the building is collecting and storing information about your visitors and clients, which could be an issue if you want to keep the identity of certain clients confidential. Further, the screening process could be annoying to your clients if it is not done efficiently and politely. Here, as in many other areas, there are tradeoffs between security, ease of access, and privacy. Good building managers will be sensitive to liability and reputational risks due to poor security, and to the business advantages of efficient and discrete security.

The Office Creeper

A great cautionary tale on the importance of physical security comes from a case I prosecuted involving a serial office thief, known as an "office creeper." For the longest time, all the evidence we had was a photo and physical description of a person responsible for about twenty separate thefts. He casually and confidently walked into the various offices as if he belonged there, strolling past receptionists like he was a regular. If there was an access control device, such as a swipe card reader to open a locked door, he circumvented it by waiting for someone to exit or enter, and then he would walk through—a technique called "piggybacking" or "tailgating."

Once inside, he walked with confidence, looked for unattended offices or cubicles, and looked for wallets, purses, or devices on the desk or in a drawer. He would steal what he could, and then make a casual exit. This thief liked cash and credit cards, using the credit cards in stores to buy clothes, electronics, or gift cards. These twenty-plus incidents were identified thanks to video surveillance systems, either in the offices, or later in the stores where he was using the stolen credit cards. Finally, he was caught in the act one day and he fled, running out of the office, down the stairs, and through the streets, while being chased by office workers. He ran past a police officer, who joined the chase and eventually caught him.

Though this thief focused on wallets and purses, there are many thieves out there who choose to target electronic devices. Many of these thieves sell or "fence" the stolen devices, never intending to steal or utilize

> the data stored or accessed by the device. But it's not inconceivable that experienced thieves might be hired by spies or cybercriminals to steal electronic devices specifically for the purpose of analyzing them for the data inside them. These kinds of specialized criminal rings have been identified in the past, and there's every reason to believe there will be more of them as devices and technology become ever more prevalent in our lives.

Even if the building's security is partly outside of your control, you do have control over your own office space. The first step to protecting your office is ensuring that anyone who steps into your office is promptly and professionally greeted by a receptionist or other employee. You don't want visitors strolling in unnoticed and walking around. A practice of escorting all visitors can be welcoming for the authorized visitor, while simultaneously deterring and detecting unauthorized intruders. Within your office, if an employee sees an unescorted visitor, they can pleasantly and helpfully ask who they are going to see and if they need assistance. Good visitor screening prevents not only cybercriminals, thieves, and spies from getting in, it also prevents unexpected visitors from appearing when you are not prepared, or have sensitive papers out in plain view.

Consider limiting access to your own office room by locking the office door when you are not there. Sensitive documents or electronic devices can be further secured by placing them inside a locked filing cabinet or desk.

2. Locks and Doors

After business hours, good physical security means making things difficult and time-consuming for burglars and thieves. You want to make it hard for them to break into your office, and set up security measures so that a burglary will not go unnoticed when you come to work the next morning. This process starts by locking the front door, office doors, and file cabinets at the end of the day. If you leave your office open, and leave your file cabinets open, you might not even notice that someone has been in your office, reading and photographing all of your files. You may not think to review your property to see what was stolen. Locking doors and cabinets means burglars need to break them open, since most burglars don't know how to pick a lock. This added inconvenience is a significant deterrent to many thieves. And even if a thief is not deterred, when you come to work the next morning, you will learn of the crime from the broken locks and you will call the police. Since police will be able to investigate soon after the commission of the crime, there is a chance they will obtain some evidence that might help them catch the thief.

As a state trooper, I investigated hundreds of theft-related cases that were reported by victims, and as a prosecutor I handled hundreds more, this time after the police were able to make an arrest. Finding out about the theft soon after its occurrence is crucial. If the time of theft is merely approximate—a range of days, weeks, or months—then the chances of solving the crime are diminished greatly because it is unlikely that any evidence will be found. If the theft occurred long ago, there may be no point in even looking for fingerprints, DNA, or video evidence. The more time that goes by, the more likely that such evidence is lost, that employee's fingerprints and DNA are comingled in the crime scene, and the video data has been deleted. In contrast, if you come in the next morning and notice your office door was broken, your filing cabinet pried open, and items stolen, you can freeze the scene, call the police, and they can take pictures, look for fingerprints, DNA, and canvass your building and the neighborhood for witnesses and video surveillance.

Thus, having and using a lock is a great first step. But not all locks, doors, and door hardware are the same, nor are they necessarily installed in the correct manner. A flimsy door secured with flimsy security features might open with a single kick, whereas a door with good security features may hold even after many kicks, or withstand specialized tools, like crowbars. A door is only as strong as its weakest link, so factors such as the material of the door (hollow core, solid core, wood, steel), the type of lock securing the door (low-security latch lock versus high-security deadbolt), the strike plate, and the door frame, are very important. The longer it takes a burglar to get in, and the more noise he has to make, the better off you are.

Good Door, Bad Door

When I was a trooper, I sought to execute a felony arrest warrant. I learned the defendant's current address but he never seemed to be home. I contacted the landlord, who said the defendant was always at home, so I asked the landlord to meet me at the apartment and let me in. The landlord didn't want to be bothered and told me to just kick the door down, the door was really flimsy, and he would come later in the day and fix it. I couldn't convince him otherwise, so I confirmed the apartment number with him and off I went to get my man. I banged on the door again to give him another chance, then I banged on the apartment next door for good measure (maybe they knew where my suspect was) but there was no answer.

I gave my suspect's door a good strong kick, expecting the door to blast open as the landlord had predicted. Instead, it didn't budge at all, and by kicking against a solid door, I almost knocked myself backwards, off the narrow stairwell landing and down the stairs. I regained my balance and I started kicking the door until it finally broke open after about a dozen kicks. I entered the apartment, ready to hunt down the suspect, but instead I found a nicely tended apartment, decorated and with family photos, and no one was home. It was clear that I was in the wrong apartment. I called the landlord back, who told me for the first time the correct apartment number of the defendant—next door.

I went next door and banged on the door again, yelled through it, but of course he didn't open it or say anything. I gave his door a single strong kick and it practically flew off the hinges, he was hiding in a closet and I apprehended him without further incident. The landlord fixed both doors, and all was forgiven by the resident of the other apartment.

Though you are not going to have state troopers kicking your door down, a burglar might try out his karate kicks on it. You are better off if your door can survive a number of kicks before failing. That noise may make the burglar nervous enough to abandon the mission. A good door has a solid core and high-security hardware and strike plate, with long screws that penetrate deep into a solid door frame.

3. Alarm Systems and Video Surveillance

An office burglar alarm can deter burglars and reduce the amount of time they are willing to spend on-site looking for valuables or data, since they will be worried that police or security will arrive quickly. It also means that you might be alerted to the break-in immediately, which helps with the investigation. A specific time and date of occurrence helps investigators gather evidence, as compared to a broad and vague time or date range. Of course, having a burglar alarm also can result in false alarms, which means you will be contacted every time the alarm goes off, and law enforcement or security guards will need to respond, and possibly you. There might be a fee for such responses, plus the inconvenience and drain on resources, so you should do your best to reduce the number of false alarms.

Video surveillance is now an inexpensive and ubiquitous option for improving workplace security. The presence of video cameras can deter burglars and thieves, and the footage provides valuable evidence in the event of a theft. Most video surveillance systems today offer conveniences such as remote access and monitoring, and communicating through an existing Wi-Fi network, reducing the need to run cables.

You should be aware that video cameras create cybersecurity vulnerabilities. If you can view your office's video surveillance via the Internet, then there's a possibility that this system could be hacked, allowing criminals to have the same clear view of your office, employees, and clients. If the security cameras communicate the video feed wirelessly, remember that wireless signal is never as clear and continuous as a wired cable, and it is subject to being intercepted, so it needs to be encrypted. You should also consider segregating the security camera Wi-Fi network from other Wi-Fi networks in the office. Remember also that poorly secured video cameras and other IoT devices can be hacked and controlled by malicious cybercriminals.

If you have a video surveillance system, you should understand the privacy and security risks that accompany it. When employees and clients are being recorded, there are privacy implications—your video footage might document every client that visits your office, and every time an employee takes a restroom break. Here are a few other physical security tips:

- Employees should promptly shred sensitive paper documents, not leave them lying around or place them in the trash where criminals can "dumpster dive" looking for sensitive information.
- Adequate exterior and interior lighting can deter crime, especially when coupled with video surveillance.
- Proper key control means keeping track of who has office keys, and changing locks periodically, including when keys are lost or former employees are a threat.

4. The "Plain View" Doctrine in Your Office

In order to maintain information security for your physical documents and notes, you should consider prying eyes, or even casual eyes, once people are in your office. You've done your best to keep unauthorized people out of your building, rooms, and cabinets; here we look at what information is available to someone who gains access. That person could be a potential client, delivery person, cleaning person, or thief.

The first step is to evaluate what is in plain view when you take a look around your office. What paper documents are readily visible? What is written on post-it notes and stuck on a wall or cubicle? Obviously, you should not have passwords written on your computer monitor, under your keyboard, on your laptop, or in your desk drawer. You should not have sensitive information posted on your walls or left out on your desk. This type of information should only be available to individuals with a "need to know." If it's out in the open, you're making it available to anyone who has access to that area.

Some offices have a "clean desk" policy. At the end of the day, or even whenever the employee leaves the desk, all work is put away so that nothing is visible to a passer-by. Some policies, for offices handling highly confidential information, even consider what can be viewed by someone outside the office peering in with a telescope, and may require computer monitors to be positioned away from the windows, and blinds to be down. On the other side of the spectrum are those who have permanent piles of papers everywhere on their desk and it's a wonder they ever find anything. Many of us have left confidential papers unsecured without thinking about it, or a confidential diagram on the conference room whiteboard for all to see. As with all things security, it's up to you to find the right balance between the extremes of no security and excessive security.

D. SECURING YOUR EMPLOYEES AND COWORKERS

When you shift your cybersecurity focus from your home to workplace, the first major change is location, and next is the addition of employees and coworkers. The presence of other people affects the security of the office in a number of ways. Each additional employee in the office increases the complexity of the IT systems, since it increases the number of devices and the amount of data to manage. Each additional person also increases the opportunities for data breach, cybercrime, or fraud by increasing the "attack surface." When more people are involved, there are more devices to secure, a larger network to maintain, and a greater risk of human error; thus, more people can mean more vulnerabilities. Fortunately, it's not all bad news, because each additional well-trained person in the workplace also presents an opportunity to detect or prevent an attack, vulnerability, or fraud.

1. Screening and the Insider Threat

Fraud prevention starts with hiring and working with people of good character who are not inclined to steal or sabotage. Try avoid hiring a problem employee who later goes on to steal money or secrets, as this will save much aggravation, time, and money. Of course, it is hard to predict in advance who will turn out to be a good hire or bad hire, but once you learn that a good hire was made, retaining that employee is important. Employee turnover means starting the screening and hiring process again, which is costly, creates disruption in the office, and adds another person to the list of those with inside knowledge of your office systems and their security.

Some employees would never do anything improper, whereas some might if the conditions allow it. For all employees, tone is important, and that is set at the top. Tone is set informally every day, and helps establish what is acceptable and proper, and what is not. Tone, properly conveyed and received, can be more important than written policy.

As organizations grow, more formality is required, and a step towards that is written policies and procedures. Briefly, a policy is a high-level guiding principle that sets a general direction, while a procedure is a granular-level set of steps that are to be followed to accomplish a task. Policies, since they are broad, guiding principles, are more lasting and changed infrequently. Procedures, however, will need to be updated more frequently since they are detailed steps that need to be adjusted to changing circumstances.

Reasonable policies and procedures can keep your business running efficiently, promote security, increase resilience against a disaster, and reduce the chances of cybercrime and internal and external fraud. These policy and procedure documents should be reasonable and practical, and should be followed by employees. It is not enough to set policies and procedures and then turn a blind eye as to whether they are functional, or if they are followed or flouted. Unrealistic policies and procedures create cynicism and confusion, because employees need to navigate between the plain written word of what the rule is, and the informal practice of determining how things "really work."

2. Training

By reading this book, you are amassing a great deal of practical knowledge. By picking up the book in the first place, you already had a strong realization of the threats you face and your responsibilities. Others in your office may not give cybercrime or fraud a single thought, nor be aware of the many threats your firm faces every day. Such employees create a risk for your firm, and that's why awareness, training, and procedure are important. Every person in your circle who has weak cybersecurity or poor anti-fraud awareness is a portal through which criminals can attack. If the managing partner or a particular employee has his or her e-mail compromised, that is a vector through which the criminal can learn secrets, gather intelligence, and impersonate selected individuals to commit a fraud. Even when you have trained all of the people within your workplace, each person needs to be vigilant to threats that can come from outside your workplace, including clients, vendors, or suppliers who have become compromised themselves.

The Security Bubble

The Secret Service keeps their protectees in a "bubble" of security, and the size and strength of that bubble is dictated by the person and the threats against him or her. This bubble might mean that anyone who gets within a certain number of feet of the protectee has been screened for weapons, or that anyone who enters the building has had a background check performed. Sometimes the Secret Service creates multiple concentric bubbles around a protected person, and as one travels closer to the center, the bubbles are of increasing security.

With this book, you created a cybersecurity bubble in your home when you evaluated all of the devices, systems, and people inside your home, and all of your data that you access outside your home. Your devices, router, e-mail accounts, and social media accounts all have potential vulnerabilities, and by now you have secured them to a degree, as well as securing your family members. These efforts have created a zone of safety, commensurate with where you have chosen to set your "security dial." But now, as you extend your review to your work office, you are coming outside the security bubble of your home that you created. So, you need to work to extend that security bubble to your workplace.

Of course, you want to keep cybercriminals and fraud-sters from getting into your bubble. They can get into your bubble in some creative ways, such as when they hack a friend or business associate's e-mail account, or even computer. Also, they may insinuate themselves into your social media network. There are many LinkedIn and Facebook profiles that are set up in fake or assumed identities, and some of these are controlled by fraudsters or intelligence-gathering spies. If you blindly accept all LinkedIn or Facebook requests, you will let fraudsters or intelligence gatherers into your bubble, allowing them an opportunity to gather information about you and all of your connections.

Training does not have to be a formal event with a lesson plan and a Pow-erPoint presentation. It can be done informally, when the issue arises, taking five minutes within a conversation or a staff meeting. When you are teaching employees about a policy or a procedure, it is highly effective to discuss *why* the procedure is important. An employee who mindlessly works through a procedure checklist without understanding the basic concepts could miss the forest for the trees. You want an employee who knows the policies and proce-dures, understands and follows them, and has good habits. Such an employee will be able to spot new threats as they evolve.

3. Shadow IT in the Office

Shadow IT describes when employees use devices, data storage, and informa-tion technology practices that are not approved by the employer. An employer might have specific IT resources which are monitored and secured, and the policy requires all employees to use these resources for all work functions. However, when employees do their work with their personal resources, out-side of the systems provided by the employer, they are doing it in the "shad-ows," and outside of supervision or oversight by the IT department. Even if we don't remember ever hearing the term, most of us have used shadow IT in some form.

Shadow IT includes the use of personal e-mail for work, such as e-mailing a work document to or from a personal e-mail account, or using (outside of an office policy) personal devices like a smartphone, laptop, or home computer to do work. In some workplaces, there may be an official policy that allows the use of personal devices for work, so-called bring your own device policies (BYOD), which mean personal device use is authorized and out of the "shadows." Often, BYOD policies mean the employer has installed significant technical controls on the employee's device.

Shadow IT can be prevalent when employees become frustrated with their existing IT resources, including with restrictive security controls, and they feel the office is not meeting their needs to get their work done. They search for and use unauthorized workarounds which are more convenient for them, such as storing and sharing company documents and data in an unapproved Google Drive or in Dropbox accounts, or using personal e-mail accounts.

The consequences of Shadow IT can be severe. If employees are poorly trained and are not aware of cybersecurity risks, they might transmit and store confidential information within personal e-mail and cloud accounts that are poorly secured. These accounts might have weak passwords and single-factor authentication, among other significant security weaknesses. Shadow IT puts workplace activity and data outside of the employer's review. If the employer doesn't know what data is there, it can't be found, backed up, secured, or reviewed in order to respond to discovery requests. Moreover, if an employee has a laptop that is infected with malware, and they plug it into the office network, that malware can spread to other devices on the network.

To avoid negative consequences of shadow IT, you should start by training your employees about good cybersecurity habits. That way, even if they use shadow IT (and violate your policy), the chances of a data breach or network infection are minimized. In other words, don't make your first priority to clamp down on the shadow IT policy violations, but instead educate employees to be secure both at home and work. This approach will, in essence, broaden and strengthen their security "bubble," and recognize that shadow IT will occur occasionally, including when emergencies arise. You want your employees' personal systems to be secure when this happens.

You should also examine the reasons, or root causes, that lead your employees to use shadow IT. Are your employees finding your systems so inadequate that they resort to using personal workarounds? At work, as at home, you need to decide where to set the security dial, and balance the need for security with the need for availability. If you set the security dial at "11" in the workplace, employees may become frustrated with a system that makes it difficult to do their jobs. They may find the work systems so locked down—and secure—that they feel the need to resort to using personal devices and accounts to get their work done.

Shadow IT

Like all of us, I have used shadow IT on occasion. While working in government, the e-mail system was not perfect, and sometimes interfered with essential communications. The spam filter was distrustful of any e-mail that contained a language other than English, and occasionally deleted these e-mails without telling me or the sender. This created confusion and miscommunication until we realized what was happening, and we started to confirm receipt of each e-mail so the sender knew it had come through. Though the spam filters blocked important e-mails from trusted senders, they somehow allowed typical spam through, promising low-price medications and performance enhancers. The work e-mail system also blocked large attachments, whereas my free personal e-mail provider had generous size allowances. These work restrictions meant that I occasionally used my personal e-mail to send or receive work-related e-mails.

Shadow IT exists in part because IT and cybersecurity are imperfect and represent a compromise between security, availability, and reliability. To ensure that systems work properly, don't crash, and are secure, IT departments and firms need to enforce certain rules and standards. Some of those rules include ensuring that certain features are locked down, and cannot be changed by the user, and that certain features are unavailable to the user. But these situations can cause frustration, and when this occurs, employees may try to find a workaround.

There is no perfect answer, but a key part of the solution lies with addressing the human component of computing—educating and training people to think about cybersecurity and the related issues. The cybersecure employee who temporarily resorts to shadow IT will do so with a secure device, secure cloud account, awareness of the digital footprint, and will delete data from unapproved locations when it is no longer needed. The employee may have violated policy, but will have minimized the risk of compromise.

Another approach centers on providing IT resources to the employees that meet their business needs, so they are not tempted to use their own methods and resources. Tools, policies, and procedures need to be reasonable and realistic to be effective. Finally, if employees are properly trained, resources are adequate, and policies and procedures are reasonable, then enforcement needs to take place to ensure employees are doing their work in the required manner. Spending time and effort to create cybersecurity and IT policies is of no benefit if they are not followed.

4. Acceptable Use of Workplace Computers

The inverse of shadow IT (using personal computing resources for work) is using workplace computing resources for personal use. Your company should have an "acceptable use" policy for the office's computing resources. You should start with the premise that any computer usage exposes the computer and network to compromise, so reduction of non-essential use will reduce risk. That said, in many work settings, it is reasonable to allow employees some personal use of workplace computing resources, whether that is incidental web surfing (such as checking the news), or perhaps checking personal e-mail occasionally. The idea is to reduce personal usage to what is appropriate, does not greatly affect the security of the work network and data, and does not interfere with job performance.

Employees should not use office computing resources in any manner that creates a high risk for exposing the computer to compromise. They should not be visiting sites or engaging in activity that is inappropriate or illegal, such as viewing information from hate groups, looking at pornography, file sharing, or harassment. Further, computer activity from your workplace might be traceable to your firm, such as through the IP address. Thus, you should consider whether it is permissible for an employee to write blogs, review restaurants, or edit Wikipedia pages using workplace devices or Internet connections, for example.

Your firm's acceptable use policy should also indicate that the user has no expectation of privacy for activities they perform with your equipment and systems. A notice of this is usually provided to the employee at every sign-in, indicating their usage will be monitored, including to ensure that policies are complied with.

E. SECURE THE DEVICES IN YOUR OFFICE

We've just covered two areas that change considerably when you shift your cybersecurity focus from your home to your work office—a new location, and the addition of employees and coworkers. Now, it's time to return to the major topics we covered in the home, starting with devices.

The first step is to conduct an inventory of your office devices. You need processes to inventory the devices you have, to purchase and configure new devices, and to securely decommission devices at the end of their service life. In the home, it may be sufficient to create a mental list of your phones, tablets, laptops, and desktops. In the workplace, with more people and more devices, a written list becomes necessary. Large companies use asset-tracking software, while a small firm could keep a list in a document or spreadsheet.

You will have choices regarding how much trust to place in each user, and to what extent options on the computer should be "locked down," meaning the user would lack the ability to change, or even access, certain settings or applications. Secure configuration means: (1) they should have only the software and features needed to perform the required tasks, (2) the operating system and software on each device should be kept updated and patched, (3) each device should be routinely scanned with anti-malware software to keep it malware free, and (4) devices should not be used for risky or inappropriate computing activities.

If your workplace has laptops or other devices that leave the office, and if they contain sensitive or confidential data, you should implement full disk encryption on them, with a strong password. Loss or theft of portable devices is all too common, and full disk encryption is your best defense against loss of data if this should occur.

F. SECURE THE DATA IN YOUR OFFICE

Here, apply what you learned in Chapter 9 to your data at work. Most importantly, make sure you back up your data regularly, and store it in a place that is safe from burglary, fire, and ransomware—probably off site.

If an analysis of all of the data in your workplace seems daunting, then be comforted by the fact that you have already evaluated and started to address the massive amounts of data you store at home. You might take thousands of photos per year, and store huge quantities of music, videos, and documents, not to mention thousands of e-mails. In that context, your work data might not seem so daunting.

Conceptually, your first thoughts should be:

- Where is my data?
- What types of data do I have? How sensitive is each type?
- When and how often is my data backed up? Where are my backups?
- Is sensitive or confidential data encrypted when it is at rest (stored)?
- Is sensitive or confidential data encrypted in transit (when transmitted through the local network or Internet)?

1. Network Storage Devices in Your Office

If you are a solo practitioner, it might be acceptable to store your data on the hard drive of your desktop computer, and back it up periodically to an external hard drive that you store in a safe location. With larger offices, it becomes necessary to store that data not on individual computers, but on a company-wide network storage device—a server. This method allows everyone's data to be backed up in a more efficient manner, since it is all stored on the company server, rather than individually on each user's computer. It also allows certain data to be shared among multiple users, which would be difficult to accomplish if data was stored on individual computers.

If you have IT professionals administering your company server and your network, they probably don't want you adjusting anything. But it is still important to review how data is stored, and this provides an opportunity for you to have a conversation with them about security.

2. Documents and Data in the Cloud

The ready availability of cloud services has changed things tremendously for small and large businesses. Before these cloud services became popular, businesses had to administer their own servers to store their data, and that required considerable expertise and effort. Companies needed their own servers, their own data center, and either in-house IT professionals, or had to outsource these tasks to an outside IT firm. Now, cloud providers offer inexpensive solutions for storing and accessing your data so that you don't need to have your own server, nor hire your own IT professionals. Microsoft, Google, and many others offer you the capability to store your data and documents in the cloud, instead of within your office. They even offer these services for free or at low cost to non-profits.

These cloud services can include an entire suite of applications designed to handle all of your business needs, from timekeeping, to billing, to document storage, and more. Not only will these public cloud companies store your data, they will also provide you with the applications to manage it. This type of service can simplify a number of office operations, and eliminate the need for many firms to have in-house IT professionals, saving time, effort, and money, if your needs fit the offerings.

In many cases, public cloud services are run extremely well and extremely securely—probably much better than you could do yourself. They have teams of experts making sure systems are patched and regulations are complied with, while continually working to keep criminals from getting in. That said, you bear the responsibility for ensuring your cloud accounts are secured with a strong password and two-step login. It doesn't matter how securely the provider runs the cloud operation if your credentials are compromised and the criminal can log in as if he were you. No matter whose services you use, and how well they say the services are secured, you bear the ultimate responsibility for the security of your credentials, data, and systems. Again, all cloud accounts, including your social media accounts, should be secured with good passwords and two-factor authentication. Chapter 9 covers that in more detail.

3. E-mail

Your work e-mail contains a lot of important and sensitive information. Chances are very good that you have tens of thousands of e-mails stored in the "cloud," plus all of your contacts' information. We discussed the cyber threats to your personal e-mail, and so it should be obvious that the threats and risks for your business e-mail are far greater. Can you imagine if the entire contents of your office e-mail account were exposed to a cybercriminal, identity thief, adversary, or the world through WikiLeaks? Two-factor authentication is necessary to keep your e-mail secure from these threats, but, unfortunately, it is not implemented by many attorneys. Take the few minutes to implement two-factor authentication for your e-mail, and spare yourself the tremendous aggravation and embarrassment of an e-mail compromise.

4. Data at Rest

If you have a server in your office, it should be physically secured, such as in a locked closet or cabinet. Backups should be securely stored as well. Of course, every device should require input of a password to access it. And if employees have laptops that they take out of the office, and those laptops contain sensitive or confidential information, those laptops should be configured with full disk encryption.

5. Data in Transit

We covered the topic of securing the data you transmit through the network and Internet in Chapters 9 and 10, and we will touch on it in the next section as well. The data you send through your internal network, through a public Wi-Fi network, and through the Internet can be intercepted, and encryption can help secure data in transit. Consider using a VPN to access your confidential data when outside the office—we'll cover that in a moment.

6. Business Contacts and Social Media

You should check your LinkedIn and other social media accounts for contacts from whom you may have blindly accepted connection requests, and who might be imposters, fraudsters, or intelligence gatherers. If fraudsters are connected to you, it gives them credibility and the opportunity to connect to your contacts, leading to bad results for you. Your legitimate contacts may be duped by the fraudster, thinking the fraudster is a real person connected to you. Or some of your contacts may spot the fraudster, and wonder why you have allowed fraudsters into your social network.

If your firm has its own social media account, consider reviewing its followers for these fakes. In addition, you may hear of companies or celebrities that pay for social media followers, but you should never pay for followers or friends. It might be tempting to amass what appears to be a large following, but it can create digital clutter in your contacts that is hard to unwind, and it can make it hard to separate real people from fake people and fraudsters.

G. SECURE THE WORKPLACE NETWORK AND INTERNET USE

In Chapter 10 we secured your home network, here we will apply that to the office network. Certain security controls that might have been unnecessary or even unhelpful in the home may end up being helpful in the workplace, and in addition, certain assumptions made for the home don't translate in the workplace. We expect to have ubiquitous Wi-Fi in the home so that we can access the Internet at any time, no matter where we are and what we are doing. However, the office environment creates different priorities.

The risks of a Wi-Fi network in the office could outweigh many of the benefits. You should decide if Wi-Fi is merely to provide Internet access for employees and visitors, or whether it is to grant access to the company's internal network and data. The principles of "least privilege" apply, in that if a person merely needs Internet access, they should not be provided with more than they need, such as access to the company network. If some employees need Internet access, and some need both Internet and network access, then you could implement separate Wi-Fi networks so that there is segmentation between levels of access and types of use. Guests should not use the same Wi-Fi network for the Internet that employees use, because the guest Wi-Fi network name and password are likely to be disseminated further. Also, you don't want those with guest access to be able to eavesdrop on the Internet activity of employees.

The traditional professional office has employees coming to their office or cubicle every day, and sitting behind their desktop computer that is connected to the network and Internet via Ethernet jack and cables wired in the walls. As long as the employees do most of their work from their office, behind their desks and computers, there may be no business need for Wi-Fi. However, many employees might like Wi-Fi Internet access to connect their business or personal smartphones and tablets. You need to evaluate the implications of the use of Wi-Fi and these personal devices at work, and whether that need should be accommodated.

Further, many companies, such as tech firms, startups, and others, are breaking from that traditional setup. Instead of working from desktop computers in offices or cubicles, employees may travel more, work from home or the road, and when they come in to the office they might not even have a dedicated workspace. Employees might rotate among available space as needed, working from their laptops while remaining connected to the Internet and company network. That's a scenario that requires a Wi-Fi network, and since it is being used to access all company data, it needs to have a high degree of security: an innocuous name, and a very strong password that is changed frequently.

When we secured your home Wi-Fi network, it was acceptable to let your Wi-Fi signal blast at maximum power, since most homes use a single Wi-Fi router to cover the whole house. But at work, you need to reevaluate that idea, and think about how to limit the distance that your Wi-Fi signal travels outside your office. Imagine your firm's wireless signal broadcasting into the parking lot, and a cybercriminal who parks there for hours on end, comfortable and undetected, as he takes his time to break into the network: don't make it so easy for the criminal.

When we secured your home, we figured it was impractical to turn off your Wi-Fi, except perhaps, when you leave for a vacation (assuming it wouldn't also disconnect any "smart home" devices). At work, that might be different. The office is generally vacant at night and most weekends, so having the Wi-Fi network on when no one is present creates an unnecessary risk of the Wi-Fi being hacked. Also, the stakes are higher when it is your livelihood in the balance, and it is your professional responsibility to limit risks and safeguard information. It's not simply a matter of personal preference, but a decision to protect your firm, employees, and clients. Thus, it might be a good practice to turn off the work Wi-Fi at the end of the workday, because the one way to ensure that no one hacks into your Wi-Fi network is for it to be off. Before shutting down your Wi-Fi at night, ensure that your security systems don't rely upon it. Also, don't name your Wi-Fi network after your firm or business name, because that makes it too easy for a hacker to target you.

In the home, we recommended against implementing MAC filtering, because this security measure can be troublesome without significant benefit. At work, it provides important security protections. MAC filtering is a control where the router only allows known, registered computers join the network. If a particular computer's MAC address has not been previously approved ("whitelisted") by the administrator, then the computer will not be allowed to join.

In the workplace, MAC filtering—or other types of network access control (NAC)—may be warranted, since it not only protects against the casual hacker, but against the unwitting employee who tries to connect an infected device to your company network. If a visitor or nighttime burglar tries to plug a laptop into an Ethernet jack to access the network, MAC filtering or other NAC can prevent them from getting network access. Similarly, if an employee tries to connect a personal computer to your network, access will be denied. This control helps protect data, and protects your systems from potential malware infections that unauthorized devices might have. MAC filtering can be implemented through your router's administrator portal, but remember that it alone will not prevent a sophisticated hacker from gaining access. Other forms of NAC are going to require an IT professional to implement.

Sometimes, a Wi-Fi network might seem convenient compared to running cable to each room and workstation, but easy setup doesn't mean it's the best long-term solution. Remember that Wi-Fi will always have a higher security risk because the data is transmitted through the air, and available for capture by hackers. Plus, wireless never transmits data signals as well as cable, because it does not work well through solid walls and doors, and there might be interference due to other wireless devices or networks. Wi-Fi might seem convenient because it allows the user to continue working seamlessly on their tablet or laptop as they move from room to room, but given the relatively low cost of devices, it may be more effective and efficient to have dedicated devices in each room, connected by cable to your network.

Depending on the size of your workplace, it doesn't take much until your network has expanded well beyond "do it yourself." Home routers and Wi-Fi devices might be inadequate for larger offices. For larger networks, you may need to rely upon IT professionals to implement solutions, but you are equipped to ask the right questions and ensure that security is a priority.

War Driving and Wi-Fi Hacking

Albert Gonzalez was a hacker who stole millions of credit card numbers by "war driving." He drove near retail stores and identified and then hacked into their wireless networks. The retail stores had committed a host of cybersecurity sins, including poorly secured wireless networks, poorly segmented networks, and poor data practices, so once Gonzalez hacked their network, he had the freedom to explore and ultimately access millions of customers' credit card account data. Of particular relevance for this section is that the retail stores' Wi-Fi networks unnecessarily broadcast too far, enabling Gonzalez to hack them from the comfort and anonymity of his car in the parking lot.

In your firm, and for your clients, the location, direction, and transmission power of each of your Wi-Fi access points can be adjusted to keep the Wi-Fi signal inside your office, with minimal leakage outside.

Gonzalez had a long, lucrative, and interesting cybercrime career, which included double-crossing law enforcement, but justice prevailed in the end.[1]

---

1. *See* Kim Zetter, *TJX Hacker Gets 20 Years in Prison,* WIRED (Mar. 25, 2010), https://www.wired.com/2010/03/tjx-sentencing/.

H. SECURE THE WORKPLACE FROM FRAUD

Quick tips:
- Know your clients and customers.
- Don't accept payment from third parties unless you have verified everyone's identity and role in the transaction.
- Have a phone call to verbally confirm any payment instructions.
- If it's too good to be true, it probably is.

Lawyers and professionals need to have cybersecurity and anti-fraud awareness so that they do not become fraud victims, and so that they do not become unwitting tools of criminals. As individuals, and in our homes, we face these same risks, but in the workplace the threats are greatly increased. In our home, we are very aware of every entity we accept money from, and every entity we send money to, but in the workplace, this is not always the case. Payments can be flowing faster and at greater volume, and we deal with people we do not know as well. The first steps in preventing fraud are being a knowledgeable user, practicing good cybersecurity habits, and exercising common sense.

1. Protecting Your E-mail Accounts

We've covered this security tip repeatedly: you must secure your e-mail accounts with strong passwords and two-step authentication. A rampant type of criminal fraud relies upon the hacking of an e-mail account, and then using this e-mail account to send fraudulent bank wire instructions to unwitting parties, under the pretense of conducting a real business transaction. Lawyers, real estate brokers, and anyone involved in sending or receiving payments and bank wire instructions are at high risk for this fraud. Some of these criminal schemes are quite sophisticated. The criminals hack an e-mail account and monitor the communications and patiently wait for the perfect time, and then impersonate the e-mail account holder and misdirect funds so that they are stolen and not recoverable. Do not allow your e-mail account to be hacked and used for this purpose. This type of fraud is called CEO fraud, CFO fraud, or business e-mail compromise fraud. An example of this is in the sidebar.

Business E-Mail Compromise Scam Example

In this fictional example, an attorney is responsible for negotiating a litigation settlement, real estate transaction, or business deal, and has negotiated the details with the other party's attorney. The next step is to communicate to the client how payment should be made to the other party.

However, the attorney's e-mail account has been hacked, unbeknownst to him, and the hacker is monitoring all the communications, waiting for an opportunity to misdirect funds. At the right moment, the hacker impersonates the attorney, and directs that the client wire funds to accounts controlled by the hacker.

Attorney: Dear Client: The seller has agreed to the price of $125,000. He'll need the payment ASAP. Send it to the bank account we previously discussed.

Client: That's great news, I'll do that today.

"Attorney":   One thing has changed. Wire the funds to ABC Corp., Bank of XYZ, Account Number 123. This must be done as soon as possible. I am unavailable by phone due to meetings but please get this done ASAP and we'll talk later.

(This was sent by the hacker, impersonating the attorney.)

Client: Thank you, I'll wire the funds.

Five hours later...

Client: There's a problem with the wire, can you call me?

"Attorney": It's OK. I checked with the bank, and seller. It's just a minor mix-up, the funds went through fine. I'll call you tomorrow.

Next day...

Client: We need to talk now. My bank says there is fraud involved.

The hacker has done a lot of work behind the scenes to delay discovery of this fraud, and to launder the funds so they are not recoverable.

2. Confirming the Authenticity of Payment Instructions Sent to You

You know how important it is to keep your e-mail secure, but others may not take the same precautions that you do. Anyone who e-mails you instructions to send funds might have had his or her e-mail hacked, thus you should orally confirm any payment instructions or suspicious requests. Most financial institutions have a policy of requiring an oral confirmation of bank wire instructions, and you should also. But don't just go through the motions, and "check the box" to conduct this oral confirmation.

Instead, use that opportunity to make or continue a personal connection with the person, not only to verify their identity and the circumstances of the payment, but as a business development technique. Ask about the payment and what it is for, and how they got the payment instructions—make sure they have had a phone conversation with anyone who directed them to make the payment. Ask about their family and what is happening in their work and life. This is a good opportunity to get to know your clients and customers, especially in an age of electronic communication where we tend to overlook the personal touch. Sophisticated criminals can spoof caller IDs, and can even redirect phone calls in certain circumstances, and they may try to impersonate someone during a phone call. If you already know the client, you will detect this scam. Of course, if the e-mail tells you the wire is needed urgently but the person is unavailable to talk by phone, then your suspicions should be heightened.

3. Escrow Operators ("Money Mules") and Money Laundering

Escrow operator and "money mule" frauds are common, and lawyers are at high risk for these crimes because one of the professional functions of a lawyer is to negotiate settlements and receive or pay funds on behalf of clients. In this fraud, the criminals hire the attorney to represent them and direct a large sum of money to the lawyer. The lawyer is asked to receive the money, pay a portion of it out, and retain the balance as payment for legal services. This seems like an easy legal engagement, minimal work, with a lucrative legal fee. The payment is received and appears legitimate and seems to clear the bank, so the lawyer issues a check or sends a bank wire to the third party as directed by the "client." Sometime later, the lawyer gets an unpleasant phone call from the bank or a victim, and realizes the initial payment to him was fraudulent, either with a forged check or from a hacked account. The lawyer is responsible to pay back this money out of his own pocket, and soon learns he has been an unwitting accomplice to a serious fraud.

Money Mule Fraud Scam Example

In this example, the attorney is contacted by a cybercriminal who purports to be a potential client. In reality, the cybercriminal wants to send the attorney a fraudulent check or bank wire, and get the attorney to wire funds to him before the funds are identified as fraudulent.

"New client":	Dear Attorney, I am located in the country of ABC, and I am due to receive a large payment in connection with a settlement. I need to hire an attorney in the United States to review the documents, and receive the payment. This is extremely urgent, and I am sure you are busy so I am willing to pay you well. Would you handle this for a fixed fee of $X?
Attorney:	Yes, I can handle that for that amount. Here is an engagement letter, please send me the documents and details.
"New client":	Thank you. Here are the documents. As I indicated, I need this sale to go through ASAP. Widgets Corp. will wire funds into your account this afternoon. As soon as you get the funds, please keep $X as your fee, and wire the remainder to me at XYZ Corp., Bank 123.
Later...	
Attorney:	Dear new client: I received the funds from Widgets Corp., then wired you the funds. Now, my bank says there's a problem with the wire from Widgets Corp. I have left messages at the phone number you provided. Please call

> me ASAP. I need you to wire the
> funds back to me.
>
> "New client":   I can't call now. Don't worry, I
> talked to Widgets Corp. and it's
> just a misunderstanding.
>
> Of course, it's not a "misunderstanding" but fraud
> committed by the "new client" and his associates. Not
> only has the attorney unwittingly assisted in a fraud
> and provided funds to a criminal, he or she may be civ-
> illy liable to repay the full amount of any funds that he
> or she received.

The solution is to know your client, payors, and payees, and ensure they are really who they say they are. If payment is supposed to come from the client, don't accept payment from third parties. If payment is coming from a third party for a good reason, the lawyer must conduct due diligence to ensure payment is really coming from that third party and is legitimate. Before sending any payments out, the lawyer should ensure there is no discrepancy between the recipient and true beneficiary, and that he knows who the true beneficiary really is.

A forged or fraudulent check that you deposit into your account may take a significant amount of time—weeks or more—until it is identified as fraudulent. You may think the check has cleared because the funds are made available to you, but if it is later identified as fraudulent, you are responsible for the full amount of the funds, even if you have withdrawn or forwarded the funds as requested by the client. Consider that an identity theft victim may not learn about an unauthorized bank wire or check until they review the bank statement, or realize their account has been drained. That could delay their reporting of the fraud to the bank, which delays the bank from notifying the recipient and requesting return of the funds. If you received a fraudulent bank wire or check and then forwarded the funds in the interim period, you will be responsible for repaying your bank, which is responsible for repaying the sending bank.

Remember, if the names and entities of sending and receiving parties do not match, and if there are convoluted explanations for why they don't match, that could be indicative of fraud, or even money laundering. As we will discuss in the next chapter, lawyers should not be used as a tool to launder funds. Applying anti-fraud principles (knowing the client, source, and destination of funds) will also protect you from being an unwitting accomplice to money laundering. If the names and accounts don't match the true identities of the sender and receiver, it could be because the client is trying to hide that true information from the banks and authorities.

4. Cybersecurity and Anti-Fraud Policies and Procedures

Your review of policies and procedures should be done with an eye toward cybersecurity, anti-fraud measures, plus the overall health and efficiency of your office. Try to look at this issue holistically. You may be able to improve your cybersecurity and simultaneously improve your IT efficiency, minimize the unneeded data you are storing, and satisfy e-discovery requirements. Traditional anti-fraud controls like dual control, segregation of duties, and proper oversight and monitoring have relevance not only to prevent and detect embezzlement, but can also help fight cybercrime.

Embezzlement can occur if too much trust and control is placed in a single individual, such as the bookkeeper, who is predisposed or otherwise tempted to steal. Many people running a business wish to avoid accounting and bookkeeping tasks, and are happy to delegate that to an individual and then forget about it. Some attorneys dislike math and numbers, and may be tempted to avoid thinking about these areas. However, a single corrupt employee who controls multiple areas in the accounting process can divert funds and simultaneously cover up this theft. The best way to prevent and detect this type of theft is to have additional people involved in those processes.

Dual control and segregation of duties involve additional people in the process, to prevent theft by a single corrupt employee. Dual control means that two people need to act together in order to make something happen, such as if two signatures are required on a check above a certain amount in order for it to be properly issued. Segregation of duties means that various functions are split up, so that a single person is not in control of the whole process. For example, a person who writes checks should not also reconcile the bank statements. Instead, a second person should receive the bank statements and handle that task. These controls make it much harder for a single corrupt employee to steal, and they make detection much easier. Another technique is to have independent oversight and monitoring, such as having an outside accountant periodically review the books and records, whether that is monthly, quarterly, or annually. It could also mean periodic review of the books by a lawyer or managing partner.

Practices that can help prevent internal fraud can also prevent external fraud and cyber fraud. If your systems ensure that multiple parties are required to independently confirm the sending of a bank wire, you are not only protecting against internal fraud, but you are protecting against social-engineering-type frauds. Thus, if a single individual's e-mail account was hacked and the hacker orders a wire transfer, the transfer will need to be reviewed by a second individual before it is authorized. In addition, verbal confirmation of financial transaction requests not only helps confirm that the initial request is proper, and was not sent by a hacker, but helps confirm the reason for the bank wire, and offers an opportunity for detection of a fraud.

I. BUSINESS CONTINUITY AND DISASTER RECOVERY PLANNING

Chapter 4 covered this topic in a conceptual sense, now is the time to do this planning for your office. You cannot predict the exact disaster, and it could be anything from a list of horribles: fire, flood, earthquake, terrorist attack, mass shooting, and cyber incidents, as discussed in the next section.

What if one of these incidents occurred, and your workplace was suddenly unavailable? What would you do if everything in it was destroyed? Where are your backups? How will you get your business going again? Businesses of varying size have different requirements and thus varying approaches. A large financial institution that needs to keep running without interruption will have redundant IT systems, and even pay for a vacant office building many miles away that is move-in ready—a "hot site" or "warm site." That might not be practical or cost effective for you, but you should find a comfortable middle ground, something that is more than just doing nothing.

Some of your most valuable assets may be your data, so having it backed up securely and available off-site is essential. Having up-to-date contact information for your employees, coworkers, vendors, and business associates can also be essential. That is one of the great benefits of cloud data storage—the provider has invested significant resources into ensuring your data remains available for you. After an emergency, you may need to reach them, post information to your website, and have your office phone number rerouted. The key is to spend a little time planning before a disaster strikes.

J. INCIDENT RESPONSE PLANNING

Quick tips:
- Think about a cyber incident (data breach, ransomware) before it happens.
- Make sure your data is backed up periodically.
- As you think and learn about incident response for yourself, it will also help you to advise your clients.

Much of the literature on data breach planning and incident response can be daunting, and it might seem tempting to delay that planning. The good news is you have made it through the book this far and you have already taken many steps towards planning for a cyber incident, perhaps without even knowing it.

Planning for your own future data breach or cyber incident provides you with multiple benefits. Thinking about these threats will propel you to take security steps that greatly reduce the risks. If security is implemented properly, it means greater efficiency for your IT systems and use. Further, working on this issue for yourself helps you to better serve your clients because many individuals and small and large businesses do not plan for, or even think about, the consequences of a cybersecurity incident. They want to believe that it will not happen to them. You are now in a position to advise them about the criminal threats they face, and the consequences, including legal and liability issues detailed in the next chapter.

Perhaps not surprisingly, data breach planning literature written by lawyers emphasizes the importance of obtaining legal counsel to help handle and investigate cyber incidents, keep communications and facts under legal privilege, and work through the aftermath. That is probably good advice for the clients; however, many cannot afford to hire specialized attorneys for this purpose, or simply won't bother to do so. This book gets you started with some of the legal aspects you need to think about for yourself, as well as your clients.

Thinking through a cyber incident before it occurs is extremely valuable for planning and efficiency purposes. Chapter 14 briefly discusses the laws of various states when it comes to data breaches and legal responsibilities to secure data to prevent a data breach. Chapter 15 discusses troubleshooting various issues.

What follows is a general guideline to get you started:

1. Preparation for incident: This is the most important phase. Preparation includes reading this book, improving your own knowledge, looking through all of the steps below and identifying who would perform the steps. Take steps to improve your security and avoid an incident, and ensure your data is safeguarded, including being backed up regularly and securely. Items to identify during the preparation phase are:
   a. People: Who will handle the incident from inside and outside your organization? Make sure contact information for the following is printed to paper and available.
      i. Designated incident handler
      ii. Legal counsel
      iii. Insurance company
      iv. IT personnel to be notified

       v.   Location of backed-up data

      vi.   Digital forensics investigation and recovery personnel

     vii.   Law enforcement agencies to be notified

   viii.   Public relations

  b. Policies and procedures: What are in place? If nothing is written down, it would be good to draft something that covers these topics.

  c. Acceptable down time: How long can you afford for your system to be down? Reducing down time will cost you money, not just now but as a monthly investment.

  d. Cyber insurance: Evaluate whether you might need cyber insurance. If you have it, write down the contact information to make a report. Evaluate what your existing insurance might cover.

2. Identification of incident: How to identify whether it is an event (an IT issue) or a cyber incident, the severity of it, and who is to be notified? Preserve evidence.

3. Containment of threat: The process of containing a cyber intrusion to keep it from spreading or causing more damage. In your home or small office, you will probably contain it by taking everything offline.

4. Eradication of threat: The process of getting rid of the cyber intruders and malware. This step could require expensive digital forensic work, or reformatting your computers and reinstalling the operating systems and applications—it could mean purchasing new computers. Then, your backups need to be restored.

5. Recovery and resumption of normal operations: Ensuring everything is back in operation and working properly.

6. Aftermath: Ensuring that laws, regulations, and good client/customer care principles are followed. In the rush of the incident and emergency, some steps may have been overlooked or forgotten. Ensure notification of law enforcement and customers was complete. Ensure follow-up requests from law enforcement, customers, and media were addressed. Consider whether there is a need to prepare for lawsuits or regulatory actions.

7. Lessons learned: Take a moment to regroup, learning from what happened to prevent it from happening again, and to improve the response next time.

K. CYBER INSURANCE

Cyber insurance is a popular topic, because many cybercrimes and incidents are not covered by traditional insurance. The selling points of cyber insurance are that a cyber incident can cost you a fortune, given the many specialists you need to hire, including lawyers, digital forensics experts, public relations personnel, plus the potential costs of lawsuits and regulatory actions. The cybercrime itself might have stolen money from you or a company with which you do business. All of those risks mean that cyber insurance sounds great—you buy it and you can be worry free, knowing the costs will be covered.

Not so fast. Of course, you can't be worry free. The thought of going through a cyber incident should bring anxiety, and actually experiencing such an incident will be a massive headache and require much of your time. You want to avoid it if at all possible, whether you are insured or not. Also, know that cyber insurance policies are usually preceded by detailed applications. These applications inquire about your IT, cybersecurity, and anti-fraud technology, policies, and practices. Much of the time, the applications ask very good questions, and good responses will reflect sound cybersecurity policy and procedure which a company is wise to follow, whether or not they get cyber insurance. If you have not yet prepared for a cyber incident, if you have not taken a good look at your cybersecurity posture, then you are probably not ready to complete one of these applications. However, the applications can be a good starting place and impetus for you to get started. That's why I've placed cyber insurance last—there's a lot you need to accomplish before you complete and submit that application for cyber-related insurance.

Cyber insurance will, of course, come at a cost. The benefit is that if you have an incident, many costs of dealing with it will be presumptively covered, and you may have a readily available network of lawyers, digital forensics firms, IT professionals, and public relations firms to assist in the incident response and investigation. However, insurance companies don't automatically approve every claim, and some claims can be more difficult than others to process, depending on the company and circumstances. When you completed the application, you put detailed information about your firm's policies, procedures, and practices in to it, and if your firm's actions before the cybercrime differed from your stated procedures in the application, expect a difficult time getting the claim approved. The insurance company may argue that they insured you based upon the information you provided, and that the information you provided was inaccurate, and thus the claim should be denied.

L. CONCLUSION

You have had a chance to apply your cybersecurity skills and knowledge to your office, and you are aware of the information security and fraud threats you face. If you rely on others to administer your IT, cybersecurity, and physical security, you are now in a position to ask thoughtful questions and evaluate the responses. By doing this, you can ensure that your "security dial" is set to where you want it to be, and that others in your office understand that their responsibilities extend to security.

CHAPTER 14

The Law, and the Role and Responsibilities of Lawyers

A. INTRODUCTION

Cybercrime, cybersecurity, and information security are issues of which everyone should be aware. We all need to secure our homes and workplaces in order to protect ourselves, our families, and our clients. As attorneys, we have special responsibilities because of our professional duties to keep the confidences of our clients—which necessarily includes keeping our data secure. Attorneys can also be specifically targeted by cybercriminals based on our occupation, the nature of our business, and our clients.[1] Some lawyers were drawn to the law because of an affinity for words and an aversion to numbers and technology, which can make the profession especially vulnerable to cybercrime threats.

Other professionals and general business owners also have specific legal obligations, and there is an evolving body of law and regulation that imposes cybersecurity and privacy requirements. In general, if a business stores personal information about others, or stores secrets or private information, it has a duty to store and secure that information responsibly. The lawyer is in a unique position, not only responsible for being secure, but also for advising clients on the legal and regulatory risks faced and how to secure oneself and manage the risks. This chapter focuses on these special responsibilities, and conducts a brief survey of the laws that pertain to cybersecurity.

---

1. *See, e.g.,* David Lat, *Beware of Big Hacking in Biglaw,* ABOVE THE LAW (Mar. 30, 2016), http://abovethelaw.com/2016/03/beware-of-big-hacking-in-biglaw; Kirk Semple, Azam Ahmed, and Eric Lipton, *Panama Papers Leak Casts Light on a Law Firm Founded on Secrecy,* New York Times (Apr. 6, 2016), http://www.nytimes.com/2016/04/07/world/americas/panama-papers-leak-casts-light-on-a-law-firm-founded-on-secrecy.html; Debra Cassens Weiss, *Don't Click! Lawyers Get Fake Emails About a Complaint; Hyperlink Installs Malicious Software,* A.B.A. J. (Dec. 5, 2016), http://www.abajournal.com/news/article/dont_click_lawyers_get_fake_emails_about_a_complaint_hyperlink_installs_mal/; Press Release, New York State Attorney General, *A.G. Schneiderman Issues Alert on Phishing Scam Targeting New York Attorneys* (Nov. 30, 2016), http://www.ag.ny.gov/press-release/ag-schneiderman-issues-alert-phishing-scam-targeting-new-york-attorneys; District of Columbia Bar, *Email Phishing Scam Targeting Attorneys* (Dec. 2, 2016), https://www.dcbar.org/about-the-bar/news/phishing-scam.cfm.

This responsibility to safeguard information exists no matter where you are working or storing your data. Your work doesn't stop at the office door; rather, it follows you from the workplace, to your home, and wherever you travel. In today's cloud computing era, we access our data no matter where we are. That's why this book urges you to create a "bubble" of reasonable security around you, from home to office to wherever your travels may take you.

Before discussing some of the applicable rules, remember that requirements may be vague, and may change and evolve. Sometimes they are good, clear, and timely, but sometimes they aren't and might be reactive and outdated. Occasionally, organizations focus on complying with the letter of the rule, and overlook the underlying purpose. If compliance is the concern that sparks you or your client to embark upon a cybersecurity review and fortification of your defenses, that's great. But don't make changes just to "check the box," simply certifying in a document that you are complying. That is not real compliance and ignores the threats you are facing. Always try to keep your eye on the underlying goal—to improve your defenses and avoid being victimized.

You'll hear phrases like "reasonable" cybersecurity measures. "Reasonable" may not seem helpful in the cybersecurity context and may cause some to wonder, "How can we know what to do if they don't tell us?" For lawyers, we are used to the "reasonable person" standard in many areas of law. Think of the "reasonable cybersecurity" standard as authorization to do the right thing, the common sense thing. Taking "reasonable" measures starts with doing *something*, evaluating your biggest threats and risks and addressing them in a prioritized manner. A good place to start this process is by addressing those employees (and partners and CEOs) who use passwords like "password." There is plenty of room for debate about where "reasonable" ends, but we know where it starts, so make sure you and your clients get going.

"Reasonable" Cybersecurity Measures

Many regulations are based upon "reasonable" cybersecurity measures. The definition of "reasonable" is subject to debate, but if you have employees or owners without cybersecurity awareness, using passwords like "123456," logging in to public Wi-Fi for sensitive and unencrypted communication, and storing customer information in an unencrypted Excel file available for anyone in the company to access, then you are exposing yourself to extreme risk of compromise. Do not be comforted by a written cybersecurity policy that is not followed, nor by a document indicating that everyone is "trained" when they did not learn anything from the training or perhaps did not even attend it.

Some clients might want to focus on written policies and procedures, and might want to ignore dangerous security habits that could be fixed promptly. From the client's perspective, regulators might seem to be a more imminent threat than cybercriminals—regulators might ask to see such policy documents at any time. It is far easier to create a paper security policy that sits in a file than to remake the security culture of all the individuals in an organization, to change the way they access documents, or to alter IT infrastructure. Of course, paper policies aren't enough to secure a client, especially if they are not followed. If the policy describes airtight cybersecurity when the practices are inadequate and have no relation to the policy, that will not be viewed kindly by regulators and insurers.

If a firm or company has poor practices, it is exposed to risks and more likely to be breached, resulting in greater scrutiny of practices and policy. It gets worse if that scrutiny reveals a sham compliance mechanism, full of security lapses and deficiencies that even a layperson would recognize. Consider how that will be received if exposed in the news, a court filing, or a plaintiff's opening statement. These types of poor practices should be corrected promptly, before a breach can occur.

That said, just because certain security measures aren't implemented doesn't mean the client is deficient—cybersecurity needs to be "reasonable" and that means room for reasonable disagreements about where the "security dial" should be set, and there is room for business decisions around the cost and benefit equation. By reading this book you have a solid understanding of where "reasonable security" begins.

Law Firms Getting Hacked

The hacking of the "Panama Papers" and publication of the stolen documents triggered the legal community to take sharper notice of cybersecurity. The law firm Mossack Fonseca was hacked, confidential e-mails and documents were publicized, and the firm and its clients were exposed to media and government scrutiny. The clients had gone to the firm for confidentiality to create off-shore corporate entities to store assets, giving the appearance that the lawyers were used to shield assets not only from government oversight and taxes, but also from controls against money laundering. Needless to say, this hack was devastating for the firm, which was itself raided by authorities.[2]

Mossack Fonseca is not the only law firm that has been hacked. Many firms are targeted by cybercriminals, many have been breached, and many have experienced the negative publicity and professional and business consequences that come with being a data breach victim. In December 2016, federal prosecutors charged three individuals with hacking into the networks of several large

---

2. *See* Kirk Semple, *Authorities Raid Law Firm at Center of Panama Papers Leak*, NEW YORK TIMES (Apr. 13, 2016), https://www.nytimes.com/2016/04/14/world/americas/authorities-raid-law -firm-at-center-of-panama-papers-leak.html.

law firms. The criminals made over four million dollars by trading on information stolen from the firms about pending mergers.[3]

Large law firms employ IT professionals to manage their devices, data, and networks, but the professional duty to keep confidential information secure cannot be delegated or abdicated. Large law firms are not the norm—half of the lawyers in the United States work in very small law firms with four lawyers or less. The IT ecosystems of such firms are much less complex, with lawyers more likely to be directly involved with IT and cybersecurity decisions.

---

3. Press Release, Department of Justice, U.S. Attorney's Office, Southern District of New York, *Manhattan U.S. Attorney Announces ... Unsealing of Charges Against Three Individuals for Insider Trading Based on Information Hacked from Prominent U.S. Law Firms* (Dec. 27, 2016), https://www.justice.gov/usao-sdny/pr/manhattan-us-attorney-announces-arrest-macau-resident-and-unsealing-charges-against. *See also*, Leslie Picker, *3 Men Made Millions by Hacking Merger Lawyers, U.S. Says*, NEW YORK TIMES (Dec. 27, 2016), https://www.nytimes.com/2016/12/27/business/dealbook/new-york-hacking-law-firms-insider-trading.html.

B. ATTORNEY PROFESSIONAL RESPONSIBILITY RULES ON CYBERSECURITY

As with everything involving cybersecurity, the rules for lawyers are evolving, but there are some clear guidelines about a lawyer's duties:

- Lawyers must keep information relating to the representation of a client confidential.
- Lawyers need to retain data, such as client files.
- Lawyers need to be competent with technology and keep current with changes.
- Lawyers need to take reasonable cybersecurity measures and exercise reasonable care.

Of course, compliance with the Model Rules and your state's rules does not mean you have satisfied all of your compliance obligations. You still need to comply with any applicable laws and regulations, such as federal and state cybersecurity laws, data breach notification laws, and data disposal laws, which are covered later in this chapter.

1. The American Bar Association and the ABA Model Rules of Professional Conduct

The American Bar Association's Model Rules of Professional Conduct ("Model Rules") are the primary professional guidelines for the legal profession, and forty-nine states plus the District of Columbia have adopted versions of them (California is the lone holdout). Though the rules of your state may differ slightly, they probably follow the Model Rules closely. Some Model Rules and accompanying comments were amended in 2012 to better address cybersecurity-related issues; over half of the states have formally adopted this change or otherwise acknowledge the ethical duty of technology competence.[4] Even if your state hasn't caught up to this change, you should be aware of it. Ingrained in the legal profession are the duties of competence and confidentiality, and the new amendment makes clear that these duties extend to technology. We will take a quick look at the relevant Model Rules, summarizing them here and providing you with a more complete excerpt within the footnotes.

The attorney duty of competence is set forth in Model Rule 1.1.[5] Though the rule does not specifically address cybersecurity or technology, the comments to the rule make it clear that a lawyer must keep up with technology and its risks and participate in study, education, and any continuing legal education (CLE) requirements.[6] Thus, cybersecurity is a professional responsibility. The CLE requirement further confirms this duty, since approved CLE courses addressing a lawyer's use of technology uniformly stress the need for proper cybersecurity.[7]

---

4. *See, e.g.,* A.B.A. Ctr. for Prof'l Responsibility Policy Implementation Comm., *Chronological List of States Adopting Amendments to Their Rules of Professional Conduct based upon the August 2012 policies of the ABA Commission on Ethics 20/20* (as of Apr. 3, 2017), https://www.americanbar.org/content /dam/aba/administrative/professional_responsibility/chron_adoption_e_20_20_amendments.auth checkdam.pdf.

5. ABA Model Rule 1.1, Competence:
> A lawyer shall provide competent representation to a client. Competent representation requires the legal knowledge, skill, thoroughness and preparation reasonably necessary for the representation.

6. Comment to Model Rule 1.1, par 8:
> (8) To maintain the requisite knowledge and skill, a lawyer should keep abreast of changes in the law and its practice, including the benefits and risks associated with relevant technology, engage in continuing study and education and comply with all continuing legal education requirements to which the lawyer is subject.

7. *See, e.g.,* David G. Ries and Ivan Hemmans, *Cybersecurity: Ethically Protecting Your Confidential Data in a Breach-A-Day World,* A.B.A. (Apr. 27, 2016), http://www.americanbar.org/content/dam/aba /multimedia/cle/materials/2016/04/ce1604lpi.authcheckdam.pdf.

This duty of competence should be viewed in the context of the lawyer's duty of confidentiality. Model Rule 1.6 requires the lawyer to keep information about the representation confidential, using "reasonable efforts to prevent the inadvertent or unauthorized disclosure" of client information.[8] The comments to this rule emphasize that confidentiality is a fundamental principle in the client-lawyer relationship.[9] The comments further stress that the lawyer must act "competently" to safeguard client information.[10]

These comments further discuss the standard of care to which a lawyer must adhere, and indicate that lawyers should take "reasonable efforts" to prevent access or disclosure. To assess what is "reasonable," one must evaluate the type of information, the likelihood of disclosure, and the cost and difficulty of safeguards.[11] The comments make clear that lawyers are also required to comply with any relevant state or federal laws, meaning compliance with

---

8. ABA Model Rule 1.6, Confidentiality of Information:
    (a) A lawyer shall not reveal information relating to the representation of a client unless the client gives informed consent ...
    (c) A lawyer shall make reasonable efforts to prevent the inadvertent or unauthorized disclosure of, or unauthorized access to, information relating to the representation of a client.
9. *See* Comment to Model Rule 1.6, par 2.
10. Comment to Model Rule 1.6, par 18:
    Acting Competently to Preserve Confidentiality.
    Paragraph (c) [of Rule 1.6] requires a lawyer to act competently to safeguard information relating to the representation of a client against unauthorized access by third parties and against inadvertent or unauthorized disclosure by the lawyer or other persons who are participating in the representation of the client or who are subject to the lawyer's supervision.
11. Comment to Model Rule 1.6, par 18:
    The unauthorized access to, or the inadvertent or unauthorized disclosure of, information relating to the representation of a client does not constitute a violation of paragraph (c) if the lawyer has made reasonable efforts to prevent the access or disclosure. Factors to be considered in determining the reasonableness of the lawyer's efforts include, but are not limited to, the sensitivity of the information, the likelihood of disclosure if additional safeguards are not employed, the cost of employing additional safeguards, the difficulty of implementing the safeguards, and the extent to which the safeguards adversely affect the lawyer's ability to represent clients (e.g., by making a device or important piece of software excessively difficult to use). A client may require the lawyer to implement special security measures not required by this Rule or may give informed consent to forgo security measures that would otherwise be required by this Rule. Whether a lawyer may be required to take additional steps to safeguard a client's information in order to comply with other law, such as state and federal laws that govern data privacy or that impose notification requirements upon the loss of, or unauthorized access to, electronic information, is beyond the scope of these Rules.

the Model Rules alone may not be sufficient. Further, attorneys must take "reasonable precautions" when communicating with a client.[12]

The comments to the Model Rules recognize that technology and norms are evolving, and what is "reasonable" should be tailored to the circumstances. The comments acknowledge that it would be impossible to specify the exact standard of care in the face of rapidly changing technology and threats; therefore, they don't seek to define specifically what "reasonable" cybersecurity or "special security measures" might entail. Further, just because an attorney has been breached or otherwise victimized does not, of itself, indicate a violation of professional duties. It is clear, however, that the attorney has a professional duty to maintain some reasonable degree of cybersecurity.

In 2014, the ABA went further when its House of Delegates passed Resolution 109, which encourages *all organizations* to develop, implement, and maintain an "appropriate" cybersecurity program, compliant with ethical and legal obligations, and tailored to the information to be protected and the type of the organization.[13]

In sum, the Model Rules—and the rules of each state—may not specify what constitutes "reasonable" cybersecurity, but the main lesson is clear, namely that doing nothing is neither an option nor a reasonable course of action. All professionals have a duty to evaluate their data and systems and take reasonable steps to secure them. For the many attorneys who have not given any thought to cybersecurity, now is the time to start. They should begin by evaluating their IT practices and correcting the most serious security issues first, like weak passwords, single factor sign-on, and unprotected networks.

---

12. Comment to Model Rule 1.6, par 19:
    When transmitting a communication that includes information relating to the representation of a client, the lawyer must take reasonable precautions to prevent the information from coming into the hands of unintended recipients. This duty, however, does not require that the lawyer use special security measures if the method of communication affords a reasonable expectation of privacy. Special circumstances, however, may warrant special precautions. Factors to be considered in determining the reasonableness of the lawyer's expectation of confidentiality include the sensitivity of the information and the extent to which the privacy of the communication is protected by law or by a confidentiality agreement. A client may require the lawyer to implement special security measures not required by this Rule or may give informed consent to the use of a means of communication that would otherwise be prohibited by this Rule. Whether a lawyer may be required to take additional steps in order to comply with other law, such as state and federal laws that govern data privacy, is beyond the scope of these Rules.
13. *See* ABA House of Delegates Resolution 109 of Aug. 12, 2014:
    RESOLVED, That the American Bar Association encourages private and public sector organizations to develop, implement, and maintain an appropriate cybersecurity program that complies with applicable ethical and legal obligations, and is tailored to the nature and scope of the organization, and the data and systems to be protected.

2. A Survey of Cybersecurity-Related Opinions and Issues

In this section, we'll briefly cover a sampling of attorney ethics opinions, focusing on some basic technology that lawyers use, such as e-mail, file storage, and social media.[14] The recommendations earlier in this book will serve attorneys well toward complying with ethical requirements.

a. E-mail

E-mail is generally considered a secure method of both sending and storing communications, including confidential communications. Attorneys would be unwise, however, to assume that they are permitted to transmit confidential information by e-mail with impunity or store sent or received e-mails within their e-mail accounts indefinitely.

As we've covered in earlier chapters, it's important to secure your e-mail account properly, including use of a strong and unique password and two-factor authentication. You should always be careful about how you address e-mails, lest they go to the wrong person. You need to be aware of the risks of an e-mail account compromise, either to your or the recipient's account. If a sensitive file is being e-mailed, consider application-level encryption of the attachments that are being sent,[15] with the encryption password shared offline (by text or phone), though this process can be cumbersome for regular use. Some opinions recommend e-mail encryption, but for an e-mail to be encrypted from sender to recipient (i.e., "end to end"), *both* parties need to be running compatible e-mail encryption software. Further, such end-to-end encryption does not provide protection if one of the e-mail accounts is hacked.

In the early days of e-mail, some questioned if lawyers could even use this new-fangled communication method. A 1999 ABA opinion held that using e-mail was an acceptable practice, and that unencrypted e-mail affords a reasonable expectation of privacy—the same level of privacy associated with U.S. mail and landline telephone communications.[16] With a better understanding

---

14. For a more in-depth view, *see* David G. Ries, *Safeguarding Confidential Information, Attorneys' Ethical and Legal Obligations*, A.B.A. (Apr. 2016), http://www.americanbar.org/publications/law _practice_home/law_practice_archive/lpm_magazine_articles_v36_is4_pg49.html. *See also* Sharon D. Nelson, David G. Ries & John W. Simek, Locked Down: Practical Information Security for Attorneys (2nd ed. 2016).

15. Such password protection prior to e-mail transmission of a file was recommended in a New Jersey ethics opinion. *See* New Jersey Ethics Opinion 701, *Electronic Storage and Access of Client Files* (Apr. 10, 2006), footnote 1, Advisory Committee on Professional Ethics, https://www.judiciary.state.nj.us /notices/ethics/ACPE_Opinion701_ElectronicStorage_12022005.pdf.

16. *See* ABA Formal Ethics Opinion 413 (Mar. 10, 1999). As this book went to press, the ABA issued a new ethics opinion that supersedes the 1999 opinion. *See* ABA Formal Ethics Opinion 477R (revised May 22, 2017). Under the new opinion, e-mail communication may remain appropriate in many circumstances, but reasonable cybersecurity risk mitigation measures are needed, and "special security precautions" may be required in certain circumstances.

of technology, evolved practices, and the booming cybercrime industry, we know that this 1999 comparison is not fully accurate today. A somewhat better technological comparison would be that e-mail has the level of privacy afforded a postcard sent through the U.S. mail.[17] But overall, e-mail is very different from postcards, postal mail, and telephone calls, and the threats and risks differ. In addition to the danger of eavesdropping or misdirected e-mails, our e-mail is at risk because there is a huge volume of stored data in an e-mail account, and e-mail account hacks are widespread.

A 1998 New York State Bar Association opinion was more cautious and held that unencrypted e-mail was generally fine to maintain confidentiality, but that lawyers must act reasonably, and keep up with evolving threats and technology.[18] Despite being nearly twenty years old, that opinion's advice is still good, since it anticipates technology changes and employs the reasonableness standard. The lesson is not to look for a rigid IT rule to follow, but to evaluate the threats and risks, and set your cybersecurity dial accordingly.

b. Storing Files

Lawyers need to store their files securely, so as to maintain confidentiality. They should also retain a copy of their files for a period of time, both for the benefit of the client and as a record in the event of an ethics complaint or malpractice claim. Depending on the state of practice, some attorneys may be required to keep certain files for a set period of time. That means lawyers need to maintain access to their files and take appropriate measures to prevent them from being destroyed through hard drive failure, fire, flood, or a cybercrime event. It also means lawyers need to keep the files secure by taking reasonable measures to prevent compromise or hacking, and not do foolish things like forget confidential papers or laptop computers in a taxi or bar. Your files include your documents, notes, letters, and e-mails, whether in electronic or paper form. Many practitioners and vendors of office management systems stress the benefits of a "paperless office" for efficiency, as well as using cloud applications to handle all legal practice needs. The more we transition from paper to electronic, the more important our information security practices become.

---

17. *See, e.g.,* Bruce Schneier, *Protect Your E-Mail,* MACWORLD (Nov. 1995), https://www.schneier.com /essays/archives/1995/11/protect_your_e-mail.html (there is no privacy or confidentiality with either a postcard or unencrypted e-mail). *See also* Lawrence R. Rogers, *Email: A Postcard Written in Pencil,* CARNEGIE MELLON UNIVERSITY, http://nwl.cc/email_postcard.pdf (unencrypted e-mail does not have any data integrity protection; someone could intercept and change the sender's words and the recipient would not know). Thus, encryption has both confidentiality benefits and can ensure integrity from unauthorized changes.

18. *See* New York State Bar Association Ethics Opinion 709, *Use of Internet to Advertise and to Conduct Law Practice Focusing on Trademarks; Use of Internet E-mail; Use of Trade Names,* COMMITTEE ON PROFESSIONAL ETHICS (Sept. 1998), https://www.nysba.org/CustomTemplates/Content.aspx?id=5550.

Storing documents in the "cloud" was at one time a scary thought; now, it is generally accepted. But, like e-mail, you must secure your cloud account properly, as we've covered earlier in the book (including with a strong, unique password, two-factor authentication, and good practices).

There are some ethics opinions on electronic and cloud storage of files that are thoughtful, but don't mandate specific practices. In 2014, the New York State Bar Association recognized the threats lawyers face from hackers, and advised that "reasonable precautions" are required; however, it noted that it was impossible to specify exactly what those precautions should be in different circumstances.[19] In 2006, the New Jersey Advisory Committee on Professional Ethics also underscored a lawyer's duty to exercise "reasonable care" in securing and maintaining files, noting that methods for adequately protecting data evolve with technological advances, and that meeting the requisite "reasonable care" standard does not guarantee absolute security.[20] Thus, according to the opinion, a lawyer who is using reasonable care and meeting all professional responsibilities could, nevertheless, be the victim of a data breach, but the fact that an attorney is breached does not necessarily mean the attorney has violated a professional standard.

c. Social Media and Websites

Social media and websites present many issues and challenges for lawyers. Because services like LinkedIn, Twitter, and Facebook are potent communication and marketing methods, they implicate existing rules on attorney advertising and communication with clients, potential clients, adversaries, unrepresented parties, jurors, and judges. These services also raise important security concerns for lawyers and their clients.

From a security perspective, social media professional responsibility starts with adequately protecting your accounts from unauthorized access. As with other cloud storage and communication platforms, your social media account should be properly secured, as covered earlier, including with two-factor authentication and a strong password or passphrase. If you or your firm has a website, the method through which you administer your website and change your website content should be similarly secured.

From a fraud perspective, try to keep your social media contacts free of fraudsters, intelligence gatherers, and bots. If you have no idea who some of your contacts are—or if you have paid for followers, contacts, or friends—you

---

19. *See* New York State Bar Association Ethics Opinion 1019, *Confidentiality; Remote Access to Firm's Electronic Files*, COMMITTEE ON PROFESSIONAL ETHICS (Aug. 2014), http://www.nysba.org/Custom Templates/Content.aspx?id=51308.

20. *See* New Jersey Ethics Opinion 701, *Electronic Storage and Access of Client Files*, ADVISORY COMMITTEE ON PROFESSIONAL ETHICS (Apr. 10, 2006), https://www.judiciary.state.nj.us/notices/ethics/ACPE _Opinion701_ElectronicStorage_12022005.pdf.

are likely to have intelligence gatherers and bots in your network. Additionally, an argument can be made that paying for followers is a deceptive practice designed to make others believe you are more popular than you really are. Of course, do not pay for positive reviews, since that could constitute a deceptive business practice.

The principle of confidentiality is repeatedly challenged when social networking sites seek to obtain access to all of your contacts within your e-mail account, which could include anyone to whom you have ever sent an e-mail. LinkedIn and Facebook repeatedly urge you to expand your connections, and to surrender access to your e-mail account, so they can review and use the data within. Just the act of granting the social media company access to your contacts may implicate client privacy and confidentiality concerns, and by granting this access, the social media site may send invitations to all of your contacts, seemingly on your behalf, and perhaps without you even realizing it.

Having a social media service send out unwanted communications to everyone you know can be annoying and, in some cases, professionally inappropriate. What if such an e-mail or "friend request" were sent to a judge before whom you are appearing or a represented or unrepresented adversarial party? This automated action could constitute a communication you weren't supposed to initiate. Perhaps you have a current or former client and either the fact of that representation or your connection with the client needs to remain confidential.

All of these potential hazards mean you need to pay close attention to what each site is asking and not provide unfettered access to your e-mail account or other authorizations.[21] If it is appropriate for you to connect with a person on social media, you should make that decision independently and not surrender your entire address book or e-mail account to a social media company.

Social media allows for posting of comments, recommendations, and sharing of content posted by others. Lawyers should review their privacy settings, review how their pages appear, and review what others might post that appears on their pages. Some general concepts are:[22]

---

21. Some social media sites can be confusing when they ask for access to our e-mail accounts, and it might seem like we are merely being asked to re-enter a social media password. Their request seems innocuous and nonchalant, but they are asking for our e-mail password to obtain our contact list and records of everyone with whom we have e-mailed. These confusing requests are another reason not to reuse the same password across social media and e-mail accounts, because it prevents you from unwittingly authorizing access to your e-mail account when you meant to enter your social media password. Of course, for a number of security reasons discussed throughout this book, the passwords to your social media accounts and e-mail accounts should be different.

22. *See, e.g.,* District of Columbia Bar Association Ethics Opinion 370, *Social Media I: Marketing and Personal Use* (Nov. 2016), https://www.dcbar.org/bar-resources/legal-ethics/opinions/Ethics -Opinion-370.cfm.

- Be accurate (including the endorsements you make, receive, and display).
- Review your website and social media pages to ensure they comply with attorney advertising rules.
- Be cautious when identifying yourself as a specialist or expert.[23]
- Be cautious responding to comments or online reviews, including false or negative reviews about you.
- While it may be permissible to write or blog about your own cases, consider doing so only with the informed consent of your client.
- Protect client confidences.
- Avoid inadvertently forming an attorney-client relationship with someone with whom you communicate. Use disclaimers to indicate you are not forming such a relationship, and that you are not providing legal advice.
- Avoid creating conflicts of interest by stating positions on issues that might conflict with a future representation.

d. Anti-Money Laundering Guidance for Lawyers

Anti-money laundering information may seem out of place in a cybersecurity book, but it actually dovetails nicely with protecting your firm from cybercrime, and there is ethical guidance on the subject. In sum, if you are holding or moving funds on behalf of a client whose true identity is unknown to you, or if you don't know who is the true sender or recipient of the funds, then you are susceptible to being a victim of fraud, as well as being used as a tool to launder money or finance terrorism. News coverage has reported on lawyers who appeared willing to assist in money laundering, tax evasion, or questionable financial practices, and there have been criminal cases in which attorneys were convicted of money laundering. Few lawyers would ever choose to engage in illegal or questionable practices, but there are great risks for the unwitting attorney. Undoubtedly, the attorney-client privilege,

---

23. For example, New York State prohibits an attorney or firm from stating they are a specialist or specialize in a particular field of law, except as specifically provided, which requires them to be certified as a specialist by an approved organization. *See* N.Y. RULES OF PROFESSIONAL CONDUCT, r. 7.4 (a, c). On the other hand, certain restrictions on making such claims have also been struck down as unconstitutional. *See* Searcy v. Florida Bar, 140 F.Supp.3d 1290 (N.D. Fl., 2015). The ABA Model Rules merely restrict statements about being *certified* as a specialist. *See, e.g.,* Model Rule 7.4: Communication of Fields of Practice:

    (d) A lawyer shall not state or imply that a lawyer is certified as a specialist in a particular field of law, unless:

        (1) the lawyer has been certified as a specialist by an organization that has been approved by an appropriate state authority or that has been accredited by the American Bar Association; and

        (2) the name of the certifying organization is clearly identified in the communication.

escrow accounts, and the ability to conduct transactions on behalf of clients and manage their assets are all factors that make attorneys susceptible to being approached by money launderers. When an attorney participates in the growing trend of meeting and communicating with clients entirely online, the danger of becoming a pawn in organized money-laundering operations can be higher. Being aware of anti-money laundering principles will protect you from inadvertently getting involved with money launderers and will simultaneously protect you from being a fraud victim.

Attorneys and the Money-Laundering Threat

In an earlier section, we talked about the 2016 hack of the Mossack Fonseca law firm and the posting of confidential client information to the Internet—the "Panama Papers." These events spawned an investigation into whether the firm, its clients, and other law firms that used its services were trying to evade government oversight of client assets and finances. The firm's practices suggested involvement in tax avoidance or evasion, but its services also carried money-laundering implications.

In 2014, Global Witness, a nonprofit whose mission is to reduce corruption and exploitation of natural resources, sent undercover investigators to meet with various attorneys to inquire about setting up companies in a manner that would disguise the true ownership. An investigator posed as an aide to a minister of mining from an African country who had apparently accumulated a lot of income from bribery. This "aide" said the minister wanted to invest a large amount of funds in the United States and needed to do it without detection or his name being attached to it. In other words, the proposal was full of money laundering red flags. But despite these signs, most attorneys who met with the "aide" appeared willing to assist with these efforts.

It should be noted that none of the attorneys were ever engaged nor did they take any action beyond the initial consultation, thus, it is possible that none of these attorneys would have performed the acts solicited. These interviews were video recorded, and in January 2016 Global Witness published a report and the recordings, which generated significant news coverage.[24]

---

24. *See, e.g.*, Louise Story, *Report Describes Lawyers' Advice on Moving Suspect Funds into U.S.*, New York Times (Jan. 31, 2016), http://www.nytimes.com/2016/02/01/us/report-describes -lawyers-advice-on-moving-suspect-funds-into-us.html. *See also* Global Witness, *Lowering the Bar. How American Lawyers Told Us How to Funnel Suspect Funds into the United States* (Jan. 2016), https://www.globalwitness.org/documents/18208/Lowering_the_Bar.pdf.

Terrorist financing sounds nefarious, and to the unaware it seems like it would be easy for the average attorney to avoid having anything to do with it. But if you aren't following basic anti-money laundering practices, then you don't really know the source of funds you might be asked to handle, or who might eventually be receiving those funds. Money laundering involves disguise and concealment. Terrorists, narcotics traffickers, child pornographers, and everyone else participating in illegal money-centered activity take steps to anonymize themselves and their funds in order to continue their business undetected by law enforcement and intelligence agencies. They may try to trick attorneys, bankers, and other legitimate professionals into transferring funds for them. These funds are sent wherever needed to support terrorist or other illegal activities, such as weapons purchases, training, supplies, travel, rent, food, and more. Halting this flow of funds starts with some basic anti-money laundering principles designed to ascertain the source and destination of funds and the identities of the parties to the transaction.[25]

---

25. The government keeps a list of people, entities, and locations to which it is illegal to send funds. The list is administered by the Office of Foreign Assets Control (OFAC) within the U.S. Department of Treasury. Terrorists know about this list and generally don't use their real names anyway, so this list is merely the start of an inquiry into a party's status. To help disguise the funds, a terrorist might employ an intermediary, a shell corporation, an attorney, or other methods. Regardless, checking the OFAC list is a prudent step for anyone and is a required step for many regulated financial entities. *See* OFAC Sanctions List Search, https://sanctionssearch.ofac.treas.gov; OFAC Resource Center, https://www.treasury.gov /resource-center/sanctions/SDN-List/Pages/default.aspx.

There is a tension between the need of the government to combat money laundering and terrorist financing, and the need of the lawyer to maintain the confidentiality and integrity of the attorney-client relationship. The lawyer plays an important role as intermediary and gatekeeper for transactions and payments on behalf of clients, and thus presents a potential money laundering avenue. Congress has proposed legislation that, among other provisions, would require attorneys to obtain and report certain information about their clients and transactions.[26] This could potentially place an attorney in the difficult position of choosing whether to disobey such reporting law or disclose a client confidence, thus potentially violating the attorney-client privilege. The ABA has opposed this legislation[27] and has developed *voluntary* guidelines for lawyers to follow to help prevent money laundering.[28]

Accordingly, lawyers should realize that the legal profession is vulnerable to money laundering and should be aware of these voluntary guidelines when representing clients in any type of financial transaction. This representation could encompass matters such as the sale or purchase of real estate, managing client funds or accounts, and forming, operating, managing, or buying and selling companies or other business entities.

e. Know Your Client

Lawyers should start with a client intake procedure that reveals the client's true identity. If the client is an individual, this procedure should include the gathering of a detailed pedigree and background information, including birthdate, addresses, occupation, and more. A government minister from a developing nation who hints that his assets are the proceeds of bribery should undoubtedly raise a red flag. If the client is a corporation, it means learning about the background of the entity, who runs it, and who owns it. A shell

---

26. *See, e.g.,* Incorporation Transparency and Law Enforcement Assistance Act (ITLEAA), H.R. 4450, 114th Congress, https://www.congress.gov/bill/114th-congress/house-bill/4450. *See also* Press Release, Reps. Maloney, King and Senator Whitehouse Introduce Bills to Stop Anonymous Money Laundering Operations by Requiring Disclosure of Shell Corporation Beneficial Owners (Feb. 3, 2016), https://maloney.house .gov/media-center/press-releases/reps-maloney-king-and-senator-whitehouse-introduce-bills-to-stop.

27. *See, e.g.,* A.B.A. Ctr. for Prof'l Responsibility Policy Implementation Comm., *President's Letter Dated May 24, 2016 to the U.S. House of Representatives Task Force to Investigate Terrorism Financing* (May 24, 2016), http://amlawdaily.typepad.com/0000brownletter.pdf. *See also* A.B.A., *Fact Sheet on Gatekeeper Regulation and the Legal Profession, ABA Opposes Anti-Money Laundering Legislation That Erodes the Attorney-Client Privilege and Imposes Burdensome Regulations on Lawyers, Businesses, and States* (Jan. 2017), https://www.americanbar.org/content/dam/aba/uncategorized/GAO /gatekeeperregandtheprofessiontf(abafactsheetjanuary2017).authcheckdam.pdf.

28. *See* A.B.A., *Voluntary Good Practices Guidance for Lawyers to Detect and Combat Money Laundering and Terrorist Financing* (adopted Aug. 2010), http://www.americanbar.org/content/dam /aba/uncategorized/criminal_justice/voluntary_good_practices_guidance.authcheckdam.pdf; A.B.A., *A Lawyer's Guide to Detecting and Preventing Money Laundering* (Oct. 2014), http://www .americanbar.org/content/dam/aba/uncategorized/GAO/2014oct_abaguide_preventingmoneylaun dering.authcheckdam.pdf.

company controlled by unknown parties should also raise a red flag. Obtaining this kind of detailed client information is known within the financial industry as "know your customer" (KYC), "customer identification program" (CIP), and "customer due diligence" (CDD). Certain clients are higher risk than others. For example, "politically exposed persons" (PEP) is a term that refers to people in high government positions who might be in a position to steal from a country or government.

Lawyers also need to consider the business activity of the client, the source of any funds, and the form of the funds, because this information makes it possible to identify financial activities that are indicators of money laundering. Traditionally, anti-money laundering specialists have focused on the risks of cash because of its role in the street crime economy as an untraceable form of payment. A lawyer who receives a duffel bag full of cash from a client would be naive not to wonder if that cash represents criminal proceeds. In today's era of cybercrime, the money laundering threats have shifted, because, with cybercrime, cash does not play as significant a role. Instead, cybercriminals rely more on the conventional financial system, digital currency, and other payment methods. Today, a lawyer who receives significant payment through digital currency, such as Bitcoin, or a bank wire of suspicious origin, should also wonder if these funds might be criminal proceeds. Payments of these types can constitute today's duffel bags of cash.

For criminals overseas who have earned millions of dollars through crime—be it by cybercrime, traditional crime, or looting their countries—the United States is an attractive location to invest these criminal profits, whether through depositing funds in financial accounts, purchasing real estate, or making other investments.

Money laundering threats relate to cybercrime and fraud threats. Think about the classic "Nigerian prince" scam, where the potential victim receives an e-mail requesting help to transfer funds from a foreign country into the United States. When you think about it, this scam has several money laundering red flags, including a request for a secret transfer of funds outside the watchful eyes of government authorities, and a potential client who is a PEP, in a position to loot his country. Of course, a real money launderer is not going to approach you in this manner, and we can laugh about the silliness of this particular scam. Since criminals are innovative and forever developing better cons, a more complex variety of this old fraud would be more believable. Applying some anti-money laundering principles to your practice will protect you from these deceptions. When you start inquiring about and attempting to verify the identity of the client and the source and destination of the funds, you will find any inconsistencies and suspicious indicators. Remember that there is a continuum of potential clients and possible transactions that might need a lawyer's help or might be tempting to represent.

C. CYBERSECURITY LAWS, DATA BREACH LAWS, AND LITIGATION

People and corporations find themselves in interesting times, thanks to cyber-crime. How are we to handle the conflicting needs and motives of business profit, security measures to defend against crime, complying with government regulations, and defending against government actions or private lawsuits that might allege inadequate security or privacy? Cybercrime threats are generally unchecked, and cybercriminals succeed frequently in their attacks and usually get away scot-free. After the crime, businesses, consumers, and the government are left to address who should bear responsibility.

A growing body of laws place responsibility on those who maintain the data to ensure that it is secured properly, requiring that victims and law enforcement be notified of a breach. Previous chapters discussed methods and steps to secure the devices and data in your home and office and to develop a plan to prevent and respond to data breaches. This section briefly covers the laws and regulations that may place legal duties upon you and your clients to do so.

1. Cybersecurity Laws and Data Disposal Laws

A fair number of states now have general information security laws that require reasonable measures to protect defined categories of personal information.[29] While the scope of the laws and definitions vary among the states, "personal information" or "personally identifiable information" is usually defined to include general or specific facts about an identifiable individual (such as name, address, date of birth, and Social Security number). The exceptions tend to be information that is presumed public and does not have to be protected, such as business information that is already available publicly (e.g., a business address and phone number).

In addition to these general cybersecurity laws, companies and individuals may have duties under other statutes or regulations. Those working in the financial industry or in the medical field (or otherwise dealing with personal health information) typically operate under specific data regulations. And if any type of company suffers a data breach, there are usually laws and rules directing what actions must be taken, as we'll cover in the next section.

In a similar vein, a majority of all states have data disposal laws.[30] You already know how irresponsible it would be to sell or donate your laptop to a

---

29. *See* NATIONAL CONFERENCE OF STATE LEGISLATURES (NCSL), *Overview of Data Security Laws—Private Sector* (Jan. 16, 2017), http://www.ncsl.org/research/telecommunications-and-information-tech nology/data-security-laws.aspx. These states include Arkansas, California, Connecticut, Florida, Indiana, Maryland, Massachusetts, Minnesota, Nevada, Oregon, Rhode Island, Texas, and Utah.

30. *See* NCSL, *Overview of Data Disposal Laws* (Dec. 1, 2016), http://www.ncsl.org/research/telecom munications-and-information-technology/data-disposal-laws.aspx.

stranger without securely deleting the data on it. You know how improper it would be to throw out confidential paper files or paper records with customer information without first shredding them. Unfortunately, companies make these mistakes all too often. Businesses move or go out of business, and files and equipment are disposed of hurriedly. Companies update their fleet of desktop computers, and hundreds of old computers are resold, recycled, or thrown away, each with hard drives containing various types of stored and residual data. Given today's identity theft risks, states have enacted laws to prohibit this careless dumping of data about others. Before discarding old computers or files, personal information must be rendered unreadable and unrecoverable. If you are dealing with a single device, you could follow the device decommissioning guidelines in Appendices 6 and 7. Otherwise, hard drives can be removed from the computer and placed into specialized equipment that securely deletes all data so that it cannot be recovered. Many companies offer services to shred paper documents and securely delete or even shred electronic storage media.

Regardless of laws, you should nevertheless be properly disposing of sensitive data. You need to protect not only your confidential information, but also that of your clients and customers. Nothing would be more careless from an information security perspective than to simply abandon your own data to strangers. Thus, while these state statutes are diverse, they generally embody common sense recommendations; to date, the federal government has not weighed in with a general cybersecurity law.[31]

2. Data Breach Notification Laws

Data breach notification laws, starting with a law passed in California in 2003, are the reason why we have begun to hear about massive data breaches. The trees were falling in the forest long before we heard them, but before these laws, there was neither any incentive for the breached corporation to let anyone know about it nor any penalty if they kept silent.

Now, nearly every state requires notifications to victims of a data breach involving personally identifiable information.[32] Just because you or your client is not headquartered in a particular state does not mean that you are exempt from that state's law; it may still apply to you. It is possible that merely having clients or customers in a specific state will subject you to the state's notification laws if that client's data is breached. Therefore, it is possible that one can

---

31. The Federal Data Security and Breach Notification Act of 2015 did not pass—nor did a similar bill the year before. As drafted, it would have required broad cybersecurity measures and breach notification protocols and would have preempted state laws.

32. *See* NCSL, *Security Breach Notification Laws* (Feb. 24, 2017), http://www.ncsl.org/research/tele communicationsandinformationtechnology/securitybreachnotificationlaws.aspx. Forty-seven states, plus the District of Columbia, Puerto Rico, and the Virgin Islands, have enacted these laws. States that currently do not have a security breach law are Alabama, New Mexico, and South Dakota.

be subject to the notification laws of many states, and those laws vary by state. Generally, all the laws require notification of a data breach to law enforcement and the customers or clients whose data was breached.

When faced with evidence of a potential data breach, some companies might be tempted to overlook certain facts and pretend that nothing happened, since dealing with a data breach is time-consuming, costly, and reputation-damaging. By reporting the breach, you will face scrutiny from the government and customers, but the penalties for failing to report encourage forthrightness.

From a policy perspective, the variety of state statutes is cumbersome, and a data breach in one state can trigger a duty to review and comply with notification laws of dozens of other states. So far, the federal government has not enacted a unifying statute, and, in this absence, there is the opportunity for states to consider working amongst themselves to enact a unifying notification law, such as through an interstate compact or uniform law approach. For now, anyone keeping customer or client data is potentially subject to numerous state laws—an added incentive to maintain data as securely as possible.

3. Data Breach Litigation

Now that victims learn (sometimes) when their personal data has been stolen, they sometimes file lawsuits against the companies who held their information. Thus, data breach litigation is a growing practice area. Given that some data breaches have exposed personal information of thousands or millions of individual victims, it is also a ripe area for class action litigation. Victims sue the breached corporation, alleging inadequate cybersecurity, and claim that the data breach caused actual damages, or perhaps that they are entitled to statutory damages if that is available.

This trend has resulted in some significant class action cases. In a particularly egregious data breach due to an IT error rather than a hacker's work, the personal information of medical patients was posted online and available for the public and identity thieves to see and copy. The resulting class action lawsuit was eventually settled for about $28 million, which included compensation of about $242 for each of the individual victims.[33] This settlement is believed to be one of the largest recoveries per victim in a data breach class action litigation, but these cases have not generated significant recoveries for individual victims.

Data breach litigation is expensive for both sides. Additionally, it can be difficult for the individual whose personal information was exposed to show actual damages, because it's often impossible to prove that a future incident of identity theft is attributable to a particular data breach. Perhaps the only way

---

33. *See* Marianne Kolbasuk McGee, *"Egregious" Breach Results in Hefty Settlement*, BANK INFO SECURITY (Mar. 16, 2016), http://www.bankinfosecurity.com/egregious-breach-results-in-hefty-settlement-a-8974.

to address this form of damage will be through a uniform system of statutory damages.

D. PRIVACY LAWS AND REGULATIONS

The United States does not have a unified privacy statute but, rather, a mix of laws that pertain to privacy. We'll touch on some of the basics here. In general, these privacy laws implicate cybersecurity because they are enacted to protect the personal information and other privacy interests of clients and customers. If companies are improperly collecting, storing, or safeguarding this data, they can face reputational, regulatory, and legal risk.

The Federal Trade Commission (FTC) does most of the federal privacy regulation and enforcement within the United States, bringing enforcement actions when consumer privacy is violated. The states also play a significant role, through each state's Attorney General. When the FTC brings an action against a company for violating the privacy of its customers, it is usually framed as addressing an unfair or deceptive trade practice under Section 5(a) of the FTC Act.[34] The FTC also has jurisdiction if it determines a company's cybersecurity was inadequate and, thus, constituted an unfair practice, or if a company's promises about security were deceptive. Of critical importance are the company's privacy policies and terms of service. If the privacy policies are deceptive or simply not followed by the company, these scenarios can constitute a deceptive trade practice. To help prevent identity theft, the FTC also enforces the "Red Flags Rule," which requires covered businesses to implement a written program to detect and combat identity theft.[35] Lawyers have been exempted from this rule, but they should be aware of it and its potential applicability to their clients.

Businesses with websites, apps, and software should be aware of the Children's Online Privacy Protection Rule (COPPA), which the FTC also enforces.[36] This rule generally requires that companies with an online presence have a proper privacy policy, a means of obtaining parental consent if any personal information is collected from children under 13, a method for

---

34. *See* FTC Act § 5(a), 15 U.S.C.§ 45(a)(1). *See also* FTC, *A Brief Overview of the Federal Trade Commission's Investigative and Law Enforcement Authority* (July 2008), https://www.ftc.gov/about-ftc/what-we-do/enforcement-authority.

35. *See* FTC, *Fighting Identity Theft with the Red Flags Rule: A How-To Guide for Business* (May 2013), https://www.ftc.gov/tips-advice/business-center/guidance/fighting-identity-theft-red-flags-rule-how-guide-business.

36. *See* FTC, *Complying with COPPA: Frequently Asked Questions* (Mar. 2015), https://www.ftc.gov/tips-advice/business-center/guidance/complying-coppa-frequently-asked-questions. *See also* FTC, *The Children's Online Privacy Protection Rule: A Six-Step Compliance Plan for Your Business* (July 2013), https://www.ftc.gov/system/files/documents/plain-language/BUS84-coppa-6-steps.pdf.

parents to review the collected personal information and to delete it, and reasonable security measures for the information.

In today's globally interconnected world, lawyers should be mindful not only of federal and state laws within the United States but also the privacy laws of other countries. Other countries and governments have privacy laws that may be much more thorough and restrictive than U.S. laws, and may restrict the transfer of data about their citizens outside of that country unless certain requirements are met. The European Union (EU) has particularly strict privacy laws, and cross-border data transfers can create thorny legal issues. If you have U.S. clients doing business in another country, and collecting data in that country, you should evaluate the laws of that country and how they relate to exporting data. Conversely, if you have a U.S. client who does business in the U.S., and collects data on U.S. residents but who outsources work to another country (such as an overseas call center), you should ensure that the overseas partner is complying with U.S. regulations, including reasonable security measures.

The EU's strict privacy rules mean that U.S. businesses must find methods to transport personal information of EU citizens out of the EU legally under the EU construct. One such framework was called "Safe Harbor;" however, in 2015 the European Court of Justice invalidated this approach as failing to provide sufficient privacy protections for EU citizens. Since then, a new framework known as "Privacy Shield" has been implemented.[37] Other methods of transferring data from the EU include "standard contractual clauses" and "binding corporate rules."

Countries outside the EU have a myriad of privacy laws as well. This underscores the importance of knowing one's data, what data is being collected and stored, and where it is stored. Once you can answer those questions, it is time to become aware of which country's laws apply and evaluate the legality of moving certain data from one country to another. This evaluation must be done with an eye to the privacy laws in both jurisdictions.

E. RULES FOR FINANCIAL INSTITUTIONS

Financial institutions and related businesses have a host of cybersecurity and data privacy rules to follow. They are designed to protect not only customer privacy, but also the integrity of the financial system.

The Gramm-Leach-Bliley Act of 1999, among other things, aims to ensure that covered businesses in the financial sector adequately protect the privacy of customers' personal information, and that businesses comply

---

37. Privacy Shield is also administered by the U.S. Department of Commerce. *See* PRIVACY SHIELD FRAMEWORK, *Privacy Shield Program Overview, https://www.privacyshield.gov/Program-Overview.*

with minimum security standards. The act includes restrictions on sharing and using personal information, as well as maintaining the information with adequate security.[38] The FTC and many financial regulators[39] enforce these provisions.

Certified Public Accountants, tax preparers, and people who work with this type of financial information, taxpayer information, or who electronically file taxes also need to comply with privacy and security rules.[40] The Securities and Exchange Commission (SEC) has regulatory and enforcement oversight over securities, in general, and over investment companies, hedge funds, and public corporations. One oversight area is information security and protection of customer records; thus, the SEC has rules to ensure these types of corporations properly secure such records from loss or theft.[41] Yet another area the SEC oversees concerns maintaining the security and integrity of technology infrastructure.[42] This means a focus on the information security triad of CIA: (1) keeping data *confidential* (imagine if information was broadcast to all), (2) ensuring data maintains its *integrity* (imagine if a hacker could alter records about account balances, who owned what, who traded what, and at what price), and (3) making certain data remains *available* (imagine if records could not be accessed or if trades and transactions could not be processed).

The New York State Department of Financial Services issued cybersecurity regulations for all financial services institutions regulated under its laws.[43] Among the requirements, covered institutions need to have an infor-

---

38. *See* FTC, Safeguards Rule, 16 C.F.R. Part 314, https://www.ftc.gov/enforcement/rules/rule making-regulatory-reform-proceedings/safeguards-rule. *See also,* FTC, *How to Comply with the Privacy of Consumer Financial Information Rule of the Gramm-Leach-Bliley Act* (July 2002), https://www.ftc.gov /system/files/documents/plain-language/bus67-how-comply-privacy-consumer-financial-information -rule-gramm-leach-bliley-act.pdf.

39. Financial regulators include not only the SEC, but also the Federal Deposit Insurance Corporation (FDIC), Office of the Comptroller of Currency (OCC), National Credit Union Administration (NCUA), the Federal Reserve, and others.

40. *See, e.g.,* IRS, *Safeguarding Taxpayer Data: A Guide for Your Business* (Oct. 2015), https://www.irs .gov/pub/irs-pdf/p4557.pdf. *See also* IRS, *Safeguarding IRS E-File,* https://www.irs.gov/uac/safeguarding -irs-efile1.

41. *See* Regulation S-P, 17 C.F.R. § 248.30, https://www.sec.gov/spotlight/regulation-s-p.htm.

42. *See* SEC, *Regulation SCI (Systems Compliance and Integrity),* https://www.sec.gov/divisions /marketreg/regulation-sci-faq.shtml. *See also* SEC, *Responses to Frequently Asked Questions Concerning Regulation SCI,* https://www.sec.gov/spotlight/regulation-sci.shtml. Regulation SCI is codified as 17 C.F.R. § 242.1000-1007.

43. *See* 23 NYCRR 500, *Cybersecurity Requirements for Financial Services Companies.* The rules were proposed in September 2016, went through a comment period, were revised and went into effect on March 1, 2017. *See e.g.,* Press Release, New York State Department of Financial Services, *Governor Cuomo Announces Proposal of First-In-The-Nation Cybersecurity Regulation to Protect Consumers and Financial Institutions* (Sept. 13, 2016), http://www.dfs.ny.gov/about/press/pr1609131.htm; Press Release, New York State Department of Financial Services, *DFS Issues Updated Proposed Cybersecurity Regulation Protecting Consumers and Financial Institutions* (Dec. 28, 2016), http://www.dfs.ny.gov/about/press/pr1612281.htm.

mation security and cybersecurity program that is overseen by an account-able individual, as well as certify compliance with the regulations and report adverse cybersecurity events within 72 hours. A cybersecurity event is defined broadly to encompass attempts, as well as completed attacks. While there may be value to having some states lead the way in certain areas, it might quickly become unwieldy if each state's regulatory agency develops individualized cybersecurity rules for the entities it regulates.

Financial institutions have long been required to file various reports that might relate to money laundering under the Bank Secrecy Act (BSA).[44] The entity charged with receiving those reports is FinCEN, the Financial Crimes Enforcement Network, an arm of the U.S. Treasury Department. In October 2016, FinCEN issued guidance making clear that financial institutions should report "cyber-events" and "cyber-enabled crime."[45] These events were already subject to reporting, but the guidance clarified that fact and increased the duty of financial institutions to detect and report these events.

F. HIPAA AND HITECH

Those in the medical field and those handling medical data of patients are required to comply with the privacy and security provisions of the Health Insurance Portability and Accountability Act of 1996 (HIPAA).[46] HIPAA was amended with the Health Information Technology for Economic and Clinical Health Act of 2009 (HITECH),[47] and was designed to increase the use of technology to store medical records, with added privacy and breach notification requirements and penalties.

These rules apply to doctors and medical offices, hospitals, and anyone else working with medical and patient data. The rules also govern lawyers handling this type of data in the context of a representation or litigation. Attorneys who provide legal services to clients regulated by HIPAA are classified as "business associates" and are subject to HIPAA regulations.[48]

---

44. The BSA requires banks to investigate, report, and combat money laundering. These requirements include mandatory reporting of certain transactions, as well as analyzing circumstances and patterns for suspicious activities.

45. FinCEN, *Cybercriminals Target the Financial System to Defraud Financial Institutions and Their Customers and to Further Other Illegal Activities*, FinCEN Advisory FIN-2016-A005 (Oct. 25, 2016), https://www.fincen.gov/resources/advisories/fincen-advisory-fin-2016-a005. *See also FinCEN, FinCEN's Frequently Asked Questions (FAQs) Regarding FinCEN Advisory FIN-2016-A005* (Oct. 25, 2016), https://www.fincen.gov/frequently-asked-questions-faqs-regarding-reporting-cyber-events-cyber-enabled-crime-and-cyber.

46. HIPAA Pub. L. No. 104-191, 110 Stat. 1936 (1996), amended and within various sections of 26 U.S.C., 29 U.S.C., and 42 U.S.C.

47. HITECH Pub. L. No. 111-5, 123 Stat. 226 (2009), codified as amended in various sections of 42 U.S.C.

48. *See* 45 CFR §164.502(e), §164.504(e), §164.532(d) and (e). The classification "business associate" is defined at 45 CFR §160.103.

G. ELECTRONIC COMMUNICATIONS PRIVACY ACT

The Electronic Communications Privacy Act (ECPA), a federal law enacted in 1986, amended certain wiretap statutes to address electronic data transmitted and stored by computers.[49] ECPA provides a framework for federal and state prosecutors in obtaining court processes (such as a subpoena, search warrant, or wiretap order) for specified data, such as transactional records, transmitted or stored electronic data, and voice conversations. Though ECPA has been amended since 1986, those amendments do not address some of its antiquated aspects. For instance, it was enacted long before e-mail was commonly used, long before the ubiquity of cloud storage, and long before the age of the smartphone. Thus, some ECPA aspects and definitions don't translate well to today's world.

An illustrative example is the ECPA provision holding that e-mails that have been stored for longer than six months can be acquired by law enforcement without a search warrant. This provision applies to e-mail "content," meaning the text within the body of the e-mail, the subject line, and any attachments. According to the statute, a subpoena would be sufficient to obtain these older e-mails, and law enforcement need not go through the process of obtaining a search warrant by preparing a sworn affidavit setting forth probable cause that there is evidence to be found and having that affidavit reviewed by a neutral judge who must then decide whether a warrant should be issued. The lack of a search warrant requirement by ECPA for e-mail content stored over six months was based upon an antiquated assumption that data stored for this long must have been abandoned and, therefore, subject to a lower expectation of privacy. Of course, today most of us store our e-mails in cloud e-mail services such as Gmail and Hotmail for years on end without any intention of abandoning the data. Hopefully, the practice is to obtain a search warrant for this data even if the letter of the law does not require it, and this law should be amended nevertheless.[50]

H. CYBERSECURITY INFORMATION SHARING ACT

The Cybersecurity Information Sharing Act (CISA) is a 2015 federal law designed to make it easier for private companies to share with the government information about cybersecurity threats.[51] Prior to CISA, private corporations might have had concern that if they shared such information with the government, in the absence of a proper legal process such as a subpoena or

---

49. ECPA is embodied in 18 U.S.C. § 2510 *et seq.* and 18 U.S.C. § 3121 *et seq.*

50. There has been legislation proposed to make this change. *See, e.g.,* Email Privacy Act, H.R. 699, 114th Congress (2015–2016), https://www.congress.gov/bill/114th-congress/house-bill/699.

51. CISA was part of an omnibus spending package, Pᴜʙ. L. No. 114-113, https://www.congress.gov/bill/114th-congress/house-bill/2029/text.

search warrant, they might have violated ECPA and be subject to civil or even criminal liability. CISA seeks to protect privacy by requiring that unnecessary personal information be scrubbed from the data that is transmitted by these companies.

Supporters of CISA argue that the law allows companies to share information about cyberthreats with the government with the hope that the government then will be able to apprehend more cybercriminals, build stronger cases, defend against nation-state threats, and set more effective national policies. To fight these threats the government must have access to relevant data for proper analysis.

On the other hand, privacy advocates and many technology companies worry that CISA tips the balance in favor of disclosure; since the corporation is protected if it discloses data to the government, the default will become handing over data, which will reduce customer privacy. This warrantless sharing of bulk data with the government could infringe upon individual liberties and enhance the government's surveillance powers. Some have argued that key privacy protections were stripped from the provisions shortly before the law was passed. At the time, some members of Congress stated that a classified memo provided good reasons why CISA should not be passed, but since the memo was classified, they could not disclose the reasons.

I. CYBERCRIME-RELATED CRIMINAL STATUTES

A brief survey of some principles of criminal statutes is important in the context of improving cybersecurity. You or a client may well become a victim of a cybercrime someday, and if you know what the applicable crimes are, you will communicate more effectively with law enforcement and better guide your client. Also, a client might consider actions that would constitute the commission of a crime, perhaps under the mistaken impression that if something is "just data" or "just a network," it is fair game for borrowing or exploring. You are in a position to give proper advice against the commission of such actions.

Conceptually, people should think of computers and networks as places like a building or home; if you don't have permission to enter or access it, you shouldn't. Military installations have fences with signs stating "U.S. Government—No Trespassing" and few people would consider climbing over that fence. That same principle should apply to a network or e-mail account. In other words, people should think of data as property, and if you don't have permission to take, read, access, copy, or delete it, then you should not. Of course, criminal law doesn't always follow those principles. Statutes specifically proscribe certain conduct, defendants are arrested, and then judges need to decide whether the statute and existing definitions apply to a certain cyber-crime. In criminal law, any uncertainty usually favors the defendant.

The federal government and the states have a wide range of laws that can be applied to the various cybercrimes and frauds. Many criminal statutes that are traditionally applied toward "brick and mortar" crimes can be applied to cybercrimes as well. For example, most cybercrimes are committed with financial theft as the primary motive and result. Thus, larceny statutes usually apply to the general conduct. Most statutes prohibit the intentional or reckless damaging of someone else's property through vandalism or "criminal mischief," as New York calls it. Those statutes might fit whether the perpetrator has thrown a brick through a window or intentionally damaged a computer network, deleted data, or maliciously encrypted a computer's contents. On the other hand, sometimes, these traditional criminal statutes don't translate well for digitally based crimes.[52]

The federal government and states have enacted criminal statutes relating to computer intrusion.[53] These statutes generally make it a crime to obtain access to a computer or data without the owner's permission. Learning or guessing a password, and then using it to log in as that other person is illegal. Some jurisdictions have statutes that specifically prohibit malicious destruction of computer data.[54]

The federal government and most states also have enacted identity theft statutes that prohibit impersonating or pretending to be someone else.[55] These

---

52. This problem is illustrated by the federal and state criminal prosecutions against Sergey Aleynikov for allegedly stealing proprietary computer source code from Goldman Sachs. Under the first federal criminal prosecution, a federal appeals court reversed the conviction and dismissed the case, holding the federal statute could not be applied to computer code. *See* United States v. Aleynikov, 676 F3d 71 (2d Cir. 2012). The State of New York then brought a second prosecution for the same conduct, but under state criminal statutes. After trial and a conviction on one of the counts, the state trial judge dismissed the conviction, holding that the state statute could not be applied to computer code either. The Appellate Division reversed and reinstated the conviction, holding that the statute was indeed applicable to this digital data. People v. Aleynikov, slip op. 00449 (N.Y. App. Div. decided Jan. 24, 2017), http://www.nycourts.gov/reporter/3dseries/2017/2017_00449.htm. This case is being appealed to New York's Court of Appeals.

53. *See, e.g.,* 18 U.S.C. § 1030(a), The Federal Computer Fraud and Abuse Act; N.Y. Penal Law §156.05; Unauthorized Use of a Computer; N.Y. Penal Law § 156.10, Computer Trespass; N.Y. Penal Law §156.29 *et seq.,* Unlawful Duplication of Computer Related Material. Unlike the federal statute, New York separates the act of intrusion and duplication of data into distinct offenses. *See also* NCSL, *Computer Crime Statutes* (Dec. 5, 2016), http://www.ncsl.org/research/telecommunications-and-information-technology /computer-hacking-and-unauthorized-access-laws.aspx.

54. *See, e.g.,* 18 U.S.C. § 1030(a)(5), The Computer Fraud and Abuse Act; N.Y. Penal Law §156.20 *et seq.,* Computer Tampering.

55. *See, e.g.,* 18 U.S.C. § 1028, Identification Fraud; 18 U.S.C. § 1029, Credit Card Fraud; N.Y. Penal Law § 190.78 et seq., Identity Theft; N.Y. Penal Law § 190.25 *et seq.,* Criminal Impersonation. *See also* NCSL, *Identity Theft* (state statute summary), http://www.ncsl.org/research/financial-services-and-commerce /identity-theft-state-statutes.aspx.

statutes are relatively recent additions, enacted to address a booming crime wave where defendants and victims were usually in very different geographic locations. Identity theft statutes can usually be applied whether the perpetrator is committing the crime at a store with a forged credit card and forged ID, or online, via the Internet using stolen personal identifying information.

Finally, and of particular importance, the federal government and most states have laws prohibiting eavesdropping and wiretapping, and sometimes these laws extend to video surveillance.[56] Under these laws, it can be a serious offense to listen in on someone's oral or electronic communications or to break into their computer or network and monitor the communications. As covered in the ECPA section, there are statutory provisions through which prosecutors can obtain wiretap orders. Companies, however, can monitor their own systems and networks.[57] There is also the aspect of consent and whether one party's consent is sufficient to allow eavesdropping or recording, or whether all parties to the conversation or communication need to consent. The federal government and most states allow listening or recording if one party consents, but in some states, listening or recording is a crime unless all parties consent.[58] An important part of the analysis is whether someone has a "reasonable expectation of privacy."[59] Thus, employer notifications, login banners, privacy policies, and terms of use can play a significant role in whether a system user has a reasonable expectation of privacy.

Without a doubt, the laws to fight cybercrime could be improved. With many laws written before the Internet age and a relative lack of cybercrime prosecutions to further develop the law, it is unclear how individual judges might apply these older statutes to current cybercrime activity. Some statutes that are specific to cybercrime and identity theft have clear application but may have been enacted before these crimes presented the threats they do today. Some carry relatively minor penalties, which may not be sufficiently severe to punish or deter the criminals who commit these crimes continually as their full-time occupation.

For criminals who make a career out of crime and who organize with other criminals, the federal government enacted the Racketeer Influenced

---

56. *See, e.g.,* 18 U.S.C. § 2511(1); N.Y. Penal Law § 250.00 *et seq.,* Eavesdropping (Wiretapping) and Unlawful Video Surveillance.

57. 18 U.S.C. § 2511 (2) (monitoring activities necessary to provide service or protect rights or property are acceptable); N.Y. Penal Law § 250.00(1): exception for "wiretapping" is "normal operation" and "normal use" by the provider and as necessary to protect rights or property.

58. *See, e.g.,* 18 U.S.C. § 2511(2) (d) (one party consent); N.Y. Penal Law § 250.00(1) (not unlawful if either sender or receiver consents, making New York a "one party consent" state). *See also* Kristen Rasmussen, Jack Komperda, & Raymond Baldino, *Reporter's Recording Guide,* REPORTERS COMMITTEE FOR FREEDOM OF THE PRESS (August 1, 2012), https://www.rcfp.org/reporters-recording-guide.

59. Katz v. United States, 389 U.S. 347 (1967).

and Corrupt Organizations Act (RICO Act) in 1970, and many states followed suit with their own versions of this statute. These statutes were aimed at traditional organized crime actors, such as the Mafia or narcotics rings, and applying these organized crime statutes to cybercrime is subject to interpretation by the courts. One state, for example, did not approve of applying its RICO-modeled statute to the newer, more lucrative, and more capitalistic cybercrime economy.[60] Perhaps laws could be updated, but that will not be enough. Law enforcement and prosecutors must dedicate sufficient resources to investigating and prosecuting cases that attack all aspects of the cybercrime and identity theft economies.

J. CYBERSECURITY STANDARDS

1. Critical Security Controls

There are various cybersecurity standards for businesses and organizations, and your awareness of them should start with the Critical Security Controls (CSC).[61] This framework, initially developed by the SANS Institute and now administered by the Center for Internet Security, is designed so that organizations can start securing themselves in a prioritized fashion, starting with CSC Number 1 (i.e., conduct an inventory of computer devices being used) and proceeding from there. Each CSC control maps to controls within more technical standards, such as NIST 800-53, which we will mention later.

You'll note that this book, in walking you through securing your home and office, has also followed an analogous prioritized method, starting with devices and securing aspects within them, then moving through data, and then moving to networks. It's good to know where to start and how to prioritize, especially when the totality of it might seem daunting or overwhelming.

These controls are common sense and threat-based; defenses should focus on the most common and damaging attack activities, security controls

---

60. New York's highest court held that New York's organized crime statute (Enterprise Corruption) did not apply to one group of cybercriminals and identity thieves that were investigated and prosecuted. The prosecution was attempting to apply an existing organized crime statute to the new cybercrime era, to defendants who committed crimes together for many years with a joint profit motive. But the court held that this was not the type of criminal conduct the statute was meant to address, because these criminals were not operating within an organizational structure as defined by the statute but, rather, were independent criminals working at an arm's length in a criminal marketplace. *See* People v. Western Express Int'l, Inc., et al., 19 N.Y. 3d 652 (2012), http://www.courts.state.ny.us/Reporter/3dseries/2012/2012_06987.htm. After the Court of Appeals dismissed the Enterprise Corruption count, the case proceeded on the remaining counts. Many defendants pled guilty, but three elected to go to trial and were ultimately convicted of all counts.

61. *See* CENTER FOR INTERNET SECURITY, *Welcome to the CIS Controls,* https://www.cisecurity.org /critical-controls.cfm. *See also* SANS INSTITUTE, *CIS Critical Security Controls,* https://www.sans.org/critical -security-controls.

should be consistent across an organization, and the basic, root-cause problems must be properly addressed.[62] Listed below are the 20 Critical Security Controls, preceded by a user-friendly description for each control. First, in bold, is a "friendly" name for the control, followed (in regular text) by the official control name:

CSC 1:   **Inventory devices (both authorized and unauthorized).**
Inventory of Authorized and Unauthorized Devices.

CSC 2:   **Inventory software (both authorized and unauthorized).**
Inventory of Authorized and Unauthorized Software.

CSC 3:   **Configure devices and software securely.**
Secure Configurations for Hardware and Software on Mobile Devices, Laptops, Workstations, and Servers.

CSC 4:   **Review vulnerabilities continually.**
Continuous Vulnerability Assessment and Remediation.

CSC 5:   **Don't use administrator accounts for normal computer usage.**
Controlled Use of Administrative Privileges.

CSC 6:   **Enable automatic logging, and use the logs.**
Maintenance, Monitoring, and Analysis of Audit Logs.

CSC 7:   **Secure e-mail and web browser use.**
E-mail and Web Browser Protections.

CSC 8:   **Use anti-malware.**
Malware Defenses.

CSC 9:   **Disable (or "lock down") services and features you don't need.**
Limitation and Control of Network Ports, Protocols, and Services.

CSC 10:   **Back up your data in a way you can recover it.**
Data Recovery Capability.

CSC 11:   **Secure your router (and hardware firewall).**
Secure Configurations for Network Devices such as Firewalls, Routers, and Switches.

CSC 12:   **Have firewalls and systems to defend your boundaries.**
Boundary Defense.

---

62. *See, e.g.,* SANS INSTITUTE, *CIS Critical Security Controls: Guidelines,* https://www.sans.org/critical-security-controls/guidelines. *See also* Russell Eubanks, *A Small Business No Budget Implementation of the SANS 20 Security Controls,* SANS INSTITUTE (Aug. 2011), https://www.sans.org/reading-room/white papers/hsoffice/small-business-budget-implementation-20-security-controls-33744; AUDITSCRIPTS, *Critical Security Controls,* http://www.auditscripts.com/free-resources/critical-security-controls/ (including free resources available for download).

CSC 13: **Protect your data.**
Data Protection.

CSC 14: **Don't give a user more access than is needed.**
Controlled Access Based on the Need to Know.

CSC 15: **Secure wireless networks.**
Wireless Access Control.

CSC 16: **Monitor accounts.**
Account Monitoring and Control.

CSC 17: **Continual training.**
Security Skills Assessment and Appropriate Training to
Fill Gaps.

CSC 18: **Secure company applications and web applications.**
Application Software Security.

CSC 19: **Have a plan for cyber incidents.**
Incident Response and Management.

CSC 20: **Test your defenses with penetration testers ("ethical
hackers").**
Penetration Tests and Red Team Exercises.

Penetration testing—so-called ethical or white hat hacking—is the last
control to tackle, *after* all of the earlier controls have been implemented. Until
a company has worked to implement the guidance in CSCs 1 through 19,
there is no point in paying someone to identify areas where the company is
deficient. Thus, companies should do their best to implement the first nine-
teen controls, and *then* employ a penetration tester to help identify weak areas
or overlooked controls.

2. National Institute of Standards and Technology

The National Institute of Standards and Technology (NIST), a Department of
Commerce agency, developed a cybersecurity framework that provides guid-
ance as to how organizations can protect themselves from cybercrime.[63] NIST
Special Publication (SP) 800-53 is a catalog of security controls for the fed-
eral government and an effective standard that all organizations can follow.[64]
NIST SP 800-53A is a guide on how to assess compliance with this standard.[65]

---

63. NIST, *Cybersecurity Framework*, https://www.nist.gov/cyberframework; NIST, *Framework for Improving Critical Infrastructure Cybersecurity* (Feb. 12, 2014), ver. 1.0, https://www.nist.gov/sites/default /files/documents/cyberframework/cybersecurity-framework-021214.pdf.

64. NIST, *Security and Privacy Controls for Federal Information Systems and Organizations*, SPECIAL PUBLICATION 800-53 Rev. 4, http://nvlpubs.nist.gov/nistpubs/SpecialPublications/NIST.SP.800-53r4.pdf.

65. NIST, *Assessing Security and Privacy Controls in Federal Information Systems and Organizations*, SPECIAL PUBLICATION 800-53A Rev. 4, http://nvlpubs.nist.gov/nistpubs/SpecialPublications/NIST.SP.800 -53Ar4.pdf.

Neither publication is light reading, but it is helpful to know they exist and are available. NIST also provides publications with helpful guidance for small businesses.[66]

3. The International Organization for Standardization

The International Organization for Standardization (ISO) is just what it sounds like, an international standards-setting organization.[67] ISO partnered with the International Electrotechnical Commission (IEC) to create standards relating to information security, resulting in the ISO/IEC 27000 series, a group of publications that includes ISO 27001, which addresses information security management.[68]

4. Other Standards (COBIT, ISA, PCI DSS)

COBIT (Control Objectives for Information and Related Technologies) is a focused framework for governing and managing information technology in large organizations, including cybersecurity and information assurance and other aspects. It is developed and administered by ISACA, an information systems security, assurance, and auditing organization.[69]

The International Society of Automation (ISA) also provides a cybersecurity framework geared towards industrial automation and control, which is known as ISA/IEC 62443.[70] There are other security standards as well, such as the Payment Card Industry Data Security Standard (PCI DSS) for use by businesses that accept or process credit and debit card payments.[71]

K. CONCLUSION

Cybersecurity is a professional responsibility that all lawyers must accept as one of their many ethical and professional obligations. Cybercrime-for-profit is an enormous industry that targets everyone, and attorneys may be

---

66. *See* Celia Paulsen and Patricia Toth, *Small Business Information Security: The Fundamentals,* NISTIR 7621, rev. 1 (Nov. 2016), http://nvlpubs.nist.gov/nistpubs/ir/2016/NIST.IR.7621r1.pdf.

67. ISO, http://www.iso.org/iso/home.html.

68. *See* INTERNATIONAL ORGANIZATION FOR STANDARDIZATION, *ISO/IEC 27001 Family Information Security Management Systems,* http://www.iso.org/iso/home/standards/management-standards/iso27001.htm. The full text of the standards is available at https://www.iso.org/obp/ui/#iso:std:iso-iec:27001:ed-2:v1:en.

69. *See* https://www.isaca.org. ISACA was previously known as Information Systems Audit and Control Association, but now goes by its acronym, to reflect its broader role. For information about COBIT see http://www.isaca.org/COBIT/Pages/FAQs.aspx.

70. *See* ISA website and webpages: https://www.isa.org; https://www.isasecure.org; https://www.isa.org/isa99/.

71. *See* PCI SECURITY STANDARDS COUNCIL, *PCI Security,* https://www.pcisecuritystandards.org/pci_security/; *The Prioritized Approach to Pursue PCI DSS Compliance* (May 2016), https://www.pcisecuritystandards.org/documents/Prioritized-Approach-for-PCI_DSS-v3_2.pdf.

specifically targeted by cybercriminals because of their occupation and access to potentially valuable client data and information. There are many laws and regulations that place duties on corporations and individuals to safeguard their data and take certain measures in the event of a data breach. Attorneys are in a position to guide their clients toward properly implementing a cyber-security program, managing the legal and business risks, and helping them after an incident.

CHAPTER 15

Troubleshooting and Responding to Your Own Incidents

A. INTRODUCTION

The short time it takes to read this chapter could save you hours of headaches in the future, because it will help you prepare for problems before they arise. Resist the temptation to skip this chapter and put the book on the shelf, thinking you will come back to it later if you have an issue. Instead, give the first few sections a read, and skim through the rest. A little bit of knowledge and planning can prevent an incident from occurring in the first place, as well as minimize its impact. This chapter is not going to rehash what has already been covered but, rather, will provide an overview of the basic steps for handling issues you might face while improving your cybersecurity, and point you to the proper chapter for more detailed reading.

B. FINDING SPECIFIC TROUBLESHOOTING HELP

The troubleshooting advice offered here is not a list of detailed instructions on how to fix something, since technology changes too fast, and we all use a variety of devices, operating systems, and software. There are a lot of great resources on the Internet, and if you are having a problem, chances are high that many other people have had that same issue, and someone has written something helpful about it. Search on the Internet and look for reputable websites. Some good websites for learning how to do something technical on your computer are:

- How-To Geek: howtogeek.com
- ZDNet: zdnet.com
- c/net: cnet.com
- YouTube: youtube.com (for walkthroughs with screen displays)
- Stack Overflow: stackoverflow.com

You should be able to find a user manual for your devices or software to which you can refer. Paper manuals are becoming a thing of the past, but you can probably find the electronic version on the company website. Your operating system or software may have an online forum where employees or customers answer questions similar to yours. Examples of websites offered by Microsoft and Apple are:

- https://discussions.apple.com/welcome
- https://support.apple.com/
- https://social.microsoft.com/Forums/en-US/home
- https://support.microsoft.com/en-us

The quality of these manuals, instructions, and technical support may vary, so try not to get frustrated. Plus, if you don't know the proper vocabulary, it's hard to know what terms to use in your search. Sometimes, a live technical support person can be helpful, and many products come with free technical support, or there may be options to pay for technical support. Unfortunately, technical support is not always as helpful as one might hope.

You may feel emotions like frustration and annoyance when you encounter a tech problem. Try to make an effort to remain calm, find your place of Zen and happiness, and remember that you *can* learn these things. Once you have taught yourself to resolve a tech issue, you will have improved your knowledge, and increased your future tech efficiency, as well as security.

C. DIAGNOSIS 101

1. Troubleshooting

Troubleshooting means trying to isolate what might be the problem, and ruling out what is *not* the problem. It's a logical process for which lawyers are well suited by virtue of our education and experience. Don't let fear of technology get in the way of learning how to resolve your own problems. Of course, no matter what one's profession or occupation, everyone uses problem-solving skills every day, perhaps without realizing it. Doctors, accountants, auto mechanics, carpenters, landscapers, and the rest of the society face daily problems that require these skills.

As you are trying to identify and fix your problem, ask yourself:

- Have you tried rebooting (or completely powering off the device) before going any further? This solves many issues.
- What is the issue you are facing?
- What exact error message or notice are you getting?
- When did the problem first occur?
- What changed prior to the problem occurring (different computer, different software, installed an update, changed a setting)?

- Can you divide the task into smaller parts and try to isolate (troubleshoot) the individual parts?
- Can you do the task—or part of the task—using a different method or device?
- What is still working normally?
- What is now abnormal and different?

2. Is It a Tech Issue or Has a Crime Occurred?

Throughout the process of troubleshooting an issue, you should be continually evaluating whether the issue you are having is a technical issue, or if a crime is occurring or has occurred. Sometimes it is not easy to determine. But if a crime is in progress, you will want to take steps to prevent it from spreading—you may want to disconnect devices from the Internet and from your network. You may even want to turn them off, though that will erase data in volatile memory, which could include evidence of the malware. If a crime has occurred, you will want to take steps to preserve evidence and possibly notify law enforcement. If it is merely a technical issue, you have more freedom about how to resolve it because you don't need to worry about preserving evidence. Remember that if you call an IT professional with an issue, his or her focus may simply be on getting your systems running properly again—on fixing the problem with minimal time and cost and with little thought about preserving evidence. If evidence should be preserved for law enforcement or future litigation, you may need to make that very clear to your IT professional or consider hiring a digital forensics and investigations firm.

Further, before you drop off your computer at the repair shop, consider what confidential information is contained on your computer or accessible by it. You need to ensure that information that is accessible by the IT professionals will be treated in a manner that is consistent with your professional obligations.

3. Device vs. Cloud vs. Other Issue

As you are troubleshooting, you will want to try narrow down the possible sources of the problem. For example, if you are having a problem accessing your data, you need to figure out if the problem is with the device that you are using, with the data that is stored in your cloud account, or with your network or Internet connection (it's hard to tell sometimes). Remember the story about the person who thought his device was being hacked because data was disappearing from it? It turned out that it was a misunderstanding, and instead the device had become disconnected from the data stored on the cloud.

Therefore, if you know your "contacts" data is stored in the cloud, for example, but all of a sudden your smartphone has no contacts in it, you should check the smartphone to make sure it was configured to synchronize with your cloud data. Then, you should use a different device (e.g. laptop or desktop) to log in to your cloud account and check to see if the contacts are there. Steps such as these can help isolate the source of the problem—device, cloud, network, or something else.

D. PRESERVING EVIDENCE OF A POTENTIAL CRIME OR TORT

With many of the issues discussed in this chapter, it is helpful to document, in some fashion, what occurred and what you did to try fix it. The question becomes how much time—or money—should be spent towards documentation and evidence preservation. Documentation can be helpful to resolve a technical support issue, and preservation of evidence can be essential towards proving a criminal or civil case. The choice is how much to document and preserve. At one end of the spectrum is documenting nothing, and preserving nothing, and at the other end is having forensic experts come and preserve all data, whether in live memory or stored on hard drives on computers and servers.

There is no better time than the present to record observations and actions, and collect evidence, since passage of time can mean lost evidence. On the other hand, there is a natural reluctance to hire experts given the expense and disruption that can occur. Preserving evidence is only the start of the expense; analysis of that data to identify root causes or restore data is also costly.

If you decide to do certain things yourself, here are some methods you can use to document actions and preserve evidence:

- Keep running notes on a notepad. Indicate the date and time, events observed, and actions performed.
- Preserve what you see on the screen.
- To preserve a webpage, use the web browser's print feature. Print it to a PDF electronic file, and give it a helpful name.
- To preserve how things appear on your screen, use a "screenshot" or "screen capture" feature.
  Windows 10:
  - Press the "PrtScn" (Print Screen) button on the keyboard to copy what is displayed on the monitor. Then paste (Control-V) the saved image into a Word or other document.
  - Press Windows Button → PrtScn to automatically make and save a screenshot within your Pictures → Screenshots folder.

- Use the Snipping Tool (SnippingTool.exe). Copy what you see on the monitor and save the image as a .JPG file, with a helpful file name (e.g. 2017-2-16--2-12pm Malware message.jpg).

Mac OS X:

- Press Shift → Command (⌘) → 3 to take a screenshot of your entire screen, and automatically save it to your desktop.
- Press Shift → Command (⌘) → 4 to be able to select a precise area, then save it to your desktop.
  - Use the crosshairs to select a desired area.
  - Press the space bar to select a window.
- The file will be automatically named and will include the date and time of the screenshot.

E. DEVICE-RELATED ISSUES

Chapter 8 covered securing your devices, so refer to that chapter for more details on how to configure them.

1. Device Not Working Properly—Can't Tell Why

Potential steps to take:

- Reboot!
- Power it off (remove battery if applicable). Wait a few seconds. Power it on.
- Scan for malware.
- If you haven't updated it in a while, update firmware/operating system.
- If you have just updated it, try rolling back the recent update, if possible.

Don't bother calling technical support until you do these things, because these are the steps they will probably tell you to do first.

2. Device Won't Turn Off, Won't Boot Up, or Won't Start

Potential steps to take:

- Power it off. Unplug and remove battery (if any). Wait a few seconds. Power it on.
- Search the Internet for special button sequence to restart it (e.g. for smartphones).
- Try booting in a "safe" mode, or to a bootable CD or USB.
  - Booting to "safe" mode means the computer operating system starts in a bare-bones fashion, with a minimum of applications running. Search online how to do this with your computer.

- Booting to a CD or USB means loading an operating system from the CD/USB, rather than from your computer. Search online about how to do this.
  - Scan for malware.
  - If you haven't updated the firmware/operating system recently, try updating it.
  - If you have just updated it, try rolling back the recent update if possible.

3. Malware Infection (Including Ransomware)

First, try to determine whether it is a serious infection or merely unwanted adware. If it is not serious, your anti-malware software can remove the threat. If it is a serious malware infection, the computer and your data should be treated as compromised, and steps include:

- Stop using the infected device. Use a clean computer unless and until the infected computer is fixed and sanitized.
- Change all online passwords.
- Ensure that two-factor authentication is implemented to protect your cloud data and accounts.
- Run multiple scans on the infected computer and its data using different anti-malware software, such as:
  - Malwarebytes (free version)
  - AVG (free version)
  - Avast (free version)
  - Spybot Search and Destroy (free version)
  - Bitdefender (free version)
  - Windows Defender (free)
  - Other free software that is reputable and has been positively rated by trusted technology websites
- If your computer continually scans clean, even after restarts and using different anti-malware software, then you may have cured it, and it may be okay to keep using the computer.
- Consider what data is available on the computer that you can access, and that you can back up to an external hard drive. Once the data is copied to an external hard drive, scan the entire contents of this external hard drive from a clean computer using anti-malware software.
- Consider wiping the computer (removing all data and software) and reinstalling the operating system and data.
- If your data was encrypted with ransomware, you will probably not be able to recover it. Hopefully, you have a recent backup of this data you can restore.

4. Lost or Stolen Device

- Activate the "find my device" feature or similar tracking feature, if possible. See if you can track the device. (Check now to make sure this feature is enabled, before it is too late.)
- If the device was stolen, and you can log in to cloud accounts that display information about the device's location and usage, preserve evidence by taking notes and screenshots of relevant information displayed on the screen.
- If the device has cellular service, log in to your cellular provider's website to see if there are clues on usage or location.
- Consider notifying law enforcement.
- Consider remotely wiping the device if possible. (Check now to make sure this feature is enabled.)
- Evaluate your desire/need to recover the device, keep your data secure, gather evidence about the thief, and engage with law enforcement.
  - Keeping connected to the lost/stolen device means you may be able to track the thief's movements and use of the device and perhaps lead law enforcement to it. However, the thief might be able to access your data.
  - Disconnecting the lost/stolen device and remotely wiping it protects your data, but means that you may not be able to track the thief.
- Access your cloud accounts, consider changing the passwords, and consider revoking access to these accounts from the lost/stolen device.
- Consider whether to cancel your cellular service for the device. Before you cancel your service, evaluate whether to remotely wipe the device (see above).
- Evaluate whether confidential or sensitive data or client/customer data is on the device.
  - Was data encrypted?
  - Consider reporting to law enforcement. Evaluate whether the type of lost data triggers a legal requirement to report to law enforcement.
  - Consider the need to report to clients/customers.
  - Consult data breach and data disposal laws.

5. Someone Untrustworthy Had Temporary Access to Your Device

If someone borrowed or otherwise used your device and now you are suspicious about what they might have done to it, you should make sure they did not install monitoring software or otherwise obtain access to your data.

- If you are concerned someone tampered with your device, assume the device is compromised, as if by a malware infection.
- Preserve evidence by taking notes and screenshots.
- Consider reporting to law enforcement and preserving evidence for them.
  - If you believe a serious crime has occurred (such as someone accessing your device or accounts without your permission), consider preserving the device "as is" (powered off) as evidence until you consult with law enforcement.
  - Recognize that law enforcement resources are limited.
- Evaluate the desire to gather evidence versus securing your cloud data.
- To secure your cloud data: From a different (known clean) device, access your cloud accounts, change passwords, review devices that have access to the cloud data, and revoke access of any unrecognized devices. If in doubt, revoke access for all devices. Enable two-factor authentication.
- On the device:
  - Scan for malware.
  - Review all installed apps/programs.
    - Consider uninstalling any recently installed applications/apps.
      — On Windows machines, in "Programs and Features," sort applications by their "installed on" date.
    - Uninstall any apps that appear suspicious or unneeded.
  - Review programs/apps running on the device.
  - Review Internet history and downloads for suspicious activity.
  - If the suspect has significant technical skills:
    - Consider taking the device to a forensics or security professional.
    - Consider not using the device again.
  - Consider what data is on the computer and can be backed up.
  - Consider wiping the computer and reinstalling the operating system and data.

6. Lack of Connectivity

If your device cannot access your network or Internet, try these steps:

- Evaluate whether the problem is with the device, network (router), Internet, or remote data source (cloud, website).
- Evaluate whether you can connect via Wi-Fi, Ethernet cable, or cellular. If one connection method works but not another, that can help you identify the problem.

- Consider whether other devices can connect via this method.
- Evaluate whether you have connected to the Wi-Fi network.
  - If you are using a Wi-Fi network, the first step is connecting and logging in to the Wi-Fi network. The next step is determining whether the Wi-Fi network is allowing you to access the network or Internet.
- Consider whether MAC filtering or other network access control is enabled. This could prevent a device from connecting to a router or network.
- Evaluate if the router and modem is functioning properly.

  - Power it off. Then restart it.
  - Upgrade the firmware.
  - See section G on network/Internet related issues.

7. Repurposing a Device

If you are selling, giving away, or changing users on your device, see Appendices 6 and 7 (device decommissioning checklists) and section O in Chapter 8, on decommissioning. Consider past use of the device, and the sensitivity of the data that it stored and accessed. Consider the future use of the device, because your relationship to the next user will also affect the security steps you need to take. Consider whether the device recipient is:

- Electronics recycling
- Stranger
- Coworker
- Friend
- Child
- Spouse

If the device is going to a family member, the steps below may be sufficient. If the device is going to a stranger, follow detailed steps in Appendices 6 and 7. Basic considerations before repurposing a device include:

- Ensure the new device is working and that all data has been copied from the old device.
- Evaluate any duties to preserve data or evidence.
- Ensure the device can no longer access your cloud data (passwords removed, etc.).
- Ensure the device can no longer access your networks (passwords removed, etc.).
- Clear all Internet history on all web browsers.

- Ensure your data is removed from the device (securely deleted).
- Delete programs/apps the new user does not need.
- Wipe any free space to securely remove "deleted" data.
- Check for removable memory cards and remove them.

F. DATA-RELATED ISSUES

Chapter 9 covered securing your data, including your e-mails and cloud accounts, so refer there for more detail.

1. Can't Find or Access the Data

Evaluate where the data really is (or was):

- Consider if the data was stored locally on a device.
  - Consider the last known location and how it was accessed.
  - Use the operating system's search feature.
    - Consider if the data was accidentally moved or deleted and whether it can be recovered.
  - Evaluate if a backup copy is available.
- Consider if the data was stored on the cloud.
  - Determine the last known location, and how it was accessed.
    - Consider if the data was accidentally moved or deleted and whether it can be recovered.
  - Evaluate if a backup copy is available.

2. Data Is Not Readable

Take the following steps if your data won't open or is corrupted:

- Consider what type of data it is.
- Consider what software is supposed to open it.
- Evaluate if your operating system recognizes the type of file it is.
- Consider if you are using the right software to open it, and whether different software might work better.
- Consider if the file is corrupted (e.g. damaged and unreadable).
- Consider if a backup copy is available.

3. Lost/Forgotten Password to Data in the Cloud

- Consider if your password is written down anywhere.
- Check the password reset process (e.g. password reset message sent by provider to e-mail account, alternate e-mail account, or text message to phone).

4. Lost/Forgotten Password to Data That Is Stored Locally

- Is your password written down anywhere?
- Have you printed out a decryption key/code?
- Is a backup copy available?
- If the data is not encrypted, consider booting to another operating system to access the data. Consider forensic analysis, which might recover your data.
- If the data is encrypted, forensic analysis will probably not be successful.

5. Cloud Account Was Hacked

Remember to preserve evidence as you go with notes and screenshots. Account hacking is a serious crime. Look for evidence of what the hacker did. Ensure that the hacker no longer has access to your data through the following steps:

- Regain control of your cloud account.
  - Conduct a password reset; if needed, call technical support.
- Change the password (if you haven't already, or if you logged in with a password that was e-mailed to you). The password should be complex and you should write it down.
- Enable two-factor authentication.
- Inspect security events, security settings, and account recovery options.
- Check recent activities, recent logins, recent changes, deletions, sent and received e-mails, trash, etc. for suspicious activity.
- Check e-mail access and e-mail forwarding options. Disable e-mail forwarding.
- Check device access. Revoke access for unknown or unauthorized devices.

6. Accidental Dissemination of Confidential Material

If you've accidentally disseminated confidential material through e-mail, hidden metadata, and so on, take these steps:

- Review what was disseminated.
- Review data breach notification laws that may apply to you.
- Consider notifying the client/customer whose information was disseminated.
- Consider notifying the recipient of accidental dissemination, requesting that the material be deleted and disregarded.

G. NETWORK- OR INTERNET-RELATED ISSUES

Chapter 10 covered securing your network and Internet access. This section discusses steps to take when an Internet connection is lost.

Use troubleshooting techniques to identify the cause of this problem. Consider:

- Can the device access the Internet for certain purposes but not for others?
  - Check software firewall settings.
- When did the problem first arise?
- What changes were made recently?
- Which devices are affected?

The problem could stem from different causes:

- Internet Service Provider (ISP): Service could be out.
  - Can you access the Internet using that ISP through other devices?
    - If yes, then the problem is not your ISP.
    - If no, the problem could be with your service, but first check your modem and router.
  - Do you have a bundled service with the Internet, such as phone and television? See if those services are working.
  - Call ISP customer service.
- Modem and/or router: Might not be functioning properly.
  - Can you access the Internet using that modem and/or router through other devices?
    - If yes, then the problem is not your modem/router.
    - If not, the problem could be with your modem/router or the ISP.
  - Consider rebooting the modem and router. Unplug it, wait about ten seconds, and then plug it back in.
- Device (smartphone, tablet, laptop, desktop):
  - Is the device properly connected to your network? The proper network?
  - Does the device have software firewalls that might be blocking all traffic?
  - Check configurations for the network and Internet.

H. SUSPICIOUS REQUESTS OR SUSPICIOUS POTENTIAL CLIENTS

You may be approached by individuals who purport to want to hire you but actually want to steal from you, or they want to hire you to assist them with criminal activity. Chapters 13 and 14 cover this type of fraud in more detail. Approaches that should raise red flags are:

- New potential client requests to deposit a large check or to send a large wire to your operating account or escrow account.
- New potential client needs assistance holding, moving, collecting, or transferring funds.
- You are offered lucrative compensation for an ordinary service.
- Existing clients or contacts demand an urgent transfer of funds, may have changed the wiring instructions, and are not available for voice conversation.

Here are some basic steps to help keep you from becoming a victim of or unwitting accomplice to a crime:

- Learn about the client, the funds, and background information.
- Know your client: name, physical address, e-mail address, phone numbers, and occupation.
- Know the source of the funds and investigate any discrepancies.
- Know the destination of funds and investigate any discrepancies.
- If the compensation seems too good to be true, something nefarious may be afoot.
- Have a voice conversation with the client to confirm the authenticity of e-mailed instructions.
- If the client is relaying bank wiring instructions from a third party, make sure that not only have you spoken with the client, but that the client has spoken with the third party. Advise the client of the need to confirm the authenticity of the instructions transmitted by the third party.

I. VICTIM OF CYBERCRIME

See Chapter 13 and your own incident plan. Take notes and preserve evidence as you go. The degree and scope of your response will depend on whether it is a hack of your personal e-mail account that has purely personal information in it or a hack of a larger corporate network or e-mail system that has client information in it.

1. Stop the Attacker and Regain Access, Control, and Security

- Regain control of your accounts. Change passwords and enable two-factor authentication.
- Contact e-mail, cloud storage, and other service providers as appropriate to notify them, and regain access.

- Contact financial institutions as needed to alert them to the scam.
- Consider hiring legal counsel.
- Consider hiring a data breach response forensics firm.

2. Follow-Up Actions

- Notify legal counsel.
- Notify insurers. You may have coverage even if you think you don't.
- Notify law enforcement.
  - Call local law enforcement.
  - Contact your local FBI office.
  - Make an online report to the FBI though the Internet Crime Complaint Center (IC3) at ic3.gov.
- Notify clients/customers, as appropriate, if their information was compromised.
- Consider public relations management.
- Consider engaging a firm for digital forensics and investigation.

J. VICTIM OF IDENTITY THEFT

Identity theft and cybercrime go hand-in-hand. If someone has assumed your identity and used your name, passwords, or account information to hack your e-mail account, use your credit card, steal from your bank account, or open up credit in your name, then you are a victim of identity theft.

- Notify local law enforcement.
- Complete a report through the Federal Trade Commission (FTC) at identitytheft.gov.
- Contact financial institutions.
- Strongly consider changing passwords and increasing your "security dial" setting.
- Order *free* credit reports from each of the three credit reporting agencies at annualcreditreport.com.
- Consider other actions, such as fraud alerts or a complete credit freeze to restrict the issuance of new credit accounts without prior approval.
- You can do this yourself, without having to pay for services or products.

K. VICTIM OF CYBERBULLYING, HARASSMENT, OR THREATS

- Preserve evidence.
- Don't harass back, don't bully back, and don't threaten back.

- Consider contacting appropriate officials and representatives (e.g. school, workplace, etc.).
- Consider contacting the provider of the service (e.g. Facebook, Twitter).
- Consider contacting law enforcement.

L. TRAVELING TO A HIGH-RISK COUNTRY

If you're traveling to a country that is at a high risk for cyber espionage, please also consult Chapter 12.

- Consult your IT department.
- Elevate your security dial, even if temporarily.
- Consider creating and using a temporary e-mail address just for this travel.
- Strongly consider using a temporary device just for this travel.
- Have strong passwords and two-step authentication.
    - Ensure that you can receive two-step authentication codes (e.g. text messages) where you will be or, in advance, obtain a "scratch pad" of one-time access codes that you can use in lieu of text messages.
        - Your cloud provider may have instructions on how to print out these one-time access codes.
- Scan your devices for malware before you leave and when you return.
- Don't accept any operating system or software updates while abroad.
- Strongly consider wiping your devices upon return.
- Change your passwords when you return.

M. CONCLUSION

These are some quick steps to think about if you are having a technical support issue or have a cybersecurity or fraud event. Earlier chapters have more details on how to protect yourself and secure yourself from these threats. And remember that serious IT and cybersecurity issues may require you to hire professionals who are experts in the field.

Conclusion

Technology is here, and it is incumbent on each of us to use it responsibly and with regard to the security and privacy concerns of our families, clients, and ourselves. You have invested considerable hours reading this book and implementing suggested changes, which will pay both short- and long-term dividends on many fronts.

Our home is the best place to learn cybersecurity, where we can practice in a smaller and simpler environment that we control. This is the place where we can protect what is most important to us—our family. Taking control means becoming educated and aware consumers and users, and starts with having an understanding of the data that is being collected and stored by us and about us. It means taking the time—at least occasionally—to read privacy policies and always consider the implications when we click "accept" or grant access to our data. It requires educating ourselves about our devices, data, and networks, how they work, and what we can do to secure them. We don't need to become tech experts, but we must become educated users, with an awareness about our data and our security and privacy settings. Many aspects of our privacy and security are within our control—if we make the time to learn.

Everything you learn and apply within the home can be translated to your firm, whether it is small or large. Securing the devices and online presence of your firm is the right thing to do from a business perspective, for yourself, and for your clients. Remember that professional obligations impose this duty upon you.

Having secured yourself and your firm, you are in a position to help your clients secure themselves, thus helping to manage their legal and cybersecurity risks. Many individuals and corporations experience trepidation around cybersecurity and privacy issues, and are in need of guidance. Too many become cybercrime victims and need help with the aftermath. Even if cybersecurity never becomes one of your practice areas, it is helpful to be able to spot the issues when they arise, to be proactive, and know where to begin.

The industry surrounding cybersecurity is developing rapidly. Many companies are vying to sell services and products to you, and the choices and marketing can be confusing. Cyber insurance policies are becoming more common, as well as services to investigate and remediate cybercrime incidents. This growing recognition of cybersecurity responsibilities is leading to legal disputes following a cybercrime; insurers may deny a claim, victims will sue other victims alleging inadequate cybersecurity, etc. Litigation of these issues will become more frequent, further evolving this area of legal practice.

We also face difficult legal and political issues with respect to cybersecurity, cybercrime, privacy, and national security. Our country has not yet found effective methods to address these complex problems, as daily news items detail the new attacks and threats that we face. There are existing laws and regulations affecting cybersecurity and privacy, but new laws and actions are proposed and debated every day. Many of these proposals have serious implications for our country and clients, and require careful consideration.

Lawyers can play a formative role in these debates, aided by a foundational understanding of cybersecurity, technology, and privacy. Lawyers can also be truth seekers and problem solvers. We can identify and separate the issues to be addressed, tackling them in a logical manner, ascertaining facts, and applying these facts within a legal framework. These controversies will require legal and political solutions—so while expertise in technology and cybersecurity is valuable, legal skills will be key. Solving the world's problems pertaining to cybersecurity, privacy, cybercrime, and national security seem like lofty goals, but it needs to be attempted, and we start by tackling their component parts.

Putting aside the broader debate, we all can use our knowledge and skills to focus on areas closer to home, to take the steps necessary to protect ourselves, our families, firms, and clients, and hopefully, to gain considerable personal satisfaction as we move forward.

Good luck, and let me know how you are doing becoming cybersecure. You can contact me at:

CybersecurityHomeAndOffice.com
John@CybersecurityHomeAndOffice.com

Your Cybersecurity Posture and Awareness

Security Posture and Awareness Quiz

Topic and statement: If statement is true, record the number of points, if any.	Points if true	Points for you
Devices		
All of my devices require a password or fingerprint to access.	1	
My devices do not require a password or fingerprint to access.	0	
All of my devices auto-lock after a period of inactivity.	1	
My devices do not auto-lock after a period of inactivity.	0	
A thief might steal my device if I leave it unattended.	1	
No thief wants to steal my device.	0	
Data and Cloud		
I know what two-step login is (two-factor authentication).	1	
I do not know what two-step login is (two-factor authentication).	0	
My e-mail accounts and important Internet or cloud accounts require two-step login.	1	
My e-mail accounts and important Internet accounts do not require two-step login.	0	

Topic and statement: If statement is true, record the number of points, if any.	Points if true	Points for you
My Beliefs		
No criminal would want to hack my cloud accounts, so I'm safe.	0	
Anyone can be a victim of cybercrime and identity theft.	1	
Cybercrime or identity theft will not happen to me.	0	
Cybercrime or identity theft might happen to me, or has already happened to me.	1	
You can't stop a determined hacker, so there's not much point in trying.	0	
I want to take reasonable measures to protect my security.	1	
Cybercriminals won't target me, and if they do, they are welcome to my data.	0	
My data has value to me and to cybercriminals, so I want to protect it.	1	
I don't know much about technology, so there's not much I can do myself to improve my cybersecurity.	0	
I can do my own cybersecurity. I can learn enough about my devices and accounts in order to protect myself.	1	
Cybersecurity is too much work.	0	
Cybersecurity can be implemented in a commonsense manner that protects me and increases my efficiency.	1	
Cybersecurity is only for experts.	0	
Cybersecurity is for everyone, just like automobile safety is for everyone (even if you are not an automobile engineer).	1	

Topic and statement: *If statement is true, record the number of points, if any.*	Points if true	Points for you
I'm so cybersecure no one could hack me.	0	
Every day, new ways to conduct hacks are being discovered.	1	
Total: Tally up all the 1s in the "Points for you" column		**TOTAL**

Analysis of score:

0–4: You should improve your cybersecurity posture and awareness.

5–9: You are generally aware of cybersecurity risks, but could do more to protect yourself.

10–13: You're doing well keeping yourself cybersecure, because you know it's an ongoing threat.

Cybersecurity Threats and Risks You Face

Threats and Risks You Face

Topic and statement: Record a point for each statement that is true.	Points if true	Points for you
Devices		
I store sensitive, confidential data on my devices.	1	
I have data stored on my devices that I cannot afford to lose (important work or personal information photos, contacts, etc.).	1	
I use my devices for sensitive or confidential communications.	1	
Data		
I have sensitive, confidential data stored in the cloud.	1	
I have data that I cannot afford to lose stored in the cloud.	1	
I am professionally obligated to preserve data and files.	1	
I possess data and information pertaining to others and I have a duty to safeguard it.	1	
If my data is breached, I might have to notify law enforcement and clients, or I might face a lawsuit or malpractice claim, or it might be bad for my reputation.	1	

Topic and statement: Record a point for each statement that is true.	Points if true	Points for you
Communications		
I engage in sensitive and confidential communications electronically (e-mail, text, etc.).	1	
If a criminal or malicious individual got access to my e-mail accounts or social media accounts, it would have very negative consequences for my work or for me personally.	1	
If I lost access to my e-mail accounts or social media accounts, that would hurt my business.	1	
I transmit or receive bank wiring instructions by e-mail, or other financial or payment information.	1	
I, or My Clients, Fall Under One or More of These Categories		
Celebrity	1	
Public figure	1	
High net worth	1	
Hold position of high responsibility or power in private sector or government	1	
Hold position relating to national security, defense, etc.	1	
Entrusted with confidential information of others, including attorney-client privileged materials, intellectual property, corporate mergers, and/or financial, health, personal identifying information (PII), etc.	1	
Total: Tally up all the 1s in the "Points for you" column		**TOTAL**

Analysis of score:

0–3: Either you don't use computers or e-mail much, or you need to improve your awareness of cyberthreats.

4–16: You seem to understand that your data may be at risk, and should set your "security dial" accordingly.

17–18: You face significant consequences if your data is breached, and should set your security dial at ten.

Home-Work Cybersecurity Connection

This evaluation helps you realize how much your home cybersecurity posture influences your work cybersecurity. Good cybersecurity starts at home.

Topic and statement: Record a point for each statement that is true. Consider it "true" even if you only do it occasionally.	Points if true	Points for you
I use work devices for personal use.	1	
I use personal devices for work purposes.	1	
I bring a personal device (smartphone, laptop, etc.) to work and connect it to work Wi-Fi.	1	
I bring a work device (smartphone, laptop, etc.) home and access it at home using my home Wi-Fi or Internet connection.	1	
I use personal e-mail for work purposes occasionally.	1	
I use work e-mail for personal purposes occasionally.	1	
I work from home occasionally.	1	
I use my home computer to do work, or access work e-mail or networks.	1	
I store information about work contacts with my personal contacts, and vice-versa.	1	
On a single device, I access both work and personal e-mails and contacts.	1	
Total: Tally up all of the 1s in the "Points for you" column		**TOTAL**

Analysis of score:

0–1 Either you keep your digital work and personal life very separate, or you're not fully aware of how intertwined your work and home digital life are.

2–10: Your work and personal cybersecurity are interrelated. Improving your home information security posture will improve your work security posture, and vice versa. Weaknesses in your home security posture can weaken your work posture, and vice versa.

Your Cybersecurity Dial

You decide where to set your "security dial." The settings on this conceptual dial range from 0 to 11, but you should avoid the extremes, and aim to be somewhere between 2 and 9.

SECURITY DIAL SETTINGS

0: Off

- You don't care who sees your data.
- You don't care if you lose all your data and accounts.
- Your password is "password" or "123456."
- You don't know, or care, what two-factor authentication is.
- You are reading this book only because of its mellifluous prose.

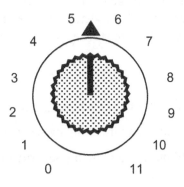

Your security dial.
Decide where to set it.
Don't turn it up too fast.

1: Barely On

- You have some concerns about keeping your data private, and about losing access to your data. However, you want to spend the absolute minimum time thinking or doing anything about it.
- You think cybercrime and identity theft only happen to other people.

5: Midway

- You maintain a law practice with clients and family that depends upon you, and you depend upon your devices, e-mail accounts, and documents to manage your professional and personal life.
- You have strong passwords and have enabled two-factor authentication on your e-mail and cloud accounts.

10: Very Secure

- You are extremely concerned with your data being stolen, about losing access to it, and want to lock everything down as much as possible, while still being able to use devices and the Internet.
- Level 10 is suitable for intelligence operatives, high-ranking military and government officials, CEOs, etc.

11: The Other Extreme

- You are willing to disconnect from the Internet. If you have a computer, it is behind five locked doors and has no Internet access.
- P.S. You will still likely be a victim of cybercrime and identity theft, since other entities that are storing your personal information will be breached.

Assessment and Goal

Currently, my security dial is set at about _____ (number from 0 to 11).

In the next month, I would like to increase my security dial setting to _____.

In the next year, I would like to increase my security dial setting to _____.

Cybersecurity Myths

Myth: If they want to get in, they are going to get in. I can't stop [insert country name] or an elite hacker from breaking into my computer and data.

Truth: Yes, a determined and sophisticated hacker probably will find a way in. But we all are targeted by cyber-crime-for-profit, and many of the threats we face can be stopped or prevented. We should take reasonable measures to ensure our security and safety by making our devices and data harder for criminals to find and access.

Myth: Cybercriminals won't target me because I don't do anything interesting; or, Cybercriminals can have it, I don't have anything to hide.

Truth: Cybercriminals target everyone and everything. Many of their tools are automated, so they often don't even know whom they are attacking. There are so many different types of cybercriminals and scammers out there, it's hard to predict what information of ours might be worth something. The bottom line: If your data has value to you, it has value to them, especially with ransomware, where the cybercriminal can hold your data hostage.

Myth: I can't do my own cybersecurity because I don't know anything about technology.

Truth: If you are able to use a computer, then you can learn to use a computer safely and properly. After all, people drive cars and may know nothing about how to repair them, but they learn how to put on a seatbelt, follow the rules of the road, and lock the doors. Similarly, you can learn and employ good cybersecurity habits while computing.

Myth: Cybersecurity is too much work.

Truth: It's work, but not "too much" work. Done properly and at your chosen level of security, it can save you work—sparing you the cost and trouble of an incident, protecting you from loss of data or theft, and increasing your awareness and efficiency.

Myth: Cybersecurity is only for experts.

Truth: Cybersecurity is for everyone, just like automobile safety is for everyone. Learn and develop good habits for doing the cybersecurity equivalent of putting on a seat belt, locking your car, and following the rules of the road.

Myth: I'm so secure no one could break in.

Truth: Every day, malefactors and honest security experts are finding holes and vulnerabilities in the hardware and software we use. These vulnerabilities are the hidden corridors that cybercriminals sneak through to get into our devices and data, and then victimize us. While no one is bulletproof, there is high value in a good and reasonable cyber defense.

How Computers Count
and Why You Might Care

People live in a "base ten," decimal world—that's how we count without even realizing it. However, computers work in a "base two" binary world, and only convert it to decimal for human users. Computers live in base two because they only know two states—on or off. Binary is impossible for most regular people to decipher, so we use the hexadecimal system (base 16) to display it for people, which converts nicely with binary. We touched on computer counting in Chapters 5 and 6, and this appendix covers it in more detail.

Don't be frightened by binary and hexadecimal. You've already mastered much more complicated counting systems—like the "English" measurement system we use. We have inches, and we divide them into halves, quarters, sixteenths, and thirty-seconds. Then we put them together with twelve inches to a foot, three feet to a yard, 5,280 feet in a mile. Liquid volume is just as confusing, eight ounces to a cup, two cups to a quart, and four quarts to a gallon. There are reasons these measurements evolved this way, but it's definitely confusing, and means we're not in as much of a decimal world as we might think. In contrast, the metric system is aligned with decimal, base-ten numbering: 100 centimeters to a meter, 1,000 meters to a kilometer, 1,000 grams to a kilogram, etc. It's a simple system that makes calculations easy. Binary is even simpler, but takes getting used to.

Computers work in a binary system, which is conveniently displayed for us in a hexadecimal format. You'll start seeing much more hexadecimal notation in the future because the Internet is transitioning from IPv4 to IPv6. The traditional Internet addressing method is IPv4, which displays IP addresses in decimal form (e.g. 69.245.51.122). It's still based in binary—that's why the numbers in each "quartet" can only go up to 255.

IPv6 is the "up and coming" Internet addressing method, which displays IP addresses in hexadecimal form, such as 2001:0de8:85b3:0000:0000: 8c2e:0272:7334. Hexadecimal needs to be able to count from zero to fifteen using just one character. After "9," we can't use "10," because that's two characters, so we start using A, then B, etc.

We can count using either decimal, binary, or hexadecimal, and the conversion looks like this:

Decimal	Binary	Hexadecimal
0	0000 0000	0 0
1	0000 0001	0 1
2	0000 0010	0 2
3	0000 0011	0 3
4	0000 0100	0 4
5	0000 0101	0 5
6	0000 0110	0 6
7	0000 0111	0 7
8	0000 1000	0 8
9	0000 1001	0 9
10	0000 1010	0 A
11	0000 1011	0 B
12	0000 1100	0 C
13	0000 1101	0 D
14	0000 1110	0 E
15	0000 1111	0 F
16	0001 0000	1 0
17	0001 0001	1 1

Smartphone and Tablet Decommissioning Checklist

Chapters throughout the book discuss the many ways computers automatically store your data in places you might not expect. Because of this often invisible storage process, secure decommissioning of devices is a key component of your cybersecurity plan. Decommissioning is discussed in depth in Chapter 8. These are some basic steps you can follow when you are getting rid of an old smartphone or tablet.

DECOMMISSIONING STEPS

1. Use the new device for several days. Ensure it is working, with all data transferred and accessible.
2. Consider whether you should preserve any of the data on the old device. Consider any business, legal, or ethical obligations to preserve the data.
3. Consider the future use of the old device (family member, friend, stranger, trash, recycle). If it is for a family member, you may want to preserve certain applications and access.
4. Disconnect the old device from Internet (but be prepared to reconnect temporarily if needed). This means disconnecting it from cellular signal, Wi-Fi, and Bluetooth.
   - Remember that you want to delete data stored on the device, not delete data that is stored in the cloud.
5. If you're in a hurry, and want to quickly delete all data in the phone/tablet (perhaps less securely), skip to Step 10.
   - To more thoroughly delete data, and to learn more about the data you have accumulated on the device, proceed to Steps 6 through 9, manually deleting data.
   - If you are giving the device to a family member or trusted friend, and want to retain certain functionality or apps, proceed through the following steps, leaving apps or accounts that will remain needed, and deleting data and accounts that will not be needed.

6. Clear all Internet history in all web browsers (Safari, Chrome, etc.). Delete all browser-stored passwords and access to cloud accounts.
7. Delete any settings that reference your cloud accounts.
   - Navigate to settings for each cloud account.
   - Accounts to consider include:
     - iCloud, iTunes and App Store, Message, FaceTime, etc.
     - E-mail, contacts, calendar
   - First, change the password stored by the device for each cloud account. Enter meaningless text into the password field (e.g. "zzzzzzz").
   - Then, change the account name for each cloud account. If the account name was "info@yourlawfirm.com," change it to "zzzz@zzzzz.com."
   - Delete any stored data for that account and remove it from the device.
   - Consider uninstalling these apps.
8. Manually delete data remaining on the device. Navigate through various settings and applications, and delete data you find, including but not limited to:
   - Documents, photos, etc.
   - References to cloud accounts
   - Voicemail, call history
   - Text messages
9. Uninstall unneeded apps/software on the device.
   - Delete all apps that will not be needed.
     - If you are leaving apps on the device (e.g. because the next family member wants to use them), make sure they can't access your cloud accounts, and that they no longer have your data in them.
   - Conduct a review of the old device for any of your personal data or information that might remain on it and delete it.
10. Use the device's "erase settings and data" feature. Then verify data has been erased.
11. Use the device's "reset device/erase device" feature. Then verify the device is reset to its factory setting.
12. Check for removable memory cards and remove them.
13. If you put the device in a closet or drawer, put a note on it summarizing what you did.
14. The final step for the paranoid:
   - Put on safety goggles and smash device with hammer! A little extreme and probably wasteful.
15. Recycle the electronics responsibly.

Laptop and Desktop Decommissioning Checklist

Chapters throughout the book discuss the many ways computers automatically store your data in places you might not expect. Because of this often invisible storage process, secure decommissioning of devices is a key component of your cybersecurity plan. Decommissioning is discussed in depth in Chapter 8. These are some basic steps you can follow when you are getting rid of an old laptop or desktop computer.

DECOMMISSIONING STEPS

1. Use the new device for several days. Ensure it is working, with all data transferred and accessible.
2. Consider whether you should preserve any of the data on the old device. Consider any business, legal, or ethical obligations to preserve the data.
3. Consider the future use of the old device (family member, friend, stranger, trash, recycle). If it is for a family member, you may want to preserve certain applications and access.
4. Download CCleaner (free version) by Piriform onto the old computer.
   - https://www.piriform.com/ccleaner/download
5. Disconnect the old device from Internet (but be prepared to reconnect temporarily if needed).
   - Remember that you want to delete data stored on the device, not delete data that is stored in the cloud.
6. If you're a Windows 10 or Mac OS X user in a hurry, and want to quickly delete all data in the laptop/desktop (perhaps less securely), skip to Step 18.
   - To more thoroughly delete data, and to learn more about the data you have accumulated on the device, proceed through Steps 7–17, manually deleting data.

- If you are giving the device to family member or trusted friend, and want to retain certain applications or functionality, proceed through the following steps, leaving applications or accounts that will remain needed, and deleting data and accounts that will not be needed.

7. Clear all Internet history in all web browsers (Safari, Chrome, Edge, etc.). Delete all browser-stored passwords and access to your cloud accounts.

8. Delete any settings that reference your cloud accounts.
   - Open and test all applications and remove cloud access, and remove locally stored data.
   - For any apps/applications that are configured to automatically connect to cloud accounts (e-mail applications, etc.):
     - First, change the password stored for each cloud account. Enter meaningless text into the password field (e.g. "zzzzzzz").
     - Then, change the account name for each cloud account. If the account name was "info@yourlawfirm.com," change it to "zzzz@zzzzz.com."
     - Delete any stored data.
     - Consider uninstalling these applications.

9. Manually delete any data remaining on the device, including but not limited to documents and photos.

10. Uninstall applications on the device that won't be needed.
    - If you are leaving apps on the device (e.g. because the next family member wants to use them), make sure they can't access your cloud accounts, and that they no longer have your data in them.
    - Conduct a review of the old device for any of your personal data or information that might remain on it and delete it.

11. Empty the recycle bin (trash).

12. Run CCleaner (free version): delete data and wipe free space (one pass is sufficient for most purposes).
    - Be overly inclusive with the things it should analyze and erase.
    - Have it fix your registry, too (and don't "back up" the old registry).
    - Wipe free space (one pass will be sufficient for most purposes).

13. Create a new user account with administrator privileges and an anonymous name like "user." Sign in to the new user account.

14. Delete all of the old user accounts.

15. Run CCleaner (free version) again, analyze and erase data, fix the registry, and wipe free space.

16. Defragment your hard drive using the operating system's built-in tool.
    - Windows: Search for "Defragment and Optimize Drives" or "dfrgui.exe," and run the utility on your hard drive.

17. Run CCleaner (free version) again, analyze and erase data, fix the registry, and wipe free space.
18. Use the operating system's shortcut to remove files:
    - Windows 10 offers a shortcut to reset your PC, remove your files, and clean the drive.
        - Navigate to and select Settings → Recovery → Reset this PC → Remove everything → Remove files and clean the drive.
    - Mac OS X recommends some steps and a utility to remove your files and clean your drive:
        - What to do before selling or giving away your Mac: https://support.apple.com/en-us/HT201065
        - Erase a volume using Disk Utility for Mac: https://support.apple.com/kb/PH22241
19. Consider using CCleaner to wipe the entire drive, including applications and the operating system. Note that this will mean you cannot use the computer again unless you reinstall the operating system and all applications.
20. If you put the device in a closet or drawer, put a note on it summarizing what you did.
21. The final step for the paranoid:
    - Remove the hard disk drive and disassemble it (or let your children disassemble it under your supervision). Or destroy it with a hammer.
22. Recycle the electronics responsibly.

View Data Flowing Across Your Network

Now we are really getting technical, so read at your own risk. Two software tools—WinDump and Wireshark—can allow you to see communication activity and data movement across your network. You would be amazed at the activity that occurs; even when you aren't touching your keyboard or mouse, your computer is nevertheless constantly communicating with the Internet. Then, when you start using the computer by accessing a webpage or downloading something, there is rapid activity.

There are some privacy and legal issues with use of these tools. Make sure you have the proper authority to run them on your network, as they have visibility into all unencrypted network traffic, not just traffic going to and from your computer. If you use these tools on a network without the proper authorization to run them, you could violate someone's privacy rights, and even arguably be committing a serious criminal offense such as unlawful surveillance, eavesdropping, or wiretapping. If you run these tools on your work network, you should first obtain proper permission, and make sure all employees have proper notice about their lack of an expectation of privacy on the work network. It probably is best to only try this robust software on your home network.

The cybersecurity lesson with these tools is that anyone else can use them to snoop on your communications, for example when you are using a public Wi-Fi network at a coffee shop, in a library, or on an airplane. These tools put the computer's network interface controller (NIC) into promiscuous mode, listening to all network traffic, regardless of who it is intended for.

You should also be aware that WinDump and Wireshark have their own security vulnerabilities. These powerful tools installed on your computer could be used by a hacker to snoop on your network's communication. Wireshark is frequently updated to patch discovered vulnerabilities.

WINDUMP (TCPDUMP) FOR WINDOWS

WinDump is a free, open source application that allows you to review network traffic on your local network. It is the Windows version of TCPDump, which runs on Linux/UNIX operating systems. You can download WinDump from http://www.winpcap.org/windump/default.htm.

It will download as an executable file (WinDump.exe), and when you run it, it will open a command prompt and start displaying a summary of all traffic across your local network. Run this way, without any options, it merely displays a summary of network traffic, without the actual packet data (the contents of the communications). WinDump has the capability to view and save all network traffic, including the content of communications ("packet data"), when run with certain options.

WIRESHARK

Wireshark is an application that is also free, open source, and allows you to use a packet analyzer. It is more user friendly and graphically oriented than WinDump. You can download Wireshark from https://www.wireshark.org.

Wireshark will display a running list of all traffic on the network, and you can save, filter, and analyze the content. It provides "packet capture," preserving the data sent across the network in chunks called "packets." You can see where each packet is from, and where it's going, so you'll be able to tell what is communicating with your computer. You'll see the IP addresses, MAC addresses, and ports associated with each packet. You can click on each packet to see the contents, the "payload." If the packet is not encrypted then the contents will be viewable to all, but if it is encrypted, the contents are encoded and, thus, confidential.

Don't expect to make sense of all of this data, which is constantly flowing across the network. Just realize that cybercriminals are able to, and that anyone on the network has access to it.

Additional Resources and Bibliography

There are many available resources about cyber threats and cybersecurity, and I would like to share some that I drew upon to write this book and which may be helpful for you.[1] First are some general resources applicable to the entire book; then we will provide resources that pertain to each chapter.

GENERAL RESOURCES ON CYBERSECURITY AND CYBERSAFETY

There are reputable websites to help you learn how to manage and safeguard your devices and software, as well as evaluate products and services, including:

> How-To Geek, howtogeek.com
> ZDNet, zdnet.com
> c/net, cnet.com
> PCMag, pcmag.com
> Consumer Reports, Consumerreports.org

Center for Cyber Safety and Education. A nonprofit educational organization affiliated with (ISC)², another nonprofit organization that, among other things, administers the Certified Information Systems Security Professional (CISSP) information security certification.

> SafeAndSecureOnline.org. For keeping families, parents, children, and seniors safe.
> IAmCybersafe.org. A more general cybersecurity reference site.

SANS Institute, sans.org. Offers cybersecurity training and resources. They have a helpful glossary, and you should consider reviewing or signing up for their newsletters.

---

1. Note that webpages and websites periodically change or are reorganized. Also, no endorsement of products or services is intended.

Glossary of Security Terms, sans.org/security-resources/glossary-of-terms/
Newsbites Newsletter, sans.org/newsletters/newsbites/
OUCH! Newsletter, securingthehuman.sans.org/resources/newsletters
/ouch/2017

National Institute of Standards and Technology (NIST), nist.gov

Richard Kissel, *Glossary of Key Information Security Terms*, NISTIR
7298 Rev. 2 (May 2013), http://nvlpubs.nist.gov/nistpubs/ir/2013/NIST
.IR.7298r2.pdf

OWASP, Open Web Application Security Project, owasp.org. A nonprofit
organization devoted to improving the security of software.

Center for Internet Security (CIS), cisecurity.org

U.S. Department of Homeland Security (DHS), dhs.gov

Stop.Think.Connect, dhs.gov/stopthinkconnect
Cybersecurity Publications, dhs.gov/cybersecurity-publications

Federal Bureau of Investigation (FBI), fbi.gov

Cyber Crime, fbi.gov/investigate/cyber
FBI Internet Crime Complaint Center, ic3.gov

StaySafeOnline, StaySafeOnline.org

Cybersecurity for the Home and Office, CybersecurityHomeAndOffice.com
A website I created to, among other things, parallel this book and include
photos and diagrams that could not be included in the book. Also, some
of the forms in this book are available for download, so you can print
them to full-size paper.

ADDITIONAL CHAPTER RESOURCES

1. The Need for Cybersecurity (Introduction)

This is a summary chapter, so refer to the general resources.

2. The Black Market for Your Data: The Cybercrime Economy

Interesting books about cybercrime include:

Cliff Stoll, The Cuckoo's Egg (1989)
Kevin Poulsen, Kingpin (2011)
Byron Acohido and Jon Swartz, Zero Day Threat (2008)
Mark Bowden, Worm: The First Digital War (2011)

Krebs on Security, https://krebsonsecurity.com. A cybercrime and cybersecurity news website by journalist Brian Krebs.

John Bandler, *Cybercrime and Digital Currency*, ABA Information Law Journal (Autumn 2016), http://apps.americanbar.org/webupload /commupload/ST230002/sitesofinterest_files/INFORMATION_LAW _JOURNAL-volume7_issue4.pdf

John Bandler, *Dirty Digital Dollars*, Fraud Magazine (July 2016), http://www.fraud-magazine.com/article.aspx?id=4294993652

3. Advertising—Another Market for Your Data

Federal Trade Commission (FTC), ftc.gov

> FTC Consumer Information Center, consumer.ftc.gov
> FTC Protecting Consumer Privacy, ftc.gov/news-events/media-resources /protecting-consumer-privacy
> FTC Business Center, ftc.gov/tips-advice/business-center

International Association of Privacy Professionals (IAPP), iapp.org. A good resource on privacy issues. Membership may be required to access certain website content.

4. Basic Information Security Principles

Shon Harris and Fernando Maymi, CISSP All-in-One Exam Guide (7th ed. 2016).

SANS Institute, sans.org

ISACA, isaca.org

(ISC)2, International Information System Security Certification Consortium, isc2.org

Center for Cyber Safety and Education, iamcybersafe.org

5. Basic Computer Principals

How-To Geek, howtogeek.com

Mike Meyers, CompTIA A+ Certification All-in-One Exam Guide (9th ed. 2016)

6. Basic Internet and Networking

How-To Geek, howtogeek.com

Mike Meyers, CompTIA Network+ Certification All-in-One Exam Guide (6th ed. 2015)

7. Start Securing Yourself

See the general resources.

8. Secure Your Devices

See the general resources.

9. Secure Your Data

See the general resources.

For an interesting book about the brain's memory, see Joshua Foer, Moonwalking with Einstein: The Art and Science of Remembering Everything (2011).

10. Secure Your Network and Internet

How-To Geek, howtogeek.com

SANS Institute, sans.org

Mike Meyers, CompTIA Network+ Certification All-in-One Exam Guide (6th ed. 2015)

Internet of Things

Online Trust Alliance, otalliance.org. Within this website is a "Smart Home Checklist" and a "Smart Device Checklist."

U.S. Department of Homeland Security (DHS), dhs.gov
- *Securing the Internet of Things*, https://www.dhs.gov /securingtheIoT
- Strategic Principles for Securing the Internet of Things (Fact Sheet), https://www.dhs.gov/sites/default/files/publications /IOT%20fact%20sheet_11162016.pdf

OWASP, Open Web Application Security Project, owasp.org

IoT Security Guidance, https://www.owasp.org/index.php/IoT_Security _Guidance

11. Secure Your Family and Children
Children

Safe and Secure Online, safeandsecureonline.org. An educational program from the nonprofit Center for Cyber Safety and Education.

American Academy of Pediatrics, healthychildren.org. Offers many resources regarding child health, including about reducing the time children spend in front of devices.

- *Kids & Tech: Tips for Parents in the Digital Age*, https://www.healthychildren.org/English/family-life/Media /Pages/Tips-for-Parents-Digital-Age.aspx
- *Why to Limit Your Child's Media Use*, https://www.healthychildren.org/English/family-life/Media /Pages/The-Benefits-of-Limiting-TV.aspx
- *Healthy Digital Media Use Habits for Babies, Toddlers & Preschoolers*, https://www.healthychildren.org/English/family-life /Media/Pages/Healthy-Digital-Media-Use-Habits-for-Babies -Toddlers-Preschoolers.aspx

NetSmartz Workshop, Netsmartz.org. An educational program of the National Center for Missing & Exploited Children (NCMEC).

StaySafeOnline, StaySafeOnline.org

Screenagers (MyDOC Productions, 2016). A documentary about the amount of time teenagers spend using their devices.

Seniors

AARP, aarp.org
Cyber Tips for Older Americans, Department of Homeland Security, https://www.dhs.gov/sites/default/files/publications/Cybersecurity%20 for%20Older%20Americans_0.pdf

12. Secure Your Travel

Mark Williams, *Staying Secure on the Road*, OUCH! Newsletter by SANS (February 2017), https://securingthehuman.sans.org/newsletters/ouch/issues /OUCH-201702_en.pdf

Cybersecurity Tips for International Travelers, Federal Communications Commission, https://www.fcc.gov/consumers/guides/cybersecurity -tips-international-travelers

Cybersecurity While Traveling Tip Card, U.S. Department of Homeland Security, https://www.dhs.gov/sites/default/files/publications/Cybersecurity%20 While%20Traveling_7.pdf; available via website through https://www.dhs .gov/stopthinkconnect

U.S. Department of State, travel.state.gov and state.gov

Personal Security—At Home, On the Street, While Traveling,
https://www.state.gov/m/ds/rls/rpt/19773.htm

Safety and Security for the Business Professional Traveling Abroad, FBI
brochure, travel.state.gov/content/dam/travel/FBI%20business-travel
-brochure%20(2).pdf. This brochure is also available through the FBI
website at fbi.gov/file-repository/business-travel-brochure.pdf/view.

Traveler's Checklist, travel.state.gov/content/passports/en/go/checklist.
html. A general purpose checklist that does not cover security but is helpful for planning.

13. Secure the Work Office

Association of Certified Fraud Examiners (ACFE), acfe.com and fraud
-magazine.com. An anti-fraud organization.

ASIS International, asisonline.org. An organization for security professionals.

Training materials from the Training Center for Internet Security (CIS),
cisecurity.org

Security education posters
msisac.cisecurity.org/toolkit/documents/2015.08.05-2016Posters.pdf
cisecurity.org/critical-controls/documents/Poster_Winter2016
_CSCs%20final.pdf

Training materials from SANS Institute, sans.org

Security education posters
sans.org/security-resources/posters/securing-the-human
sans.org/security-resources/posters/creating-cyber-secure-home/80
/download
sans.org/security-resources/posters/hooked/85/download
sans.org/security-resources/posters/target/100/download

National Institute of Standards and Technology (NIST), nist.gov

New NIST Guide Helps Small Businesses Improve Cybersecurity,
https://www.nist.gov/news-events/news/2016/11/new-nist
-guide-helps-small-businesses-improve-cybersecurity

Celia Paulsen and Patricia Toth, *Small Business Information Security: The
Fundamentals*, NISTIR 7621 Revision 1 (Nov. 2016), http://nvlpubs.nist
.gov/nistpubs/ir/2016/NIST.IR.7621r1.pdf

Framework for Improving Critical Infrastructure Cybersecurity, National Institute of Standards and Technology, Version 1.0 (Feb. 12, 2014), https://www.nist.gov/sites/default/files/documents/cyberframework/cybersecurity-framework-021214.pdf

Small Business Administration (SBA), sba.gov

Top Ten Cybersecurity Tips, https://www.sba.gov/managing-business/cybersecurity/top-ten-cybersecurity-tips

U.S. Computer Emergency Readiness Team (US-CERT), us-cert.gov

Hands-On Support for Small and Midsize Businesses (SMB), us-cert.gov/sites/default/files/c3vp/smb/Hands_On_Support.pdf
Resources for Small and Midsize Businesses (SMB), us-cert.gov/ccubedvp/smb

U.S. Department of Homeland Security (DHS), dhs.gov

Stop.Think.Connect, Small Business Resources, dhs.gov/publication/stopthinkconnect-small-business-resources

Small Business Tip Card, dhs.gov/sites/default/files/publications/Small%20Business%20Tip%20Card_0.pdf

Ten Cybersecurity Tips for Small Businesses, dhs.gov/sites/default/files/publications/FCC%20Small%20Business%20Tip%20Sheet.pdf. A joint FCC and DHS publication. Also available through the FCC website at https://apps.fcc.gov/edocs_public/attachmatch/DOC-306595A1.pdf.

Federal Trade Commission (FTC), ftc.gov

Start with Security: A Guide for Business, https://www.ftc.gov/tips-advice/business-center/guidance/start-security-guide-business (PDF download available at https://www.ftc.gov/system/files/documents/plain-language/pdf0205-startwithsecurity.pdf)

Federal Communications Commission (FCC), fcc.gov

Cybersecurity for Small Business, https://www.fcc.gov/general/cybersecurity-small-business; PDF tip sheet is available at https://apps.fcc.gov/edocs_public/attachmatch/DOC-306595A1.pdf

SANS Institute, sans.org

Mason Pkladnik, *An Incident Handling Process for Small and Medium Businesses*, SANS Institute InfoSec Reading Room (2007), https://www.sans.org/reading-room/whitepapers/incident/incident-handling-process-small-medium-businesses-1791

Patrick Kral, *The Incident Handlers Handbook*, SANS Institute InfoSec Reading Room (2011), https://www.sans.org/reading-room/whitepapers /incident/incident-handlers-handbook-33901

Information Security Policy Templates, https://www.sans.org/security -resources/policies/

14. The Law, and the Role and Responsibilities of Lawyers
See citations within chapter.
International Association of Privacy Professionals (IAPP), iapp.org

David G. Ries, *Safeguarding Confidential Information, Attorneys' Ethical and Legal Obligations* (April 2016), available on page 42, americanbar.org/content /dam/aba/multimedia/cle/materials/2016/04/ce1604lpi.authcheckdam.pdf

American Bar Association resources and publications:

American Bar Association, Section of Science and Technology Law, http:// www.americanbar.org/groups/science_technology.html

American Bar Association Publishing, http://www.americanbar.org /publications1.html

Sharon D. Nelson, David G. Ries and John W. Simek, Locked Down: Information Security for Lawyers (2012)

Jill D. Rhodes and Vincent I. Polley, The ABA Cybersecurity Handbook: A Resource for Attorneys, Law Firms, and Business Professionals (2013)

Thomas J. Shaw, Ed., Information Security and Privacy: A Practical Guide for Global Executives, Lawyers and Technologists (2011)

Stephen S. Wu, A Legal Guide to Enterprise Mobile Device Management (2014)

15. Troubleshooting and Responding to Your Own Incidents
How-To Geek, howtogeek.com
ZDNet, zdnet.com
c/net, cnet.com
PCMag, pcmag.com

Home Device Inventory

Today's date _____

- This form will help you identify and record some basic information about your devices.
- Adapt it to your own needs.
- If you include confidential information on this form, keep it safe!
- If kept electronically, password protect it!

Device #	Yr	Type	Make	Model	OS	Serial #	User(s)	Comments
Example	2016	S/phone	Apple	iPhone 6s	iOS	xyz12345	Mark Z.	Personal and work sensitive info
Example	2015	Laptop	Dell	Latitude e7450	Win 10	xyz12345	Bill G.	Personal & work and travel
Example	1991	Desktop	Apple	Mac SE	System 7	abc11234	Steve W.	In closet—need to clean out data!
Device #	Yr	Type	Make	Model	OS	Serial #	User(s)	Comments
1								
2								
3								
4								
5								
6								

Device #	Yr	Type	Make	Model	OS	Serial #	User(s)	Comments
7								
8								
9								
10								
11								
12								
13								
14								
15								
16								
17								
18								
19								
20								
21								
22								
23								
24								

Personal Device and Data Summary

Today's date _____

- This form will help you identify and record some basic information about your devices and data.
- Adapt it to your own needs.
- Confidential!! Keep in a secure place!
- If kept electronically, password protect it!

💻 **DEVICE 1** Desktop computer Password protected? ☐ Yes ☺ ☐ No ☹

_____

| Make and model | Operating System | Local user accounts, passwords, admin/user |

💻 **DEVICE 2** Laptop computer Password protected? ☐ Yes ☺ ☐ No ☹

_____

| Make and model | Operating System | Local user accounts, passwords, admin/user |

☐ **DEVICE 3** Tablet Device password? ☐ Yes ☺ ☐ No ☹

_____

| Make and model | Operating System | Device password |

☐ **DEVICE 4** Smartphone Device password? ☐ Yes ☺ ☐ No ☹

_____

| Make and model | Operating System | Device password |

DEVICE 5   Device password? ☐ Yes ☺ ☐ No ☹

Make and model   Operating System   Device password

◯ **CLOUD DATA 1** E-mail/Cloud account 1 2-step login? ☐ Yes ☺ ☐ No ☹

Provider   Account name   Password   Operating System   Date password   Date privacy/security
                                                                 last changed   settings reviewed

◯ **CLOUD DATA 2** E-mail/Cloud account 2 2-step login? ☐ Yes ☺ ☐ No ☹

Provider   Account name   Password   Operating System   Date password   Date privacy/security
                                                                 last changed   settings reviewed

◯ **CLOUD DATA 3** Social media account 1 2-step login? ☐ Yes ☺ ☐ No ☹

Provider   Account name   Password   Operating System   Date password   Date privacy/security
                                                                 last changed   settings reviewed

◯ **CLOUD DATA 4** Social media account 2 2-step login? ☐ Yes ☺ ☐ No ☹

Provider   Account name   Password   Operating System   Date password   Date privacy/security
                                                                 last changed   settings reviewed

◯ **CLOUD DATA 5**   2-step login? ☐ Yes ☺ ☐ No ☹

Provider   Account name   Password   Operating System   Date password   Date privacy/security
                                                                 last changed   settings reviewed

Data Summary

Today's date _____

- This form will help you identify and record some basic information about your data.
- Adapt it to your own needs.
- Confidential!! Keep in a secure place.
- If kept electronically, password protect it!

My most important information:

The data (information) that I cannot afford to _lose access to_ is:				
Description	**Type**	**Location**	**Comments**	**Backup location & date**
Example:	*Family photos.*	*Desktop hard drive.*		*3/1/2017 external HD*

The data (information) that I cannot afford _to be exposed or compromised_ is:				
Description	**Type**	**Location**	**Comments**	**Backup location & date**
Example:	*Secret documents.*	*Outlook cloud.*		*3/1/2017 external HD*

E-mail: My e-mail accounts are . . .   Indicate if you use these e-mail accounts to store other data.

Contacts? ☐ Yes   ☐ No | Calendar? ☐ Yes   ☐ No | Documents ☐ Yes   ☐ No

---

E-mail account 1

Contacts? ☐ Yes   ☐ No | Calendar? ☐ Yes   ☐ No | Documents ☐ Yes   ☐ No

---

E-mail account 2

Contacts? ☐ Yes   ☐ No | Calendar? ☐ Yes   ☐ No | Documents ☐ Yes   ☐ No

---

E-mail account 3

Contacts: My contacts (address book) are stored in...

☐ E-mail account 1 ☐ E-mail account 2 ☐ E-mail account 3 ☐ _____
☐ LinkedIn   ☐ Facebook   ☐ Device[s]   ☐ Paper address book

Last backup of contacts: _____
                                    Date/location

Calendar: My calendar is stored in...
☐ E-mail account 1   ☐ E-mail account 2   ☐ E-mail account 3
☐ Device[s]   ☐ Paper address book

Documents: My important documents are stored in...
☐ E-mail account 1   ☐ E-mail account 2   ☐ E-mail account 3
☐ Device[s]   ☐ External Storage

Last backup of documents: _____
                                    Date/location

Passwords: I store my passwords . . .
☐ In my brain   ☐ Written down in this location _____
☐ Password manager   ☐ Other _____

Home Network and Internet Summary

Today's date _____

- This form will help you identify and secure some basic components of your network and what's on it.
- Adapt it to your own needs.
- Keep in a secure place!
- If kept electronically, password protect it!

Internet 1 Broadband

_____

Provider company name   Customer service phone #   Account #

Internet 2 Cellular data plan

_____

Provider company name   Customer service phone #   Account #

Modem   ☐ Modem only   Owned by
                                       ☐ Modem-Router (Wi-Fi)   ☐ Me
_____   ☐ Modem-Router-Phone   ☐ Provider
Make and model

Router 1 ☐ Wi-Fi router ☐ Repeater   Owned by ☐ Me ☐ Provider

                                                 Username _____
_____
Make and model   Local IP address   Password _____

                                                 Firmware _____
                                                 last updated

Router 2 ☐ Wi-Fi router ☐ Repeater   Owned by ☐ Me ☐ Provider

Username _____

_____

Password _____

Make and model   Local IP address

Firmware _____
last updated

Wi-Fi networks   ☐ Guest (Internet only)   ☐ Full network access

_____

Wi-Fi network name 1 (SSID)   Wi-Fi password   Date pw last changed

☐ Guest (Internet only)   ☐ Full network access

_____

Wi-Fi network name 2 (SSID)   Wi-Fi password   Date pw last changed

Devices on your network

Enter some information about each device on your network.
Review devices through your router's administration interface.

Desktop computers _____

_____

Laptop computers _____

_____

Smartphones & Tablets _____

_____

Printer/Scanner/Fax _____

_____

Video (TVs, Blu-ray players, Roku, AppleTV, etc.) _____

_____

Gaming (Xbox, Playstation, Wii, etc.) _____

_____

Other (IoT devices, thermostats, home security, sensors, toys, etc.) _____

_____

Index